STANLEY
CLASSIC
CAR
YEARBOOK

STANLEY

CLASSIC

CAR

YEARBOOK

THE ENTHUSIAST'S COMPENDIUM 1997

JOHN STANLEY

OSPREY
AUTOMOTIVE

DEDICATION

To XUJ 564, my Mini, my first car, my wings of freedom.
We shared work and pleasure, fun, and dangers.
I asked a lot and she always gave. Long gone, she instilled my love of driving.
Hopefully this little blue friend has found a truly peaceful spot somewhere.
She is still missed. J.S.

Published in Great Britain in 1996 by Osprey,
an imprint of Reed Books Limited,
Michelin House, 81 Fulham Road, London SW3 6RB
and Auckland, Melbourne, Singapore and Toronto

ISBN 185532 644 2

Editor: Shaun Barrington
Sub-editors: Judith Millidge, Nick Mifsud
Diary of events and club directory: Jasper Spencer-Smith
Restoration chapter: Jim Tyler
Index: Janet Dudley
Stanley Yearbook logo: Pete Mays
Art Editor: Mike Moule
Design: the Black Spot

Printed in Spain

CONTENTS

FOREWORD BY RAYMOND BAXTER   7

INTRODUCTION   8

THE CLASSIC CAR OF THE YEAR   12
Thirteen experts vote for their favourite 1950s saloon.

A PLACE OF EXCELLENCE   16
A visit to a west country Morris Minor hospital.

THE TEST OF TIME   18
At the beginning of the 1970s several motoring
luminaries - including Lord Montagu, Paddy Hopkirk, Peter
Garnier and Graham Hill - predicted which cars would in future
years attain classic status. Were they right?

EDGE OF HEAVEN   23
The 1959 Earls Court Motor Show was a watershed:
the Mini took a bow, as did the radical new Ford
Anglia, plus some stunning new sports cars, including
the SP250 Daimler and the immortal Aston Martin DB4GT.
Original pictures of the event.

THE TOY CUPBOARD   34
So why do you like cars so much? Childhood memories of
models and toys: Halcyon days of Dinky car and Meccano.

PERSONAL DREAMS   38
A guide to race car ownership. A day out at the
John Watson Driving School, advice from the experts, contact
addresses and budget guidelines.

COMING OF AGE   44
Seeking reassurance in the kit car market. Nick
Green of NG Cars explains exactly what is involved
in building your own classic.

AN OUTSTANDING DEBT   50
An interview with Guy Griffiths, the man who played such a vital
role in establishing the historic racing movement
over three decades.

THE 1996/97 COLLECTION   54
A selection of those cars that can be considered classics
according to the RAC twenty-year rule. The best from 1976-77.

THE STANLEY 100   61
An unashamedly subjective selection of one hundred classic cars,
chosen according to the only criterion possible - personal
prejudice! Including the dangerous election of Future Classics,
and pointing the finger at some automotive betrayals of classic
marque traditions.

SMALL WONDERS   185
The best auto models on the market - including the selection of
a Model Car of the Year.

RESTORATION   190
Some stern admonitions from restoration expert and Osprey
author Jim Tyler.

CENTRES OF POWER   202
The extraordinary family history of a great engine –
the BMC A-Series.

STARS AND CARS   212
Brit Ekland, Roger Moore, David Frost, Jimmy Savile
et al; the sixties revisited.

DEJA VU   218
An examination of the responsibilities of those who
own the great marque legacies.

A DRIVE IN THE COUNTRY   224
A day out with the very last Works Austin-Healey.

HOUSES OF PLENTY   230
Analysis of the classic car market from representatives
of the leading auction houses.

PRICE GUIDE   234
An analysis of more than 1,200 classic cars, listing
current prices, prices three years ago, and percentage
swing in values allowing for currency fluctuation.

DIARY OF CLASSIC CAR EVENTS   258

STANLEY 100 CLUB DIRECTORY   262

INDEX   266

AUTHOR ACKNOWLEDGEMENTS

My sincere thanks are due to Jonathan Parker, Shaun Barrington and the OSPREY team for supporting and realising my ideas, to Paul Kime and Mike Moule for providing style, to Mike Kettlewell for his wisdom and Symon Biles for his model making.

Personal thanks to Raymond Baxter for his kind words, to the distinguished panel of judges and the invaluable input from a large number of experts and manufacturers.

For the enormous task of creating the Price Guide, my sincere thanks to Shawn Biles and Barry Sample for computer programming, to Tom Dean for specialist currency data and finally to Janis, both for her huge contribution to the guide and for her unfailing personal support throughout this project.

FOREWORD
by Raymond Baxter

The Oxford English Dictionary defines 'classical' from the Latin 'classicus' i.e. 'of the highest class ... A writer or work of the first rank, and of acknowledged excellence'.

It is therefore perhaps unfortunate, although understandable, that the RAC has decided that any car over 20 years old automatically qualifies for entry in Classic Car events. To insist upon a consideration of quality would doubtless have led to so much argument and dispute that more time would have been spent in the law courts than on the circuit.

This book, however, meets the O.E.D. definition precisely and in every sense, as well as enjoining, but without rancour, the dangerous field of personal opinion.

It so happens that the Author is a considerable expert and writer on classical music - of which the definition can be equally contentious. But his life-long love affair with the motor car is blatantly exposed on every page.

To those less passionately inclined to the subject matter, some of his writing may seem a trifle 'over the top', but this is the product of pure enthusiasm rather than ostentation. The words sometimes come tumbling over one another in an outpouring comparable only to listening to an exciting and stimulating conversation, rather than reading a textbook full of erudite facts and technical detail. Yet fact and detail there is in impressive profusion, not to mention guidance and advice based upon years of personal experience.

It could be truly said of this book that it is "Classic by name, and classic by nature" - a 'must' for the collector's motoring library, an ideal gift for the enthusiast, an introduction, and perhaps inspiration, for the beginner.

With so broad an appeal, I commend it to the huge readership which it undoubtedly deserves.

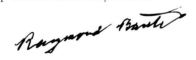

INTRODUCTION

Hard as I try, I cannot view the Morris Minor as a 'Classic Car'. I see all the magazine headlines talking it up, but it's always going to be my mother's car, the beige traveller I finally ran into the ground rushing to work. Such motor cars are not exhibits in a museum, they are cars I have known, tried, hated, fancied – they are my past. A pale blue Mini is just as vivid a milestone as my first job or my own flat. I know to some they are just a means of getting around, but motor cars are one of the few remaining ways in which we try to display our personal style, our individuality: so naturally we will remember our former steeds. The car we learned to drive in, the family wheels for holiday trips, that very first car with its impact on your popularity – even your love life! This book isn't about second-hand cars, it's about memories, it's about models that excited you, tempted you, even drove you to despair. Cynics can rightly point out that virtually any contemporary model will offer you a superior package, but there is one trait of the classic which lifts it beyond such mundane considerations – each was different, and each boasted a strong character. They may well have enjoyed common engines, chassis, sometimes even bodies, but always these cars visually stated their purpose in life, who they were, what kind of respect they deserved. A big

Healey never pretended to be a shopping car, a Frogeye always promised fun, big Humbers and Rovers naturally drew up directly at front doors. This highly defined motoring kingdom, coupled with our inevitable nostalgia for times past, is enough to spark interest. However, there is another spur to classic car enthusiasm: modern saloon car designs have become so monotonous that it is sometimes difficult immediately to differentiate amongst manufacturers. This may suit accountants and the design logic of computers, but fortunately the human imagination is not so easily crushed into conformity. As the years roll by, we become less scared about being individuals. It is a splendid convergence of this spirit with decreasing financial demands from families that has really sown the seeds of what is now termed the Classic Car movement.

As if to support the point, our distinguished judges for the Classic Car Of The Year all shared their first cars with us: the Chairman of a publishing empire holding the torch for his first car – an A35 – a distinguished motoring journalist for 40 years still recalling the time his Dad let him drive a Rover 75. Our love affair with the motor car comes from the same well spring within all of us.

For just about everyone there is a huge chasm between now and those heady days with the hood down on the scarlet MG, or the hub caps and bumpers stripped from that Cortina GT. The years in between are filled with careers and families, the world of company cars and practical family transport. It's no wonder the memory of a pair of jeans, a T shirt and that little Healey Sprite take on such resonance. Although in the 1990s the same Austin-Healey can still seduce us with its timelessness, so much else has changed. Originally we learned the detailed shifts from Mark II to III through the pages of the two bibles – *Motor* and *Autocar,* now merged. Many others such as *Hot Car, Sporting Motorist, Drive* and whole clusters of manufacturer-funded magazines also kept us informed. I contributed to many of these, and in particular *Autosport,* which drew me ever closer to the competition world. Each Saturday and Sunday I would find myself at another circuit or sitting in a different car – leaving me a rich inheritance of motoring experiences, for which I will always be grateful.

Values too have changed since those days, with thousands now being asked for cars you remember costing perhaps just a few hundred in the show room. Numerous classic car magazines, high profile auction house events, programming on television, all pitch for the returning enthusiast who might be contemplating the purchase of a car from their youth: it has become very big business.

The ambiguities of current classic values are partly the result of the investment fever of the late 1980s. Following that freakish excursion, the figures eventually re–stabilized, but even now accurate valuation is a minefield, with huge and unexplained discrepancies in prices and advice. In our own price guide (page 234) we have tried to rationalise the confusing information, insofar as that is possible, by cross matching all prices from 1993 – the market had steadied again by then – to the present-day figures and then adding a precise percentage swing indicator for every listed car, adjusted for inflation. We lay no claim to infallibility! The volatility of the market and of course the endless lists of model variants and unimaginably varied condition of specific cars means that prices are a pointer only, best considered relative one to another. But despite these caveats, I bet the first thing you did with this book was look up your own car! (Or your dream car.)

Where to look, which car dealer is best, is an auction the answer? Like antique bargain hunting there is always the dream prospect of discovering a neglected but complete classic in some scrapyard or tractor shed. Just once in a while such discoveries are indeed made, but a full restoration project could mean years of investment and work. Forecourt cars

and free advert listings tempt with economical pricing but it's important to remember such a car won't be a nearly new version with active guarantee – it's a twenty- or thirty-year-old machine quite likely to need a lot of attention.

After decades of successfully buying yourself modern vehicles without outside help, it might feel odd to seek advice. However, still far and away the best starting point for a purchase is contacting the Owners Club who will steer you on model subtleties, danger areas, possibly even connect you with a member selling just what you want. That first-hand advice is ultimately of far more direct use to you than mountains of magazines and guide books which will rarely cover your precise quest.

The romance of scrapyard discoveries like this TR must be tempered with research into restoration costs.

STEPPING OUT OF THE SHADOWS

Though intervening years may have interrupted hands-on experience, knowledge – and the thirst for

Burning the midnight oil; a common experience for amateur motor sport enthusiasts over the years, in this case rebuilding a Cooper S ahead of the weekend's hill climb.

knowledge – remains. The new and growing range of classic magazines has further awakened appetites. There is also a big rise in the number of finely detailed collectors models of classics, (which we briefly touch upon in this book) yet another signal of the burgeoning interest. In fact, collectors and modellers often possess astonishingly detailed knowledge of a car's specification changes, even the dates and drivers for particular competition cars. A Works car in full livery is something of an enthusiast's icon and both modellers and enthusiasts are drawn to the excitement of these cars. It is no accident that cars such as the scarlet and white Coopers, the factory racing MGB, Works rally Healey or powder blue Works TR are frequently modelled – for these were the competition stars of our era, dream cars dressed in familiar bodies. An extreme example of competition car adulation is the thirty-year obsession of songwriter Chris Rea, fuelled solely by black and white TV pictures and some Express newspaper cuttings. So deeply etched are his visions of Von Trips driving the shark-nosed F1 Ferrari that he has funded a stunning replica and involved it in the semi-autobiographical motion picture *La Passione.*

One of the most exciting aspects of the expanding world of classic cars is the increase in event participation. This embraces the now traditional `runs' such

as the RAC Norwich Union event, which nearly 1800 enthusiasts enter – just 31 not completing the distance in '96. Asking little of your `at least twenty-year-old' car and proving enormous fun, these runs now include excursions into Europe to sample drives around some of the most famous circuits. More robust are the re-runs of the blue riband rally and

track fixtures which blossom under the banner of historic events. For these the enthusiast can prepare an ex–road car in a lock–up and then line up on the same grid or starting line as an owner/driver with retained mechanics and liveried transporter. The competition is part of the enjoyment, but the main attraction is definitely the coming together of so many like-minded enthusiasts.

Perhaps the greatest revelation is the extraordinary spread of ages amongst the competitors. The impression that historic racing grids are restricted to just young blood eager to impress is seriously wrong. As teenagers we may have fleetingly fantasised about driving a racing car but Real Life ensured that nothing came of it. Decades later, it seems grown ups have retained that dream – mediated perhaps by the understanding that a historic car need not, indeed should not, be pushed to within an inch of its venerable life. The starting grids reveal generations of enthusiasts enjoying activities they neither had the self-confidence nor funds to explore in their youth.

Whether you own (or dream of owning) a modest Ford Anglia, a neglected sporting legend, or a one-time Formula 1 car, the essence is the same – you admire individuality. We hope that this book celebrates and comments in the self-same spirit.

CLASSIC CAR OF THE YEAR

A Battlefield of Memories

ALEX DICKSON OBE
Managing Director Radio Clyde.
First Car – Vauxhall Wyvern

TOM LEAKE
Motoring journalist, Chairman of Guild of Motoring Writers 1979/80/81 and 1986.
First Car – Singer 4AB

MICHAEL WARE
Curator National Motor Museum, Beaulieu and motoring author.
First Car – 1931 Austin 7

The dominant feature of our months of research preparing the price valuation section was the almost unnoticed advance of the domestic cars. With Ford Populars, Standards, BMC Farina saloons and the like presenting stronger investments than the most exotic sports cars, it was a sharp reminder of the power of nostalgia. To explore the true strength of this force I decided to invite a distinguished panel of judges drawn both from centres of design influence outside the car world, and a collection of hardened professionals – unlikely to be swayed by over-romanticised views of the past – to consider the merits of some of these cars. The results were revealing. They graphically confirmed that our early motoring experiences remain a powerful influence on our adult thinking and that however often we are told that a fire-eating Supercar is the ultimate, our very first car is stiff competition.

We created a list of twelve models on sale between 1st January 1950 and October 1959 – which was when the London Motor Show unveiled the 1960 ranges. All the cars were UK domestic by design and all had to cost under £1,000 – excluding Purchase Tax. The direction to the judges was that period styling and affection were as important as performance or innovation. It was not to be a purely technical assessment, although appreciation of the cars according to their era was valid – the then current US influences for example, or the UK's need for basic utility transport.

A brief reminder of specifications (and distinguishing marks) helped to jog memories, eg 'Wolseley 15/60 1958-61, 1489cc, 4 cylinder, 77mph, 4 seater, 28mpg, 4 speed. First of the BMC Farina family, a cocktail of burred walnut and traditional illuminated grille badges with fifties tail fins and bench seating.' Similarly: 'BMW Isetta 1955-62, 247/298cc, single cylinder, 55mph, 2 seater, 75mpg, 4 speed. BMW motorcycle engine, sun roof, superb access, unmatchable economy and easy parking.'

I sought their reason for their first choice and asked that they then graded the other eleven, and in a final box asked each of them what had been their very first car.

THE FULL VOTE

AUSTIN A35	1	5	6	3	4	2	2	6	5	5	11	4	10	64
AUSTIN A40 FARINA	11	8	10	1	12	8	7	10	4	2	9	6	4	102
BMW ISETTA	9	4	7	10	10	1	12	7	12	7	2	5	11	97
CITROEN 2CV	5	1	2	9	5	5	10	2	3	2	6	2	12	64
FORD ZODIAC MK II	3	10	11	8	8	7	5	4	8	4	3	10	2	83
HILLMAN MINX CONV	10	6	8	7	9	4	8	8	7	6	4	11	7	95
MORRIS MINOR 1000	4	2	3	2	2	3	1	1	1	3	8	3	6	39
ROVER 75	7	7	1	5	3	10	6	3	6	8	5	9	3	73
STANDARD 8/10	6	12	9	12	11	9	11	11	10	9	12	7	8	127
VW BEETLE	2	3	5	4	6	11	9	9	2	1	1	1	1	55
VAUXHALL CRESTA PA	8	9	12	11	7	6	4	12	11	10	7	12	9	118
WOLSELEY 15/60	12	11	4	6	1	12	3	5	9	11	10	8	5	97

Despite individual workloads there was a generously prompt response and it quickly became clear that strong views prevented any runaway leader. The VW Beetle, the Citroen 2CV and the Morris Minor began accumulating consistent scores, but no less than eight of the twelve nominees received a first place nomination. These were …

VW BEETLE

The most successful 'people's car' by a mile! Boldly innovative technically, the design met almost every target requirement, including ease of production. Alex Issigonis admired it – as he did the 2CV. But this approach to the Minor 1000 and the Mini had to be modified by a different concept of "social acceptance" He got that right too!

RAYMOND BAXTER

Difficult to judge it on technical appreciation as I've driven only a few of the cars. But as a marketing person I've selected on the basis of enduring appeal. I'm indebted to my 17-year-old daughter who helped with the selection process but who confirmed my original thought that the VW Beetle remains the 'coolest' choice: We'd both drive one today!

PAUL LEONARD

Simply because it was the only model amongst all of these that I actually owned – two of them in fact, during the '60s.

ANTHONY PEAGAM

Beetles conquered the World! Still do. Noise, shake, rattle 'n' roll, and an engine you could lift out by yourself. I've had one, loved it, and made money when I sold it. Pity about bursting into flames that time though … adults who want to be Peter Pan still hunt them down. Even Caption Hook figures like me turn to look in envy at a well preserved one, winding back their speedos, sorry time-clocks, in the process. When I retire, I shall buy one again. Fool!

ALEX DICKSON

ROVER 75

My dad had one – and he let me drive it just once!

TOM LEAKE

BMW ISETTA

As a school kid I loved bubble cars and wanted my father to buy one, he didn't. Well, my mother was large, I was over 6 ft and there was my sister and the dog. I collected all the brochures and thought the Isetta the prettiest of the bubble cars. By the 1960s when I did buy a car, all thoughts of an Isetta had evaporated — I got a Mini.

MIKE KETTLEWELL

WOLSELEY 15/60

It might not be an automotive icon like the Minor, 2CV or Beetle but the Wolseley 15/60 bristles with tingly, sturdy BMC British quality and has a wonderfully friendly aura. Traditional Englishness meets Pininfarina styling and well proven, unbreakable mechanics.
What a combination! NICK LARKIN

AUSTIN A40 FARINA

Has the good points of the Morris Minor and the A35, plus good looks and a hatchback. A bold experiment that really worked.

MICHAEL WARE

CITROEN 2CV

Anyone can design and manufacture an expensive car – all it needs is money. It takes real genius to conceptualize and build an effective machine for little money. The 2CV Citroen is brilliant minimalism.

ROBERT COUCHER

AUSTIN A35

Lighter than the Morris Minor and narrower – therefore more manoeuvrable in tight traffic when humiliating more expensive, more modern cars. Cheeky, charming looks. As James Hunt (an A35 owner at the end of his life) always said, it feels exciting even at 30mph.

SIMON TAYLOR

ANTHONY PEAGAM
Group Public Relations Director – AA, Ford Times, Drive Magazine, TV Times editorship.
First Car – 1935 BSA Scout

MIKE KETTLEWELL
Mill House Books, Autosport, Sporting Motorists, Speedway International, Brands Hatch.
First Car – Mini 850

PAUL LEONARD
Head of Marketing Communications – Cellnet.
First Car – Ford Anglia 1200cc

JOHN COOPER
Cooper Car Company.
First Car – MG TA. (The car in the background is not fifties domestic)

CLASSIC CAR OF THE YEAR

MORRIS MINOR 1000

2ND VW BEETLE 1200
3RD CITROEN 2CV & AUSTIN A35
4TH ROVER 75
5TH FORD ZODIAC MK II
6TH HILLMAN MINX CONVERTIBLE
7TH BMW ISETTA & WOLSELEY 15/60
8TH AUSTIN A40 FARINA
9TH VAUXHALL CRESTA PA
10TH STANDARD 8/10

RAYMOND BAXTER
*BBC Motoring Correspondent,
Director of BMC Publicity,
host of Tomorrow's World, author.*
First Car – MG J2

CHRIS POLLARD
*Editorial Director of Gramophone
Publications.*
First Car – Triumph Herald 13/60

NICK LARKIN
*Features Editor Popular Classic and
Practical Classics.*
First Car – Ford Anglia 105E

Great memories of
driving up and down a
twisty hill in a friend's
Minor – our own
private hill climb in
that wonderful car.
JONATHAN ASHMAN

Morris Minor 1000 was
the first of the great
small cars after the War
thanks to Sir Alex
Issigonis.
JOHN COOPER

JONATHAN ASHMAN
Director of Major Events –
RAC MSA.
First Car – Sunbeam Imp Sport

SIMON TAYLOR
Classic and Sportscar columnist,
BBC commentator, Chairman
of Haymarket Publications.
First Car – Austin A35

ROBERT COUCHER
Editor of Classic Cars, Your Classic.
First Car – Lancia Aurelia B20 GT

Mechanically straight-
forward, rugged,
honest and beautiful.
Spacious, airy and with
comfortable interior,
the perfect vehicle for
Mr and Mrs England
to drive through their
finest years.
CHRISTOPHER POLLARD

A PLACE OF EXCELLENCE
Re-visiting the Morris Minor

One of the two great names of the British motor industry; the other is Herbert Austin.

The Morris Minor actually received one less first place nomination than the VW Beetle but its constantly high positions earned this much loved car the eventual accolade of our Classic Car Of The Year. For a great many of us, Alec Issigonis' simple design brings back waves of nostalgia. They were so familiar on our roads, they were reliable, economical, indeed they were in production for 25 years, offering middle England its most trusted workhorse. It is not hard to understand why it should have eased its way into our affections, but it is extremely unwise to allow this nostalgia to persuade us that it would be a great car to own now. There have been many press cuttings which suggest the venerable Minor makes a perfect second car – I've even seen one which suggested it as a good company car. It all makes compelling reading: but just how practical would it be in real life?

The central danger is treating its pretty shape and smattering of front wing and sill rust as the only

issues. Many of the articles praising the car are perfectly correct in that it is a good investment, the engine is wonderfully reliable and there is indeed an extraordinary camaraderie amongst the army of Minor owners. However, before convincing yourselves it's a wholly practical car to own, it really is important to actually drive one again. It comes as something of a shock to many well-read enthusiasts that when traffic snarls up in front, you are going to have to work that bit harder to stop the Minor. Again, when it all begins to crawl forward you may well still be trying to persuade it into the traditionally tricky first gear. Items such as a lack of synchromesh or ponderous drum brakes were not originally points of criticism, because all production cars performed in much the same manner – or worse. On the other hand, in the middle of a line of computer-designed N and P plate cars, a classic is going to give you the odd moment or two of stress! This is a general warning for anyone flirting with the acquisition of a classic car – but particularly

Minor surgery at the Bath workshops can range from a once-over for the MOT to a five-speed gearbox and new 1300cc engine.

relevant to the Minor because it is so often praised for being a practical '90s car.

The other critical point when contemplating purchase is that any prospective car's true value is under the skin. It is not the body panels or paintwork that count but the condition of the floor panels, the sills, the internal rusting in the shallow doors. If these areas are still sound or have been correctly restored then you have an extremely good investment. One that will serve you well and increase in value as you subsequently restore the more cosmetic aspects. If you only attempt superficially to improve an ageing car you are ultimately wasting your money.

In order to balance such issues with the ownership delights of one of these true British Classics I visited the renowned Morris Minor Centre in Bath who for 20 years have specialized in just this car. It might appear an exaggeration, but this sprawling company truly is Minor Heaven. Founded in 1976 by a young one-time property entrepreneur Charles Ware, it houses Minors and workshops in profusion. For their 10th anniversary, the company published a paperback of press cuttings largely featuring the proprietors' emergence from various financial traumas! Reassuring as this success story is, the real equity in the Morris Minor Centre, the assets which make it the perfect place to approach successful Minor ownership, are the staff. These men live and breathe Morris every single day, they thoroughly restore 20 examples every month, affording them priceless knowledge. Wander up to them in the workshops and they exhibit an almost schoolboy enthusiasm for their work, instilling utter confidence in their restoration.

If you have a love for Minors and wonder where to look for a safe example, you need look no further than this Centre. When you learn that receptionist Jean opens your sales file using the nick name you have christened your Minor – you just know that the after-sales attention and the future restoration detailing will be wonderful.

In recent years, there has been a marked move in the Minor market with increasing numbers of new owners using these cars as their daily transport. Even the vans and pickups are sought after by independent tradesmen needing cheap economical transport, something that costs a fraction of the outlay for a modern van and naturally draws rather more public attention. The Minor Centre has built its reputation by observing individual customer's requests over the years and then creating services for all along the same lines. The problem of period handling on modern roads is tackled head-on by a host of improvements.

Discs brakes with or without servo are a very good idea, suspension kits, alternators, halogen lighting, twin-speed heater motors, steering locks, 1300cc engines, two-speed wipers and even marriage of the existing engine to a modern five speed gearbox, via custom-built bell housing, are all available. A complete upgrade is what they loosely term a Series III Minor, but every aspect is individually available and with very few exceptions the integration of modern equipment is not visibly too obvious.

True, any of these items could be seen as compromising a pure Minor, so they will happily restore to actual factory specifications. However, if you plan to use your Minor on a fairly regular basis then some of these upgrades will transform your classic into a car you can drive without constant alarms and excursions. Mr Ware is fond of drawing analogies between Minor restoration and property development. The argument being you would upgrade heating, windows and decor in your house to maintain and improve the investment; whereas a conventional car purchase just sees an instant outlay and instant depreciation, the Minor, he feels, offers an opportunity for something akin to that property improvement.

The basic model range is the two door which is the most common and thus the most affordable, the four door, the convertible and the distinctive wood-trimmed traveller. The Morris 1000 is the most practical – being the later incarnation – and I renewed my acquaintance with a green two-door example. It must have been more than 25 years since I sat in the driver's seat of a Morris Minor and yet it only took the turn of the ignition key for it all to flood back: the driving position, the big steering wheel, even the crude and tiny twist lock on the passenger door. The car and I ventured into the sunlit Wiltshire countryside, I smiling once more at its simple charms, it offering that distinctive rasping exhaust boom on overrun. It was a return to many thousands of miles from my own past: and it was extremely seductive.

The 1000, power for 'the first of the great small cars after the War.' (John Cooper)

TEST OF TIME

1970s Predictions

What was happening at the time of these predictions is nicely encapsulated by the Auto Car show report (right). The Citroën D models (above) were also cited by Charles Bulmer, Editor of Motor.

According to the official Swedish Vehicle Testing authority, AB Svensk Bilprovning, the natural life expectancy of the most durable motor car during the early 1970s was 14.2 years; not surprisingly, the car was a Volvo. The last place in this organisation's research list was claimed by Simca with a modest 9.9 year projected lifespan, which would suggest that there ought not to be too many Simca 1100s running – when, incidently, did you last see one? Such statistics are a reminder that modern cars are increasingly designed for limited lifespans and that those cars which continue to survive in reasonable numbers must therefore be loved enough to prompt the instinct to preserve. Future classics will depend almost entirely on public affection – and the prevailing logistics of restorations – in order to survive. 20 years on from any point of departure we can judge true classics by the numbers of those which have been preserved.

The alternative way to predict 'Future Classics' is to turn to any newspaper or magazine and find the inevitably over-used 'classic' headline. It has been so abused as to be virtually meaningless – at least for enthusiasts. I am mindful of falling into the trap within this book, but the handful of possible future classics have been chosen extremely carefully, and are largely driven by public loyalty – without which no car gets preserved.

The main problem with future predictions is that no-one takes them very seriously – who is going to keep a cutting for 20 years to assess the judgements? That's what makes it so safe for experts to constantly predict anything that pleases them.

By a twist of fate, at the beginning of the 1970s I prepared an entire feature on future classics, seeking the opinion of the leading motoring figures of the time. I never delivered that planned work, and the research material has remained hidden in a file, surviving no less than seven house moves. While hunting background material for this book, I discovered the forgotten feature. The passing of the years has created an utterly unique opportunity to consider these experts' opinions – both in their own right and in the harsh glare of reality. More than 20 years later a classic choice ought to have come into its own, or at least be treated with respect by the cognoscenti. These, then, are the nominated future classics according to some of the country's leading motoring figures of the early 1970s.

RAYMOND BAXTER

Renowned for hosting *Tomorrow's World*, his BBC motor racing commentaries and his stint as a motor industry PR, it took him just minutes to elect the original Mini. 'It is unquestionably the most important single motor car now in production. You only have to try and count the numbers of other cars which have followed in the technical footsteps of Issigonis' little brainchild'. He paused, and then added that both the Rover 2000 range and the Citroën D models were also milestones which should be listed as future classics.

Did the Rover 2000 range survive the passing of the years with its reputation as a technically sound option intact?

It just had to be at the forefront of many of the predictors' thoughts. Interestingly, journalist Gordon Wilkins pointed out that the Mini's transverse engine position was not a completely new idea.

GORDON WILKINS

Distinguished motoring expert, presenter of BBC TV's *Wheelbase*, motoring correspondent to *The Observer* for 18 years, and former technical editor of *Autocar*. When I invited his nomination over the telephone he asked for time to consider his choice. I called him later as arranged and he explained his immediate thought would have to be the Mini for breaking such completely new ground, but he pointed out it was in no way a new idea. He had studied an experimental car at the Paris Motor Show in 1947 designed by Charles Dechaux which featured front wheel drive, full independent suspension and a transverse engine. He explained that 'Issigonis' achievement wasn't thinking up the Mini idea – it was getting it through to be a production motor car'. However, he went on to decide that his first choice would actually have to be the Citroën

GS which was breaking genuinely new ground. He felt it was a significant motor car offering a totally new body design, with technical refinements inherited from the more expensive D range which were certainly new to a £1,000 family car.

LORD MONTAGU

Founder of the National Motor Museum, he was even then working tirelessly to build up his exhibition halls. He was emphatic that the then new V12 Daimler Double Six was the future classic, qualifying easily on both technical and aesthetic grounds. It was, he explained, 'the most eligible car for future inclusion in [his] growing museum'. The other future classic had to be the Ford Cortina Mk III, which he felt offered new standards in mass production family cars. He, too, mentioned that the Mini was a natural choice, but he already had two at Beaulieu! There is, however, no Daimler Double Six currently in his excellent museum.

GRAHAM HILL

The racing legend immediately began eulogising an extremely exotic Ferrari, before settling for the slightly less rarefied Citroen SM. 'The sheer logic of all the design had to make this the collector's car for the future', he enthused. He went on to underline features such as its six headlights, some turning with the steering, the famous suspension and the interior styling; ironically, the only aspect he didn't list was the Maserati engine.

PETER GARNIER

Then the editor of *Autocar*, he felt the choice ought to be a collective one with his staff. The debate which followed was apparently quite extensive and when he called me it was still going on in the background. However, the consensus was that 'the Lotus Elan in any of its forms was a beautifully conceived and balanced motor car and certainly a future classic'. The Lotus shared its status with *Autocar's* other choice, the Ferrari Dino 246GT. This Garnier explained 'offered a compact, and relatively speaking, cheaper Ferrari sports car without losing the character of its larger stable mates. With its 2418cc engine resting squarely mid-ships, it's a work of art'.

PADDY HOPKIRK

This internationally famous rally driver won the 1964 Monte Carlo Rally and drove for the Rootes, Standard Triumph and BMC teams. He, too, wanted time and eventually explained that he felt both the Frogeye Sprite and the Mk II 1275cc Cooper S – which Leyland had recently ceased to produce – were both obvious future classics. However, he finally decided that his nomination ought to be the Bristol 411 with its hand-built body, the 6.3-litre engine and 'its old fashioned standards of perfection'.

CHARLES BULMER

The editor of *Motor Magazine* took his time and was then equally cautious with his nomination. His actual first choice was the NSU Ro80 which, he explained, 'will be looked back on, and marvelled at, for being the first with the Wankel engine'. With technical innovation in mind, he went on to praise the Citroen D range, but in the end elected the tiny Fiat 500 which he cited as 'truly the car for the people'.

1959 and at long last the emphasis switched from exports to the home market. Now you could dream about, maybe even buy, one of the dazzling range of 1960 models.

EDGE OF HEAVEN

The 1959 Motor Show

I t may have been the year they photographed the dark side of the moon and the Dalai Lama fled Tibet, but for me 1959 was the brink of freedom. Art school was just around the corner and prospects of being 17 – driving age – were finally measurable in months. There was a then brand new Austin-Healey Sprite living down Oxford's St Ebbes. I cycled to and fro, waiting on the street corner until the owner came out, so I might ask question after question. Finally, one day, he offered me a ride.

So, with Cliff Richard's *Travellin' Light* dominating the pop charts, the 1959 motor show unveiled its treasures to an eager public and one restless teenager. In fact, the industry itself saw this particular show as important. The previous few years had seen the lion's share of post-1940s investment in research and design: significant new models were now rolling into the spotlight. The export drive had been strong and virtually half the UK's production was being shipped overseas. Some manufacturers such as Jaguar didn't even bother to show key models such as their XK150 sports car – simply because export orders had filled their books. Now it was felt the home market could grow – encouraged that spring by Chancellor Heathcote Amery's announcement of important reductions in Purchase Tax. Just days after the then Minister for Transport Ernest Marples opened the motor show, the first section of the MI came into service. Modern motoring was the talking point.

Retrospectively, this particular show was certainly

Dr Fidel Castro triumphs, Charles de Gaulle becomes President, and the author is still on his bike.

Ford's important newcomer, the 105E Anglia offered a new, high revving engine, four-speed gearbox, electric wipers and a controversial reverse rake windscreen.

something of a watershed year for models. There was naturally a swathe of new and revitalized models, but this show featured three distinct milestones. It witnessed the birth of the Issigonis vision with the Mini – still influencing motoring today – and the arrival of the radical Ford Anglia, boasting one of the industry's most important new engines: one which would even go on to power Grand Prix cars.

The third milestone was more generic. It was the confirmation of the order of battle for the great 1960s British sports cars. As money

again began to flush through the economy and all we teenagers became young men and women, the demand soared. The Austin-Healey 100 had sold 28,000, the Triumph TR2/3 80,000 and the MGA a further 60,000 – both UK and export markets welcomed the two seater concept. Now the Frogeye Sprite, the rapid MGA Twin Cam, and the shiny new Healey 3000 were to be challenged by both Daimler and Sunbeam. Daimler unveiled their SP250 – an extraordinary gamble. It was their one and only sports car venture, using all new parts, engine and body shell. The new V8 engine and distinctive aerodynamic styling were actually pluses; but simpler, more appealing designs would eventually prevail. On the Sunbeam stand just such a sports car was unveiled – the Sunbeam Alpine, with long graceful lines, high specifications and excellent road manners. With its long, high rear fins, bright body colours and continental lines, it successfully captured the spirit of the new.

Radical styling was clearly the mark of the all new Ford Anglia 105E and although there were mixed feelings about the reverse angled rear window and curious headlight eyelids, the basic package was universally welcomed. Not least by me: it would be the

The Americans were there in force, trying to redress the balance a liitle following a period of significant levels of British imports. The Dodge Polara was never going to find many buyers in the old country though. It was just nice to gawp at the chrome.

car in which I was to pass my driving test. Excellent accommodation, trustworthy gearbox, dependable new Kent engine, all combined to tempt over 1,000,000 customers eventually.

If Ford planned to steal the show then BMC's star offering was the perfect counter. On the Austin stand the stunning new Austin

Seven Mini simply took people's breath away. Commendably under-styled body work had been half cut away to show the exact configuration of the engine bay, seating and luggage. Had such specifications merely been boasted of in a press release, no one would have believed it possible. Front wheel drive, transverse mounted engine, gears in the sump, four seats, all independent suspension, tiny road wheels – all brilliantly drawn together by designer Alex Issigonis and offered for sale by BMC for just

Undoubtedly one of the main attractions, showing off one of its revolutionary features to best advantage, the transverse engine.

£496. The car's very existence must have sent most of the industry rushing off for their calculators and draughtsman. Just as Elvis Presley had touched the nerve of restless teenagers and Mary Quant would embody the new style freedom, so the Mini touched the very pulse of the decade ahead – and indeed those which followed. So important are such creative stimuli to us all, that the Mini, alongside those pop and fashion idols, has actually become part of the fabric of social history. The Mini was the '60s and the '60s were in part the Mini. That 1959 Earls Court Show was the beginning of a sea change.

Early in that year, Triumph too had launched its own radical concept in the form of the Triumph Herald. This Italian Michelotti design was based, unusually, on a separate chassis frame, incorporating all independent suspension, an extraordinary 25-foot turning circle and the power plant from the Standard Ten. Onto this package were bolted, quite literally, detachable body panels with a one-piece front end hingeing away to give spectacular engine bay access. Like the Alpine, the design and bright colour schemes appeared to hint at the good times of the swinging '60s – just a few months away.

Interestingly, BMC had also looked to Italian flair to create excitement in the family car sector with the Farina-styled A40, which had been launched into the British market twelve months earlier. Clean, crisp

The timeless beauty of the Jaguar Mk II. At the show the 3.8 cost a mere £1,800. Our price guide indicates that one would cost you about £20,000 today, and prices are rising.

modern styling gave a completely fresh life to what was in effect still an Austin A35. The 1959 motor show was used to unveil the more important Countryman version which boasted both upper and lower tailgates – effectively pioneering the '80s hot hatchback.

An overview of the show reveals a division between the perceived safety of the traditional and the vibrance of the new. Armstrong-Siddeley made one last attempt to stay afloat with their excellent new Star Sapphire, while over on the Daimler stand was the stately Majestic Major – brand new, with 4.5-litre engine offering 120mph and 220bhp in what is all too often thought of as just a funeral car. Rolls-Royce finally succumbed to American tastes by fitting the 6230cc V8 engine into their new Silver Cloud II, Bentley SII and Phantom V models, while the Humber Super Snipe moved up to 3 litres in Mk II form. Not to be out-gunned, BMC developed a C Series 6-cylinder range based upon the Farina styling. The Wolseley 6/99, the Austin A99 Westminster and the Vanden Plas Princess all elbowing into the crowded executive marketplace which, years later, Jaguar and BMW would claim as their own.

Not to be ignored, the Rover's range personified the traditional approach to transition from old to new, with 'new' 80s and 100s based upon the decade-old P4 body styling rubbing shoulders with their

The planned replacement for the Morris Minor was scrapped, but a by-product was the 1957-launched Riley 1.5 and Wolseley 1500, sporting four seaters on the Minor floor pan. At the 1959 show BMC highlighted the B-series engine and facelifts for the spring of 1960, but the Mk IIs never really caught the public's attention.

New world motor racing champion Jack Brabham's winning Cooper Climax was a special feature at the show.

year-old P5. This 3-litre car became a favourite of dignitaries and officials and successfully reinforced the image of Rover as establishment transport. Although extremely heavy, the car employed an upgraded P4 engine, and later models would utilize the glorious lightweight V8 engine.

One brand new alloy engine unveiled at the show was Chevrolet's air cooled flat–six, lodged in the rear of their new Convair. On May 4th that year, 7,200 American showrooms simultaneously revealed this six-seat family `compact', conceived to counter the surge of European models into their market – it failed to impress.

One of the more eyecatching features of the show was the sight of a racing car perched on top of a display pyramid. Competition cars were not normally permitted, but to celebrate victory in the World Sports Car Championship Aston Martin were allowed to display their awesome DBR1–300 still wearing its racing numbers. Not to be outdone, Jack Brabham had become the Grand Prix World Champion and so Cooper were permitted to show their title-winning Cooper Climax.

Bristol cars were showing their new 406 model with a slight engine enlargement to try and propel this increasingly overweight town carriage. The new

*Limited offer: David Brown offered an £800 sporting option on the
DB4, without any fanfare, in order to qualify his competition cars.
These rare DB4GTs are now worth well over £100,000.*

body had paid lip service to some of the contemporary styling ideas, but the use of slightly angular panels didn't really suit this large, two-door model and less than 300 were actually sold. Interestingly, another specialist marque caught at a crossroads was AC, showing a new four seater – The Greyhound. Less than a hundred were made of this largely Bristol-powered sports tourer from the Ace family. The body styling was not radically inspired, although the ideas behind the model were sound enough. Resources within a small factory were inevitably limited and the famed Cobra was just around the corner. The year after the Cobra's 1962 launch the Greyhound was withdrawn.

Looking back on classic motor shows will spark any enthusiast's imagination – the very thought of buying a brand new 3.8 Mk II Jaguar for £1,800, or an MGA Twin Cam for under £1,000, can stimulate a pleasant reverie. The prices are of course all relative to their times. Mind you, given enough funds there was definitely one bargain at that show that no astute enthusiast could have resisted. On the David Brown stand there was an Aston Martin DB4GT which offered a more sporting package than the `standard' DB4 for the additional sum of just under £800. What they didn't tell you was this was something of a `special offer' in order to generate just enough sales to qualify the car for competition under the Homologation rules. The investment of £4,500 would have matured into six figures – that is, if you could ever be parted from such a masterpiece.

Healthy exports now allowed the manufacturers to cater for the Englishman. Perhaps these two gentlemen would not be signing on the dotted line for the Dodge ...

AC launched the Greyhound four-seater model, but just a year later all the factory's resources would be switched to the famous Cobra.

THE TOY
CUPBOARD

Why include this brief interlude between the 'adult' automotive facts and figures? As a reminder, perhaps, of some of the reasons for classic car enthusiasm, a partial explanation of why you are reading this book; and – perhaps – to suggest that those reasons are not entirely adult! Childhood is – with luck – free of responsibilities and all too soon adult life shrinks our horizons, imagination and freedom. My brother Richard and I enjoyed our childhood world enormously. Initial collections of teddy bears soon created twin territories with individual passports, currency and monarchy. We fashioned everything from armaments to postage stamps acting out fragments of a big world we thought we understood. The more 'realistic' delights of Dinky meant that we could engage in military manoeuvres just like those in the films, we could achieve great speeds on the kitchen lino,

Eight huge carb intakes feed the American V8 prototype Lola GT. One of the author's favourite models.

Modelling taught you about the chassis, the bulkhead form, the radiator position, long before you were old enough to get close to the real thing.

take precocious risks cornering cars on the roadways of patterned carpet. In the absence of computer games and multi channel TV, parent, toy and each other were the stimuli to all play: each time fresh material was presented our world expanded. Plasticine, Viewmaster and the ever expanding world of Meccano were milestones. (Ring any bells? If so, we can begin to guess at your age; how many children do you know who actually have a Meccano set?) At the age of eight I joined the illustrious Meccano Guild and received a certificate reminding me that a 'Meccano boy undertakes to be Obedient, Patient, Truthful, Persevering and Helpful'. Not content, it also required the humble member to be 'Alert & Vigorous, Helpful to others, Clean in thought & Habit, Determined to make Progress, Observant & Ambitious'. I imagine at eight I had probably rather hoped to just get news of new bits of Meccano. I tried … My school report for that year did announced I was 'a very practical child and skilful with my hands' which must have earned me some merit marks: though the same report went on to commend my sewing, which doesn't sit so easily within the Meccano ethos!

As the early years drifted by, I became increasingly absorbed with my cars. Among the very few personal possessions to accompany me to boarding school was my cherished set of five Dinky racers. On quiet moments at weekends they achieved quite astonishing speeds along the stone corridors by the kitchens. I know I was not alone in my miniature motoring

adventures and that modest set of five grand prix cars i now worth £1,000 – if any one still has the box!

From Dinky cars and Meccano constructions it was the usual short step to model kits and real freedom o choice. At long last I could lie in bed and consider which car I might save up and buy next, what were my preferred colour combinations, whether I should convert i to a competition model.

The kits, the detailing, and the costs all increased unti that awkward point in growing up arrived which require regular checks in the mirror. Old hobbies fell away as the prospect of real life motoring became a more tangible fixation. I restored and hand-painted a barely roadworthy Standard 10 which never took to the roads. However once that licence was in the hand, things relaxed and I fel confident enough to return to models. Scalextric had a solid hold by then, but the models were pretty poor. I began building or converting Cobras and Ferraris, even a racing replica of my own Mini, and the satisfaction of celebrating such machines for a few pounds was very real. I had begun to visit motor sport events, to take pictures even contribute to the local Motor Club magazine, and the desire to recreate what I saw led me further and further into static models, to paint detail, to fit miniature flexi navigator lamps in the rally cars, to paint simulated muc where it belonged. I knew the shape of a Healey 3000

The author's photograph
taken for the Ford Times
magazine of his 1/32nd
scale K & B model
Mustang 350 GT on a
Scalextric circuit..

chassis, the bulkhead's form, the radiator positioning, long before I had the opportunity to roam around the real thing. Soon enough, real life consigned these simple, 'virtual' motoring pleasures to the past. During a house move 25 years later a wooden orange box from a garage loft turned up, covered in dirt. In it were many of those motoring daydreams – now a little worn. I have no idea how they came to have been saved and presumably must thank the stout wooden box for at least their partial preservation.

Nowadays most of those cars I know well, have road tested and one or two even owned, yet somehow the models remain exciting. There is a box of wheels and I know in time I shall find a moment to begin sorting out which set belongs to which car, which steering wheel goes where. I shall convince myself it will only take an evening to reconstruct a damaged race car, and almost imperceptibly the intervening years will have disappeared. Constructing detailed models of classic cars is to escape. Just for a little while you can again choose a car of your dreams, fit it out, paint it exactly as you wish. The model choice now is breathtaking and magazines, books and video all provide incredibly detailed information. The high ideals of Meccano Guild membership may be beyond my reach, but that box

of cars remains evidence of a genuine continuity of interest in motor cars.

The individual that owns a Ferrari, those that follow its fortunes and others that recreate it in miniature – all are enthusiasts. All, thank goodness, have not lost that childhood zest for things that stir imaginations.

Living room Grand Prix; a motorised Lotus waits on the grid.

PERSONAL DREAMS
A Guide to Race Car Ownership

The joy of the open road, when you can find one, is some recompense for the nightmares of day-to-day road travel. Every weekend millions watch race drivers extend that freedom beyond Ministry of Transport rules. Most of us are quietly confident drivers and the knowledge that with the right car – and with a clear road – you too could test your skill, and experience the same excitement first-hand, is ever present. Until recent times motor racing schools have been the exclusive domain of young bucks eager for professional recognition. However, the phenomenal growth in classic cars has changed everything. The sheer numbers of the generation of 'Baby Boomers' has turned classic eventing into the fastest growing area of UK Motor Sports. Significantly, reaching the freedom of their middle years, with fewer demands on finance,

has led many real enthusiasts to ignite their dream. Classic car rallies, timed hill climbs and historic racing are all swelling with competitors eager to stretch personal skills, rather than indulge in do-or-die dicing. There are often single seater race grids with average ages of 40 or 50, simply because they have the funds, and the urge to have serious fun.

If this hasn't been your whole life, how do you start?. Like so many things, it's easier than you think. Motor sport worldwide is governed by the FIA who vest British control in the RAC's Motor Sports Association (MSA). All but the major international events are then organised under RAC MSA supervision by one of the 750 individual motor clubs. Joining one of these recognised clubs will open up a great many closed competition opportunities without need for more than an RAC MSA Clubman licence. However, getting properly qualified and licensed is everyone's real ambition. Because of the huge growth of interest, the RAC MSA created an introductory pack which has proved a runaway success. For £35 you receive a plastic folder containing a superb 30-minute video showing all the steps; their 372 page bible *The Competitors' Yearbook;* a booklet helping you select your preferred strand from the 22 different motor sport disciplines, and another listing the fixtures. There's personal insurance help, the important application form for a National B Competition licence, and a list of the approved Association of Racing Drivers Schools (A.R.D.S) by whom your application has to be endorsed. A staggering 75 per cent of all those who buy these introductory packs go on to successfully gain a genuine Competition Licence.

Schools are the vital key to any competitive career. Because they also provide exciting corporate VIP days out, introductions for teenagers, even great birthday presents, the teaching staff are reassuringly flexible. The lure of Silverstone, the home of the British Grand Prix, plus the astonishing choice of 90 vehicles, prompted my decision to approach the John Watson Driving Centre.

Sitting with John Watson himself in the pits' hospitality area, while Formula 1 Williams and McLarens screamed by, was an interesting experience. Watson had been a works driver for that

Passing on his racing knowledge, John Watson waits with the author for the Formula One cars to clear the track.

same Mclaren team and stood on the winners' podium at this very circuit as victor in the 1981 British Grand Prix. He's taken the chequered flag as a Works driver for Porsche, for TWR Silk Cut Jaguar, and was one of the Toyota team for the World Sports Prototype Championship. This considerate man is virtually unique in the sport for, unlike many others who have taken the money and run, Watson is passing his knowledge on to further generations.

The school has instructor teams available for everyone, from children taking pre-instruction in Peugeot 106s, through to adults wishing to control fully prepared single seater racing cars. It's a complex organisation based within the nerve centre of the Silverstone circuit and using its famous facilities.

An impressive line-up at the John Watson Driving School at Silverstone. Touring cars are of course the mainstay and the starting point, but the single seaters beckon.

"Keep it smooth, retain the racing line ... "

under supervision. Further high performance training in Caterham Sevens, touring cars or single seater Formula Fords depends on ability and your piggy bank.

According to Watson, clients often display a mixture of nonchalance and honest nerves. The major obstacles are really the initial bombardment of the senses, the reality of staring up the pit road towards the open track, the unknown machine, strange harness and race wear, unfamiliar corners and cambers – a continuous intake of new information. According to this Grand Prix ace, the initial stress levels are high and so his instructors are geared to pace individuals according to the speed at which they can absorb information.

Watson himself took me round the initial introductory laps, calmly threading the car from corner to corner, talking me through braking points. Of the same breed as Alain Prost, he prefers the approach of perfect, smooth lines, of treating the car like a horse, imposing control while letting it exercise its own strength. In his assured hands the only real sense of speed was the pendulum sensation of the car being 'allowed' the full track width when leaving corners: giving the car its head.

The value of being talked around a course is huge, the exhilaration when you have to swap seats is even greater. It's only really then that you begin to understand the value of such expert lessons.

Touring cars may represent the backbone of such tuition, but there is absolutely no doubt that approaching a single seater race car is something very special. This is where reality blurs with dreams, where fantasy rushes to confront the present moment.

Watching two dozen racing cars weaving into a corner on television is not the same thing as walking up to this tiny machine standing millimetres from tarmac, defying you, challenging you. Over the next ten minutes you will face perhaps a dozen hurdles.

How to climb nonchalantly into the cockpit, and negotiate the full harness? More importantly, how to start it? The car's body virtually disappears once the driver is in position, and the two exposed front wheels and suspension dominate forward vision. The engine fires immediately, though idling sounds disappointingly like a rough road car. You are now at

Watson is shrewdly aware of the growing band of enthusiasts who neither wish to become a Michael Schumacher, nor unduly bruise their motoring pride. They do, however, want to challenge themselves, extend their skills and learn track competence. Owning a 1960s classic sports car is rewarding, but to feel confident enough to don a helmet and drive 10 laps alongside others requires instruction. A completely new world of pleasures is probably only eight Watson school lessons from reality. The basic RAC MSA qualifying instruction and examination takes less than a day, costing £135, plus licence fee.

He stresses that track disciplines are vital, and these are taught in their fleet of safe modern racing cars. The introductory lesson involves instructor circuits in a 155bhp Peugeot 2-litre touring car, followed by your own efforts

the point of no return. You casually flick down the helmet visor as though it were a regular occurrence, select what you pray will be first gear, withdraw the fierce clutch … and stall it! Just like any other car, you gradually learn its characteristics.

The first few laps or so are a blur, trying to recall your touring car instruction, guessing when a gear change is needed, trying to give the car its 'head'. Gradually, it all falls into a rhythm and the full magic of the experience dawns on you. The tiny right hand gear change feels like it was made for your palm, the precision of the steering, the power, and sounds of the engine just behind your head are overwhelming. It has to rank among the most full- blooded moments

available in life. Some of the most famous racing landscape in the wotld rushing past your visor, the great ribbon of grandstands and pits, the circuit bridges: it is the fulfilment of those personal dreams, living at ten tenths. You eventually draw into the pits, half expecting mechanics to battle with tyre changes – though the faces of the Watson school staff are just as welcome.

In the privacy of this high speed classroom, you quickly learn an enormous amount both about your driving and yourself. The sense of self-esteem which follows is very powerful. I was fortunate to experience the Watson school car during the lunch break of a private Formula 1 test day. After my laps I walked back along the shiny lines of McLaren, Williams and Benetton wagons still wearing my full kit. The race wear is the ultimate in power dressing, the sense of personal triumph irrationally strong – John Watson likens the metamorphosis to that of a gladiator.

Race schools will loan you personal equipment for training, but properly fitting racewear of your own is then essential. Although incredibly few people are injured in motor sport, this is because safety is taken so seriously and getting the right gear is imperative. If your classic competition interest is ever likely to embrace trips to any of the legendary European circuits (most historic series do) then it might be wiser to invest in International rather than National grade items. There are a

Another single cockpit (and on page 38), Merlyn Formula Ford at Snetterton; originally built by Colchester Racing Developments.

Before the single seater, first a few laps in the Peugeot 2-litre touring car.

cars forgive, handle well and look good, there are also 50 different marques from which to choose. The engines are traditionally reliable and access to all mechanical areas is wonderful. Specifications have to be as original, except for modern safety aspects, but this doesn't mean they are tame; as Chris points out, he can lap most UK circuits five seconds quicker than monsters such as the AC Cobra. This is real single seater racing, and the formula helped propel the careers of masters such as James Hunt and Ayrton Senna.

Chris explains that he could get you onto a race circuit with what he terms a scruffy but safe car for around £7,000, while £15,000 would buy you a race winner. As to general overheads, it is possible to run a full season of 12 races at an average cost of £250 a meeting – barring accidents!

The obvious names such as Lotus come with a premium for the badge, but the most reliable and forgiving car – the ideal newcomers' racer – is the Merlyn, which was made in the hundreds by Colchester Racing Developments. They are great engineers who got caught up building a Formula 3 car, adapted it to conform with Formula Ford, and discovered this formula suited the car perfectly. Chris brought his own 1966 Merlyn to Snetterton Circuit where I was able to see what the £15,000 price tag represented. Not only does it breed confidence on the circuit, but it also looks like a real race car. The cockpit is a snug fit, but once in place everything falls easily to hand, and underway, handling, visibility and the gears – all destined from the outset for abuse – prove to be superlative. Strangely, however, the lingering impression months later hasn't been the obviously impressive car, but the thought that for the price of an Escort, I could own one and belong to this great club. The comradeship between the Formula Ford drivers was palpable. Few were mechanically minded, some just keep their car at home and called a garage for help, but I saw three generations of men in race suits enjoying life, sharing jokes, problems and tools. It was cold, there were periods of track closure, and yet when they were talking about that next week's drive to Spa and arriving early to catch the best pits, I felt envious. Yes, circuit racing is exciting, but beyond that, simply belonging to this world is a whole new experience.

considerable number of suppliers and not everything on display meets regulations. I use Demon Tweeks, who offer a worldwide service, have an excellent catalogue and have been successfully helping drivers for 25 years. Incidently, they also sponsor the Historic Rally Championship.

The final, and most exciting possibility, is owning a real racing car. Various formulas exist, with huge differences in cost. Given the traditional hazards of just buying a second-hand road car, it's essential to purchase competition machinery from an expert. The leading light in 1960s racing cars is Chris Alford, who as a child watched the likes of Moss and Fangio battling and whose first racing car was a tiny 500cc Formula 3. His first love is for Formula Junior (1959–63) which was a golden era. FI and FJ were so similar that many juniors were successfully re-engined to become Grand Prix cars. Really good examples are now worth £40,000 to £50,000. The simple two-tier racing brought good drivers quickly to the surface, and earmarked them for FI. Junior was so successful it split into two levels – Formula 2 and 3 – and priced itself out of the enthusiasts' reach. Racing schools needed practical cars – as did pupils – and Formula Ford with its 1100cc production engines emerged, offering plenty of excitement and economical spares back-up.

Formula Ford is over 25 years old and the Historic S.C.C. now runs thriving race series for pre–31st December 1977 cars. This is the perfect starting formula, for not only do the

CONTACTS

The ARDS race pack, video and list of all clubs from

RAC MSA
Motor Sports House
Riverside Park
Colnbrook
Slough
SL3 0HG

Leading general club for period competition

Historic Sports Car Club
Silverstone Circuit
Silverstone
Nr Towcester
Northants
NN12 8TN

International race wear suppliers

Demon Tweeks
75 Ash Road South
Wrexham Industrial Estate
Wrexham
Clwyd
LL13 9UG

Period racing car sales

Chris Alford Racing
Newland Cottage
Hassocks
West Sussex
BN6 8NU

John Watson Performance
Driving Centre

Silverstone Circuit
Silverstone
Nr Towcester
Northants
NN12 8TN

BUDGET GUIDELINES

RAC MSA "'Go Racing' Information pack £35.00
RAC MSA National B Competition Race Licence £35.00
RAC MSA Clubman Licence
(covers most non-race events) £10.30

Typical Demon Tweeks kit package
International Standard

Sparco FIA 2 layer sprint suit	£175.00
Sparco FIA budget gloves	£24.00
Sparco FIA racing shoes	£58.15
Sparco balaclava open/eyehole	£9.00
Sparco underwear set top/pants	£55.00
Sparco socks	£6.00
Sparco pro racing full face helmet	£206.00
Demon Tweeks motorsports kit bag	£22.22
Chronus 602 M100R stop watch	£29.95
Demon Tweeks digital pit board	£26.95
TOTAL (excl VAT and delivery)	£584.62

DT have kindly offered the above Inernational package to readers at the reduced price of £530 plus carriage and VAT. The National Standard package is also available, reduced from £356.25 to £325.

Typical John Watson Race School charges

Single basic day course for RAC exam/licence £135.
Various 3 & 4 day intensive courses are available which include all driving skills, sponsor/promotion education, a F1 factory visit, personal race kit and licence fees. These vary in price and a budget plan is available.
Personal racewear loaned by school.
Opportunity for inter-pupil race experience is available through their new, season-long championship linked to the school.

Typical race car from Chris Alford Racing

Cars generally found to customer's budget.

The featured Merlyn Formula Ford built 1966 by Colchester Racing Developments costs £15.000.
Lesser Formula Fords start from around £7,000.

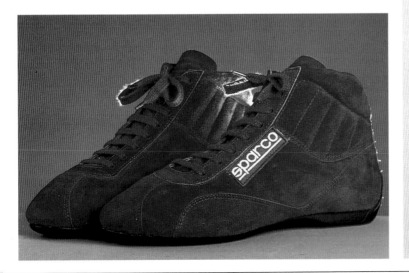

COMING OF AGE
Seeking reassurance in the kit market

The very mention of the words 'kit car' sends shudders down the spines of many hard core motoring enthusiasts. It's a curious reaction given that assembling a decayed sports car is considered commendable, but perhaps this dismissal is because the cars don't have a formal tradition. Certainly there are some extremely suspect kits in the market place and an understandable sense of recoil from poor replicas of great cars. However, it is very unfair to tar all kit cars with the same brush – after all, if the mass of older manufactured cars were viewed as one, all of the great cars would be lost amid the morass of the poor and the ugly. As to a lack of tradition, we should question our basis for objection very closely: Lotus came from kits and they were certainly not always reliable or well manufactured. A Caterham Seven is definitely kit; as are TVR, Ginetta – we appear to let some under the wire yet without a logical qualification.

Even if you are drawn towards a kit car project, there is uncertainty over exactly what is involved, the level of skill required, the

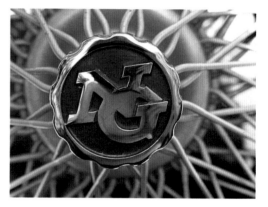

Stubby gear lever to the left, long, louvred bonnet to the fore; the look and the feel challenge you to define the word 'authentic'.

equipment, and the back-up each time you encounter a problem. Despite all these questions and misgivings, when you climb into something like a well-built Caterham Seven you get all the satisfaction of driving a highly individual car, yet an inner knowledge that all the bits that matter have been recently – and properly – screwed together, which is certainly not automatically the case when you buy a legitimate classic. One recent innovation which provides some reassurance is the advent of the Association of Specialist Car Manufacturers, a deliberate alliance of the firms now pressing for higher standards and the best possible back up for customers.

The basis of the TF is the MGB.

One such ASCM member is NG Cars of Epsom who produce a small range of traditional open sports cars with long louvred bonnets,. The initial preconception that NG Cars was a rather bare-faced journey around the edge of Abingdon is confounded when you learn that all the cars were designed by the original owner, Nick Green, and two of the four models were actually inspired by the Aston Martin International and the 'Boat Tailed' Ulster from the 1930s. Green was a graduate of mechanical and aeronautical design and having worked on other kit cars elected in 1979 to design and manufacture his own – initially the Aston-inspired TA, then the 'Boat tail', which was very much his private baby. Indeed, he still keeps this TC and claims his intention is to be buried with it eventually. The two remaining models, the TD and TF, followed shortly afterwards and were variations on a 2+2 – all of them MG B-based. One of his customers, John Hoyle, bought a TF, spent 16 months constructing it and began winning show awards for its build quality. By 1986 Nick had also began work on a Ford Sierra but then started systematically selling on his models to Peter Fellows who eventually changed the trading name to Pastiche and the donor car to the Ital/Marina. The MGB was then sharing in the mad valuation surge towards the end of the 1980s. Pastiche over-stretched and GTM bought out the rights to the TC, TD and TF trading them again as NG Cars with enthusiast John Hoyle helping GTM get to grips with their new acquisition. However, a satisfactory financial settlement with his multi-national corporation employer meant John was able to switch his energy and experience to his hobby. He approached GTM with new ideas and to his surprise was offered the NG Cars company.

Since 1993 he has carefully stabilised the business and engaged a network of over 30 suppliers to ensure there are never unacceptable supply delays. His objective is to offer the highest possible manufacturing standards, to create cars steeped in traditional motoring style, while providing modern reliability and creature comforts. The range is based on MGB donor cars which provides all that car's reliability and instant sports car performance without the need for additional tuning. It also gives you an MG without all that rust and bodywork trauma. Because of Nick Green's engineering training the fibreglass body and strong tubulat steel cruciform chassis are light but immensely rigid, and combining this with the torquey 1800cc twin carburettor provides excellence performance, particularly in the vital mid-range speeds: It also sounds good.

He had three built examples at his Surrey headquarters and I selected a striking metallic grey TF which proved to be the original award-winning model which John had bought as a kit

from Nick Green. Nothing looked tatty, nothing suggested a home build. Driving it around the Surrey countryside frankly made me forget it wasn't a new car. The tiny gear lever offered delightful short changes and the general levels of trim and comfort were commendable; attention was even paid to detailing such as a push button starter on the dash alongside. It is

easy to see it as a desirable motor car, but I returned to NGs inhibited by the prospects of hand-building to such levels. Hoyle explained that roughly 200 hours' work is involved, and great care has been taken to ensure no specialist tools or facilities are required. Obviously a build book is provided, but I gather customers build up great friendships with him by calling by, or phoning for detailed advice. It appears he enjoys the customer contact as much as selling the cars.

Who buys? According to Hoyle his customers range from one who runs two trucks, right through to £100,000 Mercedes owners. In particular, there is a strong following from those running company cars who are looking for something more exciting for their leisure time. NG can help steer you to towards donor cars and an increasingly popular alternative is supplying prepared rolling chassis with either the MGB or Rover SD1 V8 engines. It is also possible to arrange a pre–built model. If however, you are considering a second-hand example, it's important to check exactly what you are buying, for during its interim production at Pastiche it was adapted and sold for Marina/Ital parts.

The challenges of a home build are very real and most of the time you will only have yourself to blame for troubles. 200 hours of anyone's time isn't to be wasted, and so make sure the basic car and the supply route for parts are good. If you can also find a concern such as NG which actually welcomes calls for support, then you are really fortunate.

NG Cars Ltd
Unit One
Eclipse Estate
30 West Hill
Epsom
Surrey
KT19 8JD
Tel: 01372 748666

The other initial members of the ASCM are:

Marlin Engineering
01363 773772
Chesil Speedsters
01308 897072
Ultima Sports Ltd
01455 631366
Quantum Sports Cars
01384 834422
Gardner Douglas
01949 843299
Grinnall Cars
01299 822862
Dakar Cars
01322 614004
Beauford Cars
01695 622608

OUTSTANDING DEBT
Just a man with a camera

Historic motor sports are a very real success story, and classic eventing is the fastest growing area of RAC-governed eventing, with two generations of enthusiasts now competing together on historic grids. The Historic Sports Car Club now thrives with around one thousand members, of which a staggering two-thirds are actively engaged in racing. This has not only brought enormous entertainment to both drivers and race-going crowds, but perhaps more importantly, it has meant the preservation of an enormous number of historic sports and racing cars.

As a result many businesses have prospered and whole ranges of specialist magazines emerged to accommodate the interest. It is, however, to our eternal shame that we have taken all this growth for granted and not once within the thousands upon thousands of motoring magazine pages seen a proper tribute to the lone figure who fought to popularise post-war historic motor sports. In the 1950s historic sports racing cars were outclassed within the existing racing categories and owners were left with nothing but club racing activity. As a result, a large number of historically interesting racing cars were neglected

A rare picture of the camera shy Guy Griffiths (centre) alongside friend Sam Clutton (left) at the 50th anniversary Prescott Hill climb meeting. Guy and Sam drove the same Itala at both the very first and the 50th Anniversary events.

A guy Griffiths picture from 1967, showing some of the marvellous cars, Ecurie Ecosse D-Type to the right, which he did so much to preserve. In May that year, the Griffiths Formula was invited to provide a support race to the Tourist Trophy at Oulton Park.

or simply broken up. Even more tragically, the handfuls of truly significant historic examples such as the racing Jaguars were simply being sold overseas by frustrated owners. It was a potential melt down situation for these British racing cars. A solitary figure fought the general apathy to prevent the inevitable loss of these models to Britain. This extraordinary gentleman, a discreet and familiar trackside photographer, is Guy Griffiths. Through my work for *Autosport* I met with Guy frequently during 1960s and 1970s events, and enjoyed his friendship and occasional hospitality. Whether being driven across the Cotswolds by his skilful daughter Penny in the 1950 Healey Silverstone, or dining surrounded by impeccable art and furnishings, one always left Guy Griffiths with a profound sense of well being – the lasting enjoyment of a good vintage. However, he is essentially a retiring man and it takes years to extract any true sense of his contribution to motor sports, the aviation industry, and photography. It is this reticence, this unfashionable modesty, which has conspired, along with the silence of motoring commentators, to conceal Guy's important contribution to the vigorous health of historic motor sports.

In July 1966 I wrote a feature in *Sporting Motorist* entitled 'Lest We Forget" which began:

'We are a nation of hoarders, sentimentalists, steeped in a curious sense of historical showmanship. There seem to be few limits to the trouble we will go to to preserve the old, the famous and the unusual.

Occasionally, quite unexpectedly, we lapse and something important is forgotten. Just so with our famous wartime fighters like the Spitfire, who earned universal admiration in their active career yet now number only a handful of flying examples. The motoring enthusiast is generally a good custodian of his or her particular obession and groups like the Vintage Sports Car Club do a great deal to preserve active examples … This satisfactory situation does not however exist with one of the most interesting and important classes of competition cars – Sports/racing cars from 1945 to 1955 … "

The article went on to describe the then brand new Griffiths Formula which was the outcome of Guy's campaign for a race classification which would provide decent competition events for a virtually ignored range of cars, including Aston Martin DBs, HRGs, Healey Silverstones, Frazer Nash, Cooper Bristols, Jowet Jupiters, and Jaguar C- and D-Types.

Guy, who has also spent decades collecting important cars, could see the increasing lack of incentive for owning or restoring these cars, and so approached Tim Carson of the Vintage Sports Car Club and suggested that they should open up a new class of membership/entrant for these ignored models. The rationale was that they were currently relatively inexpensive to buy and would thus open up a new, wider membership as well as introducing a fresh crowd attraction to VSCC race events. Informally his idea was given support but when

The unique collection of Jaguars that Guy Griffiths had created through the years. From left to right:

C-Type *Works Le Mans car, led 1952 Goodwood nine hours with Moss/Walker; Mille Miglia car with Moss and Prescott Sports Car record with P. Walker.*
D-Type *Works spare car. Holder of six records at Monza driven by Major Baillie.*
E2 A *Works prototype; Le Mans 1960 with Briggs Cunningham and first American Can-Am Series with Cunningham and Jack Brabham.*
Lightweight E *First sold to a private entrant, Tommy Atkins, and driven by Roy Salvadori; Silverstone and Spa Sports Car lap record.*
E-Type *Racer built on Protheroe shell using light-weight works parts.*
The red E-Type is the pro-duction offspring of all the above cars!

placed before the formal VSCC Committee it was turned down. Again, the proposition was presented and yet again these 'far sighted' individuals turned Guy and his idea away. Griffiths, a man more likely to raise a topic of cultural interest than his voice, was not to be beaten. He wrote to the Science Museum suggesting that the technical and commercial signif-icance of cars such as the Jaguar D-Type ought to qualify them as museum items. The proposition actually included giving these awesome cars to the museum – but they never even replied.

With no one sharing his vision of their significance he was left with the single option of somehow creating a new club which would qualify for events under RAC MSA regulations, yet be able to open up competitive racing classes for these important cars. He was one of the first members of the VSCC, as well as other clubs including the Frazer Nash C C – one which had recently become the charge of famous owner and international rally driver Betty Haig. Pre-war she had studied at the Slade Art School and wenr

on to become a leading international driver both in rallies and on race circuits such as Le Mans where she drove a Ferrari. A friend of Guy's, Betty offered the Frazer Nash Club as the surrogate parent to his project, and so the Griffiths Formula was born for 'Internationally famous types of car made or raced between 1945 and 1955'.

At 4.15pm on 14 May 1966, a modest field of eli-gibles gathered on the Castle Combe grid, starting a movement which has evolved into today's feast of historic events and festivals.

I was at that Wiltshire meeting which listed a handful of Healey Silverstones, Betty in her famous Le Mans Frazer Nash, an Aston Martin DB2 and 3-S, Allards, an HRG, a Jowett, a Cooper Bristol, a Healey 100S, a HMW Jaguar and three D-Types including Guy's own car. Neil Corner had recently bought his D-Type and drove 300 miles just to get this chance to race. There was also Bernard Worth who owned the rare 1953 Type 166 Ferrari sports car – a thinly disguised V12 2-litre Grand Prix machine.

It was the only example in Britain and until then had only been used for his annual holiday and the odd hill climb. Guy had just opened the competition door to many more enthusiasts than he had imagined. A wide range of owners, from the most impoverished DIY restorer/competitor, to richer drivers in shinier cars all owe a huge debt of gratitude to the insight and quiet tenacity of Griffiths.

The momentum grew naturally. Invitations arrived, such as that to provide a support race to the big Tourist Trophy at Oulton Park – and even offered welcome starting money. The Griffiths Formula as such ran for a few years until the formation of the present Historic Sports Car Club, and in typical Griffith style, Guy quietly bowed out, leaving the movement he rescued to grow and prosper.

After a quarter of a century's silence I unexpectedly received a personal note from Guy sent via a national newspaper. He had read something of what I had been doing and dropped me a line of good wishes and support. It was typical of this mercurial man and I grasped the opportunity to visit him once more.

Living on a hill top with views out to sea, Guy Griffiths has a range of knowledge and interests wider than that of the average car buff. We sat in the kitchen tackling sandwiches and talked of the past, aviation engineering … and cars. We spent hours in his study discussing opportunities, lost friends … and cars. The man's intellect, his spirit for life, his interests are boundless. We recalled his famous and unique collection of Works racing Jaguars which he gave to Penny, his close friendship with 'Lofty' England, of W. O. Bentley's remarks as a house guest, 10-year-old Penny's habit of sitting in Bernie Ecclestone's Cooper 500, even Alex Issigonis' mother! His spheres of interest and influence are extraordinary, and all the while his fingers trace rows and rows of colour slides with the same affection and familiarity as a pianist over keys. 'I can always remember the pictures I have taken', he muses, before opening a drawer of perhaps a hundred large scale portraits of just about everybody you might have ever heard of within motor sport during the last half century or so.

I asked him how he viewed the present-day popularity of historic motor sports and indeed if he gained personal satisfaction from it. I received the customary non-committal and modest response. I asked him what had inspired his own passion and he instantly cited the awesome post-war Jaguars – hence his subsequent unique racing collection, which includes the one-off experimental prototype E2 A and the lightweight C-Type, which actually appeared as the Works car under three different specifications, as well as his true Lightweight E and the D. Early Alfas, too, are much favoured and for over 30 years Guy owned the extremely important 1933 8C–2300 Berlina with its stunning Carrozzeria Viotti bodywork. This car came third in the 1933 Le Mans just eight days after its registration. As with all his cars he tried to ensure they were as original as possible – he is not a fan of over-restored historic vehicles.

Griffiths will never seek accolades. He was central to developing the vital wartime 24-cylinder, sleeve-valved Napier Sabre which powered the Typhoon fighter aircraft. He will proudly hand you the sample sleeve in his study, yet his sole declared professional status is as a simple photographer. With highly commercial summer festivals of historic motor sports attracting thousands upon thousands of fans, it would be fitting, indeed appropriate, for some of those now enjoying the benefits of this popularity to commemorate Guy's pivotal role. Surely something like a Griffith's Trophy is not beyond their imagination.

Eventually the clock overtook events and drew my lengthy visit to a close. As I drove away my mind raced over the variety of topics discussed, the depth of information exchanged, the resonating sense of having been privy to so many intimate first-hand fragments of history. His friendship is a rare privilege.

A rare photograph of the late Betty Haig, who helped to establish the pioneering Griffiths Formula in the face of 'official' indifference.

1996/7 COLLECTION
New Eligibles

The phrase 'Classic Car' means different models to each of us according to our interests. Although there are obvious core masterpieces, the majority of any one person's list would not match another's. This is part of the joy, for it celebrates individuality as well as offering chances to revisit less complicated periods in our own lives.

In more formal terms 'Classic' has become an accredited word trying to define exactly what is and isn't a qualified model. Most of the time this is a very unimportant point, as decisions are really entirely subjective. The phrase itself was largely born of journalism, but it has now taken firm root even within the hallowed halls of the RAC. The huge growth in sporting competitions and classic runs has required the RAC

MSA, who govern all UK motor sports, to define a qualifying category for events such as the huge Norwich Union RAC Run each summer. Reading the entry papers still reveals an easy going attitude, allowing more recent cars of appropriate types and histories. The formal position, however, is that cars must be at least 20 years old to qualify as Classics. This means that every year a completely new collection of cars fall eligible – some of which are already highly desirable. The march of time also re-introduces forgotten models which have yet to become fashionable – or expensive.

The 1996/7 vintage offers a wide cross-section, from the exotic Boxer Ferrari to humble Triumph Dolomites: all now formally become Classics.

OWNERS' CLUB
Triumph Dolomite Club
TDC HQ
39 Mill Lane
Arncott
Bicester
Oxon
OX6 OPB

SPECIFICATIONS
ENGINE: 1296cc/1493cc
GEARBOX: 4 Speed
POWER: 58bhp/61bhp
BRAKES: Disc/Drum
SUSPENSION: Ind wishbone/coil
                Live axle/radius arm/coil
TOP SPEED: 90mph
FUEL: 34mpg
LENGTH: 161.2in/411cm

CURRENT PRICE – £1,000

NEW ELIGIBLES

TRIUMPH DOLOMITE 1850

Unobtrusive Michelotti styling and confusion surrounding the small Triumph saloon range have largely kept these cars in the shade, and some believe that is where they should stay. Quentin Willson consigned the later models to the abyss in the BBC *Good Car Guide 1995-6* as 'Another Leyland folly. Leave them to the classics boys.' But reliable components and quite reasonable degrees of luxury actually brought them closer to BMW than was appreciated. Initially a mid-1960s front wheel drive 1300, it grew to 1500cc before development costs required a wholesale shift to the more economical rear wheel drive. The Toledo 1300cc and 1500cc cars led to the Dolomite 1850 and 2 litre Sprint which used the 1500 body shells and the Triumph-made Saab 99 slant-four engine. The smaller-engined cars were suburban transport but the later two litre Sprint – an uprated version of the 1850 – created the best Dolomite balance with good city manners, a reasonably refined interior and open road enjoyment with its 100mph capabilities. All these cars are now eligible classics and their lacklustre image has kept the prices low enough to make them a potentially very rewarding first classic. The alloy engine is prone to overheating, which, if unchecked, can become expensive.

ALFASUD SPRINT

In the 1980s and 1990s the Japanese dominated the attractive three door hatchback market with sporting derivatives of their family saloons such as the Honda Civic and CRX. Back in the mid-1970s, however, Alfa did just the same thing - putting the Alfasud floorpan and power plants with the beautiful Giugiaro coupé bodywork. Though at first glance similar to the GTV, the Sprint offers its own considerable charms. Though not as long or spacious as its bigger brother, it is still beautifully proportioned and actually much more agile. It was launched in 1970 with the responsive 76bhp 1.3 litre engine (which became 1.5 litre in 1978) and a Veloce tuning option which lifted the output further to 95bhp. It weighed just 1148lbs; the statistics don't give a true impression of the sporting performance from this pretty GT which even in basic form could propel you to 100mph. If you are seeking an economic classic with a fine sporting tradition and a little class, then you will be hard pressed to improve on this model among the new intake of eligibles. Perfect for entering those civilised and sociable classic runs, and the fact that it has only just passed through the qualifying door means that good examples are exceptional value for money.

SPECIFICATIONS
ENGINE: 1286cc
GEARBOX: 5 Speed manual
POWER: 76bhp
BRAKES: Disc
SUSPENSION: Ind MacPherson/coil
Rigid axle/Watt linkage/transverse linkage/coil
TOP SPEED: 103mph
FUEL: 35mpg
LENGTH: 157.9in/401cm

CURRENT PRICE: £2,600

OWNERS' CLUB
Alfa Romeo O.C.
97 High Street
Linton
Cambs
CB1 6JT

LANCIA GAMMA COUPÉ

The Gamma was originally introduced in 1976 as a replacement for the Fiat 130, and the coupé was a brilliant adaptation of the dull Gamma saloon. The wheelbase was shortened by 4.5 inches and the saloon platform squeezed under a brand new Pininfarina two door, four seat coupé body which offered considerable space as well as Italian style. The 2.5 litre boxer engine and the all-synchromesh five speed gearbox makes this a fast and comfortable long-distance express with a 120mph top speed. All independent suspension, electronic ignition, servo assisted disc brakes, power steering, alloy wheels, tinted glass, electric windows and velour seating – a long list of quality extras making good condition examples wonderful value for money. Inevitably the main concern with 1970s Italian production is rust – if you buy carelessly, restoration will be more expensive than the car. However, reduced numbers mean that the good ones will certainly rise in value. It is not a DIY candidate and with any thrashed example a drive belt break can chew the entire engine. Chosen carefully, this Lancia can give you highly practical and stylish transport – and a chance to catch a real bargain. Currently the very best examples are available for just under £3,000, which represents a lot of car for your money.

SPECIFICATIONS
ENGINE: 2484cc flat four
GEARBOX: 5 Speed manual; automatic option
POWER: 140bhp
BRAKES: Servo discs
SUSPENSION: Ind wishbone/coil
TOP SPEED: 121mph
FUEL: 25mpg
LENGTH: 176.4in/448cm

CURRENT PRICE – £2,900

OWNERS' CLUB
Lancia M.C.
David Baker
Mount Pleasant
Penrhos
Brymbo
Wrexham
Clywd
LL11 5LY

OWNERS' CLUB
Alfa Romeo O.C.
97 High Street
Linton
Cambs
CB1 6JT

SPECIFICATIONS
ENGINE: 1962cc
GEARBOX: 5 speed manual
POWER: 130bhp
BRAKES: Disc
SUSPENSION: Front – Ind wishbone/torsion bar
Rear – Rigid axle/trailing arms/transverse
Watts linkage/coil
TOP SPEED: 120mph
FUEL: 28mpg
LENGTH: 165.4in/420cm

CURRENT PRICE: £3,700

ALFA ROMEO 2.0 GTV

Although officially a Bertone styling, it was actually the last design from Giugiaro before he left Bertone to start his own consultancy. The Fiat 850 Spider, the Fiat Dino, the Iso Griffo, the BMW 3200C, and the ill-fated Gordon Keeble were all contributions he made to the Bertone house, though none more important than this classic Alfa coupé which first appeared in 1967. The 1970s incarnation was based upon the Alfetta and this 2.0 GTV version now becomes an eligible classic. It was the fastest four-cylinder Alfetta, and would eventually be joined by an excellent 2.5 litre V6 in 1981. The Alfetta GTV was launched in 1974 with a 1.8 engine, then 1.6, followed by the 1962cc, 130bhp which offered around 25mpg and a top speed of 120mph. The initial dashboard layout was curious, with most of the instrumentation in the centre, but the space and visibility were exceptional, while the four headlights and frontal grille treatment were pure Alfa. Over 120,000 were produced, so even allowing for many neglected examples falling prey to rust plenty of choice still exists. Spares are still good, many minor parts now exist to actually improve details and your main objective is hunting out cars with regular services – something Alfas benefit from particularly.

OWNERS' CLUB
BMW C C.
John Kinch
PO Box 328
Andover
Hants
SP10 1YN

SPECIFICATIONS
ENGINE: 1990cc
GEARBOX: 4 speed
POWER 122bhp
BRAKES: Disc/Drum
SUSPENSION: Ind MacPherson/coil
Ind semi trailing/coil
TOP SPEED: 112mph
FUEL: 27mpg
LENGTH: 171.3in/435cm

CURRENT PRICE: £2,000

BMW 320

The company's post-war fortunes really improved with their best selling Series 2 cars which were launched in 1966 with the 1600–2, and continued in various forms until 1977, surviving the oil crisis to win an increasingly loyal following. Best illustrated with their more glamorous 2002 variants, these cars were fast, handled well, and remained very understated in styling. Between 1968 and 1975 the 2002 spawned several successors. In 1975 BMW introduced the Series 3 and surpassed themselves selling over 1.5 million cars in just seven years of production. The formula remained the same, but this time it involved a longer wheelbase, trimmer body styling, and progressive engine improvements from the initial 90bhp power output. After just two years of production BMW introduced the M60 versions which replaced the four cylinder engine with two small six-cylinder power plants. These were the 320–6 developing 122bhp via natural carburation and the 323i generating 143bhp thanks to fuel injection. These are fast cars and like other mid-range BMW saloons required driver concentration in wet conditions. There were just a few convertible versions but these were never sold in the UK. Well built, understated Q cars, the 320 now qualifies as an eligible classic, but such performance – and handling – demands that you thoroughly check its past before buying.

MATRA RANCHO

This was a really good idea – when dogs, kids and a boat were dominating my life I very nearly bought one myself. By 1977 Range Rover had already begun its relentless creep towards luxury-viewing cabins from which to enjoy the countryside. The Rancho actually looked prettier than the eventual Discovery, and, being French, had the style and courage to provide the maximum interior space, hardy trim that didn't need dirty shoes removed, and the simplest of mechanical parts to reduce engine problems. Critics belittled it for not boasting the macho ingredient of four wheel drive, but many four wheel drive owners wouldn't even know how to engage full drive – or indeed if it's permanent. I live deep in the country and yet I can't recall ever needing it. Certainly higher ground clearance is useful, and the Matra enjoyed just under seven inches, but it was their brilliant interior accommodation which excelled. Borrowing from the straightforward front-wheel-drive Simca 1100, it offered 80bhp and a top speed of around 90mph. Three doors were provided, with folding rear seating, excellent interior headroom; fibreglass was used to preserve the exterior panels. It's a practical vehicle, with all the Gallic simplicity and logic of the legendary 2CV. Like that car, it has enduringly useful qualities, and enters the classic lists at an attractive price.

SPECIFICATIONS
ENGINE: 1442cc
GEARBOX: 4 speed
POWER: 80bhp
BRAKES: Disc/drum
SUSPENSION: Ind wishbone/torsion bar
　　　　　　　 Ind Trailing arms/transverse torsion bar
TOP SPEED: 90mph
FUEL: 25mpg
LENGTH: 169.7in/431cm

CURRENT PRICE: £3,200

OWNERS' CLUB
Matra Enthusiasts' Club
Mr T Martin
6 Woodlands Court
Woodlands Road
Harrow.
Middlx
HA1 2RU

FORD ESCORT MKII RS 2000

An enormous range of model variations were involved in the five-year life of the Escort Mk II. Over 2,000,000 Mk I sales set the pace and Ford launched the Mk II with an astonishing 19 model range and went on to underline their conviction by generating a further 2,000,000 Mk II sales. A huge number of these were modest road transport, while a handful were the highly successful RS 1800 with 115bhp BDA 16-valve engines; everything was enhanced to create homologation status for front line competition machines. Ford's second sporting version was an attempt to cash in on their competition success by marketing the German-built Mexicos, but this time enthusiasts quickly rejected it for its cosmetic shortcomings. The Mk II RS 2000 was a different matter, however, for this was a skilful mixture of road and rally car. It employed the 110bhp Pinto engine and its main distinguishing feature was the plastic raked front grille – although competing enthusiasts sometimes removed it. Needless to say model detail gets confusing, with some early Mk IIs in Mk I body shells, while in 1978 the Mexico and RS 1800 ceased, but the inferior Mexico interior went straight into the RS2000, and a Custom RS 2000 version went upmarket. Find a good one and enjoy its down-to-earth performance and handling, but be careful as most are likely to have been driven hard.

SPECIFICATIONS
ENGINE: 1993cc
GEARBOX: 4 speed manual
POWER: 110bhp
BRAKES: Disc/drum
SUSPENSION: Ind MacPherson/coil
　　　　　　　 Rigid axle/semi elliptic leaf
TOP SPEED: 110mph
FUEL: 28mpg
LENGTH: 161.8in/411cm

CURRENT PRICE: £4,250

OWNERS' CLUB
Ford RS O.C.
Stuart Niland
8 Heron Close
Lower Halstead
Sittingbourne
Kent
ME9 7EF

OWNERS' CLUB

Panther C.C.
91 Fleet Road
Farnborough
Hants
GU14 9RE

SPECIFICATIONS

ENGINE: 2279cc
GEARBOX: 4 speed, 5 speed optional
POWER: 108bhp
BRAKES: Disc
SUSPENSION: Ind wishbone/coil
Rigid axle/trailing radius arms/transverse linkage bar/coil
TOP SPEED: 110mph
FUEL: 25mpg
LENGTH: 142.1in/361cm

CURRENT PRICE: £5,300

PANTHER LIMA

Having created expensive specialist cars such as the J72, (inspired by the Jaguar SS100) Panther needed a more affordable model. The Lima was their answer, deliberately targeting the Morgan and Caterham 7 customers. Its sparse two seater body was loosely based upon a 1930s look; it was constructed mainly of fibreglass, with MG Midget doors which were generally concealed by duotoned paintwork. Though it looked highly individual, it was actually based upon the Vauxhall Magnum floorpan and mechanicals. A square, tubed structure attached to the Magnum base provided the strength to support the non-stressed body shell, although the 1979 Mk II version used a separate box frame. The Magnum 2300 engine and gearbox gave it a top speed of around 110mph, although Vauxhall DTV tuning and even a turbocharged version were possible. Around 900 of the Lima were built, with the early cars actually offering better performance than the later Bedford CF engine versions. Passenger and luggage space were pretty minimal, while the extremities were hard to protect when parking. It was Panther's first attempt at volume sales, and it has remained popular as a fun car. Spares are not a problem, but for the same price it's tempting to hunt out something with more tradition and resale appeal.

OWNERS' CLUB

Lotus Owners' Club
90 Coppell Lane
Stanstead Abbotts
Nr Ware
Herts
SG12 8BY

SPECIFICATIONS

ENGINE: 1973cc
GEARBOX: 5 speed manual
POWER: 160BHP
BRAKES: Disc
SUSPENSION: Ind Wishbone/coil
TOP SPEED: 135mph
FUEL: 20mpg
LENGTH: 165in/419cm

CURRENT PRICE: £5,500

LOTUS ESPRIT SI

A beautiful, timeless wedge design from Giugiaro, and the Lotus sporting tradition, elevate this car – while so much else should warn you off it. Launched in 1976, it followed in the footsteps of the mid-engined Lotus Europe and looked wonderful. However, you could not see to reverse, even hand luggage was homeless, the interior trim was almost amateur and frustrations such as heaters not working, or windows jamming, were all too frequent. The Esprit followed the Lotus principle of a steel backbone frame with the 1973cc, 160bhp engine mounted amidships behind the driver's seat. It used fully independent suspension, plus disc brakes front and rear, which combined with the lightweight plastic body to offer tantalising road holding. Unfortunately this means many over exuberant owners have left the road at some point. Reliability problems plagued Lotus, but the car's actual specifications progressively improved with the 1978 S2, then the 1981 S3, the 1986 HC and on into the world of turbos. However it's the early Mk Is which have become eligible, and these need very careful checking, particularly as the early chassis was not galvanised, so rust may become a serious problem. In the end a good looking example at a low price may well seduce and leave you simply trusting to luck!

PORSCHE 924

This car went into production in 1976 and reached Britain the following year. It would have been a much praised car if it hadn't been called a Porsche – indeed it was originally going to be an Audi. This really is a bargain classic and becoming eligible for classic competitions and runs makes it even more attractive. Much fuss was made about it not being a *real* Porsche and having a water-cooled front-mounted engine – which was rather mindless given that the critics already knew it was a VW/Audi project before Porsche hijacked it. Actually, a 2+2 coupé complete with hatchback, enjoying a top speed of 125mph and returning 28mpg is pretty seductive. Add to that four wheel disc braking, fully independent suspension, five speed gearbox (after 1977) and later engine enlargements, plus a turbo version, and the package becomes exceptional. It's true the body styling is simple, but that is entirely compatible with Audi and only disappoints boy racers who would have 911 fishtail turbo wings out of choice. As you would expect of cars built at the Audi plant, structural condition is good, though early 924s need checking for some rust, particularly around sills. Areas most likely to need attention are overworked engines and gearboxes, though rough interior trim is costly and all spares prices are high owing to that Porsche badging.

SPECIFICATIONS
ENGINE: 1984cc
GEARBOX: 4 speed manual (5 from 1978)
POWER: 125bhp
BRAKES: Disc/drum
SUSPENSION: Ind coil
                Ind Torsion bars
TOP SPEED: 126mph
FUEL: 28mpg
LENGTH: 166in/421cm

CURRENT PRICE: £5,000

OWNERS' CLUB
Porsche 924/944 Club
Mr G Downs
P O Box 3000
Woodford
Salisbury
Wilts
SP5 4UF

ASTON MARTIN LAGONDA

This may have just qualified as a classic in the RAC's rule book, but virtually from the moment this Lagonda was unveiled its startling design commanded attention. Designer William Towns believed sporting 2+2s should be designed to their natural length and never involve grafting on extra inches – such as the 2+2 Jaguar E-Type. He managed to get his ideas across within the financially troubled Aston Martin and got support to create a full length 2+2 and a sports coupé car. The shorter model was the Aston Martin DBS which would house the V8 engines and, indeed, start a fresh Aston dynasty, while the longer version was the stunning Lagonda, first glimpsed at the 1976 motor show. This car was as technically advanced as it was ultra modern to the eye, but development problems, and Aston's financial plight, held production up until 1978. Only four complete cars were built before the company went into receivership, and another three were built with alterations under the new owners. The car's highlights were razor-edged styling, an extraordinary narrow frontal wedge, and initially an entire electronic dash, (later replaced with less troublesome dials), although it could also hurtle four people from A to B at 140mph – turning every head en route.

SPECIFICATIONS
ENGINE: 5340cc
GEARBOX: Automatic
POWER: 340bhp
BRAKES: Discs
SUSPENSION: Ind wishbone/coil
                Rigid axle/trailing arms/transverse watt
                linkage/coil
TOP SPEED: 145mph
FUEL: 15mpg
LENGTH: 208in/528cm

CURRENT PRICE: £22,150

OWNERS' CLUB
Colin Bugler
Wintney House
London Road
Hartley Wintney
Hants
RG27 8RN

FERRARI 512BB BOXER

It hardly needs the passage of 20 years to establish such a masterpiece as a classic car. Virtually every model Modena produces is the stuff of legend, yet even that proud factory is never free from the competitive pressures of the market place. Italian rivals Lamborghini and Maserati had both produced show-stopping mid-engined cars with the Miuri and the Bora, leaving Ferrari still offering front-engined V12s. Ferrari's central passion was always engines, and so to compete it naturally turned to a new engine adapted from Grand Prix experience. The Boxer unit was a V12 with each bank of six cylinders laid horizontally, and this engine went into the 365GT4 BB in 4.4 litre form. The BB stood for Berlinetta Boxer, and the 365 rested between the famed Daytona and the mighty Testarossa. In 1976, the 512 Boxer was unveiled, which was the result of Ferrari's 365 development and took capacity up to five litres, though BHP remained at 340bhp to achieve an improved power band. Ferrari never forgot the driver's experience was the key. Twelve carburettors behind the seat, the growling engine, and exquisite Pininfarina bodywork took the owner close to heaven. The fuel-injected 512i version followed in 1981; which presaged the 1985 launch of the immortal Testarossa.

OWNERS' CLUB
Ferrari Owners' Club
35 Market Place
Snettisham
Norfolk
PE31 7LR

SPECIFICATIONS
ENGINE: 4942cc
GEARBOX: 5 speed manual
POWER: 340bhp
BRAKES: Disc
SUSPENSION: Ind wishbone/coil
TOP SPEED: 175mph
FUEL: 13mpg
LENGTH: 173.2in/440cm

CURRENT PRICE: £68,500

MORE ELIGIBLE CLASSICS

ROVER SD1 2.3 & 2.6 £900
1976 saw the brand new V8 powered SD1 and the following year came the six-cylinder versions. Good 110mph-plus top speed, five door, interesting styling. Early examples need careful checking.

MASERATI KYALAMI £12,300
Nobody's child. Owners Citroën had just gone bust and De Tomaso stepped in with Ghia restyling the front of the De Tomaso Longchamp and fitting 4.1 litre and 5.0 litre Maserati engines.

PORSCHE 928 £10,000
Unloved, sleek and characterless, this front-engined 140mph plus V8 armchair cruiser offered virtually everything, including automatic, but suffered from a severe image problem. As a result, prices are extremely low for such a luxury sporting car.

PORSCHE 3.3 TURBO £25,650
1975 saw the 3 litre turbo and in 1977 the 300bhp, 3299cc version was unveiled, offering undeniable status and performance to its owner, along with new levels of rust prevention.

TOYOTA CELICA £2,100
The second generation Celica was a two-door, four-seat hatchback with a four-cylinder engine, five speed gearbox and a good record in competition rally work. The fastback styling and interior accommodation was pitched to rival the Ford Capri.

TVR TAIMAR £7,150
This is a 3000M series hatchback body option, using the Ford V6 power plant and makes an attractive buy. Roughly 30 were turbocharged. The external access to the boot was a first for TVR and it became a best seller.

THE STANLEY HUNDRED

History, specifications, advice

Most of us have quite firm opinions on motor cars. Which look good to you, which offend, which would be worth a portion of that inevitable lottery win. Like sport, it is a universal source of conversation. It therefore seems very strange to me that the classic car guide books, in the main, continue to remain void of any personal voice. If you're in the pub and a friend tells of grief with his car, that's fine and you will remember the problem, even though it won't necessarily change your own view of the car. Personal opinions are the staple diet of the enthusiast and so I have tried to introduce a voice to the Stanley Hundred. Some times you might agree with me, other times I'm sure you won't, but surely that is far better than a cold parade of names and specifications. However, one thing which all existing classic car owners will agree upon is the value of the Owners' Car Club. They are founts of knowledge and advice – often used by manufacturer's press officers shaky on their own marque's past. If you are even *thinking* of buying, talk to them, they will steer you, perhaps even help find a reliable car. They have no commercial axe to grind – just a common love for the car you are considering.

The Stanley Hundred is a purely personal choice of 100 cars which I feel are worth talking about, whether it's because they are under-exposed, over-exposed or just plain misguided. Having said that, the basic information is still given about each model's evolution, its place in the production family tree and which particular examples have appeal. I also apologise for a bias toward BMC Farina cars, the B series and the larger C range; yes, there are too many examples of what might be dismissed as mere badge engineering. But that bias is partly the result of an examination of the price movements in those cars exposed during our value investigations.

VALUATION

The Star System for valuations is drawn, quite simply, from our own price guide which, thanks to months of data imputing represents the most balanced figures we could produce. We have studied all the valuations for these cars from three years ago and again as to current price, created the mean average and then taken the brave step of adjusting for the change in the value of the pound – as provided by the Bank of England – to show a percentage swing. Just eleven cars qualified for five stars, representing substantial increases in market value. Virtually all the four star candidates were on a par, except the slightly under-performing Honda CRX. From there to break-even qualifies for three stars, while one and two stars chronicle the fortunes of those losing value: with the Quattro claiming the very lowest spot – a 33% loss over the three years. (The cars have been put in approximate price order.) The point to bear in mind of course, is that the star rating must be interpreted according to your own lights: the Quattro, it could be argued, is the best bargain around today!

SPARES

Consider the spares heading as really a shorthand for the level of problems that you might encounter if you own any specific model. Virtually no classic is trouble-free and ownership often provides a parable of the heart ruling the head. However, it is important to know what you are heading into and so hopefully through this gradation you will begin to assess the risks. It is not merely the *price* of spares which is being evaluated; which would be pointless. In this star system, a Ferrari can beat a Ford Consul.

STANLEY RATING (SR)

The Stanley Rating (SR) is entirely personal. We all favour some cars over others and yet might well find it hard to explain why. Grading feelings for 100 models certainly proved extremely hard. Each of these cars were considered separately for their looks, ideas and for personality, and then the accumulated scores converted into the five star segments. The Mini Cooper S just secured top place ahead of the Mazda MX–5. I was surprised at the generally domestic nature of the high scorers but since preparing this material, both the views of the Car of The Year panellists and the evidence of the price guide database point to a deep-seated love affair with the road cars that surrounded our youth.

MANUFACTURER
CITROËN

The prototype 2CV (above) bears no comparison with the Dyane (below), which has er... two headlights.

Cost (Dyane 6)	£1,100
% swing	5
Spares	★★★★★
V.F.M.	★★★
S.R.	★★★

Conceived in the 1930s to the design brief "transport passengers and eggs across a ploughed field", the aluminium and canvas-built prototypes with the single headlights, were concealed during the German occupation of France in World War II and emerged as the famous 2CV in 1948. (Everyone knows what the Dyane looks like, so for interest we have pictured the prototype 2CV above.) French taxation on power favoured tiny engines, and the 375cc engine gave birth to the 2CV name – two being HP, CV or *cheval vapeur,* literally meaning steam horse. In 1968 engine power was increased to 602cc and 3hp and the name remained. Well over 7,000,000 cars were sold worldwide, seducing drivers with their simplicity, pure logic and extraordinary economy. In its first 30 years there were over eleven models including the Dyane, which first entered the UK in 1968. The 435cc Dyane 4 model initially featured inboard front drum braking and lacked rear quarter lights, while the Dyane 6 enjoyed front discs and a heady 602cc engine. Essentially it was the 2CV with a slightly more conventional five-door body, full length sun roof, air cooled flat twin engine and minor refinements like integrated headlights, greater visibility, sliding windows. The 4 offered 58mpg, while the 6 returned 46mpg and a top speed of 70mph.

The Dyane offers incredible space. The back seat can be unclipped to provide space for an entire bath-

room suite, including the plumber. Brilliant gears are positioned directly on the dash, providing a large amount of leg space, and the soft, passenger-friendly suspension brings a sense of fun to cornering. I've owned four Dyanes, and while they all took their time going uphill, loved going flat-out. In an average working life, they can tot up over 200,000 miles and still perform with reliability.

SPECIFICATIONS

ENGINE: 425cc; 602cc flat twin	**BRAKES:** Drum; front discs 61 onward
BHP: 21; 28.5	**SUSPENSION:** Ind inter–connecting front/rear
FUEL: 58–46mpg	
GEARBOX: 4 speed manual	**YEARS:** 1967–1984
SPEED: 60 – 70 mph	**PRODUCTION:** 1,443,583
BODIES: 5 door	

RELATIONS

In addition to the Ami 6 of the 1960s, there was a large 2CV-based family of commercial vans, special editions, multi-purpose pick-ups, and even a twin engined model, with production in 18 countries.

BEST BUY

Front floor panels are prone to rust and king pins need regular greasing. The engine and gearbox survive high mileage. Body panels just unbolt: the entire 2CV body only requires 20 bolts and two sets of hands to lift it away from the chassis. With so little to go wrong choice is really down to condition.

MANUFACTURER
ROOTES

SUNBEAM ALPINE I-V

60S STYLE, COMFORTABLE AND UNPRETENTIOUS

Big Austin-Healeys, TRs, MGAs and MGBs all dominated the late 1950s and early 1960s. The image problems of the Rootes Alpine – it never quite matched the speed, elitism or, more importantly, the sales of its rivals – are its greatest assets as a classic car. It was over-engineered, heavy, and consequently slower than its competitors. However, the body offers more period style and grace than any of the others; the 7mph loss of speed to the contemporary MGB is hardly important now, and the Alpine's extra strength and passenger comfort are great advantages. The Rootes concept utilised existing elements from the Hillman Husky and Sunbeam Rapier. With a fashionable sporting body, the Sunbeam Alpine offered interior comfort with wind-up windows, overdrives, automatic options, detachable hardtops.

Essentially, the 1959 Mk I used the 1494cc engine with an improved cylinder head; the 1960 Mk II had the 1592cc; the Mk III in 1963 had changes to windscreen, doors and quarter lights, a refurbished interior, and a much larger boot. There was also a new detachable GT hardtop version. In 1964 the Mk IV brought slightly improved power to both the sports and GT, reduced rear fins, a changed grill and improved gearbox. The Mk V of 1965 offered 1725cc, five bearing cranks, and a power-plant shared with the Mk V Sunbeam Rapier. A limited number of fastback Alpines were also produced by the coachbuilders Harrington between 1961 and 1963.

RELATIONS

Key elements, including the floor pan and rear suspension, were taken from the Hillman Husky estate, while the engine, gearbox and front suspension were from the Sunbeam Rapier. The beautiful body was an original design by Ken Howes.

The Sunbeam Tiger, a Ford V8-engined rival to the AC Cobra, was sold between 1964 and 1968.

BEST BUY

Everything mechanical is fairly reliable, but uncontrolled body rust is a problem. Sunbeams are full of water-traps, so check the undersides, suspension points and sills, but better still, (as is always the case) get an expert to come with you. Regular servicing is advisable. Early cars, particularly the Mk III, are extremely collectable.

The spectacular new **SUNBEAM** *Alpine*

SPECIFICATIONS

ENGINE: 1494 / 1592 (II, III & IV) / 1725
BHP: 78 / 80 / 82 – (77 GT) / 92.5
FUEL: 26 / 22 / 25 / 22 auto/ 25mpg
GEARBOX: 4 speed – Automatic option post -64
BRAKES: Disc–drum
SUSPENSION: Coil/wishbone – semi-elliptic

SPEED: 98 / 97 / 98 / 92 auto / 98 mph
BODIES: 2 door open – Detachable GT hardtop – post-63
YEARS: 1959–1968
PRODUCTION: 11,904 / 19,956 / 5863 / 12,406 / 19,122

N.B – 400 Harrington Alpines built 1961–63

Nomenclature is confusing. Because of Lago-Talbots, Sunbeam-Talbots were sold in France as Sunbeams; the name was then adopted by the '53 Alpine sports car.

Cost	£1,300
% swing	19
Spares	★★★
V.F.M.	★★★
S.R.	★★★

MANUFACTURER
BMC

'We have been given orders to go out and make it into a rally-winning machine', the newly appointed BMC competition manager Peter Browning said in 1967. His first Works car was a black development 1800, nicknamed the 'Mobile Coffin' by the Competitions Department. The car used full Group 5 modifications (equivalent to a full Group 6 competition works MGB) and driving it was exhilarating. The Landcrab rally car became a legend.

The strongest BMC car ever built, the 1800 was voted Car of the Year at the 1964 Motor Show, and *Autocar* declared it "undoubtedly one of the most important cars of the motoring world". What went wrong? Early Austin/Morris versions gained a poor reputation for clutches, driveshafts, bearings, pistons, and oil consumption. Issigonis, back from the still-born Hydrolastic Alvis project, expected a V4 and V6 for the new family car but both were cancelled and the faithful BMC B series used. The body was to be a beautiful Pininfarina design but BMC rejected it and Citroën took advantage of the design for their GS.

The 1798cc 5 bearing engine married to a new all synchromesh gearbox, Hyrdrolastic suspensions and truly incredible interior space eventually pushed it into the UK Best Sellers list. The Austin, Morris and Wolseley versions were launched, peaking with the 100mph 1800 S Sports versions. In 1972 all but the basic 1800 were replaced with the 6-cylinder 2200.

RELATIONS

The body drew on the Mini and the Hydrolastic Alvis; the 1800 engines variation on the Series B unit

within MGB. The 2200 version derived from the Maxi E series.

BEST BUY

A strong sill structure and sub-frames that do not catch water reduces rust slightly. The 1800cc engines are much more reliable than the 2200s and the automatics; clutch replacements can be costly. Sparse interiors, a strange driving position and heavy non-power steering on some models. With spares plentiful, it is ideal for daily use. (Competition Chief Peter Browning is shown below, with the 'Mobile Coffin.').

Cost	£1,400
% swing	59
Spares	★★★
V.F.M.	★★★★★
S.R.	★★

SPECIFICATIONS

Engine: 1798cc,	**Suspension:** All Ind
BHP: 80 – 96	Hydrolastic
Fuel: 24 – 22 mpg	**Bodies:** 4 door
Gearbox: 4 speed manual	**Years:** 1964–1975
Brakes: Disc/drum	**Production:** 408,953
Speed: 90 –99 mph	

MANUFACTURER
ROOTES

IMP COUPÉ

PRETTY, MINIATURE GT SCARRED ONLY BY HUMAN FAILINGS

In the mid-1950s two men in their early twenties designed the excellent Hillman Imp, and Rootes bought adjacent factory land for a new production line. The plan was to counter Ford's 105E Anglia and BMC's FWD revolution, but at the time the governement was trying to encourage a wider dispersal of employment, and the planned factory site was declared a Green Belt area. Ten million pounds of governement loans encouraged the manufacturers to move to a new £22 million factory in Scotland. Having lost a certain degree of market initiative, the model finally appeared in 1963. Built rather hurriedly by a workforce of ex-ship builders, the early Imps suffered from niggling engineering problems, and inevitably lost ground to the growing band of Ford and BMC followers.

The Imp boasted a glorious engine pedigree based around the legendary Coventry Climax FWM 750 which in FWMV form was the F1 Grand Prix power plant. Initially 875cc, later 998cc, this alloy engine and gearbox weighed roughly half that of some of its rivals. It was slung behind the rear axle, but through skilful suspension and steering set–ups it created excellent handling characteristics – particularly in poor conditions. The homologation-seeking Rallye model enjoyed much competition success, and the Imp even claimed outright victory in the Tulip Rally. Rootes skilfully marketed saloon, estate, commercial and sports versions, along with coupés under Hillman, Sunbeam and Singer badges. The coupés were pretty, lowered models with reclining seats, folding rear squabs and lacked some of the marque's initial teething troubles. The three coupé

versions were the Hillman Californian (1968–70) and Chamois Coupé (1967–70), which were rebodied Imp saloons, while the Sunbeam Stiletto coupé (1967–72) boasted the fast 51bhp sports engine, suspension set-up, servo brakes and amazing quad headlights.

RELATIONS

Uniquely original, it bears no direct lineage to former models. The designers, Mike Parkes and Tim Fry conceived a conventional three box body which concealed a space saving rear-mounted engine.

BEST BUY

Early models have problems such as throttle linkage and the auto choke, but later coupés were less suspect. As cheap classics, expect to undertake some restoration on cylinder heads, for example. With a little care, and limited cash, they make brilliant miniature GTs, and the sports-based Sunbeam Stiletto is probably the best bet.

SPECIFICATIONS

ENGINE: 875cc; 998cc	**SPEED:** 87–92mph
BHP: 51; 65	**BRAKES:** Drum
FUEL: 34–38	**BODIES:** 2 door coupé
GEARBOX: 4 speed manual	**YEARS:** 1967–72
SUSPENSION: Ind coil/wishbone / ind semi-trailing	**PRODUCTION:** 440,032 – all Imp variants

Cost	£1,700
(Imp Stilleto)	
% swing	-2
Spares	★★★
V.F.M.	★★
S.R.	★★

POPULAR 100E
A 'WELL SORTED' BASIC CLASSIC

MANUFACTURER
FORD

While the old perpendicular Popular 103E continued to sell, the Prefect and Anglia were replaced in 1953 by the modern-bodied 100E. Borrowing design themes from the larger Fords, the two door (Anglia) and four door (Prefect) cars were powered by a reworked 1172cc unit. Big Ford thinking also introduced independent MacPherson strut front suspension and hydraulic brakes, among other mechanical improvements. The old three speed gearbox remained, but the improved engine and gear ratios brought steady 60mph cruising and a maximum speed of 70mph. My first rally was in a friend's 100E, and I vividly recall our climb up Porlock Hill in the pouring rain. Former owners will remember that these willing cars always got there in the end, but in their own time, and any pressure on the accelerator slows, or sometimes stops the quaint vacuum-driven windscreen wiper.

The De Luxe versions, introduced in 1955, were followed by the Escort/Squire estate bodies in 1957. However, in 1959, the brand new Ford Anglia 105E, complete with cut back rear window and brilliant Kent engine, caused the retirement of the Prefect/Anglia 100E and old Popular 103E. Intriguingly, Ford chose this moment to launch a 'New' Popular in the dropped 100E body. A De Luxe option was really a variant on the deceased 100E Anglia. Six years of production ironed out all the niggles before the late entry of the 100E Popular which remains a cheap and eminently usable classic.

RELATIONS

With scaled down Consul body style and running gear from the previous Popular 103E, the cars had improved suspension, and braking mirrored the Zephyr. The same 1172cc side-valve engine was much improved. Anglia and Prefect 100Es, and Escort/Squire estates were in parallel production.

BEST BUY

Despite their original cheapness, these cars have lasted well, and there are many examples of the Popular/Prefect/Anglia in existence. Watch for rust problems on sills and rear suspension points, otherwise be guided by the basic rules for buying. Any concerns over suspect engine symptoms can be checked with the Ford Side-valve Club.

Cost	£1,500
% swing	76
Spares	★
V.F.M.	★★★★★
S.R.	★★

SPECIFICATIONS

ENGINE: 1172cc	**SUSPENSION:** Ind coil – semi elliptical
BHP: 36	
FUEL: 32 mpg	**SPEED:** 70mph
GEARBOX: 3 speed manual – no 1st synchromesh	**BODIES:** 2 door saloon
	YEARS: 1959–1962
BRAKES: Drum	**PRODUCTION:** 126,115

MANUFACTURER
FORD

ANGLIA 105E
DISTINCTIVE, SURE-FOOTED FRIEND

SPECIFICATIONS

ENGINE: 997cc; 1198cc
BHP: 39; 48.5
FUEL: 30–40mpg
GEARBOX: 4 speed manual
BRAKES: Drum
SPEED: 75–80mph
SUSPENSION: Ind MacPherson strut & semi elliptics, live axle
BODIES: Saloon, 2 door estate and commercial
YEARS: 1959–67
PRODUCTION: 1,083,960

Reliable, forgiving and full of individuality, the Anglia 105E was Ford Motor Company's counter-attack on the simultaneous launch of BMC's Mini and Triumph's Herald. They sold 1.2 million before the Escort took over, and both that model and the Capri continued to use the inspirational new Anglia engine, known as the Kent. This fabulous oversquare OHV 997cc power-plant remained a star of road and track for 25 years, making the Anglia utterly trustworthy. The body styling, though highly original, was far from a gimmick, with the reversed back window providing cleaner glass, improved passenger headroom and a wider arc for the boot lid.

The initial models, launched in 1959, were a Standard, on sale for £589, which had a small grille, scanty amount of chrome and basic interior trim, while for another £21, the De Luxe offered luxury items such as a passenger sun visor and locking glove locker. Two years later, commercial models and a family estate version were launched, followed in September 1962 by the Super – the 123E - which used the 48.5 bhp 1198cc version from the Mark I Cortina. This model offered additions such as dual paintwork and side stripes, as well as pleated pvc upholstery, and carpets.

Common to all models were features such as the first electrically operated windscreen wipers – previous Fords were powered by vacuum and tended to stop with hard acceleration. Then there was the first four speed gearbox, complete with high gearing to make for stress free motorway travel. The suspension was MacPherson strut with semi elliptic sprung live rear axle. The car could be driven hard for long periods without any repercussions - it actually thrived on hard work.

RELATIONS

An original. The style of the 1959 Anglia 105E was completely new, with only the name and some of the running gear in common with the pre-war mechanics of the 1954 100E Anglia. This was the first car from Ford UK's new Research & Development centre in Birmingham, with some input from the American designer Elwood Engel.

BEST BUY

Earlier engines are slightly more rugged, but all Anglias are mechanically reliable. Of the one million built, over 750,000 were De Luxe models, and 130,000 were Estates. The reason they are uncommon now is rust – examine the front apron and headlight moulding areas carefully. Previous repairs tend to reflect the car's relatively humble status. The basic Standards are rare, while the last 500 were 'Specials' finished in a vibrant metallic gold or blue. The Super 123E represents the best all-round model for the classic car collector.

Cost	£1,700
% swing	-8

Spares	★★★★
V.F.M.	★★
S.R.	★★★★

MANUFACTURER
STANDARD

STANDARD 10

In the commercial gloom of the early 1950s, austerity was still the watchword in Britain, and private transport was something of a dream. Standard launched the humble Standard Eight in 1953 to compete with the new wave of A30s and Morris Minors. They named it the Basic Eight; it had no chrome grille or trim, and access to the boot was via folding rear seats. However, then as now, it answered drivers' needs: it was a simple car with an economic and virtually unbreakable engine and gearbox. These features, and the independent suspension units, would remain a factory influence on other models for over 25 years. This four door model deliberately lacked any frills, but small refinements were added over the years to make driving a little more comfortable. Spring 1954 saw the Eight De luxe; 1955, the Family Eight and the Super Eight, then in 1956 the Family Eight Phase II and the ultimate version, the Eight Gold Star. New items such as sun visors, wipers, a heater and finally, a chrome grill appeared.

Born eight months after the Basic Eight, the Standard Ten had a larger engine at 948cc, and frills such as wind-up windows, an opening boot and chrome trimmings. Progressive minor upgrades largely echoed those of the Eight, while from 1954 there was also an estate version known as the Companion. A further reckless extravagance on later cars was the optional Standrive – a solenoid-triggered centrifugal clutch arrangement.

RELATIONS

These cars brought new design to the company and passed engines and suspension down the design lines to the Herald, Spitfire and even the Dolomite.

BEST BUY

Standards are inexpensive to buy and run, and, like the 2CV, are so fundamentally pure in their purpose in life, that trim levels and outright performance are almost superfluous. If you are tempted to own a genuine classic, try to find an early Basic Eight and boast of its spartan values. Standard engines are sound, although steering and gear levers can feel tired.

Cost	£1,800
(Eight/Ten average)	
% swing	46
Spares	★★★
V.F.M.	★★★★
S.R.	★★

SPECIFICATIONS

ENGINE: 803cc; 948cc
BHP: 26; 33
FUEL: 44; 40 mpg
GEARBOX: 4 speed manual– no 1st synchromesh
BRAKES: Drum
SPEED: 61–69mph
SUSPENSION: Ind coil – semi-elliptical
BODIES: 4 door saloon, estate, commercial
YEARS: 1953–60; 1954–60
PRODUCTION: 308,817

MANUFACTURER
STANDARD TRIUMPH

Introduced as a replacement to the Standard 8 and 10, the Triumph Herald (originally known as the Zobo project) had a new chassis with the old Standard engine, gearbox and final drive. Despite modern body styling by Giovanni Michelotti, the early cars inevitably suffered from teething troubles.

The initial 1959 models both used the old Standard 948cc engine; the two door saloon offered 70mph and 34.5bhp, while the pretty twin SU carburettored two door coupé enjoyed 45bhp. Raised gearing and compression ratios pushed this model's speed up to 80mph. Although the old gearbox lacked synchromesh on first, the independent suspension at least was a new design – albeit utilising a rather basic swing axle which could confuse handling. The Herald turning circle was an impressive 25ft, aided by excellent rack and pinion steering, while fuel economy for the Coupé was 40mpg. In 1961 Leyland took over the ailing company and injected fresh enthusiasm. That year an upgrade to 1147cc gave the saloon the Coupé carburetters, and both enjoyed power boosts, higher gear ratios and an option of front disc brakes.

SPECIFICATIONS

ENGINE: 948cc; 1147cc
BHP: 45
FUEL: 40mpg+
GEARBOX: 4 speed, 3 syncromeshed
BRAKES: Drum; front disc – post 1961

SUSPENSION: Ind with transverse leaf/swing axle
SPEED: 80+
BODIES: 2 door fixed head coupé
YEARS: 1959–64
PRODUCTION: 20,472

The Herald concept of bolt-on panels and a forward-swung front body assembly suited an easy expansion of body styles, and now greatly helps modern DIY maintenance work. Slightly over 20,000 coupés were built (only 5319 of which were 1200s) before this body style was dropped in 1964.

RELATIONS

The engine, gearbox and final drive were brought forward from the elderly but reliable Standard 8 and 10; the original body styling came from Turin. Everything else was essentially original Herald except the coupés' own roof sections.

BEST BUY

Bolt-on bodywork means easy DIY, but consequently there are lots of badly fixed-up examples. A good chassis is essential, as are sound mountings, and, like the Frogeye Sprite, that one-piece front end is an expensive replacement. However, if you can find a disc-braked 1200 Coupé, it will provide a highly individual, yet practical, day-to-day classic without breaking the bank.

HERALD 1200 SERIES

Cost	£1,900
% swing	1
Spares	★★★★★
V.F.M.	★★★
S.R.	★★★

AUSTIN A40 FARINA

SIMPLE, YET EMINENTLY PRACTICAL '60S DESIGN CLASSIC

MANUFACTURER

BMC

BMC launched this car in the teeth of unprecedented competition with the new Triumph Herald, Ford Anglia 105 and the Mini, rapidly followed by the 1100 series. The three previous post-war A40s had all been BMC series B-engined, but this new model boasted only the smaller A unit. Worse still, virtually everything mechanical was from the A35 with roots dating back to 1951. It ought to have sunk without trace, yet the very virtues which sustained public affection for the A35 gave the A40 creditability, while the totally new body styling set it apart from any other British post-war model. The A40 marked the beginning of a commercial link with the Turin design house of Pininfarina, and the resultant unique two box A40 design paved the way for generations of future 'Hot Hatchbacks'. The folding rear seats, the tailgate feature, excellent visibility, and fuel economy all transformed this off-beat car into a mainstream contender. The commercial implications of the impending BMC FWD cars reduced the A40's lifespan to eight years, leaving us to wonder how many subsequent BMC models might have been born of the Farina A40 stable without the radical period of white heat instigated by Alex Issigonis. A year after the launch in 1958, the Countryman version appeared, which incorporated both upper and lower tailgates. With flattened rear seating, it offered considerable storage for a 12ft long family car, and these two versions continued in production until 1961.

The A40 then profited from a wheelbase that was four inches longer, extra power from Morris Minor carburation, improved suspension, and upgraded interior trimmings – including proper wind-up windows. Just a year later the Morris 1100 was launched and the A40 was bequeathed the new 1098cc engine, an improved gearbox and additional interior improvements. FWD had become the BMC shibboleth and the Farina A40 was laid honourably to rest in November 1967.

RELATIONS

Under the skin it is a trusted A35 with the BMC A 948cc engine, gearbox, basic suspension, braking and interior fittings; the Morris Minor 1098cc engine variant was used in late Mk II form.

BEST BUY

Although sixties' tuning kits were common, the A40 is not a sporting car. It is an excellent classic, simple to work on, and economic to run. The post-1961 longer wheel base Mk II offers better handling, while the post-1962 model – still termed Mk II - has the extra performance of the 1098cc engine.

Cost	£1,750
% swing	-1
Spares	★★★★★
V.F.M.	★★
S.R.	★★★★

SPECIFICATIONS

ENGINE: 948cc; 1098cc
BHP: 34–48
FUEL: 38–32 mpg
GEARBOX: 4 speed manual– no 1st synrchromesh
BRAKES: Drum
SUSPENSION: Ind coil & wishbone – half ellipitic leaf
SPEED: 75–80 mph
BODIES: 3 door hatchback
YEARS: 1958–1961
PRODUCTION: 364,064

MANUFACTURER
BMC

MORRIS OXFORD V & VI
A SENSIBLE FAMILY CARRIAGE

The Morris Oxford was the basic model within the Farina range, and was directly aimed towards the family. It was sold as ideal for everything from golfing trips to black-tie evenings. Based upon the same package as the Austin Cambridge, with the BMC B engine and running gear, the Oxford evolved from the earlier 1950s' Austin. The initial model, the Series V, replaced the previous lineage of Oxfords, and was, in the eyes of existing enthusiasts, a retrogressive announcement: the superior steering and front suspension of the new Oxford did not match that of the old model. However, the brand new Farina styling did bring enormous improvements in space and visibility. The Oxford cost £14 more than its rival, the Austin Cambridge, and the differences included a horizontal chrome grille design, a slightly more elaborate dashboard style which incorporated a full width parcel shelf, and an elegant half-circled steering wheel horn bar.

The Series V was the 1489cc version with pronounced rear fins and average handling characteristics, while the joint update of Austin and Morris to 1489cc in 1961 improved wheelbase, track and the handling. The estate car had been launched a year earlier at the London Motor Show, and this gave BMC's marketing men a further chance to promote the family potential of the model. They insisted that everything from kids and dogs, to china and eggs would be safe travelling within this spacious model, which also offered horizontally-split tailgates, foldaway rear seating and an opening quarter light on all four doors. The estate model was discontinued in 1969, and the four door saloon ran until 1971 with customer loyalty rather than BMC attention maintaining its presence.

RELATIONS

The body style is purely Italian from Pininfarina, although the personalising of the cars for each marque was orchestrated by BMC. The trusted BMC B series engine and basic running gear, including suspension, was carried forward from the 1954 Austin A50 Cambridge.

BEST BUY

Morris Oxfords were solid, well built touring cars, with trustworthy engines. Rusting tends to be in fairly obvious places. The earlier Series V are more economical to run, but handling and improved performance of the 2.2 litre overhead cam engine makes the later Series VI versions the better bet. The Morris Oxford trim level was marginally better than the Austin Cambridge.

SPECIFICATIONS

ENGINE: 1489cc; 1622cc
BHP: 52;61
FUEL: 28–26mpg
GEARBOX: 4 speed, 3 syncromeshed
BRAKES: Drum
SPEED: 78–81mph

SUSPENSION: Ind coil & wishbone / Half elliptic
BODIES: 4 door saloon, 5 door estates
YEARS: 1959–71
PRODUCTION: 900,000 – all Farina family

Cost	£1,800
% swing	10
Spares	★★★
V.F.M.	★★
S.R.	★★

FIAT 850 COUPÉ

A FUTURE VINTAGE

MANUFACTURER

FIAT

Few enthusiasts grieve as decades of family Fiats reach their rightful incarnation as mounds of rust. Inferior steel, questionable build qualities and little corrosion prevention all helped erase large numbers of indifferent models. However, Fiat had the knack of creating small cars that everyone loved and, as squadrons of Morris Minors illustrate, loved cars get preserved. The tiny Fiat 500s and 600s sold close to 6,000,000 in the 1950s, 1960s and 1970s, while giving birth in 1964 to the slightly larger Fiat 850. This model, too, used a three-bearing, water-cooled engine installed beyond the rear wheels, but with its sleek new body providing valued extra interior space. Motorists again voted with their feet, buying over 800,000 in the first couple of years' production. Coachbuilders, too, recognised the saloon's potential offering variations such as the Bertone Spyder, but it was the ideas of Fiat's own in–house design team which emerged in 1965 as the beautiful little 850 Coupé. Based upon the saloon underpan and running gear, it offered one of the very best proportioned miniature Grand Tourers with disc brakes, slim pillars, lots of glass and classic sporting good looks. The high revving 850cc engine enjoyed a revised head, with higher compression ratio, new cam shaft, valve gear, manifolds and twin choke Weber carburation – all prescribed by the Grand Master of Fiat tuning, Abarth. It was a brilliant sporting car, instantly adopted by press and public alike for its looks, performance and character.

Then, at the 1968 Geneva Motor Show, Fiat put the icing on the cake by increasing the power output

to 52bhp raising acceleration, top speed and even fuel consumption figures. Although its name remained, the 850 Coupé, it was by then 903cc, and external changes included a second pair of headlights and even more side glass. These excellent cars handle well and are eminently usable in congested towns or speeding at 90mph on the open roads – still returning 30 to 40mpg.

RELATIONS

Fiat's own body styling added to the 1964 850 Saloon, itself derived from the hugely successful Fiat 600 formula. Components such as disc brakes are from the Fiat 124.

BEST BUY

The passage of time has simply made good examples scarce – and thus more collectable. Obviously, post-1968 models enjoy more power and refinement, but it's really more about condition. Buy the best and enjoy wonderful motoring.

SPECIFICATIONS

ENGINE: 843cc; 930cc	**BODIES:** 2 door coupe
BHP: 47 – 52	**SUSPENSION:** Ind transverse
FUEL: 35 – 40mpg	leaf/wishbone – semi-trailing
GEARBOX: 4 speed	arm/coil
BRAKES: Disc – Drum	**YEARS:** 1965 – 72
SPEED: 87mph – 94mph	**PRODUCTION:** 380,000

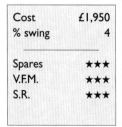

Cost	£1,950
% swing	4
Spares	★★★
V.F.M.	★★★
S.R.	★★★

MANUFACTURER
ROVER

ROVER SDI

VITESSE – A CLASSIC 130MPH FAMILY HATCHBACK

Somehow this car virtually escaped the appalling BL philosophies. Right from its launch during that 1976 heatwave, this Rover looked, and was, a winner. True, the early models still suffered from BL's tendency to use the public to iron out teething troubles, but as this sleek five door car developed, it grew in status. Initially it used the lightweight Buick-based V8 from the Rover 3.5 Coupé and 3500, which gave 120mph performance and up to 30mpg when driven carefully. An OHC 2300cc, a longer stroked 2600cc, a 2.4 Turbo Diesel and another with the ex-Morris Ital 2 litre O series engine, all added choice. The V8 was the best equipped, with power steering, electric windows and central locking, while the most humble was the 2300. All models were upgraded during 1979-80, with a new top of the range 3500SE and a Vanden Plas version dressed in real leather. One curious choice was the 1979 V8 S, which boasted gold wheels and shag-pile carpets. The undoubted classic was the Vitesse, unveiled in 1982. This was a 192bhp, 130mph five-seater hatchback on lowered suspension, complete with fuel injection and ventilated disc brakes. Few genuine family cars were ever made with domestic niceties such as folding rear seats and self levelling rear suspension with a V8 growling under the bonnet. The Vitesse and the Vanden Plas Efi, which lacked the lowered suspension, have increasingly been recognised as future classics.

In competition form these 300BHP racers were dominant until a technical disqualification caused the team to withdraw, leaving privateers to enjoy the victories. The SD1 even beat off the factory BMWs to win the 1986 European Touring Car Championship. To competition homologate certain specifications the factory sold a late Vitesse with 'Twin Plenum' chambers unofficially worth another 20bhp which has added mysticism and value to these rare examples.

RELATIONS

A brand new Rover design reputedly inspired by Pininfarina's Ferrari Daytona using the Rover P5B and P6 Buick V8 engine. The smaller engines were designed by Triumph.

BEST BUY

There are superficial rust problems and BL 'quality-control' means good and bad examples are available. Watch for occasional water damage under carpets and blocked sunroof channels causing rust. Some fuel injection can be troublesome, so can oil leaks, while early plastic trim deteriorates. A late Vitesse is a brilliant classic for the price of a second hand Escort.

SPECIFICATIONS

ENGINE: 3.5 V8; 2.3; 2.4 Turbo D; 2.6; 2
BHP: 100–155
FUEL: 42–20 mpg
GEARBOX: 5 speed manual– 3 speed auto
BRAKES: Disc/drum
SUSPENSION: Ind MacPherson strut – Live axle, coils
SPEED: 104–133 mph
BODIES: 5 door hatchback
YEARS: 1976–1987
PRODUCTION: 191,762

Cost (SD1 3500)	£2,000
% swing	-59
Spares	★★★
V.F.M.	★
S.R.	★★★

WOLSELEY 15/60 & 16/60
TRADITIONAL BRITISH COMFORTS

MANUFACTURER
BMC

Extra power ... rock-steady roadholding ...
the new Wolseley 16/60

The Wolseley name is one of the most respected in the history of British manufacturing, despite never having been an independent company. The 15/60 was the car which launched the Farina range in December 1958, replacing the old 15/50; it didn't let the side down. Critics may sometimes belittle the Farina cars, but the more traditional 15/50 sold a little over 12,000 cars in total, while the initial 15/60 Farina variant alone sold 24,579, and the collective Riley 15/60 & 16/60 sold an impressive 87,661 – despite ever diminishing interest from the soon to be defunct BMC. Just as the basic Austin/Morris were the workhorses of the company, so the better equipped Wolseley and Riley were the more civilised motor cars. Morris Minors have proved that being a classic car is as much about dependability and character, rather than glamour. Likewise, the Wolseley offered the all the advantages of a modern Italian five-seater saloon, along with practical features such as a 19 cubic capacity boot, which was increased by spare wheel stowage underneath the car. Driver visibility was a significant improvement on previous Wolseleys, with modern wrap-around front and rear windows. Overall, the Wolseley carried the kind of high trim levels associated with the later Riley, but without the twin carburettored power-plant. The traditional Wolseley grille treatment looked good on the Farina bodyshell and included a traditional integrated Wolseley badge, while the early 15/60 version boasted the more flamboyant tail fins.

Inside, there was English leather seating, carpets, polished wood door cappings and a splendid burr

walnut veneered fascia with glove locker and semi-circular chrome horn bar. The sales brochures may have revelled in the association with a famous Italian designer by showing background drawings of Rome and Pisa, but climbing into the car instantly showed that it was both very British and traditionally Wolseley.

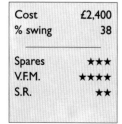

Cost	£2,400
% swing	38
Spares	★★★
V.F.M.	★★★★
S.R.	★★

Interior 'fashioned for the fastidious.' Despite having such an immediately recognisable and evocative name, Wolseley was never actually an independent manufacturer, owned by Vickers for the first 26 years and Morris thereafter.

SPECIFICATIONS

ENGINE: 1489cc; 1622cc
BHP: 52;61
FUEL: 28–26
GEARBOX: 4 speed,
  3 syncromeshed
BRAKES: Drum
SPEED: 77–81mph

SUSPENSION: Ind coil & wishbone / Half elliptic
BODIES: 4 door saloon.
YEARS: 1958–71
PRODUCTION: 900,000 – all Farina family

Like the others in the range, the initial model lacked qualities introduced with the upgrade to the Wolseley 16/60. Once it enjoyed the later benefits of a longer wheel base and the engine elevation to 1622cc, it became an excellent buy, although extravagant BMC claims that it enjoyed 'Faultless Performance', and was 'Fashioned for the fastidious' were bold ones to make for any mid-market family car … even today.

RELATIONS

The body style is purely Italian from Pininfarina although BMC personalised the cars of each marque with badge-engineering. The trusted BMC B series engine, gearbox and some of the running gear stemmed from former BMC models. 'Wolseley' evokes the spirits of three motor magnates: Herbert Austin, John Davenport Siddeley and William Morris.

BEST BUY

They are well-built cars, with trustworthy engines while rusting tends to be in fairly obvious places. As the Wolseley enjoyed high levels of trim, it was not blessed with the more sporting engine; the earlier 15/60s are naturally slower than the later 16/60s. A late 16/60, along with the equivalent Riley, makes an excellent and economic classic car.

MORRIS MINOR
STILL THE BENCHMARK FOR A DAY-TO-DAY CLASSIC

MANUFACTURER
BMC

Morris 1000 convertible (above) with new full-width screen, 1957 model year.

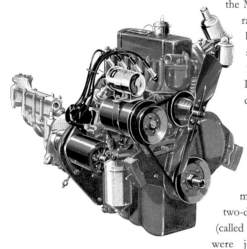

One legendary car with two distinct followings. So brilliant was it that there is still a present day, non-enthusiasts, market for models as daily transport. Aficionados hunt out the initial 1948 version, called the Minor MM, which incorporated low integrated headlights and a split screen along with the Morris 8's 918cc sidevalve engine. Issigonis's friendly yet spacious design favoured a strong unit construction, while advanced rack-and-pinion steering, and torsion bar independent front suspension won many new fans. The initial two-door saloon and convertible (called the 'Tourer' until 1951) were joined in 1953 by the Traveller van and pick-up, further widening the appeal. The only significant alteration was in 1951, when the headlights were moved up into a more conventional wing position, complying with North American requirements.

1952 had witnessed the merger of Austin and Morris, and within months BMC had replaced the ageing sidevalve engine with the Austin A30 BMC A 803cc engine and transmission. Then there were only

nominal changes to grille and dashboard before the Series II ended its run in the autumn of 1956.

The new Minor 1000 enjoyed greatly improved visibility with large wrap-around front and rear screens, upgraded interior trim and more significantly, the new 948cc version of the A series engine corresponding to the Austin move from A30 to A35. Adding improved performance to great handling simply iced the cake, and sales roared on past the 1,000,000 mark (350 commemorative two-door cars were built). The only further real change was the launch of the BMC 1100, which meant that 1098cc unit went into the Minor, thus becoming 1.1 litre. 1970 ended its distinguished career and the Traveller ran until 1971.

RELATIONS

An original Issigonis design, with engines from the Morris 8, then briefly the Austin A30, the A35's

SPECIFICATIONS	
ENGINE: 918cc (sv); 803cc; 948cc; 1098cc	**SUSPENSION:** Ind torsion bar – semi elliptical
BHP: 27.5; 30; 37	**BODIES:** 2 &4 door saloon,
FUEL: 40;36;38mpg	estate, convertible,
GEARBOX: 4 speed	commercial pick up
BRAKES: Drum	**YEARS:** 1948–71
SPEED: 61; 62;75mph	**PRODUCTION:** 1,303,331

Cost (1000)	£2,400
% swing	-14
Spares	★★★★★
V.F.M.	★★
S.R.	★★★★★

948cc, and ultimately in 1956, the 1098cc BMC 1100 version. Some running gear was common to other models, such as the MM rear axle from the MG TD.

BEST BUY

Classic heaven. Lots of Morris Minors are in circulation, with oceans of parts, many specialists and no trouble for your local garage. The early MMs are the rarest, making these and the Series II the collector's choice, while the 1000 and 1.1 litre cars are a joy to own and use daily. Many saloons turned into convertibles, so make sure you know what you are actually buying. Front wings rust frequently, but more importantly, check under floors and the suspension hanger areas – rotten undersides can be expensive.

The first Morris Minor 'traveller's car' was completed at Cowley in spring 1951. The Traveller was identical to the other Series II Minors, except for the Austin A-type rear axle.

The overseas market was resistant to composite bodywork, preferring steel, which influenced the Light Commercial Vehicle range of May 1953. The LCVs have a true chassis to compensate for lack of rigidity in comparison with saloons, with extended box sections either side of the engine.

the **MORRIS MINOR** *1000*

Now better than ever

IMPROVED PERFORMANCE · INCREASED SAFETY

Fact and fiction: the author's old Traveller being craned aboard a Scottish ferry (above), while BMC sales literature suggests a more elegant departure. The 1000 certainly was 'better than ever', with the overbored A-series engine, a new gearbox and less significant, but still pleasing, updates: thinner windscreen side pillars for example and larger back screen, for better visibility. A word of warning from restoration expert Jim Tyler: an awful lot of Minors have been badly bodged, so dig around.

POPULAR 103E
A MODEST FOOTNOTE IN MOTORING HISTORY

MANUFACTURER
FORD

Cost	£2,250
% swing	18

Spares	★★★
V.F.M.	★★★
S.R.	★★★

A significant part of the classic car culture is the way period styling and mechanics instantly conjure up former eras – be it in your memory or just imagination. Extended fins or aerodynamic wedges, razor-edged panels or flowing curves, these are as essential as the performance. One of the true classic automotive shapes, the Sit Up and Beg Utility Ford, is captured in the 103E Prefect. Those who remember them will fondly recall that this Ford provided much needed transport – freedom rather than excitement. The factory policy was to continue employing what was, in effect, the 1930's Model Y body style, and to re-use common running gear so they could afford to promote claims to the world's lowest priced car. In 1954 the 103E was being advertised at just £275 less tax.

The Popular was the last incarnation of this traditional upright styling, married to the larger 1172cc sidevalve engine previously employed in the export Anglia and Prefect cars. With 36mpg and 60mph top speed, it was essentially a pre-war engine packaged together with the most deliberately basic trim levels. Painted bumpers and hub caps, reduced headlights, only the passenger seat tipped forward, one wiper, plastic finished floor coverings. Struggling for trim selling points the sales brochure boasted 'Window and windscreen space is generous. Both driver and passengers are well catered for'. More telling were lines such as 'The man with a tired pre–war car and increased running costs now drives and saves in a Popular'. This was Ford's key to over 150,000 sales

during times of great austerity. Even publications get model variants confused. The 1948–53 1172cc Prefect was the E493A, while the 933cc Anglia was E494A; the 1953–59 Popular, the 103E, was 1172cc.

RELATIONS

Its roots are in the pre-World War I Model T, its grandparent, and body style was influenced by the 1932 Model Y and 1949 Anglia, but without the trim, and with the addition of the 1172cc engine.

BEST BUY

Purely utilitarian, reliable and economic, it suffered rust chiefly to the rear, while the back axle was prone to wear. Vague steering is quite normal and a starter handle is insurance against 6 volt electrics. Ageing engines can smoke, notably from the oil filter. Virtually unbreakable, and with great pre-war character, it's a case of finding the right car. Approach the Ford Side Valve Owners Club for help.

SPECIFICATIONS

ENGINE: 1172cc	**SUSPENSION:** Transverse leaf
BHP: 30	springs
FUEL: 36 mpg	**SPEED:** 60mph
GEARBOX: 3 speed manual–	**BODIES:** 2 door saloon
no 1st synchromesh	**YEARS:** 1953–1959
BRAKES: Drum	**PRODUCTION:** 155,350

MANUFACTURER
BMC

The last genuine Austin-bodied model range, the A40/50/55 Cambridge, was withdrawn in the midfifties and replaced with this Farina design. It was launched in January 1959 as the A55, a four-door saloon using a 1489cc version of the B series engine. They kept the reliable elements of the retired model, while cleverly offering a touch of Italian flair with the Farina bodywork. The Austin and Morris versions were launched with the most pronounced tail fins of the range, along with individually adjustable bench seating, optional Borg Warner automatic gears, and a choice of floor or column gear change. The De Luxe version also boasted sun visors, a heater, screen washer, a clock, leather trim and full carpets. There was liberal use of fashionable chrome on bumpers, headlight surrounds, etc. and a bold, square meshed, full-width grille boasting the Austin badge. The dashboard was pretty basic, however, with two principal dials set into the painted facia with black vinyl on the top, a glove locker and a parcel shelf. The Countryman Estate version was launched the following spring, and in 1961 the A60 appeared. The 1961 revamp included handling modifications such as 1.5 extra inches on the wheelbase and wider tracking, while the engine was enlarged to 1622cc. The dashboard gained a simulated wood finish, the rear fins were reduced in scale, the front grille was widened to virtually full width, and the bumpers were also altered.

RELATIONS

The body style was from Pininfarina, although BMC personalised the cars for each marque. The BMC B series engine and basic running gear, including the suspension, came from the 1954 A50 Cambridge.

BEST BUY

They were well built cars, with trustworthy engines and rusting tends to be in obvious places. The earlier A55s are more economical, but improved performance makes the later A60s the better buys.

SPECIFICATIONS

ENGINE: 1489cc; 1622cc
BHP: 52; 61
FUEL: 28–26mpg
GEARBOX: 4 speed, 3 syncromeshed
BRAKES: Drum
SPEED: 78–81mph

SUSPENSION: Ind coil & wishbone / half-elliptic
BODIES: 4 door saloon, 5 door estates
YEARS: 1959–69
PRODUCTION: 900,000 – all Farina family

Cost	£2,750
% swing	55
Spares	★★★
V.F.M.	★★★★★
S.R.	★★

MG MAGNETTE MK III & IV
SUPERIOR PERFORMANCE AND TRIM

MANUFACTURER
BMC

This car and the Riley 4/68 were fashioned as the two sporting versions of the Farina family but the MG in particular suffered from snobbery. The true heyday of the pre-war MGs was well and truly over, so reusing the Magnette name was hardly a criminal offence. The retiring Mk II Magnette Z Series looked very pretty, but it, too, was the product of factory rationalisation. A designer had been brought in to create a common concept for the Wolseley 4/44 and MG Z – the MG without any significant MG parts which inevitably looked virtually identical to the Wolseley. However, the basic inadequacies of handling and performance in the initial Mk III model simply fuelled enthusiasts' discontent. The MG grille was inserted into the body shell and the rear fins raked in a suitably sporting style – no MG Farina ever had vertical fins. The interior trim levels were quite good, with a dashboard of Indian walnut, capped with leather, and incorporating imaginative little touches such as an electric clock and an integrated chrome bevelled loudspeaker. With adjustable leather bucket seats, the car's rear seats were divided by a central folding arm rest. Under the bonnet the BMC B series engine was enhanced by a pair of SU carburettors, and the resultant performance was roughly a match

for the venerable Z series. With the Farina range upgrade in October 1961, the MG actually became a good package, with greater engine power and improved handling (but no change to the fin design). By then however, the combination of disgruntled MG enthusiasts, and the dwindling fortunes of BMC itself, had damaged the car's reputation almost irreparably.

RELATIONS

The body style is by Pininfarina, and BMC orchestrated personalising the cars for each marque. The trusted BMC B series engine, gearbox and axle were carried forward from the old Z series cars.

BEST BUY

MG Magnettes were well built cars, with trustworthy engines, and rusting tends to be in fairly obvious places. The earlier Mk IIs are more economic to run, but handling and improved performance makes the later Mk III versions the best choice.

Cost	£2,400
% swing	10
Spares	★★★
V.F.M.	★★★
S.R.	★★

SPECIFICATIONS

ENGINE: 1489cc; 1622cc	**BRAKES:** Drum
BHP: 64; 68	**SPEED:** 84–86mph
FUEL: 28–26	**BODIES:** Four door saloon.
GEARBOX: 4 speed, 3 syncro-meshed	**YEARS:** 1959–68
SUSPENSION: Ind coil & wishbone / Half elliptic	Production: 900,000 – all Farina family

MANUFACTURER
BMC

300 FFC

In April 1959 this Riley was the last of the Farinas to be launched, and entered manufacture at Cowley alongside its brother, the MG Magnette. The individual grille arrangement was rather more successful than that of the MG with which it shared the same raked rear fin design. The factory's existing philosophies of rationalisation had already meant that the Pathfinder badge was virtually common to an MG and Wolseley. Additionally, the little Riley 1.5 was effectively a Morris Minor in terms of engine parts, so the Riley individuality was already wounded and indeed would die after one further round of badge engineering, based on Issigonis's final front wheel drive variants.

The 4/68 inevitably suffered the known deficiencies of narrow tracking, a short wheel base and only average performance, but even in this initial guise the Riley was staking a claim to the luxury end of the range. Deep pile carpets, leather seats, a polished walnut facia and door cappings were complemented by distinctive instrumentation, which included a temperature indicator and even a rev counter (not an MG fitting).

Then, in October 1961, the upgraded version appeared as the 4/72 which really turned the Riley into an attractive car. The combination of relative luxury, brisk performance with the twin carburettored 68 BHP engine, a spacious boot and excellent visibility, made the Riley an excellent touring car. Its 4/72 sales brochure boasted 'Elegance, Luxury, Comfort and Convenience', and although our perceptions of these things change over the years, the claim still stands to some extent. Although BMC was losing interest in everything except the front wheel drive projects, the Riley represented good value and it soldiered on a full year after the MG Magnette was pensioned off.

RELATIONS

The body style is classical Italian from Pininfarina, although the personalizing of the cars for each marque was BMC orchestrated. The trusted BMC B series engine, gearbox and running gear were rooted in the earlier 1950s. Will BMW be bringing back the Riley name? Rumours abound …

BEST BUY

Like all Farinas, the Rileys were soundly built with sturdy engines. The interiors were good on both the 4/68 and 4/72, but the former was less well set up. A good 4/72 represents one of the best of the Farina family and is an excellent classic. An automatic gearbox was also an option.

SPECIFICATIONS

ENGINE: 1489cc; 1622cc
BHP: 64; 68
FUEL: 27–26mpg
GEARBOX: 4 speed, 3 syncromeshed
BRAKES: Drum
SPEED: 84–86mph

SUSPENSION: Ind coil & wishbone / half-elliptic
BODIES: 4 door saloon.
YEARS: 1959–69
PRODUCTION: 900,000 – all Farina family

Cost	£2,700
% swing	30
Spares	★★★
V.F.M.	★★★★★
S.R.	★★

R5 GORDINI

FASTER THAN A COOPER S – WITH FRENCH FLAIR

MANUFACTURER
RENAULT

5,000,000 Minis breed a sense of invincibility and there is no doubting the car's unique values. Yet across the Channel the Renault 5 has achieved the same figure, despite being launched 13 years after the ubiquitous Mini. This does nothing to distract from the originality of Issigonis's ideas, but does serve to remind us that while we exalt the Mini, there are clearly merits within the Renault. Rust, poor quality, and abused examples are equally common to the Mini and the Renault 5. Yet the Mini Cooper and the Renault R5 Gordini perhaps provide a more interesting parallel. England's 'Swinging Sixties' and a successful BMC Competition Department naturally reinforced Britain's allegiance to the Mini Cooper, leaving the interesting Gordini in the dark. They are now being valued at less than half the figure of a standard Mini Cooper, yet the Gordini offers 93bhp against the Cooper's 55bhp or indeed 76bhp from the mighty 1275 S. Having owned two 1275s I later bought a bright blue Gordini which offered many of the same driving pleasures with the welcome additions of passenger refinements.

Around the rest of the world this sporting 5 is known as the Renault Alpine, but as Chrysler owns that name in the UK, it became the R5 Gordini. The engine is a bored out version of the Renault TS, with alloy cross flow head, a sports camshaft and a twin choked Weber carburettor. With the optimum power band around 4000 revs, a five speed gearbox used in the larger 16TX and 17TS was installed. The resultant 93bhp gets to the road through 5¼-inch lightweight wheels which are almost impossible to keep

clean. A good sized tailgate and folding rear seats are infinitely more practical that the old Cooper S, while the high backed, side hugging front seats are really well upholstered competition seats. However, to anyone committed to the sporting front wheel drive principle, the real joy is in travelling fast through the gears…and the corners. It's a grown-up's Cooper S and a bargain at current prices.

RELATIONS

Clearly Renault 5-based, with elements drawn from the larger Renault models such as the 16 and 17.

BEST BUY

The main danger is the car's ability to be driven hard – which inevitably means examples may be abused. Luckily with the Gordini Turbo and the fire-eating rear-engined Turbo T2 offering raw excitement, it leaves this rapid and civilized French car for those seeking fun.

Cost	£2,350
% swing	-14
Spares	★★★★
V.F.M.	★★
S.R.	★★★

SPECIFICATIONS

ENGINE: 1397cc	**SPEED:** 107mph
BHP: 93	**BODIES:** 3 door 4 seater
FUEL: 30mpg	hatchback
GEARBOX: 5 speed	**YEARS:** 1976 – 81
BRAKES: Disc/drum	**PRODUCTION:** (5,471,709)
SUSPENSION: Double wish-	Gordini 63,814
bone – Torsion bar and	
trailing arm	

MANUFACTURER
FIAT

The early 1960s gave Fiat over 2,000,000 sales of their 850 range, and its last incarnation, the pretty Bertone-designed Spider, sold most of its 140,000 examples to the USA. Naturally, both Bertone and Fiat looked for another project and the design work culminated at the 1969 Turin Motor Show where they showed their 'Runabout'. Close to the eventual X1/9, this was a design exercise based upon the Autobianchi A112 chassis. It was the same year Bertone's breathtaking Lamborghini Miura was released, and the central principle of that Supercar was compressed into the diminutive Fiat X1/9 – the transverse mounted mid engine. The final car was unveiled after the 1972 Turin Motor Show and was based upon Fiat 128 Coupé components including the 1290cc engine. This fresh new sporting car offered a good deal including quite excellent handling thanks to the central engine position, a detachable Targa roof, all round disc brakes and independent suspension, plus two different luggage areas. Its problem was Fiat itself, who had reputedly been less convinced about its potential – they even deferred its announcement until after that Motor Show. They concentrated on reviving the American market and thus ignored Britain – despite the MG/Sprite/Spitfire boom. For the first five years UK models were imported and converted by Rathbourne, the Fiat and Abarth specialists.

From 1977, official RHD models began to filter in, and a year later Fiat announced the 1500 using the more powerful 85bhp Strada 85 unit. Along with the extra horsepower came a new five speed gearbox and overdrive. From the spring of 1982 Bertone took over the building and the 1983 VS1500 model boasted both electric windows and leather upholstery. Quick, nimble and highly individual, these cars suffered from lacklustre Fiat marketing and so still offer excellent value for money as a classic.

RELATIONS

The Fiat X1/9 has original Italian design house styling based upon the Fiat 128 Coupé engine, gearbox and general specifications. The later 1500 model utilised the Strada 85 power train.

BEST BUY

Opinions are divided between the two models. The interiors of all except the final version are very basic, while the 1500 suffered the US-imposed impact bumpers. Rust and Fiat were synonymous, so check carefully as panels are expensive. However, if you find a sound example and enjoy DIY, try boring out to 1650cc and adding twin Weber 40 DCNIF carbs.

SPECIFICATIONS

ENGINE: 1290; 1498cc	**SUSPENSION:** All Ind
BHP: 75 – 85	Macpherson strut
FUEL: 30 – 37mpg	**BODIES:** 2 door sports Targa
GEARBOX: 4 & 5 speed	**YEARS:** 1972–89
BRAKES: Disc	**PRODUCTION:** 180,000
SPEED: 106mph	

Cost	£2,700
% swing	-9
Spares	★★★★
V.F.M.	★★
S.R.	★★★

SUNBEAM RAPIER IIIA
ECONOMICAL AND SPACIOUS SPORTING BARGAIN

MANUFACTURER
ROOTES

Pure Sunbeams were pre-1935 motors cars which were turned into disguised Hillmans and Hunters by the new owners, Rootes, who salvaged Sunbeam from the chaos of STD (Sunbeam, Talbot, Darracq) in that year. Under corporate ownership there was little respect for individual badges or traditions, and marque personalities were systematically eroded. The initial 1955 Sunbeam Rapier was very similar to a two door Hillman Minx even down to its radiator grille – which was all the more confusing as it pre-empted the actual Minx launch by seven months. The initial car used an up-rated 1390cc Hillman Minx engine, a four speed gearbox with standard overdrive, and conventional, but effective suspension and handling. This natural performer managed to finish fifth overall in the Monte Carlo Rally, and immediately afterwards Rootes launched the Series II. It had a new, more powerful, overhead valve 1494cc engine, the overdrive was reduced to an option, and the car had a grille design of its own as well as distinctive rear fins. Both this and the Series III were also offered in convertible form. The next stage in its development mirrored the newly launched Alpine. Thus, the Series III Rapier enjoyed the Alpine's close ratio gearbox, new aluminium cylinder head and front disc braking. The II and III sold well, but it was the Series IIIA which ultimately was the bestseller, despite the appearance of a Series IV with general improvements borrowed from the new Humber Sceptre, and even a Series V, which added a five bearing 1725cc unit. The IV actually had slightly more power, a new gearbox and different road wheels, but it was the Series IIIA which offered performance while retaining the classic hood-

ed headlights, the higher bonnet line and the option of a full convertible – although the saloon's pillarless side windows were also a nice touch.

RELATIONS

In essence the Rapier was a Hillman Minx – including the drive train. Later models borrowed the engines and developments of the new Sunbeam Alpine and the Humber Sceptre. Many panels and parts were common to the Minxs and Gazelles.

BEST BUY

They were built with generously thick metal so the inevitable rust ought not be terminal, though check particularly around the screen base and suspension mounts. Poor servicing may lead to worn steering and suspension if greasing has not been maintained. The overdrive is a real asset, though watch for oil leakage around the gearbox. Broken dash instruments can be costly to replace. Good convertible IIIAs are like hens' teeth now, and the saloon is also becoming a desirable classic.

The IIIA will actually cost considerably more than the average for the whole range quoted below – particularly the convertible.

Cost (I-V)	£2,700
% swing	26
Spares	★★
V.F.M.	★★★
S.R.	★★★★

SPECIFICATIONS

ENGINE: 1592cc
BHP: 75
FUEL: 24mpg
GEARBOX: 4 speed
BRAKES: Disc/ drum
SUSPENSION: Ind Coil/wishbone – semi-elliptic

SPEED: 90mph
BODIES: 2 door saloon, convertible.
YEARS: 1961–63
PRODUCTION: 17,354 (total Rapier 65,050)

MANUFACTURER
ROOTES

Humber was one of the original pioneering manufactures and were the subject of a takeover by the Rootes brothers in the late 1920s. Eventually in 1976 the company was bought by the Chrysler Corporation and it was then that both Humber and Sunbeam ceased to exist. Having created such distinguished transport it's sad that the final car to carry its proud badge was a re–badged and trimmed Hillman Minx – the Humber Sceptre. The penultimate Humbers, the Super Snipes, were a far more fitting tribute to decades of elegant transport.

Launched in 1958 the Super Snipe Mk I revealed a modern, slightly Americanised, monocoque constructed body using a new 2.6 litre engine supplied by Armstrong Siddeley. This engine was similar to the Sapphire 346's unit and its supply was part of commercial arrangements whereby Armstrong also worked on the Rootes Sunbeam Alpines. A three speed automatic gearbox, extensive interior fitments, plus both limousine and vast estate car variants, completed the initial two years' thrust until 1960, when the Series II gained a bored-out 3.0-litre engine and front disc braking.

A year later the Series III got the four headlight treatment, and this was followed by the Series IV, again upgrading both trim and performance. The final incarnation was the 1965–67 Series V, which involved much crisper roof line styling, dropping the wraparound rear window and further enhancing details. This was joined by the ultimate Humber Imperial version with all the traditional de luxe features undertaken by Thrupp & Maberly. The new American owners gave brief hope of a further V8 upgrade but instead the marque was laid to rest. They are discreet motor cars – a cocktail of elegant veneer, leather and picnic tables with just a twist of Americana in the chrome and body styling. Driving one is like drinking a good claret – something to savour rather than rush.

RELATIONS

The engine was from the Armstrong Siddeley Sapphire 246, while the bodyshell was shared with its four cylinder twin, the Humber Hawk – all made on the old Sunbeam-Talbot production line at British Light Steel Pressings.

BEST BUY

Spares for the initial 2.6 litre engine are getting scarce, though the larger engine/gearbox is little trouble. Rust is likely around wheel arches and sills. A poor body means some searching for panels. Buy the best you can afford – a IV or V offers greater performance, although there's a rewarding restoration project with any of them.

SPECIFICATIONS

ENGINE: 2651cc; 2965cc
BHP: 105; 121; 124; 128.5
FUEL: 20 –18mpg
GEARBOX: 3 speed; Auto on Imperial
BRAKES: Drum/ Disc; Drum Series II onward
SUSPENSION: Ind Coil/wishbone – semi-elliptic
SPEED: 92 –100mph
BODIES: 4 door saloon, estate, limousine.
YEARS: 1958–67
Production: 30,013

Cost (II-III)	£2,900
% swing	12
Spares	★★
V.F.M.	★★★
S.R.	★★★

FORD CAPRI

POCKET GT ... THANKS TO DIANA & A COMMITTEE

MANUFACTURER
FORD

The Capri was a Detroit concept which evolved from a Ford think tank called the Fairlane Committee, so-called because it met at the Fairlane Hotel! Aimed at swelling the numbers of car-buying European 'baby boomers', it deliberately set out to create multi-package options with a long bonnet and short tail styling in the footsteps of the legendary Ford Mustang. Germany and the UK entered production in 1968 and the resulting car was an immediate success. The Mark I proved to be the lighter car with sculpted side panels and even dummy air vents in front of the rear wheel arches. Essentially, there were 1300cc and 1600cc + GT versions, as well as a V4 2000GT and a V6 3000GTS, plus a de luxe V6 called the 3000E. In addition, there was a German bored-out 150bhp racer, the RS2600, and briefly a UK homologation qualifying Cosworth version – the RS 3100.

The Mk II development programme was called Project Diana (after an inspiring Ford secretary) and the 1974 model changes included dropping the V4 in favour of the 2.0 litre Pinto unit, with four headlights, upgraded trim and a hatchback option – all designed to capture the young family market. There were S versions, Ghias, even one painted to match a leading package of cigarettes – every conceivable choice. The bodywork was slightly longer, higher, wider, and the trim was simplified. The 1977 Mark III took matters further with a changed grille and an altered bonnet line over the four headlights. Again, with this last incarnation there was a veritable roll call of options such as Capri Calypso, Cameo, Cabaret, Laser, Brooklands, even a Tickford.

Mid-way through the Mark III's lifespan, the interesting and very desirable high performance 2.8i was developed by Ford UK's Special Vehicle Engineering.

With sales approaching 2,000,000, Ford's concept was proved absolutely right. The Capri is still such a common sight on our roads it is hard to perceive its classic status. However, it is a pretty design, it is reliable and will increasingly evoke past times: All sure signs and even now, they are beginning to win concours show awards.

RELATIONS

The Capri was an American design based upon the Mustang. The multiplicity of engines, gearboxes, etc. were drawn from US and European Ford factories.

BEST BUY

The 'wide boy' image is already fading and their classic potential is still unrealised. Ford reliability and spares are good, while rust, lack of servicing and general abuse need considering. Choose the original sporting mid-Atlantic Mk I, the more domesticated Mk II or any of the refined Mk IIIs. If you like the original design, and a big engine then the underrated 3000E makes an interesting prospect.

Cost (3000E)	£3,000
% swing	-21
Spares	★★★★★
V.F.M.	★
S.R.	★★★

SPECIFICATIONS

ENGINE: 1297; 1593; 1996; 2994; 3091cc
BHP: 72 - 148
FUEL: 20 – 30mpg
GEARBOX: 4 speed
SUSPENSION: MacPherson strut– semi-elliptcal

BRAKES: Disc/ drum
SPEED: 86 - 140 mph
BODIES: 2 door 2 + 2 coupe; hatchback coupé
YEARS: 1969–86
PRODUCTION: 1,886,647

MANUFACTURER
STANDARD TRIUMPH

VANGUARD PHASE I

A REAL PERIOD GEM FOR AN INDIVIDUALIST

This is not a simple 1950s runabout just attaining classic eligibility, but the real thing, an example of new post-war styling and all the more interesting for it. The Standard Vanguard was the first genuine new post-war British car and was the result of impressive forward thinking. Money and resources were in very short supply, and so it was decided to create a single world car and push exports to draw in valuable foreign exchange. Two years in planning, the Phase I Vanguard closely resembled American styling, with items such as column gear changes increasing US sales. The immensely strong chassis, and even the generous ground clearance, were deliberate decisions to favour countries with poor road conditions. Because of export successes, it was not until 1950 that production capacity allowed British sales in any number. Effectively a six seater with a good boot, it proved successful in all walks of life. Estate versions were both cavernous and sturdy, giving them a long working life. The likes of HRH the Duke of Gloucester, Lord Mountbatten and Lord Brabazon all favoured the Vanguard. A competition team even entered the Monte Carlo Rally. The very first cars used only 1849cc, but all of these are thought to have been exported. The replacement 2088cc engine had wet cylinder liners and was actually common to the successful Ferguson tractor which Standard also manufactured. The basic model offered vinyl trimmings, while a fully-fledged example had leather, a heater, a radio and overdrive. In 1951 a change of bumpers, grille design, enlarged rear window, rear wheel spats and revised bonnet – termed the Phase 1A – helped keep customers interested until its final replacement in 1953 by the more conventional Phase II.

Somehow the car manages to address the period American bias while retaining a very British, stately, presence. When you climb into one you know you are in a real car. A fascinating classic to own or restore with few problems – providing you don't expect 1990s responses from it.

RELATIONS

Standard visited the American Embassy to sketch current US car styles before creating the Phase I although the body is a Standard design. The 2088cc engine was also used in the Renown and would find its way into the TR2. With less stylised bodywork the Vanguard would continue in various guises through the 1950s.

BEST BUY

A wonderfully strong chassis and body. Check for rust around the lower edges of the bodywork and in particular the rear – behind the wheels there is no chassis support. The post-1951 Phase 1A encapsulates all the model's best features. Reasonable spares and a good UK club are in support.

SPECIFICATIONS

ENGINE: 2088cc	**BRAKES:** Drum
BHP: 68	**SPEED:** 80mph
FUEL: 25mpg	**BODIES:** 4 door saloon, estate,
GEARBOX: 3 speed	van, pick–up
SUSPENSION: Ind coil – semi-	**YEARS:** 1947 – 53
elliptic	**PRODUCTION:** 184,799

Cost	£3,100
% swing	4
Spares	★★★
V.F.M.	★★★
S.R.	★★

MANUFACTURER
RENAULT

Louis Renault had witnessed the launch of the VW Beetle at the 1938 Berlin Motor Show and spent the years of the Nazi occupation planning his own super-economical model. Work started discreetly in 1940 and rear wheel drive was one logical decision for the secret prototypes. The little 4CV was unveiled at the 1946 Paris Motor Show. The engine was 760cc, water-cooled and married to a three speed gearbox, but such raw statistics have little to do with the car's central appeal. In a deeply depressed France the sight of an affordable four-door, four-seater car, must have been very seductive. It was frugal to run and positively glowed with Gallic charm. Within a year a Luxe version had been announced and the car's roof line rounded; a now rare convertible model was introduced in 1949 along with slight engine increases. As 14 years of production rolled by, numerous changes took place, including renaming the Luxe the Affaires, a Grand Luxe becoming the Sport; and in 1952 a Service model was launched. This was an absolutely basic version with no interior trim, hammock seating and just a dark grey paint option. At the other end of the scale, racing activity – including two Le Mans class wins - led to a competition model. Just 80 were made of this 1063cc, 32bhp car with specially constructed engines and four or five speed boxes, while the road-going Sports 4CV offered speeds into the 80s. The 4CV was a huge success, becoming the first Renault to sell a million examples and reaching over 500 produced in a single day. A Japanese production line made over 50,000 examples and another in London produced the model named the Renault 760 and 750. The slight cc change was to put the car into a 750cc category.

RELATIONS

An original Renault concept which gave birth to many coach-built models including drophead, coupés, two door pillarless cars, and even a Gullwing coupé. The 1956 Dauphine also used the 4CV engine, gearbox and suspension.

BEST BUY

Naturally with such a basic car many have rusted away; particularly watch floors, engine and suspension mountings. Body panels are difficult to find, but engines were made into the 1980s.

Cost	£3,100
% swing	-5
Spares	★★
V.F.M.	★★
S.R.	★★★★★

SPECIFICATIONS

ENGINE: 747cc; 760cc	**SPEED:** 60mph
BHP: 17–21	**BODIES:** 4 door saloon; convertible
FUEL: 50mpg	
GEARBOX: 3 speed	**YEARS:** 1947–61
BRAKES: Drum	**PRODUCTION:** 1,105,547
SUSPENSION: Ind wishbone/ coil – swing axle/coil	

MANUFACTURER

VAUXHALL

The first HA Vivas appeared in 1963, becoming HBs five years later; these spawned a staggering 26 variants before turning into HCs in 1971. One further year and the factory was celebrating their millionth Viva. However the rewards of this, and incidently passing the 2,000,000th Bedford, were marred by Ford's devastating launch of the Capri. Vauxhall had no immediate answers, but focused their best efforts on creating the 1159cc Firenza Coupé. This was really the Viva HC clothed in an indifferent two-door coupé body. Within a year they tried adding larger engines, extra trim, instrumentation, fashionable wheels and even the using the 110bhp 2300 Sports SL engine – but that Ford still turned the enthusiasts' heads. Vauxhall tried parallel marketing de luxe versions called Magnums but they were not convincing.

Then through aerodynamic testing they found that a different Firenza nose panel boosted performance. This simple addition involved low frontal air damming, streamlining the four headlights and adding a rear spoiler. This was the David Jones-designed Droop Snoot. The 2.3 litre overhead camshaft engine was further tuned, twin Stromberg carburettors and a five speed ZF gearbox added, creating a 120 mph coupé that reached 60 in just 8.5 seconds

This was serious motoring and this model together with competition success help improved a flagging period in Vauxhall's history. Unfortunately, its production took place during the era of the three day week and lasted only long enough to built 204 cars. Just as the Firenza coupé had accommodated a variety of engines to suit Vauxhall's production plans, so

the Magnum soldiered on for a final year with the same Droop Snoot nose, while a never-listed additional Sportshatch model based on the 2.3 litre engine with Magnum interiors utilised the last remaining 197 nose cones (effectively a Viva estate). This was not a distinguished period for Vauxhall, but this small Firenza coupé was a high point.

RELATIONS

Various Vauxhall engines were used along with many parts from the Ventora. However, the basis for the Firenza is firmly the HC specification Viva.

BEST BUY

The inevitable rust needs checking, particularly around sills and surrounding the wheel areas. The carburation may need to be re-set and the gearbox almost certainly will take getting used to – it did when new. Above all, try and establish you are buying a real one rather than a DIY upgrade.

SPECIFICATIONS

ENGINE: 1159-1256-1599-1759-1975-2279cc	**SPEED:** 80–100–120mph
BHP: 62.5 – 80 – 131	**BODIES:** 2 door coupé, Droop Snoop coupé
FUEL: 26–34mpg	**YEARS:** 1971–76
GEARBOX: 4 & 5 speed	**PRODUCTION:** 20,013 (+1889 Magnum Droop Snoots & Sportshatch)
BRAKES: Disc/drum	
SUSPENSION: Coil/wishbone – trailing arm	

Cost (Droop Snoot)	£3,500
% swing	-14
Spares	★★★
V.F.M.	★★
S.R.	★★★

CONSUL CAPRI
A RARE DESIGNER FORD ANGLIA COUPÉ

MANUFACTURER
FORD

With the Ford Anglia rapidly accumulating sales, and the still secret Cortina under development, Ford took the commercial gamble of launching a freshly designed interim model – the Ford Classic. Despite its transatlantic flavour, this was a Dagenham concept with plenty of chrome, four headlights and their latest gimmick, the Anglia's reversed rear window. Ford knew this was only a short term production, and did not develop a weight-saving policy, which resulted in really strong metalwork. Essentially, this was a highly individual style exercise in a four door Anglia – complete with vast boot. The car's initial performance was poor until 1962, when the new 1500cc five-bearing engine was installed. This unloved car actually sold over 111,000 in its brief two year life but its offspring, the Consul Capri, generated a different reaction. It may have been commercial suicide offering two bodies of an interim car, but the resulting Ford Consul Capri showed real flair. Below the waistline it was pure Classic, but the pretty coupé roof line and the pillarless curved side windows transformed the controversial styling. The interior was all new, although the rear seating was lost to the 40 degree rear window angle and the lower roof line.

The Classic's change to the 1500cc engine also improved the Capri, but it was seven months later in February 1963 when it began to perform as it looked.

The Capri GT boasted a twin choked Weber carburettor, servo-operated front discs, floor gear change, a Duckworth designed cam, four branch exhaust – specifications to please any enthusiastic Anglia owner. Naturally this specification was off-set by the sheer weight of the standard Ford Classic structure but it left you wondering what might have developed had Ford given the car a chance.

RELATIONS

The original design was influenced by the 105E Anglia; the Capri used much of its running gear including the 1340cc engine. The later 1500cc unit was similar to the Mk I and II Cortina. Otherwise, the Consul Capri was a re–roofed Consul Classic.

BEST BUY

All increasingly rare and collectable. The initial 1340cc ones are slower, the 1500 an improvement and the late GTs by far the most desirable. Watch out for body rust.

Cost	£4,000
% swing	41
Spares	★★★
V.F.M.	★★★★★
S.R.	★★★

SPECIFICATIONS

ENGINE: 1340cc; 1500cc
BHP: 54; 59; 78(GT)
FUEL: 30; 27(GT)mpg
GEARBOX: 4 speed
BRAKES: Disc/drum
SPEED: 81; 82; 95(GT)mph

SUSPENSION: Ind MacPherson strut – semi-elliptic
BODIES: 2 door coupé
YEARS: 1961–64
PRODUCTION: 20,013

MANUFACTURER
VOLVO

VOLVO PV444 & 544

A STRONG, AGILE, HIGHLY INDIVIDUAL CHOICE

'We design and we improve – but we do not invent', a philosophy declared by Gustaf Larson, one of the founding fathers of the Swedish Volvo organisation. True to his words, Volvo's history charts progressive improvement through just a handful of models. In the last 25 years they have relentlessly perfected transport for labradors and their owners – and it has worked. Now they are heavily investing in correcting that image through racing and advertising the 850. It has impressed new fans while the better informed just smile in the knowledge that Volvo's real sporting heritage pre dates the current macho chest beatings.

The distinctive PV544 has its roots in the Second World War. Sweden was neutral and allowed factories to continue manufacturing, so in 1944 Volvo unveiled their PV444 – named after the year of its launch. The car incorporated a 1414cc four-cylinder engine, independent front suspension, plentiful space for passengers and luggage (the seats even converted into beds), and an American-influenced body styling. Shadowing the Amazon specifications, the PV444 was then upgraded as a Sports version to an 85hp, 1.6 unit which went on to achieve class wins in race meetings across the USA. In 1958 this car became the impressive PV544, initially with the same 1593cc engine. and then from 1962 using a larger 1780cc powerplant. The sales pitch emphasised 'The car renowned for its repeated racing successes', stating that the PV544 was designed 'specially for passenger comfort and safety', and even listed rear seat belt attachments – perhaps current Volvo marketing isn't quite so innovative after all.

A great rally car in its day, strong, responsive and predictable, it makes an indestructible day-to-day classic which still enjoys a little competition. Sadly, import taxes made it too expensive to justify any right hand drive versions.

RELATIONS

Volvo designer Erik Jern had previously concentrated on streamlined cars which, coupled with Volvo factory fascination with the USA, naturally led to the distinctive 'Hunchback' style, as it was nicknamed. The engine was rationalised with Amazon parts.

BEST BUY

PV544s love to be driven, and mileage should not be a concern – the engine is so willing you can actually start in third! There was a factory option of three or four speed boxes. Bodywork was sturdy heavy gauge metal, the interior has uncomplicated trim. The Sports version is a lighter car.

SPECIFICATIONS

ENGINE: 1414; 1598; 1778cc	**SPEED:** 59 – 98mph
BHP: 40 – 90	**BODIES:** LHD 2 door saloon, estate & van
FUEL: 33 – 28 mpg	
GEARBOX: 3 or 4 speed	**YEARS:** 1944–58; 1958–65
BRAKES: Drum	**PRODUCTION:** 440,000
SUSPENSION: Ind coil/wishbone – coil/rigid axle	(Various basic & sports versions of each engine necessitate compression of figures)

Cost (PV544)	£3,900
% swing	-11
Spares	★★
V.F.M.	★★
S.R.	★★★

VANDEN PLAS 4 LITRE R

A SATISFACTORY MARRIAGE OF CONVENIENCE

MANUFACTURER

BMC

By the beginning of the 1960s BMC's predilection for repackaging every available configuration of marques and engineering was legendary. Their Farina saloon range, first revealed as the 1958 Wolseley 15/66, was beginning to lose ground to rivals, and both the trusted BMC B and larger C series engines were showing their ages. However, the government had just announced a tax allowance on company cars of £2000 and all the manufacturers raised mid-range car specifications to capture that market. BMC were to price this Vanden Plas 'Princess' R at £1998.

The C series-engined Austin A99 Westminster and Wolseley 6/99 had been supplemented in 1959 by a Super De Luxe model – the highly trimmed Vanden Plas 3 litre. Meanwhile, Rolls-Royce were quietly developing their future monocoque Shadows and were testing both the V8 and a version of their aluminium 4 litre B60 – a 6 cylinder version of the B40 which powered the military Austin Champ. Rolls-Royce took the V8 route and a willing BMC entered negotiations for the spare B60 engine for their Farina model. Incidently, they also flirted with using it in an Austin-Healey 3000 replacement. The resulting car was the interesting Vanden Plas Princess 4 litre R, which used the regular Austin/Westminster/Wolseley/Vanden Plas body, but with a vertical grille, horizontal tail lights and an even higher standard of interior trimming. An automatic gearbox was standard, so was power steering, picnic tables, built in fog lights, reclining front seats and plenty of leather. Despite weighing 32cwt, it performed well and the level of refinement made it an interesting prospect only lacking sufficient visual distinction from the rest of the BMC Farina range. Future development and a new Farina body could have created fascinating

prospects. As it was, R-R were shifting unwanted engines, BMC had a Farina flagship and Vanden Plas were left trying to create a BMC production car to match Rolls-Royce's legendary standards. Numbers of the earlier ones suffered from some irritating build quality defects.

RELATIONS

The basic concept is an Austin A99 Westminster/Wolseley 6/99, with enhanced trimming as a Vanden Plas 3 litre, united with a 4 litre Rolls-Royce engine conceived for military application, to become the Vanden Plas 4 litre R. Simpler than it sounds.

BEST BUY

With relatively few produced, these finite BMC/Farina cars are now desirable. Rust usually concentrates on the bottom sections of the bodywork and naturally, the sills. The engine and the gearbox are both built to last and last, but don't be surprised if the engine is noisier than you might have expected of a Rolls-Royce. As with so many BMC products, it pays to buy late models when the bugs had been ironed out.

Cost	£4,000
% swing	-8
Spares	★★
V.F.M.	★★
S.R.	★★

SPECIFICATIONS

ENGINE: 3909cc	**SUSPENSION:** Coil/wishbone – semi-elliptic
BHP: 175	
FUEL: 18mpg	**BODIES:** 4 door
GEARBOX: Automatic	**YEARS:** 1964–1968
BRAKES: Disc/drum	**PRODUCTION:** 7000
SPEED: 113 mph	

MANUFACTURER
HONDA

Born out of brilliant motorcycle success, Honda's initial entry into sports car production involved a two seater with a twin–cam four-cylinder 356cc engine with four carburettors. Weighing only 1122lbs (509kg) this prototype offered an impressive 33bhp and a top speed of 75mph. The commercial version was known as the S500 and was followed in 1964 by the S600 which provided 57bhp from its enlarged 606cc unit. Honda's sporting ambition blossomed the following year when their white F1 car scored its first Grand Prix victory; while the 1966 F2 was dominated by Hulme and Jack Brabham with the 140bhp 1 litre Honda-engined Brabhams.

This stunning little engine was designed by Tadashi Kume, who was also responsible for the extraordinary 791cc powerplant installed in the 1966 S800 development of their sports car. This was an advanced, largely aluminium unit employing twin overhead camshafts and twin exhaust for each cylinder pair, along with four sidedraught Kei–Hin carbs. It screams. It generates all its power in the upper rev bands around 8000rpm, while it will reach a staggering 11,000rpm. This kind of action requires a love of real driving and abundant use of its willing four speed, all synchromesh gearbox. There is independent suspension all round, with only early S600 examples employing a short axle and drive chains to each wheel. The body draws upon European 1960s design, yet retains its individuality. The dash offers very full instrumentation and quality trim abounds both inside and out. Lessons Honda learnt from the prototype S600 and from F2 racing and S800, were then carried

forward to the best-selling Civic range. The S800 was set to make high sales when in 1967 the pound was suddenly devalued, making the Honda price tag way above even bigger cars such as the MGB. Production ceased in 1970.

RELATIONS

There was evolution of Honda's initial models and competition development for the engine. There were no direct descendants.

BEST BUY

Of 26,000 worldwide sales only 1500 were officially imported to the UK, and only 300 were the open sports which naturally command more money. Check rust around wheel arches, wings edges, doors – fortunately thick gauge metal has helped floor areas and chassis. Watch for corrosion around the aluminium engine and replacing the needle roller bearing crankshaft is expensive. Certain main Honda dealers carry spares and an S800 club exists in support.

SPECIFICATIONS

ENGINE: 606cc – 791cc	**SPEED:** 100 mph
BHP: 70	**BODIES:** 2 door sports; coupé
FUEL: 35mpg	**YEARS:** 1966–70
GEARBOX: 4 speed	**PRODUCTION:** 26,000 –
BRAKES: Disc/drum	all S variants
SUSPENSION: Ind Coil/wish-	
bone – live axle/coil	

Cost	£3,750
% swing	38
Spares	★★★
V.F.M.	★★★★
S.R.	★★★★

VAUXHALL CRESTA PA
1950s STYLING MASTERPIECE

MANUFACTURER
VAUXHALL

Car manufacturing history is packed with indifferent models pretending to be grand sports cars, badge-engineered to suggest that they go faster. Many tried to bait the US and home markets simultaneously; the Cresta PA had an up-front American style that caught the social mood to perfection, and brought transatlantic street culture to Britain. The Crestas were striking cars with long, low bodies, generous wrap-around windows, excesses of chrome, fins, and rear lamp clusters to match anything on American highways. The initial 2262cc in line six was replaced in 1960 with a larger 2651cc version, increasing power by 25 per cent. Both these units were tilted slightly downward at the rear to help provide identical headroom to the older and larger F series. – despite being 4.5 inches lower overall. These were fast cars for their day and comfortably accommodated six. A Velox version provided basic transport, while the Cresta with its heater/demister, washers, leather trim, carpets and underlays and a varieties of secondary lighting, was Vauxhall's rightful flagship. Distinguishing features included name-badging in gold, bonnet motifs, white wall tyres, stainless steel window trimming and gloriously flamboyant choices of duo-toned paintwork. Other markers were the 1959 changes from three to one piece rear window and replacing the initially straight grille with a larger curved version. From March 1958 there was also a Friary-bodied estate offering volumes of space.

RELATIONS

The body style is original; the engine until 1960 was the same powerplant as in the old E series, but with automatic choke carburation. The Velox and Cresta were basically identical. Prefixes for the PAs pre-1960 are Velox – PAS and Cresta – PAD, while after 1960 they were PADY and PADX respectively.

BEST BUY

The early smaller engined cars had unique elements such as the triple rear window, while the later ones were more powerful and actually boasted larger grilles and fins. Good examples are now rare and body panels are scarce.

Cost	£4,100
% swing	15
Spares	★★★
V.F.M.	★★★
S.R.	★★★

SPECIFICATIONS

ENGINE: 2262cc, 2651cc	**SUSPENSION:** Ind Coil - semi - elliptic
BHP: 83 – 113	
FUEL: 21–25mpg	**SPEED** 90–95mph
GEARBOX: 3 speed or 2 automatic	**BODIES:** 4 door saloon; estate
	YEARS: 1957–62
BRAKES: Disc /drum	**PRODUCTION:** 81,841

MANUFACTURER
TRIUMPH

The idea of combining the essence of the Spitfire, the Triumph 2000 engine and a diminutive E Type-styled coupé body was excellent. It was a 'Parts Bin' dream – which nearly turned into a nightmare simply because Triumph refuse to react to criticism.

In 1966, the year of the Mk I launch, there was a flood of orders but soon afterwards all the old Herald handling complaints magnified around the GT6. Despite knowing the limitations of the rear suspension in a modest family saloon, they pressed ahead selling the same specification in a 100mph+ sports car. To compound matters, the Spitfire front suspension had been softened on the GT6 to appease the American market – further aggravating the unpredictable handling. A leading British magazine reported that one US reaction was to ask if it was 'George III's revenge?'

Triumph capitulated, and the 1968 Mk II was a different story, with the rear suspension a Rotoflex double wishbone and a different suspension set up. It was expensive remedial action, but meant the Mk II suddenly brought the pretty coupé into bloom. Providing 30mpg, and over 100mph top speed, it had a sweet four-speed gearbox often with the overdrive option on 3rd and 4th – effectively giving it six gears. The cockpit was quite confined, but the rear storage was always useful.

In October 1970 the Mk III was born out of a Spitfire facelift. The body work was de–seamed, a larger windscreen added, and the rear chopped short which actually rather suited the coupé body. However in February 1973, with falling US sales, the factory reverted to a modified variant of the cheaper original rear suspension. The Rotoflex versions completed a very attractive coupé with excellent cruising manners and quite safe progressive handling. It also costs a fraction of its inspiration – the Jaguar E Type.

RELATIONS

It had a Herald chassis, the Vanguard Six/Triumph 2000 engine, and Mk II engine improvements from parallel work on TR5. The Rotoflex double wishbone was inspired by the Cooper F1, while the GT6 gearbox was used in the Spitfire and Dolomite.

BEST BUY

Unless it's an ambition, leave the Mk I alone. The Mk II and Rotoflex suspended Mk IIIs are definitely the best cars. Late Mk IIIs had marginally inferior handling, but improved trimmings. Lots of rust, but with a full-opening front end you can easily see many of the trouble areas. Mk I dash boards and seats are tricky to find, and many examples have acquired fibre glass bonnets. Engine/gearbox generally reliable.

SPECIFICATIONS

ENGINE: 1998cc
BHP: 95; 104
FUEL: 24; 30mpg
GEARBOX: 4 speed, optional o'drive
BRAKES: Disc/drum
SPEED: 106; 112mph

SUSPENSION: Ind coil/ wishbone – MkI swing axle MkII/early III Rotoflex: Later MkIII swing–spring axle
BODIES: 3 door coupé
YEARS: 1966–73
PRODUCTION: 40,926

Cost (MkIII)	£4,750
% swing	-3
Spares	★★★★★
V.F.M.	★★
S.R.	★★★

TRIUMPH HERALD VITESSE

TOWN MANNERS – OPEN ROAD ENJOYMENT

MANUFACTURER

STANDARD-TRIUMPH

Standard-Triumph's enforced decision to bolt on (Michelotti-designed) Herald body panels to a separate chassis proved useful. It did mean occasional rattles and leaks, but at least panels were easily replaced. To the factory, convertibles, estates, and sporting versions were thus primarily a matter of bolting on differing non-stressed body parts. Perhaps the most successful of these variants was the Vitesse range which first appeared in May 1962. Superficially, it took just a side flash of paint and replacement front panels to provide four headlights and a fresh grille. It cost little and looked good, but the real bonus was that instead of just upgrading the Herald engine they installed a reduced bore 1596cc in–line six from the Standard Vanguard 6 model. Coupled to a pair of Solex carburettors, improved gearing, 9 inch front discs (and enlarged rear drums), this offered 90mph performance on a stiffened chassis – even though it was a full 1cwt heavier than the Herald. It was, indeed, sports car performance from an economical saloon platform. With the Vitesse, Triumph were revisiting their 1930s role as manufacturers of small sixes for the discerning. After carburettor changes, in 1966 came the 2 litre engine from the Triumph 2000 saloon, with 95bhp performance married at last to a new full syncromeshed gearbox and generally improved trim. This improved performance, however, accentuated the unpredictable behaviour of the rear swing axle and the factory were finally forced to remedy matters. The Mk II was announced in October 1968 with some trim changes, improved engine performance and the lower wishbone system

from the GT6 sports car. The Vitesse had reached its final form with 100mph+ performance, four seats, good storage and in–town manners. Through a fusion of models and ideas Standard-Triumph had moulded a thoroughly enjoyable, practical motor car.

RELATIONS

Its roots are in the basic Herald. The Vitesse 6 engine came from the Standard Vanguard 6, while the later 2 litre models used the Triumph 2000 powerplant. The final Mk II versions employed improved suspensions from the Triumph GT6.

BEST BUY

Bolt-on bodywork means easy DIY and some poor restorations. A good chassis is essential, next are sound mountings and front bonnet. Gearboxes do wear and body panels rattle. The Vitesse 6 is the poor relation, the 2 litre Mk II definitely the best, a Mk II convertible something to savour.

Cost	£4,200
(MkII Convertible)	
% swing	-3.5
Spares	★★★★★
V.F.M.	★★
S.R.	★★★★

SPECIFICATIONS

ENGINE: 1596cc; 1998cc
BHP: 70; 104
FUEL: 30 – 24mpg
GEARBOX: 4 speed (early no syncro on lst)
BRAKES: Disc/Drum
SPEED: 91; 101mph

SUSPENSION: Ind with transverse leaf/swing axle (post-1968 change to wishbone system)
BODIES: 2 door saloon; 2 door convertible,
YEARS: 1962–71
PRODUCTION: 51,212 disputed

MANUFACTURER
BMW

ISETTA
A GENUINE CITY BMW FOR THE 1990s!

A classic 1950s BMW you can store at the end of your garage, that won't break the bank, that you dare to practise DIY on, you can remove an entire engine from in half an hour, tax for around £50, and cruise at 50+mph. The Isetta may have been a 'Bubble' car but the post-war recovery of BMW depended heavily upon this little Italian machine, and now their scarcity value, nostalgia for the 1950s and the enormous fun they offer make them a very serious classic choice for some. These micro saloons blossomed from a combination of limited manufacturing materials, a financial crisis, and the extreme petrol shortages following the Suez Crisis in 1956. A two seater with luggage storage, reduced road tax, 60 mpg and small enough to park at right angles to the curb is an attractive prospect, especially in our crowded 1990s cities. The Isetta originated from Iso in Milan and was launched in 1953 using a 236cc, 9.5hp two stroke engine with the paired rear wheels 26 inches closer together than the front ones. Its ingenious jointed steering column allowed the entire front of the car to hinge away as a wide single door. A year later BMW undertook German production using their 247cc four stroke yielding 12hp and as Milan production fell away the BMW model catered for exports. By 1957 BMW had opened a UK production line in Brighton's old railway buildings where employees negotiated a hundred steps to work and materials could only arrive by rail. In 1959 they switched to a three-wheeled configuration exploiting UK tax laws which considered any three wheeler under 8cwt a motorcycle, which paid less road taxation. Right-hand drive followed and then a two-door, four-seater model. Isetta means 'Little Iso' reflecting its originators, and it remained the quintessential mini car until in 1959 the Mini rewrote the rules.

RELATIONS

Designed by the Italian motorcycle and scooter company Iso, the Isetta was licensed to bike producers BMW who installed their own engines. The 700 followed the 600, another rear engine in 1960. Soon after, the BMW 1500/1800 saw the Bavarian company enter their contemporary realm.

BEST BUY

The Brighton factory produced around 30,000 using suppliers such as Lucas and Girling. The British Isettas had sliding side windows and swivelling quarter lights and used BMW 250 and 300 engines, which are strong; DIY should not be threatening, though rust can attack floors and lower bodywork.

SPECIFICATIONS	
ENGINE: 247cc; 298cc	**SPEED:** 52–58mph
BHP: 12; 13	**BODIES:** 2 seater saloon;
FUEL: 65mpg	roll top cabriolet
GEARBOX: 4 speed	**YEARS:** 1955–62
BRAKES: Drum	**PRODUCTION:** 161,728
SUSPENSION: Dubonnet Ind	(UK 30,000)
coils – Quarter	
elliptics/dampers	

Cost	£4,700
% swing	-14
Spares	★★
V.F.M.	★★
S.R.	★★★★★

MGB GT

PERFECT AFFORDABLE BRITISH SPORTS CAR

MANUFACTURER
BMC

The front end (above) is of course non-standard, but not that unattractive – certainly not as unsatisfactory as US regulations made the factory issue in 1974.

Cost	£5,200
(GT 65-74 average)	
% swing	-13

Spares	★★★★★
V.F.M.	★★
S.R.	★★★

BMC had struggled to find a suitable replacement for the MGA which utilised the existing 1622cc unit. Fighting off competition from cars like the Triumph TR3, young designer Don Hayter's simple 1958 design disposed of the restrictive MGA chassis, and within 10 weeks a full scale mock-up revealed the excellent lines of the MGB. At the next drawing table Dennis Williams battled deadlines to design the MG Midget, and ironically, a smaller MGB rear appeared on the Midget before the Roadster B itself was launched in 1962.

The MGB GT was unveiled in 1965 by which time the new BMC 1800 five bearing crankshaft was added to the MGB. So good was the B's design that no significant mechanical changes occurred until the late experiments with big engines. Excellent rack-and-pinion steering, the sturdy Series B engine, and the car's sheer versatility made it an instant favourite. Many consider the GT has the more graceful lines, yet on the classic market they are usually around 25 per cent cheaper than the roadsters.

In October 1969 there was a cosmetic update with Rostyle wheels, reclining seats, interior trimming and a revised chrome and matt black grille. 1967 had seen the start of a two year experiment marrying a strengthened MG to a 145bhp six-cylinder engine.

The MGC was to be twinned with an Austin-Healey 3000 replacement but Donald Healey would not co-operate. The resultant MG was not well balanced and certainly the Abingdon press car of the time (below right) gave me an eventful week. The regular B GT's popularity rolled on until threatened American legislation prompted the 1974 change to the large energy absorption black bumpers and raised suspension. Both these changes spoilt the car, reflected in much lower classic car prices. From 1973 to 1976 there was also an MGB GT V8 version using the 3.5 Rover engine which had more potential than the ill fated C but within a year it too was saddled with the damaging American modifications and lacked the visual excitement of the works racing Sebring bodywork.

RELATIONS

With a modified MGA engine, gearbox and front suspension, the MGB GT used an updated version from the BMC 1800 from 1964; a new BMC Series C

SPECIFICATIONS

ENGINE: 1798cc, 2912cc; 3528cc V8
BHP: 95 bhp; 145bhp; 137bhp
FUEL: 22 mpg; 18mpg; 25mpg
GEARBOX: 4 speed
BRAKES: Disc/Drum
BODIES: 3 door coupé
SUSPENSION: Ind coil/ wishbone – semi elliptic
SPEED: 103 mph; 120mph; 125mph (B, C,V8)
YEARS: 1965 – 1980; 1967–69; 1973–76
PRODUCTION: 125,597; 4,449; 2,600

engine for the MGC, and a Rover 3.5 for the MG GT V8. The Austin 3 litre gearbox was introduced from autumn 1967. The body styling was original.

BEST BUY

The only drama is rust within the central body construction, so inspect prospective purchases carefully.

Repair can be extremely costly, but in dire situations new bodyshells are now available. Otherwise they are a joy to own. They are eminently practical, spares abound and the car lives up to John Thornley's dream (formerly of MG) of creating a 'poor man's Aston Martin'. Nearly forty years on, these cars are guaranteed to turn heads and are among the most popular classic cars around.

… plus another 9000 who opted for the MGC in the same bodyshell (half GT), with the 6 cylinder ex-Austin-Healey 3000 engines, from late '67 to late '69. Top speed was impressive at 120mph, but the low-speed torque was found wanting by the motoring press at the time. Autocar considered that 'somewhere in the large BMC complex it has lost the "Abingdon touch"'. Prophetic words.

MG MAGNETTE ZA & ZB

Simple and elegant Nuffield swansong

MANUFACTURER
BMC

Having designed the Jowett Javelin, Gerald Palmer was persuaded to create the 1950s generation of MGs, Rileys and Wolseleys. Commercial pressures required that he embrace as many existing factory parts as possible and standardise all three car designs. The resulting Wolseley 4/44 (1952) and MG Magnette ZA (1953) were a skilful union of factory needs and Palmer's own passion for simple, sleek Italian designs. The MG was the first car to enjoy the new BMC Series B 1498cc engine and the twin carburettor, 60bhp set-up offered a then impressive 85mph top speed. It was four-door, four-seat motoring with excellent light steering and reasonable levels of interior luxury, including quality carpets and leather seating – although the 'wooden' dashboard proved to be painted metalwork until timber materialised on 1955 models. Some purists announced that it was not a proper MG, but customers flocked to buy this low, swift sporting saloon. BMC had become the overseer by then and rationalisation was the new commandment. Fortunately the Magnette's appeal kept intervention at bay and in 1956 the car became the Magnette ZB. Wisely, little was changed apart from a slight increase in power to 64bhp, an optional two pedal Manumatic system and a de luxe model called the Varitone, which offered fashionable two-tone bodywork and a considerably enlarged rear window. Far from sales falling for this upgraded model, ZB sales actually surpassed those of the earlier ZA, and these would continue until BMC grouped all their mid-range cars under one 1960s Farina design, with the MG Magnette Mk III contribution actually

slightly slower than the ZB and selling less well. The ZB would be the last Abingdon-built MG saloon.

Original owners were practical sporting motorists who might now consider a BMW 325, an Audi or Volvo 850, while prospective classic buyers now see the MG Z series cars as still agile and elegant.

RELATIONS

It shared the Wolseley 4/44 floor pan and monocoque – although only the roof and door panels are actually the same. The engine and front suspension were Austin, while the steering was from Morris.

BEST BUY

The BMC Series B engine and the gearbox are generally trouble free and parts are no problem. The reason few are seen on the roads is rust and it is important to find good examples or a sensible restoration project. Check all the obvious places in particular the floor areas and the prone sill sections. If you can find a good one, buy the late Varitone.

Cost	£5,000
% swing	22
Spares	★★★
V.F.M.	★★★
S.R.	★★★

SPECIFICATIONS

ENGINE: 1489cc
BHP: 60–64
FUEL: 25mpg
GEARBOX: 4 speed
BRAKES: Drum
SPEED: 80–86mph
SUSPENSION: Ind Coil/wishbone – semi-elliptic
BODIES: 4 door saloon
YEARS: 1953–58
PRODUCTION: 36,650

MANUFACTURER

AUDI

This ground-breaking Audi is a pinnacle of ingenuity. It merged the basic three million selling Audi 80 production car and the 1960s Ferguson Formula four-wheel drive concepts as used in the Jensen Interceptor FF. The four-wheel drive they were to use was adapted from the Iltis, a military vehicle Audi made for their parent company VW. By September 1979 the Audi 100 had become the 200, and the fastest front wheel drive saloon car. The 130mph, 170bhp engine then received intercooling to power the initial 1980 200bhp Audi Quattro. It was an immediate success, with simple, powerful styling and technical leadership from fixed four-wheel drive, Bosch fuel injection and KKK K26 turbo. Audi had managed to create a car subtle enough to be a five seater 'executive express' as well as an international competition car. The Quattro became an 1980s icon, and single-handedly caused the motor industry and the public to re–think the road-going values of FWD. In reality it was one of the most successful 'Parts Bin' cars, with Audi 80 basics, VW Polo interaxle diffs, and Audi 200 saloon powerplant.

During 1981 the inevitable homologation production provided just enough semi-competition models to qualify for eligibility. These Group 4 cars were made with a variety of engine configurations, built-in roll cages, larger spoilers and limited diffs, while the 1983 AI offered turbocharged, larger bore, 2145cc or 2178cc units within a much lighter yet strengthened body. The Group B A2 version went even further, providing a 400bhp rally monster, which was, in turn, overshadowed by a short wheel based Sports version

with sophisticated differential options – the victorious works rally cars were actually achieving 500bhp. The road cars stayed with the 2144cc until 1987, when it rose to 2226cc, while a 1989 20 valve head offered 220bhp until the Quattro's demise in 1991

RELATIONS

Originating from the bestselling Audi 80, the Quattro is a direct descendent from the 80 coupé. It has Audi and VW components, with the basic engine from the Audio 200 saloon.

BEST BUY

The early cars lacked acceleration until the turbo kicked in, while the last 20 valve models lost the Quattro's aggressive aura. The latest 10 valve, 2226cc versions are fractionally slower, but more economical to run, while still enjoying the bulging wheel arches and turbo excitement. The 80 Coupé dashboard is uninspired, gears notchy but rust is not a huge problem. Major repairs are expensive.

An opentop will cost you a whole lot more than the coupé – if you can find such an exotic beast. The example pictured was produced by the Tresser company of Germany with the full blessing of Audi. Tresser have worked with Audi on various projects.

SPECIFICATIONS

ENGINE: 2144cc; 2145; 2178; 2226cc
BHP: 200 to 500
FUEL: 24 to 5mpg
GEARBOX: 5 speed: F.W.D
BRAKES: Disc

SUSPENSION: Ind MacPherson Struts all round
SPEED: 135mph to 188mph
BODIES: 2 door coupé
YEARS: 1980 – 1991
PRODUCTION: 11,452

Cost	£5,000
% swing	-32
Spares	★★
V.F.M.	★
S.R.	★★★

ROVER P5

SOLID CREATURE COMFORTS

MANUFACTURER
ROVER

As the Rover 75 to 110 era – the P4 range – was nearing its end, the replacement plan was for a light, mass appeal model. Concepts included a V6 engine, front-wheel drive, rear-wheel drive, four-wheel drive, rear-engined – even a plan to place the gearbox under the seating. As time passed, and Rover failed to gain planning permission to expand production buildings, it was decided the P5 should be a quality car generating limited demand and thus less factory pressures. The V6 engine was dropped and the initial Rover 3.0 saloons were launched in 1958 using a revised 2995cc P4 unit. The strong design appealed to the more conservative customers and indeed prime ministers and royalty all favoured these charismatic cars. It employed unitary construction with a rubber isolated front sub-frame for the engine, gearbox and front suspension. This feature, and the exceptional

The 1949 P4 had been known as 'Auntie Rover' – the kind of car your maiden aunt drove – upgrade to three litres, then V8, on the P5 helped to lose the tag.

levels of interior comfort, made it supremely comfortable transport. The interior boasted three-way front seat adjustments, hide upholstery, mahogany veneers, a pull-out tool tray under the dash – it was simply the most luxurious car Rover had made– and immensely British. In 1962 the Mk II was given another 12bhp by a Weslake head, the suspension was lowered and a shorter gear lever fitted. Although identical to the saloon, the Coupé was also launched boasting a 2½ inch lower roof line. To survive, however, they needed a more powerful engine and by

Cost	£5,300
% swing	39
Spares	★★★
V.F.M.	★★★★
S.R.	★★★

SPECIFICATIONS

ENGINE: 2995cc, 3528cc
BHP: 105, 160
FUEL: 20mpg – 18mpg
GEARBOX: 4 speed; automatic; overdrive option
BRAKES: Drum;Disc/drum (after 1959)

SUSPENSION: Ind wishbone & live axle semi-elliptic
SPEED: 96mph; 110mph
BODIES: 4 door saloon & coupé
YEARS: 1958 – 73
PRODUCTION: 48,241

That doughty Buick 3.5-litre V8 engine would prove to be significant for Rover, not just in the P5 and P6; it powered the 1970 Range Rover and was an option in the Land Rover from 1979.

chance an unloved aluminum V8 was spotted during a visit to Mercury Marine in Wisconsin and the engine design was licensed to Rover by Buick. In the interim, Mk II models provided even more creature comforts including individually sculpted front and rear seating with separate rear heating controls. The P5 was phased out in 1967 and the P5B (B for Buick) arrived bringing a massive 46bhp power increase, turning these cars into very desirable executive expresses. No existing gearbox could sustain the levels of torque, so only automatic was offered.

RELATIONS

Designed by Rover, the car's initial engine was from the out-going P4 range, while the V8 came from Buick. MGB GT V8s, Morgan +8s, Range Rovers, TR8s, and the Rover SD1 all used this engine.

BEST BUY

The serious danger is rust, particularly in bulkheads, wings, and sills – the usual concealed areas. The drive trains of both versions ought to be good for around 200,000 miles. Though these cars are excellent value, the quality of construction means that any major works can get expensive – buy the best you can and don't be seduced by the delightful American V8 power without considering that miles of hard driving gives an expensive 17 miles per gallon. A post-1965 3.0 litre is still good for around 100mph and in the same comfort.

RELIANT GTE

HONEST AND INTERESTING STYLESETTER

MANUFACTURER
RELIANT

Model families:

SE5 – 1968-71
SE5a – 1971-75
SE6 – 1975-76
SE6B – 1979-86
SE8b (GTC) – 1980-86
Middlebridge – 1988-90.

Cost	£5,600
(Scimitar GTE SE6)	
% swing	1

Spares	★★★★
V.F.M.	★★★
S.R.	★★★

The innovative GTE attacks both head and heart. With all the basic bugs ironed out in the Ogle designed Reliant SE Coupé this subsequent sporting estate was very appealing. Fast, sturdy and exceptionally roomy it led others such as Volvo with its P1800 and Lancia Beta's HPE to copy the concept of practical, high speed transport. The strong fibreglass bodywork couldn't rust, the chassis was strong, the running gear all proven Ford. It appeared to have everything, yet never fully captured public imagination. In the '90s the heart recognises a highly individual sporting car, with good spares, plenty of room and best of all – extremely good value for money.

However, the head dispassionately records warnings of mixed build qualities and missing glamour. The attributes of reliability, together with the fold down rear seating meant many worked hard and so look tired. They also remain a bargain and so the costs of major restoration may well not sit easily with overall values. It would be wrong to assign the GTE's to serious DIY owners only, but tired cars could damage bank accounts.

The initial SE5 model ran until 1971 and featured the UK Ford V6 which was uprated from 128bhp to 138bhp in 1971–75 SE5a form. This minor revamp covered the dashboard, new tail lighting and a grille but left the four 5¾-in headlights – a hallmark of the first body styling. SE6 and SE6b ran 1975–76 and 1976–79 respectively, using a 4 inch stretched body style, larger outer headlights, black grille and eventually an improved braking set–up. A 1980 convertible – the SE8b, used Ford of Germany's 2.8 V6 which

kept interest alive until 1986. The cars undulating commercial fortunes saw two years in abeyance and then another company try one last incarnation – the Middlebridge, using the 2.9 Ford engine, 1988–90.

RELATIONS

Body work an original Ogle design. The engines and some gearboxes were Ford, front suspension from the Triumph TR4/5/6, with Vitesse steering rack.

BEST BUY

A realist's classic car usable day-to-day. Rustless bodywork doesn't mean the vital chassis and metal supports aren't vulnerable. Fibre glass patching, rippling, and cracks need watching – a good repaint is four figures. Interior trimming was never that durable and a major retrim too will be costly. If you are not too concerned about the thickness of burred walnut furniture but want honest, economical and practical classic transport then the GTE is just right. The early style body looks prettiest and feels more agile.

SPECIFICATIONS

ENGINE: 2994cc – 2792cc	**SUSPENSION:** Ind Coil –
BHP: 128 – 150	live axle/coil
FUEL: 22–28mpg	**SPEED:** 116 – 123mph
GEARBOX: 4 speed, overdrive	**BODIES:** 3 door sports estate
standard post 4/74	**YEARS:** 1968–86 / 1988–1990
BRAKES: Disc/Drum	**PRODUCTION:** 9,705

MANUFACTURER

BMC

After the war Austin's new managing director Leonard Lord was anxious to meet the inevitable demand for new cars. While many – including Austin – carried forward old designs, he also pushed development of new a brand new Austin A40 Devon saloon, launched in 1947. A strong chassis cradled a brand new 1200cc overhead valve engine and an equally new independent front suspension set up under a very modern 4 door body shell. The car and its derivatives sold roughly 450,000 in its five years.

Meanwhile the Jensen Brothers were evolving the luxury PW with the Austin Sheerline 4 litre unit. It was not ideal and Jensen returned to Austin with drawings for another sporting car based upon Austin's A70 chassis. There was an interesting solution: Jensen's 1950 4 litre Interceptor shared a body design with the 1950 Austin A40 Sports – which Jensen constructed. It was more an open tourer than a sports car with wind up windows and rear seating for children. Naturally it was based upon the A40 Devon rolling chassis with a modified 1200cc unit and twin SU carburettors for an additional 10mph. The initial cars were constructed with floor placed gear change but with the Devon's switch to column change in August 1951, so too did the A40 Sports. Indeed the entire interior was virtually the Devon and this same basic equipment would in time also appear in the A40 Somerset. During 1952 Leonard Lord also

encouraged Donald Healey to create an outright sports car based upon the Austin A90 Atlantic engine and that year's motor show saw a prototype Healey 100: the little A40 sports was dead in the water. Jensen's production line went on to build the Austin Healey 100. Subsequent years proved open touring cars were just as appealing as sports cars – the A40 Sports was the right idea at the wrong moment.

RELATIONS

An Austin A40 Devon through and through with bodywork shared with Jensen's 1950 Interceptor.

BEST BUY

Rare, simple, with common Devon mechanics for spares. So worth work. Engines good for 75,000 miles before anything serious; gearboxes sometimes tricky.

SPECIFICATIONS

ENGINE: 1200cc	**BRAKES:** Drum
BHP: 50 bhp	**SPEED:** 78mph
FUEL: 29mpg	**BODIES:** 2 door convertible.
GEARBOX: 4 speed	**YEARS:** 1950–53
SUSPENSION: Ind Coil/wishbone – semi-elliptic	**PRODUCTION:** 4,011

Cost	£5,100
% swing	4
Spares	★★
V.F.M.	★★★
S.R.	★★★★

PEUGEOT 205 GTI

EUROPEAN STYLE AND CLASS

MANUFACTURER
PEUGEOT

Development of the M24 – as the car was initially known – took six years to the February 1983 European launch. Peugeot could hardly have dreamt of selling in excess of 4,000,000 205s over just the first decade; but in addition, their Gti model set a trend for the 1980s, transforming Peugeot's lack lustre image. Volkswagen had lain down the challenge with its 1975 Golf Gti and Peugeot replied by creating a slightly smaller and cheaper range which didn't roll, stuck to the road like paint and was equally at home dropping the kids off at school or roaring cross country like a semi-competition car. The 205 Gti was one of those moments in motoring history when everything fell together just right. Armies of 80s drivers didn't just want performance but real style and the car's major trump card was its pretty and dateless Italian body styling from Pininfarina.

The first Gti was the 1.6 launched in March 1984. This had a Citroën 1580cc unit offering 105bhp and subsequently a higher 115bhp version which combined with excellent steering and well balanced handling to make it a joy to drive. The 205 passed the one million mark in December 1985, won the World Rally championship the same month, an attractive Cabriolet version was launched and then in September of 1986 the rapid 1.9 litre Gti was unveiled. A month later two million had been sold and it went on to win the World Rally Championship again the following year, as well as the next two Paris–Dakars. The 1.9 Gti was fitted with stronger alloy wheels, rear disc brakes, low profile tyres and an awesome 130bhp under the bonnet – that's virtually twice that of a Mini Cooper S. The `Hot Hatchback' combination will certainly create a future classic and the 205's styling, as much as its performance, economy and accommodation, will see demand for the Peugeot outlast the more austere Golf shape.

RELATIONS

An original design for a range of 205s, including Cabriolets and a mid-engined competition machine – the four wheel drive Turbo 16. The Gti engine has similarities to the Citroën BX Gti engine.

BEST BUY

Loyalty is divided between the 1.6 and the 1.9 but both do a great job. Naturally brakes and suspension work hard, as do tyres but the weak point is the timing chain which needs replacing every 30-40,000 miles. Rust ought not to be a problem but check the tailgate and lower door edging and try to buy with a good service record. They all sound noisy idling. A brilliant present-day car with classic status assured.

Spares	★★★★
V.F.M.	★★★★★
S.R.	★★★★

SPECIFICATIONS

ENGINE: 1,580cc; 1,905cc	**BODIES:** 3 door Saloon
BHP: 105;115;135	**SUSPENSION:** Ind MacPherson
FUEL: 35mpg – 27mpg	strut/coil – Torsion/trailing
GEARBOX: 5 speed	arms
BRAKES: Disc	**YEARS:** 1983 – 1994
SPEED: 120mph –125mph	**PRODUCTION:** 300,000 (est)

MANUFACTURER
BMW

It was BMW's development of their 1960s coupés which formed the foundations of their 1980s status. Fine engineering and a huge investment in competition ought to have been their magnetism but in the 1980s 'me' decade the password was style. It was the functional elegance of BMW coupés which was to cast its glow across even the most uninspiring 1980s BMW saloons. The pedigree began with the 1966 2000CS Coupé styled within BMW by Wilheilm Hofmeister. The car was based upon the standard 2000 saloon but these Karmann-built coupés were actually heavier than the saloon with consequently rather more style than performance. However the next generation of saloons presented two brilliant new 2,494cc and 2,788cc engines; and in September 1968 the first six-cylinder coupé appeared. They selected the 2788cc engine and front suspension from the big saloon and utilized the basic 2000 Coupé body but with a more aggressive front end treatment. This was the 2800CS which unlike the 2000CS both looked great and touched nearly 130mph. The quality interior with its panoramic visibility and elegant pillarless side windows simply added to the allure of what was really only an interim model: in 1971, BMW announced the larger 3.0 Coupé. The concept of rapid, refined, transport was now synonymous with BMW and the new 3.0 Coupé was able to offer over 130mph top speed while returning an average consumption of around 20mpg. Not content, later that year they added fuel injection creating a 200bhp, 140mph Executive Express. A complex game of option shuffling provided extra costumer choice.

Pursuing further competition success they created a homologation model to qualify their race cars. These 1000 lightweights, (CSL) used perspex and aluminium along with highly tuned engines. The few that were imported to the UK were reportedly refitted with some luxuries making rapid and strange hybrids..

RELATIONS

The 2000CS was based on 1960s four-cylinder saloons while the coupés from the 280 onward used the later saloon mechanics and powerplants. The factory designed 2000CL body extended through whole range with frontal amendments.

BEST BUY

Despite all the build quality rhetoric these BMWs are prone to rust. Karmann failed to fully protect the body shells and concealed mud traps didn't help. Check sills carefully, the upper mountings of front suspension and test bulkhead through glove locker. 2.8 CS/3.0CS look alike, but old suspension inferior.

The 3.0CSL (for lightweight) was a particularly fine example of the breed, but will cost you considerably more than the CS.

SPECIFICATIONS

ENGINE: 2788cc – 2985cc – 3003cc – 3153cc
BHP: 170; 200; 206
FUEL: 16 – 20mpg
GEARBOX: 4; 3 speed auto
BRAKES: Disc/drum – All disc
SUSPENSION: Ind Macpherson strut/coil – semi trailing/coil
SPEED: 128mph – 139mph
BODIES: 2 door 4 seat coupé
YEARS: 1966 – 75
PRODUCTION: 39,427

Cost (3.0CS/CSi)	£7,400
% swing	0
Spares	★★★★
V.F.M.	★★★
S.R.	★★★★

UNIPOWER GT
TINY, PRETTY AND VERY FAST

MANUFACTURER
Universal Power Drives

The Unipower was designed by Ernest Unger and Val Dare-Bryan, both racing enthusiasts, both of the Ford Motor Co. The 1964 aluminium prototype was styled by another Ford employee. The last 15 cars were built by Piers Weld-Forrester, or PWF.

When you find the speedometer on the passenger side and a tiny gear lever set in the right door sill, you know it's a car that means business. So it was with the Unipower, the very best of the specials born of the sporting Mini. I was asked to try one for the opening feature of the very first British Leyland magazine *High Road*. It drew a crowd on the forecourt of what was the London BL service centre in Holland Park – it's now a Hilton! Just 40 inches high, deep door sills, a gearbox with every gear position upside down and a choke behind your left ear all conspired to prevent a convincingly nonchalant departure.

However, it took very little time to appreciate that you were sitting in a real driver's car. The useful dials were before you, the driving position was semi-reclining full arm, full leg style, the powerful engine amidships and the whole thing set upon full independent suspension. In effect, you were sitting in what was a sparsely covered Formula 3 car. This space frame and fibreglass GT was developed by Universal Power Drives in Perivale who specialised in forestry tractors. Two years after its 1966 Racing Car Show launch it was taken over by PWF who maintained production for a further 12 months. The GT was Unipower's one successful foray into car production, though they were persuaded to construct a few Quasar–Unipowers, the dream of fashion designer Quasar Klanh: sort of Mini-based mobile greenhouses.

The GT used either the 998cc Cooper or, as with my test car, the 1275 S unit and within such a low

and light machine it flew. Indeed, over 100mph the steering would go light and the front considered following suit. Cornering was heaven, firm reassuring suspension and an excellent forward, if not rear, view of everyone else's bumpers. For the original article an equally tiny actress – starring in a Ken Russell Debussy film, posed with the car – more crowds.

RELATIONS

An original body styling with either Mini Cooper or 1275 S equipment, though own suspension. Some items from elsewhere, eg the Triumph windscreen.

BEST BUY

Very rare: just 75 plus one aluminium prototype. Given the opportunity, it's an excellent investment. The transversely mounted engine behind the seating was echoed two years later in the Ferrari Dino, and in the '71 Maserati Bora. Good thinking, evidently.

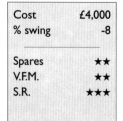

Cost	£4,000
% swing	-8
Spares	★★
V.F.M.	★★
S.R.	★★★

SPECIFICATIONS

ENGINE: 998cc, 1275cc	**SUSPENSION:** Double wishbone & coil
BHP: 55, 76	
FUEL: 32 – 40mpg	**BODIES:** 2 door coupé
GEARBOX: 4 speed	**YEARS:** 1967 – 70
BRAKES: Disc/drum	**PRODUCTION:** 75
SPEED: 103mph; 117mph	

MANUFACTURER
TVR CARS

One obstacle to classic TVR ownership is confusion among the multiplicity of models. Just one of the guide books shows 17 models and 11 engines – all looking familiar. Founded back in the 1950s by Trevor Wilkinson (TreVoR) they used a multi–tubular chassis onto which various engines, gearboxes and fibre glass bodies were bolted. By the end of the decade a more focused company were creating a kit car – the Grantura, using VW suspension, Healey brakes, Ford Consul windscreen and various engines. Supply and demand fluctuations caused problems (including company collapses) until in 1965 Arthur and Martin Lilley took over and the Grantura was re-developed with fashionable cut-off tail and renamed the Vixen. The Lilleys standardized on Ford and BMC Series B engines. Named after Martin, the M Series was to be their trading backbone for some years, sustaining them when the 1973 tax changes virtually destroyed the kit car sector of the market and through the aftermath of a huge factory fire in 1975 The new M Series 90-inch chassis was stronger and initially carried an American-emission compliant TR6 engine under a lengthened body. This 2500M was chiefly aimed at America while the UK were given two options using the Ford Cortina GT or the V6 Capri engines. These were the 1600M and the 3000M respectively and offered front disc braking, good rack and pinion, wide wheels and various ongoing improvements. Three years after the 3000M launch came a V6 Turbo – potent, thirsty and tricky to drive.

Then, just in Capri engine form, the rear of the 1976 3000M was reworked as a hatchback, the Taimar. 270 Convertibles were also produced, 13 Turbos.

RELATIONS

The M Series largely relied on Triumph TR6, Cortina and Capri components; earlier TVRs more mongrel. Body styling was their own, as was the chassis.

BEST BUY

A traditionally hard ride creates rear suspension troubles, so care is needed. Spares situation good, Ford parts readily available. The 3000M is really a rewarding lightweight version of a V6 Capri: limited DIY skills may be useful. Taimar has a 'proper' boot.

SPECIFICATIONS

ENGINE: 1599cc; 2498cc; 2994cc	**SUSPENSION:** Ind wishbone/ coil – all round
BHP: 86bhp – 265bhp	**BODIES:** 2 door coupé; convertible
FUEL: 18 – 29mpg	
GEARBOX: 4 speed	**YEARS:** 1967 – 79
BRAKES: Disc/drum	**PRODUCTION:** 2,465
SPEED: 105mph – 130mph	

Cost (Taimar)	£7,100
% swing	-3
Spares	★★★
V.F.M.	★★
S.R.	★★★

LANCIA FULVIA COUPÉ

DISCREET SPORTING PLEASURES

MANUFACTURER

LANCIA

Lancia entered the 1960s as one of the Italian aristocrats. Unlike most companies they designed their Flavia range in–house complete with authentic boxer engine – Italy's first front wheel drive production car. Their next target was a replacement for their ageing Aprilia to be based around a new V4 power unit. This was the Fulvia and would become the last real company triumph before it was sold to the giant Fiat. The FWD Fulvia family stemmed from the 1963 Berlina saloon with its 1097cc version of the V4 and rather square body styling. Six years later, the second series saloon enjoyed engine development and some refinements but the gem was the coupé derivative unveiled in 1965 and which would become Lancia's flagship competition car. The coupé was based on a shorter wheelbase than the saloon, used a great many of the new Flavia parts and, much to the enthusiast's delight, that brand new Lancia V4 engine. Alongside the standard 80bhp model there was a tuned 1.2HF (High Fidelity) version sporting a matt black bonnet and no bumpers. In 1966 a similar pairing had the 1.3S Coupé at 1298cc with 93bhp while the faster 1.3 HF Rallye version pushed both bhp and top speed over the 100 mark. Considered by many to be the most desirable was the bored out 1969 1.6HFS which in rare instances were sold with a 132bhp output. It was in this year that Fiat took over and a Series Two

was developed for 1971. Detail refinements included raised outer headlights and kinder suspension. A UK de luxe trimmed model known as the 1600HF Lusso. A 1300 shell with 1600cc engine – the Fulvia Sports, also appeared in 1971 and became the fastest non-competition version. A final 1974-76 Series 3 model offered only minor alterations. Free revving, agile with excellent gearbox and handling plus good accommodation – almost a Cooper S in Italian garb.

RELATIONS

Lancia's own body with transmission, steering, suspension and brakes from Flavia; V4 engine was brand new. The last true Lancia made. 2,600 special Zagato Sports version were also made between 1970–72.

BEST BUY

Beautifully engineered cars and so most have been loved. Buy through Owners Club sources, to avoid rust – particularly costly around subframes. Many examples will have lightweight body panels which are prone to denting. Hand brakes a traditional grief.

A very different front end treatment for the Zagato Sports special.

Cost (HF SII)	£9,000
% swing	10
Spares	★★
V.F.M.	★★★
S.R.	★★★★

SPECIFICATIONS

ENGINE: 1216cc; 1231cc; 1584cc; 1298cc	**SUSPENSION:** Wishbone/ transverse leaf spring & dead axle/half elliptic
BHP: 80p – 115	
FUEL: 34mpg – 22mpg	**BODIES:** 2 door, 4 seat coupé
GEARBOX: 4 & 5 speed	**YEARS:** 1965 – 76
BRAKES: Disc	**PRODUCTION:** 140,205
SPEED: 90 – 119mph	

MANUFACTURER
FORD

Promoted as 'The Three Graces', wisely, Ford's MkIIs were a direct development from the successful Mk I. The monocoque bodies were 3" wider, 6.5" longer, although the central passenger section remained identical to the Mk I. Exterior trim helped differentiation, from the humble Consul to gold-plated trim on the Zodiac. The traditional bench seating fore and aft permitted six occupants, there was a column gear change and the engines were enhanced. An optional overdrive was available and carefully selected higher final drives helped fuel economy – ultimate cruising status came with any one of the three convertibles. The luxury Zodiac version was released some months later than the Consul and Zephyr soft tops, offering a number of extra fittings and the prestige of a power-operated roof. Naturally, there were continual detail changes over the years including a 1957 de luxe Consul with duotone paintwork and many dashboard refinements.

One really conspicuous alteration was the 1959 change to the car's profile, reducing the slightly bulbous roof pressing by 1.5". A disc brake option had become so popular it became a standard fitting from May 1961. Somehow those bench seats and the column change *inter alia*, chimed with the huge transatlantic invasion of UK culture. During May 1961 the Consul became officially known as a Consul Classic 315 which was part of plans to use the name Consul as a prefix to Ford family cars – The Ford Consul Classic and Capri is as far as it went.

RELATIONS

Mk I! Improved engine, 'box, suspension, steering.

BEST BUY

All three were strong working cars and the less stressed 6-cylinder versions in particular are solid.

Rust inevitably is a problem, particularly around the floor, sills and front suspension mounts, and trim is becoming harder to replace.

SPECIFICATIONS

ENGINE: 1703cc; 2553cc	semi-elliptic
BHP: 59; 85	**SPEED:** 80mph; 90mph
FUEL: 25mpg; 22mpg	**BODIES:** 2 door, 4 door
GEARBOX: 3 & 4 speed	saloon, convertible, estate
BRAKES: Drum (front discs post 61)	**YEARS:** 1956–62
SUSPENSION: Ind	**PRODUCTION:** 682,400
Macpherson strut –	(1st figures – 4 cylinder Consul & 2nd – 6 cylinder Zephyr/Zodiac)

Cost (Consul MkII)	£7,200
% swing	6
Spares	★★★
V.F.M.	★★★
S.R.	★★★

MINI COOPER S

TURNS DRIVERS INTO ENTHUSIASTS

MANUFACTURER
BMC

From its spectacular entrance in 1959 the Mini's place in motoring history was secure, and subsequent major competition triumphs defined the mythology; but its obsessive hold over enthusiasts appears illogical, given that almost every modern hatchback can comfortably outperform the very best. Certainly, the Mini represented optimum fun for an entire generation's youth and nostalgia is the wild card with any classic. However, there were genuinely special qualities about the sporting Minis which stood them apart. Grand Prix's wizard John Cooper identified the potential when loaned a pre–production Mini to attend the Italian GP. Race driver Roy Salvadori in that early Mini beat team manager Reg Parnell in his Aston Martin DB4GT down to Italy: and even at the circuit, the former chief Ferrari engineer disappeared in it for a run. The result was the 1961 997cc Mini Cooper and its 1964–69 998cc replacement, utilizing the ex-Riley and Wolseley Mini unit.

The real power and glory was within the confusing world of the Mini Cooper S range. I've been lucky enough to own two glorious examples and drive almost all the possible variants – indeed at one time

had the Rauno Aaltonen/Henry Liddon Works car, my all black 60s show stopper, and a custom-built Wood & Pickett de luxe version. The major difference between the fun Coopers and the more serious Cooper S's was the engine. All John Cooper's success with both Grand Prix racing (double World Championships) and his inspired work on the same BMC A engine in Formula Junior meant that the Cooper S engine was specifically created to perform. Everything was stronger, disc brakes bigger, wheels wider on the differing S models. The initial 1963 1071cc S was deliberately aimed at motor sport and offered a 70bhp high revving engine with bags of torque in the upper ranges. Just 4,017 were produced in its 13 month production life. However, in 1964 two new S's were launched. The 970 S was a

The Cooper Car Company earned a small royalty on every car bearing their name; in 1971, when the original 'consultancy agreement' lapsed, about £2.

Cost (1275 S)	£6,300
% swing	-8
Spares	★★★★★
V.F.M.	★★
S.R.	★★★★★

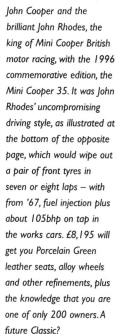

John Cooper and the brilliant John Rhodes, the king of Mini Cooper British motor racing, with the 1996 commemorative edition, the Mini Cooper 35. It was John Rhodes' uncompromising driving style, as illustrated at the bottom of the opposite page, which would wipe out a pair of front tyres in seven or eight laps – with from '67, fuel injection plus about 105bhp on tap in the works cars. £8,195 will get you Porcelain Green leather seats, alloy wheels and other refinements, plus the knowledge that you are one of only 200 owners. A future Classic?

The author taking delivery from rally ace and car dealer John Sprinzel of his new modified black 1275 S, complete with gold minilites. In the middle is Spencer Davis, pop star and Mini enthusiast.

RELATIONS

Mini 1959 onward
Mini Cooper 1961–64 : 997cc
Mini Cooper 1964–69 : 998cc
Mini Cooper S 1963–64 : 1071cc
Mini Cooper S 1964–65 : 970cc
Mini Cooper S 1964–71 : 1275cc

BEST BUY

It's a Mini so check rust in front and rear subframe mounting points, footwells, sills and around A posts. The enormous torque was always destroying the engine's top steady bar and thus damaging exhausts. Drive couplings too worked very hard: but the main issue is confirming exactly what you are buying: many Mini Coopers have been `upgraded' and there are few visual clues. The 1964 Hydrolastic suspension upset some of the older enthusiasts. The 1968 Mk II range brought the larger disc braking and a valuable all-syn-chromesh gearbox, which points to a post '68 1275cc S as the best option, but beware – if you buy an S, your driving outlook will never be the same again.

homologation exercise producing a mere 967 over just 10 months in order to claim a production class for 1 litre competition, with a screaming 6,500 rev range and an appetite for sprints and hill climbs. The other new S was the famed 1275cc version which remained in production until June 1971 – the last few were unbadged as British Leyland boss Donald Stokes thought that John Cooper's name was putting customers off! Very minor visual changes took place through the years other than the cosmetic 1967 Mini range upgrade to Mk II; but in late 1964, there was the controversial addition to all Minis of Hydrolastic suspension which altered ride characteristics.

Basic interiors, super discretion (virtually identical to the standard Mini) and sporting action within a runabout shell were the S characteristics but its divine status stemmed from the handling and through-the-gears performance. It was so responsive, so forgiving, it allowed us all to develop our own driving skills in a way no other affordable car could.

SPECIFICATIONS

ENGINE: 970cc; 1071cc; 1275cc
BHP: 65; 70; 76
FUEL: N/A; 27mpg; 30mpg
GEARBOX: 4 speed – all syncromesh post 1968
BRAKES: Disc – Drum
SPEED: 92mph; 95mph; 97mph

SUSPENSION: Ind cones/wishbone & Ind trailing arm/cone Hydrolastic inter-connection after 1964
BODIES: 2 door saloon
YEARS: 1963 – 71
PRODUCTION: 45,442

MANUFACTURER
GINETTA

The Ginetta is one of a small number of specialist cars which have earned a classic status through manufacturing in component form. Names such as Lotus, Marcos, and TVR all used the one-time kit car tax concessions to undercut rivals. Many kit manufacturers were extremely suspect but the passage of time has erased most of these from memory. Ginetta cars was the brainchild of the four Walklett brothers based in Essex. Following the initial G2 and G3's the Ford Anglia-engined G4 racing sports car established their credibility as a pure performance manufacturer. Derivatives followed, then a brief detour trying MGB and Ford V8 models to attract the Americans, before the beautiful little G15 was launched at Earls Court in 1967, their most successful model. Rootes knew that with the lightweight engined Imp Coupés there was potential, but Ginetta with their race car experience knew exactly how to take full advantage of that brilliant engine – itself born of a competitive past. The G15 mounted the aluminium 51bhp 875cc engine ahead of the back axle – unlike the Imp – and married it to the excellent Imp gearbox. It used Triumph Spitfire front suspension, steering and disc brakes while the independent rear suspension was again the Imp's. It all sits in a lightweight tubular chassis onto which the pretty fibreglass two-door, two-seater body is bolted. Gradually over its six years in production, small refinements were offered with items such as a sun roof and even a heater. This tiny 11cwt package could provide 100mph while returning around 40mpg. A few G15S cars were also made offering a breathless 115mph from the increased

998cc engine. G15s have beautifully proportioned lightweight bodies and rapid yet economic engines – they are not however trimmed and sold as plush touring machines. The Walketts sold out in 1989 and there have been attempts to re–establish the marque.

RELATIONS

Body style evolved from Ginetta's previous models. The majority of the components including engine and gearboxs were Hillman Imp with front suspension, disc brakes and steering from the Triumph Spitfire.

BEST BUY

The car was launched for £799 in component form: good ones now sell for nearly 10 times that... Prospective buyers will either fancy modest competition use or be quite accomplished drivers – recognising the body/ mechanical assets rather than the missing creature comforts. Check doors hang well and that the fibreglass has not been patched or is defective. Initial cars used an unsuccessful rear radiator.

Cost (G15)	£6,600
% swing	52
Spares	★★★
V.F.M.	★★★★★
S.R.	★★

SPECIFICATIONS

ENGINE: 875cc	**SUSPENSION:** Ind coil/wishbone – Ind semi trailing
BHP: 51	
FUEL: 42mpg	**BODIES:** 2 seater coupé
GEARBOX: 4 speed	**YEARS:** 1968–74
BRAKES: Disc – Drum	**PRODUCTION:** 796
SPEED: 94 mph	

MANUFACTURER

LANCIA

As a Classic this ought to be a disaster. It's just a Lancia Beta saloon with an iron Fiat engine, legendary rust problems, braking so tricky they interrupted production and many have hit things. Not reassuring: yet there are qualities about this car that demand affection. I suspect it falls into the same category as anti-heros or troubled pop idols. The Monte Carlo had a difficult life but actually presents a most appealing classic – providing you find a good one or have the time and patience for a restoration project.

Owners Fiat wanted to capitalize on the Fulvia and Stratos competition success and christened the Monte Carlo because of the marque's successes in that rally. In 1972 Lancia launched the Beta range which included a saloon, coupé, spider and the Beta HPE. It was inevitable they would join the 1970s mid-engined fashion race and began assembling ideas around the strong platform of the Beta and the 2000 Coupé engine. Many parts bins were raided to build this 2-litre, twin cam machine but the whole package rested beneath a pretty, understated Italian coupé body from Pininfarina. The 120bhp engine provided crisp not startling performance, although the emission controlled US version, the Scorpion, was embarrassingly slow. The car's weight distribution combined with over zealous servo-operated front disc brakes resulting in lock up and numerous accidents. After 1978 the model was tactfully withdrawn and reappeared as an improved Mk II in 1980. This boasted a new front end treatment, glass-filled rear quarters, a freshened interior while the handling benefitted from removal of both the rear anti-roll bar and ill-mannered brake servo and the addition of larger discs and road wheels. The corrected model couldn't overcome its former reputation and it faded away. In fact its small and powerful-looking bodywork is probably the least dated of any of the 1970s mid-engined sports cars, visibility is good, the performance fun rather than frantic – in fact a clean example gives highly individual classic motoring for very little outlay.

RELATIONS

Original Pininfarina styling with five bearing Fiat engine and rolling chassis from Lancia Beta range. Initially conceived as a big brother for the X 1/9.

BEST BUY

This period of Italian production marred by rampant rust, so inspect very carefully. Check for any front end impacts. Mark II clearly the model to select though some of the Mk Is have enjoyed braking conversions. Mechanically basically sound but unloved, ergo not maintained, but not expensive = bargains!

SPECIFICATIONS

ENGINE: 1995cc
BHP: 120
FUEL: 23 – 30mpg
GEARBOX: 5 speed
BRAKES: Disc/disc
SPEED: 118mph

SUSPENSION: Ind wishbone/ coil all round
BODIES: 2 door Coupé; Targa
YEARS: 1975 – 78: 1980 – 84
PRODUCTION: 7,595

Cost	£6,600
% swing	23
Spares	★★
V.F.M.	★★★
S.R.	★★

HONDA CRX SERIES II

SLEEK, 130MPH GO KART

MANUFACTURER
HONDA

The Japanese gift for analysing western consumer products and then producing quality versions is part of commercial history. German cameras, American electronics and European cars have all succumbed. Yet this analytical approach often excludes individuality – so frequently a cornerstone of public affection. A Frogeye Sprite, a Ford 105E, Anglia would never have been thought logically desirable. It's cold standardization which debars many Japanese cars from classic status. However this little Honda qualifies. To begin with it's virtually unique – tiny, low, fast, neither a hot hatchback nor a Spartan sports car. Then it's rare because of import restrictions, so few were sold into the UK. Further credibilty for the Series II came from the subsequent CRX (1992) which destroyed the charismatic body styling. However, all this is secondary to sitting behind the wheel and enjoying what's on offer. Having lived with one, I know its performance and reliability were exceptional.

The Series II car is both wider and lower than its predecessor, the old suspension was replaced resulting in a lower bonnet profile. Though the same overall length as the initial CRX, the Series II wheelbase is four inches longer which offers improved interior space and true `wheel at each corner' handling. The 130 bhp, 1.6 twin cam injection engine is basically the same but developed to offer an even wider rev range. You just flick the sweet gearbox and smooth, endless power takes the revs towards 8,000 before another flick and more of the same. The well-built and extremely pretty coupé body is desirable but it is this drive train that is the car's magic. Creature comforts

are good, fold-down occasional seating and the hatch are useful. However hard you drive it (and you will) the fuel consumption remains pleasing. Such blistering performance through the gears and its mere 12ft length demands a lot of the handling. Considering speeds taken through corners the roll is well contained. The V-TEC version was identical except in offering a variable value timing as used in the NS-X, increasing the bhp, revs and top speed.

RELATIONS

Sits between initial less attractive Mk I and the rather aimless Targa-based Mk III. All were derived from the hugely successful Civic range.

BEST BUY

Still youthful, so should still be in reasonable order. Honda owners look after cars and re-buy so best CRXs through Honda dealerships. All will have been driven quite hard so keep an eye on brakes and shocks. Honda parts dear, but rarely needed.

Spares	★★
V.F.M.	★★★★
S.R.	★★★★

SPECIFICATIONS

ENGINE: 1590cc	**SUSPENSION:** Ind coil/wishbone all round
BHP: 125 – 150	
FUEL: 32mpg	**BODIES:** 3 door coupé
GEARBOX: 5 speed	**YEARS:** 1986 – 1991
BRAKES: Disc	**PRODUCTION:** Unknown
SPEED: 125 – 130mph	

MANUFACTURER

JAGUAR

One Christmas day during this car's production life it snowed and I had to make an early morning drive to family in Oxford. Snowy landscapes, empty roads and the factory test Daimler V8 made that journey one of the more memorable ones in my life. Naturally it wasn't a classic then – just the first Daimler following Jaguar's takeover. Traditionalists discarded it as being just a Jaguar-bodied Daimler, oblivious of the fact that prior to the takeover a struggling Daimler had been seriously experimenting with this engine in a Vauxhall Cresta PA – now that really might have upset them. The Edward Turner-designed V8 was the key to everything. It had attracted fans in the flamboyant SP250 sports car, but both Daimler and Jaguar knew its value, and once the takeover was complete its installation in the current Jaguar sporting saloon was an obvious move. Fortuitously, this marriage created one of the most perfectly balanced cars, uniting glorious V8 power, a good Borg-Warner automatic gearbox, the classic Jaguar Mk II body and excellent levels of interior luxury.

Although outwardly only the traditional fluted grille distinguished the two models, the V8 provided an entirely different feel to the car. Everything from the racing Mk II Jaguars to Inspector Morse have conspired to keep this excellent Daimler something of a secret in the shadows of the Mk II – thus making good ones really excellent value.

There were changes to the automatic gearbox and axle ratios in the spring of 1964, and three years later the Jaguar manual box and overdrive became options. The only visible changes came in 1967 when it was re-named the V8–250, bumpers were slimmed down and interior trim slightly altered. By this point Jaguar had become part of British Motor Holdings and in July 1969, production ceased.

RELATIONS

Glorious engine from the 1959 Daimler SP250 sports car, everything else from the famed Jaguar Mk II except the Daimler grille and badge work.

BEST BUY

Buy a good one and you'll never want to sell it again, but take care in choosing – a mistake could make for costly restoration. The engine and gearbox are traditionally pretty trouble-free although corroded heads can give grief. The body naturally suffers from all the rust areas customary on the Jaguar cars. Check wings, sills, boot lid, the floor and the bottom of doors where drain holes can become blocked. The automatic suits the car and the post-1964 box had the extra D2 option, restricting it to 2nd and 3rd.

SPECIFICATIONS	
ENGINE: 2548cc	**SUSPENSION:** Ind Coil/wishbone – semi-elliptic
BHP: 140	
FUEL: 20mpg	**SPEED:** 110mph
GEARBOX: 3 speed automatic; rare 4 speed manuals	**BODIES:** 4 door saloon
	YEARS: 1963–69
BRAKES: Disc	**PRODUCTION:** 17,620

Cost (V8-250)	£7,500
% swing	14
Spares	★★★
V.F.M.	★★★
S.R.	★★★

SUNBEAM ALPINE
'OH LORD CHRYSLER PRAY FOR ME ...'

MANUFACTURER
ROOTES

Car enthusiasts aren't stupid. Corporations spend millions of pounds reassuring us that we'd get their car if our relationship busts up, or that we'd hear chart-topping music if we drive through fields of fire. As far back as the 1950s Hillman promised 'Every day in every way you'll be happier in a Minx', while a thrusting, high heeled, sweater girl — complete with chained peacock - leant against a partially seen Healey above the caption 'Beautiful fast'. Imagery is certainly part of the motoring dream, but the central contract which binds enthusiasts and corporation is loyalty. The likes of Mercedes or Volvo enjoy repeat custom because their products hold to a vision, a style, a standard. The public stick rigidly to these unspoken rules, so if Jaguar announced a 2 + 2 E-Type, or Ferrari install an automatic box, they challenge the public's trust. Even British Leyland taking John Cooper's name off the fast Mini, as it 'wasn't needed and affecting insurance rates' (not true), was seriously misreading us. In the end poor sales make the point, but by then the damage is done.

There is no doubt Rootes suffered bad luck devolving the Hillman Imp. Misplaced government encouragement led them to use distant, untrained labour, resulting in strikes and huge debts. Added to poor management decisions, it all conspired in the 1960s to place Rootes in bad shape. This was the backdrop to a final recovery effort. Unfortunately the crisis-stricken company failed to remember critical public loyalty, while the American Chrysler Corporation was simply concentrating on gaining control. Many years of Hillman Minx, Sunbeam

Rapier and Alpine sport cars provided the essential lifeline of trust, and the initial plan was for the Arrow range to take over from these famous names while a second scheme, the B Car, would be the Avenger range. A third project, the C car, was a tie–in with Simca, replacing the ageing Humbers, and it was that which foreshadowed Sunbeam's demise under Chrysler. An anonymous worker's poem ended prophetically 'Lord God Chrysler pray for me, and those in peril on the "C"...' The Arrow project created a successful Hunter, but destroyed the sporting Sunbeam Alpine allegiance by taking the basic car and sticking a vast, ugly, four seater fastback body over it. Nothing could have been further from that sporting tradition, with its Plymouth Barracuda styling crushing the tiny Hunter saloon road wheels. A Rapier version added insult to injury. They duplicated the classic pillarless side windows, but no one was convinced. A desperate image repair job saw a Holbay racing engine and Rostyle wheel trims added to produce the Rapier H120, but the damage was done. Companies ignore public perceptions of marques at their peril.

SPECIFICATIONS

ENGINE: 1725cc	live axle
BHP: 74	**BRAKES:** Disc/drum
FUEL: 28mpg	**SPEED:** 91mph
GEARBOX: 4 speed	**BODIES:** 2 door, 4 seater fast-back
SUSPENSION: Ind	
Macpherson strut/coil –	**YEARS:** 1967 – 75
half elliptic/	**PRODUCTION:** 46,204 (A+R)

MANUFACTURER
PORSCHE

PORSCHE 944
WORLD CLASS PERFORMER FOR THE PRICE OF A BASIC FIESTA

Porsche designers have shown little original thinking for many years, but marketing men, seeking to fill a gap between their modest VW-commissioned 924 and its Turbo version, stumbled into creating probably the best all-round sports car of the 1980s. Becoming a classic requires a mix of excitement, trustworthiness and affection. Convincing evidence of its status comes from past and present owners, even motoring writers, singing the car's praises.

Using the basic 924 bodyshell with wheel arches sculpted to accommodate the wide wheels, various engine options were considered. After the cool reception for the 924's Audi powerplant, it was felt important to use a Porsche design. A V6 was considered, but eventually half the powerful V8 928 engine block was transformed into a superb four cylinder alloy unit using twin balanced shafts rotating at twice the engine speed to iron out vibrations. The 1981 launch model used a 163bhp 2479cc unit married to a five speed rear mounted gearbox creating 50 – 50 weight distribution and near perfect handling characteristics. In 1985 they released the long-expected 220bhp turbo version with generally improved mechanical detail to handle the 150+ mph performance. As if to further ridicule Porsche's notion that the 944 was just a 924 range filler, an even hotter Limited Edition Silver Turbo SE (Sports Equipment) appeared in 1988. This offered 0–60 in nine seconds and a top speed of 161mph combined with awesome handling to shame many Supercars, particularly its sacred 911. Meanwhile, from 1986 there was a 16-valve 944S with higher rev range, 190bhp, sports suspension and

140mph top speed. This became a 2990cc S2 in 1989, adding yet another 10mph, while a Cabriolet version rounded off overall production. Build qualities, discreet good looks, wonderful handling and Supercar performance figures all suggest that these cars will become highly collectable.

RELATIONS

Porsche design work with basic bodywork, some equipment and the interior from the 924 cars, while the engine was engineered from half a 928 block.

BEST BUY

As 944s are not yet eligible classics, and newer modern cars exists, prices are excellent. Despite the performance, beware of Turbo purchases without getting a second opinion. The later 16-valve is an excellent choice. Camshaft belts need replacing every 48,000 miles and inspect the suspension set-up. Good galvanising means few rust problems.

SPECIFICATIONS

Engine: 2479cc; 2681cc; 2,990cc
BHP: 163 – 250
Fuel: 22 – 32mpg
Gearbox: 5 speed; 3 speed automatic
Brakes: Disc – Disc
Suspension: Ind wishbone & Ind torsionl
Speed: 137 – 161mph
Bodies: 3 door 2 + 2 Coupé
Years: 1981 – 1991
Production: 100,000

Spares	★★★★
V.F.M.	★
S.R.	★★★

CITROEN DS
GAMBLING ON HIGH STYLE

MANUFACTURER
CITROEN

This car has glamour and danger in equal measures. A jet black fully restored DS23 Pallas Décapotable (Drophead) is probably the most chic eligible classic car in the world – a triumph aesthetically and technically. Unfortunately, major repairs or restoration could cost you the price of another classic car. Inevitably, rusting combined with awesome levels of technical innovation, mean you need to buy with great care and guidance in order to enjoy the civilised pleasures of DS ownership. I've run three including a DS23 Pallas and the car's ride and comfort surpassed even that of the modern Bentley. However

unconventional, Citroëns – like equivalent humans – require an open mind and drivers quickly become enthusiastic or completely disenchanted.

The origins of this advanced car go back to André Citroën himself who lost money – and control of his beloved company – in the 1930s while struggling to develop and launch the Traction Avant with its revolutionary front wheel drive. After decades of the TA, the Bertone-designed D was presented to a stunned world at the 1955 Paris Motor Show. It was aerodynamically inspired, had an unstressed body of steel, fibreglass and aluminium, with disc braking and

The top-of-the-range DS19 Pallas arrived in 1964, four years after the first production convertible. The subsequent DS23 Pallas was even more luxurious.

Cost	£7,300
(20/21/23 Pallas)	
% swing	12
Spares	★★
V.F.M.	★★★
S.R.	★★★★★

Autosport's review of the 1955 Paris Salon provides some indication of the impact Flaminio Bertoni's and André Lefebvre's design made, together with the technical brilliance the car evinced. 'The Paris Salon is the most important motor show in the world … Even more brilliant than usual, the tone of this year's show is set by the incredible new Citroën DS19. Futuristic but entirely functional, this startling machine at once renders half the cars of the world out of date.'

an engine evolved from the TA. A one-spoke steering column, eye-level rear indicators, safety placement of the petrol tank and a super sensitive valve-controlled break button instead of a pedal, all contributed to its technical edge. Its famous hydropneumatic suspension ironed out every bump by combining pressurized gas and liquid while, as a by–product, creating variable ride height. The DS19 was joined by a basic ID19 in 1957 and then ID/DS minor developments took place until finally reaching the DS-only 23 model with 2347cc fuel injection. As you would expect from a French de luxe version, the Pallas offered great comfort, with limousine derivatives transporting successive French presidents during the 1960s.

RELATIONS

Italian body design with Traction Avant-inspired engine and hydropneumatic suspension principles. Many D ideas appeared within subsequent Citroën based models such as the Citroën/Maserati SM, the Citroën CX and the GS.

BEST BUY

Despite alloy, fibreglass and bolt–on body panels, rust is still an enemy, with the platform chassis particularly vulnerable at the rear and around sills. Engines last a long time and the suspension system is either fine or dreadful. The modest IDs are basic, but have less to go wrong. The self-levelling suspension is useful on the rare Safari estate car, while the dropheads are gold dust. Many good Ds were made at Citroën's Slough factory. The main body change was encasing the headlights from 1967 and incorporating swivel spotlights linked to the steering.

SPECIFICATIONS

Engine: 1911cc; 1985cc; 2175cc; 2.347cc
BHP: 75 – 141
Fuel: 34 –18mpg
Gearbox: 4 & 5 speed; semi automatic
Brakes: Disc/drum

Suspension: All ind Hydropneumatic springs
Speed: 92mph – 120mph
Bodies: 4 door saloon; 2 door Cabriolet; 8 seater estate
Years: 1956 – 75
Production: 1,456,115 (disp)

A CHRONOLOGY

1955 The Goddess is born: replete with constant height hydropneumatic independent suspension, variable ground clearance and removable panels on integrated bodywork. Length 4.81m. Weight 1215kg.

1956 Paris Motor Show. ID19 on sale from May 1957.

1958 DS Prestige and ID19 Estate.

1959 Monte Carlo Rally. Victory for Coltelloni-Alexandre-Desrosiers team. New front wing ventilation grilles.

1960 DS convertible.

1961 83bhp SAE engine.

1964 DS19 Pallas.

1965 SD19A and DS21. New radiator.

1966 Pauli Toivonen victory at Monte Carlo.

1968 DS20, ID20.

1969 Fuel injection for DS21, D Super and D Special. Robert Neyret victory in Morocco Rally.

1970 5 speeds for DS21. Citroën-Maserati SM 2 + 2 sports saloon launched at Geneva, using Deesse technology and experience.

1975 The last DS in the spring, the Maserati link broken in the autumn, and the SM abandoned as well.

BMW 6 SERIES

FAST, SLEEK AND COMING OF AGE

MANUFACTURER

BMW

Still prestige cars today, it seems incredible that the range is now twenty years old and formally eligible to be deemed classic. This is an intriguing period for prices of these fine machines. Just beginning to date now as a 'modern' car, and yet barely installed as a formal 'classic', the BMW 600 series presents an incredible bargain for enthusiasts.

Announced in 1976 to replace the equally classic 3.0 coupé, the car was an amalgam of the old 5 Series floor pan, with much engineering work in common with the then still secret 7 Series and an engine stemming from the outgoing 3.0 Coupé. All this was wrapped up in a sleek and purposeful Karmann body, resulting in an exciting new Coupé with proven components underlining BMW reliability. Initially a 633csi, then a 3.5 litre 635csi, it became a 2.8 litre 628csi in September 1980. Detailing came and went until in June 1982, improved suspension, ABS and a 3430cc graced the 635; the 628 collected ABS and improved seating in October 1984. By then the German market was already enjoying the awesome power of the M635CSi which was finally imported into the UK in January 1985. Although the 1986 Germany-only turbo powered Alpina B7 generated a staggering 330 bhp, it was the M635 which really presented the definitive BMW sporting coupé. At the heart of this discreet racer was a 24 valve twin cam engine derived from the M1 Supercar and, combined with a fine close ratio gearbox, it created a car of real urgency with silky smooth streams of power. I ran a 635csi in California and loved it, but nothing prepared me for the outright excitement of the M6.

RELATIONS

Karmann body styling with construction elements from the Series 5, power units derived from the outgoing 3.0 coupé and the M1 Supercar while aspects of the 6 would be revealed in the subsequent 7 series.

BEST BUY

Early cars were Karmann-built, slightly more prone to rust and occasionally cracked cylinder heads. Watch for rust around wheel arches, footwells, sills and damaged rear subframe mountings.. Buying the smaller 328 represents no real economy while between the 633 and 635 just choose the best example. Three-quarters of the cars were fitted with an excellent automatic box while the others were divided between a four speed with overdrive and a close ratio five speed. Spares are moderately priced, but buy the best you can afford. The M6 is the Boss but almost any of them will mature into a classic while still providing you with modern prestige transport.

Cost (635CSi)	£6,300
% swing	9
Spares	★★★★
V.F.M.	★★★
S.R.	★★★★

SPECIFICATIONS

ENGINE: 2788cc, 3210cc, 3453cc, 3430cc, 3453cc
BHP: 184 – 286 (330)
FUEL: 25 – 17mpg
GEARBOX: 4 speed, 5 speed close ratio, automatic
BRAKES: Disc

SUSPENSION: Ind coil/MacPherson Strut – Coil & trailing arm
SPEED: 122mph – 158 mph
BODIES: 2 door 4 seat coupé
YEARS: 1976 – 90
PRODUCTION: 86,216

MANUFACTURER
FORD

Just as the Mini represented the youth culture in Britain's 'swinging sixties', so their contemporaries in the US had settled their own, very different allegiances. Chevrolet had the Corvette, but Ford had nothing but an ageing Thunderbird on offer. This prompted Ford's young vice president Lee Iacocca to take the initiative, and the result was the birth in 1964 of the famed Mustang. It was actually nothing particularly special mechanically, using the engine, drive train and suspension from their basic Falcon and Fairlane ranges. However, what Ford did offer to the post-war baby boomers were great lines and freedom of choice. It was launched at the New York World Fair and offered open or closed versions as well as a Fastback, thus capturing young families as well as the lonesome cowboy. They presented a truly massive list of options so that each car felt special; somewhere within the list was always an affordable car for customers. In an inspired moment the company bought prime time on NBC, ABC and CBS to unveil the Mustang to an estimated 30 million viewers. Within 24 hours every Ford dealer across the US had sold all their stocks. It was possibly the most brilliant piece of automotive marketing ever, for all sales records were broken. The plan had been 100,000 sales for the year – it took 4 months. 680,992 sold in just over the year, a million within just two years.

It was not just the marketing genius, but the fact that a major manufacturer was allowing individuals to order the exact car they wanted, whether a humble 6 cylinder 90mph 3277cc basic, or one of four other engines up to 4.7 V8s. Then there was the separate semi-competition Shelby Mustang on offer. Shelby described the car as "chum," bait to get people into the showrooms to buy the standard options.

RELATIONS

A Ford body styling with the essential engine, gearbox and running gear drawn from existing factory models such as the Falcon and the Fairlane: 30 years of cars using the Mustang name – if not its sporting precepts – have followed.

BEST BUY

Apart from the Shelby, the original 1964-66 car is much the most desirable Mustang. A wide choice of body styles and equipment exist, and Ford still carries a great many spare parts. An automatic will mean a less stressed engine/gearbox. Remember, it's not a European sports car but a standard American motorcar with style. that will transport you to the Big Country.

An early publicity shot at Dearborn, one of the Wild Ones posing in 1964. The publicity got a lot better, a lot quicker. According to the editor, this car is 'a paradigm of the greatness of the United States: democratic individualism, all for one, a special one for all.' Then again, he was always obsessed with Uncle Sam … He is also mortified by the Stanley rating below!

SPECIFICATIONS

ENGINE: 2.8 & 3.3 in line 6 – 4.3 & 4.7 V8s
BHP: 101– 271
FUEL: 14mpg – 18mpg
GEARBOX: 3 & 4 manual; 3 speed automatic
BRAKES: Drum; Disc optional from 1965

SUSPENSION: Ind coil/wishbone & live axle/semi elleptic
SPEED: 90mph –120mph
BODIES: 2 door sports hardtop; convertible & fastback
YEARS: 1964 – 66
PRODUCTION: 1,288,557

Cost (289)	£7,500
% swing	14.5
Spares	★★★★
V.F.M.	★★★
S.R.	★★

VW BEETLE
THE STREET CHAMPION

MANUFACTURER
VW

This, the world's bestselling car, emerged out of two still-born projects from Ferdinand Porsche's design company. These ideas eventually found an outlet within pre-war Germany for a state-funded 'People's Car'. After hostilities ended in 1945, the factory – within British-occupied territory – was encouraged back into production, and the first export model appeared in 1949 complete with 25bhp 1131cc air- cooled flat four engines. Mounted in the tail along with the gearbox, it used swing axles and torsion bar suspension all round. The original intentions were for the car to transport two adults and three children at up to 100kph (62mph) consuming not more than 33 mpg and priced at no more than RM 1000 (around £90). During the decades of production the car's appearance has changed very little, but around 78,000 individual changes have actually been made. Some, such as the larger rear window in 1957, were obvious, while four years later (less visibly) the engine was improved to 34bhp, lifting the top speed to around 70mph. In 1965 the De Luxe 1300 appeared with 1285cc, moving the bhp up to 40bhp; steering joints were also improved. By 1966 it had a 1493cc engine, taking the car to 80mph+ with improved suspension, disc brakes and a wider track; a year later a new 1200cc Basic was created without all the trimmings, but with improved suspension. The early 1970s witnessed a flood of changes with the arrival of the 1600cc 1302s and 1303s with disc brakes, and a move to Macpherson strut suspension. on the S. Although German production ceased in 1978 , it continued in Mexico, reopened in Brazil and in America a lookalike is rumoured for 1998 production. It's an extraordinary story of a car full of idiosyncrasies and flaws, yet essentially providing reliable transport – a true classic.

RELATIONS

The Beetle is one of a kind, owing little if anything to anyone outside the Porsche studio's initial inspirations, although you can see a hint of the Beetle in the curvy silhouette of VW's later Karmann Ghia Ironically, those first still-born concepts involved motor cycle companies searching for new markets in the pre-war depression – hence the air-cooled engines.

It is interesting to note that the cabriolet 1300s have actually fallen in value (below). The less fashionable older 1100s, in contrast, have shot up by more than 30% over the same three-year period.

Cost	£8,800
(Cabrio 1301/2 L/S)	
% swing	-20

Spares	★★★★★
V.F.M.	★
S.R.	★★★★★

You can still buy a new Cabriolet today – the Bieber Cabriolet – providing an open four seater at a far lower price than, say, the Golf convertible, with a whole lot more character and none of the drawbacks of classic car ownership.

Why the less than professional snap shot below? Unashamed editorial corruption. This 1972 Beetle belonged to the editor's brother, and its imminent starring role here maybe helped the sale! More relevantly, one option for UK buyers is to import rust-free Beetles from California like this one. £4,000 to the door, a pricey respray, five year's trouble-free motoring, a tearful farewell for £3,800, private sale.

BEST BUY

The Beetle has a sub-culture all of its own. Overall, the mechanics are generally safe, though check the crank case pulley to judge engine wear. Rust gets into the floor areas, sills and wings particularly on the desirable Cabriolets. Buying a Beetle is a great adventure, but first try one as the driving position is an acquired taste and performance limited.

SPECIFICATIONS

ENGINE: 1131/1192/1285/ 1493/1584cc	(post 1970 Macpherson strut/semi trailing)
BHP: 36 – 50	**BODIES:** 2 door, 4 door saloon
FUEL: 25mpg; 22mpg	**YEARS:** 1949–78 (1st export model to end of German prod line)
GEARBOX: 4 speed	
BRAKES: Drum (front discs Post '70)	**PRODUCTION:** 21,000,000+
SPEED: 65 – 80mph	
SUSPENSION: All Ind torsion	

ALFA DUETTO SPIDER

BEWARE OF LOVE AT FIRST SIGHT

MANUFACTURER

ALFA ROMEO

The unofficial name of the Duetto was 'Osso di Seppia' – cuttlefish bone – a nickname that stuck, at least in those lucky countries where a cuttlefish bone, and its shape, meant something.

Cost	£9,600
(1750 Spider Veloce)	
% swing	21.5
Spares	★★★★
V.F.M.	★★★
S.R.	★★★★★

This is an extraordinary car. Like the Mini and Beetle its long production run (27 years), has automatically earned it a powerful classic status. It was never the fastest car around and many critics were unkind about even its appearance and yet it captures the hearts of enthusiasts and romantics in equal parts.

Based upon the Giulia Sprint GT platform, this Italian two seater was launched at the 1966 Geneva Motor Show under the name Duetto – the result of a 140,501-entry competition to name the new Alfa. The body styling was the last complete design project undertaken by Battista Pininfarina and had roots in both the early fifties sports racing Alfa, the 6C 3000M, and the 1962 Giulette-based Super Flow 1 concept car. The heart of the Duetto was Alfa's all alloy 1570cc twin cam engine offering 109bhp and a memorable exhaust note. This, coupled with all round disc brakes and a beautiful five speed gearbox, made it an advanced model. While the Healey 3000 was revelling in its reputation as a wild sports car, the Duetto was creating a new sophistication with light gear change and steering, a relatively comfortable ride and a particularly successful folding soft top. In 1968 the Duetto name was dropped, and the engine slightly bored out to create the 1750 Spider – actually enlarged to 1779cc and adding another 9bhp. A number of additional changes were made to the suspension, electrics and braking, but nothing conspicuous occurred to the Pininfarina bodywork until the radical face lift in 1970 when the charismatic long tail was simply chopped off and replaced by an abrupt vertical rear reducing the boot by a full six inches.

The interior too was updated and the general tone of the car was more luxurious. The same year saw the launch of a 1300cc Spider Junior, with a more economical version of the same body, though only a few came to Britain. A year later the 2000 Spider was launched, taking the trusted engine to 1962cc. General refinements continued until it finally ceased production in 1993.

RELATIONS

An original Pininfarina body style. The mechanics belong to the Giulia family of Alfas – the engine taken from the Sprint GT model.

BEST BUY

The drive train is excellent, but rust eats into the complex body structure making it a dangerous car to buy in a hurry. The 1600s are the hard-core fan's choice, late models give more comforts. The initial 1750 Spider combined the most responsive engine with the last of those long boat–tails.

SPECIFICATIONS

ENGINE: 1290cc, 1570cc 1779cc 1962cc	**SUSPENSION:** Ind coil/wishbone & coil live axle
BHP: 89 – 132	**SPEED:** 106mph –118mph
FUEL: 24mpg	**BODIES:** 2 door sports
GEARBOX: 5 speed	**YEARS:** 1966 – 93
BRAKES: Disc	**PRODUCTION:** 82,500

MANUFACTURER
STANDARD

Standard-Triumph attempted to buy the Morgan Car Company in the early 1950s and having failed, rushed to assemble a competitive model. A pre-war Flying Nine chassis, Triumph Mayflower suspension, axle and steering, together with the Standard Vanguard 2 litre engine and gearbox, were all modified and squeezed into a new body for the 1952 Motor Show. The same show premiered the new Healey 100; a redesigned TR2 was finally unveiled at the 1953 Geneva Show. Reactions were good but work continued. The 1955 launch of the TR3 was really the model's coming of age. It gained a wider egg box styled grille, sliding side screens, a useful triple overdrive option and token extra interior space along with larger carburation and a step up in bhp. Within months there was also improvement to the back axle and front disc brakes added. Critical exports built up and the TR3 achieved virtually twice the TR2 sales in roughly the same life span. In 1958 further changes

unofficially created a TR3A – though it was not the factory term. These included a full width grille integrating the side lights, recessed headlights, lockable door handles and new seating. They also began to offer the enlarged 2138cc engine used in the successful works competition cars. In 1959 they re–tooled but waning US interest was pushing the company towards certain disaster – until Leyland bought in 1961. A brief US- only TR3B was released.

RELATIONS

A cocktail of Flying Nine, Mayflower and Vanguard models and initial TRI prototype and TR2. Body style ends with TR3A but mechanics extend to TR4.

BEST BUY

Pre 1956 Mayflower back axles can be troublesome as can the early front drum brakes and many will have been changed to match Triumph's upgrades. Best choice would be a 1958–61 TR3A enjoying 100bhp, disc brakes and those low cut door panels.

During the industry rush to create affordable sports cars in the early 1950s, TR3 built much of its solid reputation through competition success. A staggering 90% of sales were exports. The engine and particularly the gearbox of most examples should be bomb proof, but beware poorly serviced front suspension.

SPECIFICATIONS

ENGINE: 1991cc
BHP: 95, 100
FUEL: 30mpg
GEARBOX: 4 speed
BRAKES: Drum; Disc/drum (after 1956)

SUSPENSION: Ind wishbone/ coil & live axle semi-elliptic
SPEED: 103mph
BODIES: 2 door sports
YEARS: 1955 – 61
PRODUCTION: 71,613

Cost	£11,100
% swing	-7.5
Spares	★★★★
V.F.M.	★★
S.R.	★★★

TRIUMPH TR5 PI
IMPERFECT STAR

MANUFACTURER

BRITISH LEYLAND

The methodical improvement of the TR range proved commercially rewarding, despite more exotic competition from cars such as the Austin-Healey 100. The simple, solid engineering of the early TRs, and the reliability of such well tested parts generated many fans, but by the 1960s the body styling was losing appeal. September 1961 saw the unveiling of the TR4 which disappointed some by continuing most of the old engineering, but did present a startling new Italian body from Michelotti. It may have used the trusted Vanguard engine, but it also boasted innovative features such as dashboard air flow ventilation years ahead of Ford, and a two part Targa hard top, preempting Porsche by some years. The body itself was much wider and created an improved boot area. Winding windows, adjustable steering column and in 1965, independent rear suspension, all gradually turned the TR into a comfortable touring car. Clearly next, the ageing Vanguard engine had to be replaced, particularly with strong new competition from cars such as the MGB. This pushed Triumph towards the next incarnation – the TR5.

At the heart of this model change was the six cylinder powerplant from the Triumph saloon which was shoe horned into virtually the same body as the TR4. What distinguished this installation was the first use of fuel injection in a British mass production car. It provided Triumph with excellent press reviews and the enthusiast with a smooth and powerful car capable of over 125mph. Coupled with the extra wide and spacious cockpit, those winding windows and the Targa roof options, this was a package which pushed

Triumph ahead of their rivals. Sadly, the Lucas fuel injection proved troublesome, and nervous garages did little to calm the mood of unease. The TR5 was the nearest Triumph got to an outright winner; production lastied just one year, so the car remains rare.

RELATIONS

Italian Michelotti body styling, with most of the model carried forward from previous TRs. The engine came from the Triumph 2000 saloon range.

BEST BUY

It's the rarest and the fastest TR, yet buy with some care. The separate chassis does multiply rust dangers and a careful inspection will save you many later shocks. The engine is not as robust as the old Vanguard unit and that fuel injection seriously bruised the car's reputation. Specialist TR firms have finally ironed out the problems which means you can now probably get more carefree enjoyment out of this very British sports car than the original owners.

Cost	£11,200
% swing	-2
Spares	★★★★
V.F.M.	★★
S.R.	★★★

SPECIFICATIONS

ENGINE: 2498cc	**SUSPENSION:** Ind wishbone/coil & Ind semi trailing arm
BHP: 150	
FUEL: 22mpg	
GEARBOX: 4 speed	**BODIES:** 2 door sports
BRAKES: Disc/drum	**YEARS:** 1967–68
SPEED: 125mph	**PRODUCTION:** 2947

MANUFACTURER
BMC

Stuck with the dated pre–war T series design and with BMC bosses giving priority to the new Donald Healey deal, MG were rapidly losing ground to their competitors. With racing privateer George Phillips, they explored a streamlined racing-bodied TD at Le Mans in 1951, and spurred on, quietly constructed further prototypes. BMC were concentrating on the Healey 100, and refused to consider developing the new car until 1954. To underline the car's racing roots, the launch was June 1955, and coincided with a Le Mans team of three MGAs. The fatalities that year, tragically, undermined further publicity, but the launch was, nevertheless, a huge success.

With solid chassis, steel bodies with aluminium bonnet, boot and doors, this MG was powered by a 68bhp, 1489cc Series B engine with sensitive rack and pinion steering and good drum brakes. Initially launched as a roadster with detachable hard top, Fixed Head Coupé versions followed in 1956. A powerful 108bhp Twin Cam version appeared in 1958 with disc brakes, bored out to 1588cc, but it proved unreliable and was dropped after just 2111 cars had been manufactured, and only 360 were sold in the UK. The following May, a pushrod version of the ill-fated Twin Cam became the hugely successful MGA 1600 MkI; the final incarnation was the 1961–62 1622cc Mk II version. A true MG, born out of sporting traditions, and reflecting the 1950s preoccupation with streamlining, it has become a true classic. 101,081 MGAs were made – more than any other previous MG – and 80 per cent of them were sold in the USA!

RELATIONS

Completely unlike any previous MG, body styling came from George Phillips' TD Special and the subsequent MG prototypes. The chassis was initially from the T series, and then evolved through racing experience. Competition successes with the MG Magnette ZA prompted the use of its engine, gearbox, back axle, and brakes. Steering and suspension was from the TF.

BEST BUY

These cars are so good, that virtually any sound example will be a delight to own and drive. Unless you are mechanically experienced, steer clear of the Twin Cam versions. Inevitably, later cars had improved performance, but the body styling remained intact, apart from the recessed grille of the Mk IIs. A factory surplus of dropped Twin Cams produced a rare and very desirable de luxe version (1960–62) which was effectively a TC without the troubled powerplant: Only 395 were made.

In comparison with the lack of movement of the 1500 Roadster price as indicated below, the price for a 1600 De Luxe has increased by about £5,000 over the last three years, which takes it quite comfortably into the four-star value-for-money category.

SPECIFICATIONS

ENGINE 1489cc; 1588cc; 1622cc; (TC 1588cc ohc)
BHP 68; 80; 93; (TC 108)
Fuel 25–30mph (TC 22mph)
BRAKES Disc–drum; TC & De Luxe disc–disc

SUSPENSION Ind–leaf sprung
SPEED 95–113mph
GEARBOX 4 speed manual
BODIES Open & coupé
YEARS 1955–62
PRODUCTION 101,081

Cost (1500 roadster)	£11,600
% swing	-1
Spares	★★★★★
V.F.M.	★★
S.R.	★★★

LOTUS CORTINA MK I

BEWARE OF THE RACE PASSPORTS

MANUFACTURER
FORD

This car basks in former glories such as the 1964 British Saloon Car Championship, and with around a million roadgoing Mark I Cortina owners longing to emulate drivers like Jim Clark, Jack Sears, and Sir John Whitmore, its desirability was assured. The sporting Cortina GT was a workhorse offering disc brakes and Webers alongside four door practicality and even an Automatic. The Lotus Cortina was a more precious item.

Ford wanted motor sport association and Colin Chapman needed a new engine for his forthcoming Elan. Using the basic Ford 1500 Kent engine, adding a twin cam cylinder head and uniting it with a close ratio gearbox created the 105bhp drive train that would grace both the Lotus Cortina and the Lotus Elan. Ford's interest in the Group 2 racing category meant quite a lot of race customization but homologation required 1000 models to be produced. So the initial Lotus Cortina bodies were transported to the Lotus factory for conversion. Aluminium housing for the diff, parts of the gearbox and clutch also saved valuable weight. The suspension was lowered, the steering ratio adjusted and a complete rebuild of the rear suspension replaced the leaf springs with coil and dampers, trailing arms and an A bracket. Externally, the classic white and green striped livery, the wider wheels, quarter bumpers and Lotus badging remained the same until production gave way to the Mk II in 1967. However, this was not the case under that bodywork. The 1000 qualifying cars were semi-racing examples, providing a track passport for the real racing Lotus Cortinas. Inevitably, many of these 1000

cars succumbed to weakness. The lightweight panels would crease if touched, and the rear suspension was fraught with troubles and wrecked differentials. Suspension reverted to leaf springing in 1964-5, panels were strengthened and a Ford gearbox replaced the tricky close ratio version. Thus, this hugely practical Cortina trailing competition glories made an interesting, if fickle classic.

RELATIONS

Essentially a Ford Cortina with a Lotus Elan engine and gearbox.

BEST BUY

Most value is placed on the early Lotus-built homologation cars, but these are potentially more troubled. The later cars are cheaper, still exciting and far more practical. Inevitably cars will have been driven hard and engine builds can be expensive. Rust attacks floors, sill, the engine area and suspension mounts, but fortunately the car is easy to work on.

Cost	£12,000
% swing	16
Spares	★★★★
V.F.M.	★★★
S.R.	★★

SPECIFICATIONS

ENGINE: 1558cc	**SUSPENSION:** Coil/MacPherson
BHP: 105	strut & semi-elliptic (see
FUEL: 21mpg	above)
GEARBOX: 4 speed	**BODIES:** 2 door saloon
BRAKES: Disc/drum	**YEARS:** 1963–66
SPEED: 106mph	**PRODUCTION:** 4012

MANUFACTURER
LOTUS

Colin Chapman was one of the country's most enterprising designers whose endless visions often ran ahead of business support. Outside the Lotus competition success, his dream was to create a sports car with wide appeal. His initial Lotus Elite was very desirable, but too expensive to produce. In 1958 he gained US orders for 1000 cars, but his body suppliers were contracted to supply just 250 per year and were already falling behind that quota. He adjusted to a far simpler concept, nearer to that of the Lotus 7, using a monocoque fibreglass body and the newly developed Lotus Ford twin cam engine. The Elan, launched at the 1962 Motor Show, had a simple backbone chassis, fully independent suspension, rack and pinion steering, disc brakes all round – everything beneath a beautifully simple open two seater body. It was replaced two years later by the Series II, which incorporated a number of customer-requested changes. In 1965 the first Fixed Head Coupé emerged as a Series III, complete with electric windows, while the Series II Sports continued, gaining a a Special Edition luxury option from January 1966. This SE package involved servo brakes, a close ratio gearbox and uplift to 115bhp. The inevitable open Series III arrived in June 1966, and both the Coupé and Sports synchronised again as Series IV in March 1968. Changes this time involved squared-off wheel arches, low profile tyres, a bonnet bulge to accommodate the Stromberg carburation, facia and rear light alterations. Some later examples reverted to Webers, and from January 1971 the final Elan – the Sprint – used Webers along with a big valve 126bhp

engine until a last change to Dellorto carbs: Sprints were duo-toned. These cars were perfectly balanced, lightweight sports cars, with great agility and a knack of making good drivers feel like great ones.

RELATIONS

A Ford Cortina-based engine, original Lotus chassis and body, and with components from various sources such as the Triumph GT6, and suspension parts from the Ford Cortina.

BEST BUY

It has a terrible reputation for fragility, but the body should be reasonable. Check the chassis for rust, particularly around the front suspension. Trim was always poor. Patchy engine reputation was never reflected when new, but is underlined by clumsy rebuilds or tuning. Set up properly, it is a sweet car, appreciated by, and ideally suited for the mechanically minded. The pretty fixed heads are cheaper and a good Series IV is a great classic.

SPECIFICATIONS

ENGINE: 1498cc; 1158cc	**SUSPENSION:** Ind wishbone/ coil –Wishbone/coil
BHP: 105 – 126	
FUEL: 20mpg – 30mpg	**BODIES:** 2 door sports; fixed head coupé
GEARBOX: 4 speed	
BRAKES: Disc	**YEARS:** 1962 – 1973
SPEED: 115mph – 120mph	**PRODUCTION:** 12,224

Cost (Sprint dhc)	£14,000
% swing	-8.3
Spares	★★★★
V.F.M.	★★
S.R.	★★★★

ALPINE A110

IT'S BEATEN FERRARIS, PORSCHE AND SOME DRIVERS

MANUFACTURER
RENAULT

The term "real sports car" is often used by owners of overweight sporting legends massaging ageing egos. Just a precious few cars – like race horses – are genuine thoroughbreds requiring skilful mastering. One such car is the Alpine-Renault A110. It was rooted in competition and throughout its lifespan searched for the perfect engines for each task.

Jean Redélé, the son of a Dieppe Renault agent began competing in a Renault 4CV, particularly the sporting Type 1063 version. In his search for victory

he discarded the heavy body and replaced it with a fibreglass shell. A Michelotti design pre–production model followed and a finished commercial version was unveiled at the 1955 Paris Motor Show. After some initial cars Redélé's vision finally crystallized in 1963. The A110 formula for success was a central backbone chassis, proven Renault components and literally a one-piece, lightweight fibreglass body. The engine was slung low behind the axle but cambered wheels, race-proven suspension and an incredibly light body conspired to create a true winner – competition versions were virtually transparent. It won races and rallies – even achieving a spectacular one, two, three victory in the 1971 Monte Carlo Rally. All independent suspension, 4- or 5-speed gearboxes, all-round disc brakes and a

truly bewildering selection of engines were employed. As with the Donald Healey/BMC union, so Renault increasingly supported Alpine, turning them into the national sports car – even competing in the French colours. Naturally, Renault's involvement led to the subsequent cars, the GTA Turbo, the A310 and the final A610 becoming heavier and more comfortable; which leaves the lithe, undeniably beautiful yet fast A110 as the true classic masterpiece. If you are looking for something different, a connoisseur's classic and have the driver skills to get the best from its power and sensitivities, then the Alpine could well become your passion.

RELATIONS

Italian Michelotti-inspired design with approximately 750 Renault components in every car, including a variety of their engines (see separate box above right). Francophiles might spot those Citroën Dyane front indicators! The history of Alpine Renault includes the engineering groundwork for the success of Williams Renault in Formula One today.

Cost	£16,500
(1500/1600)	
% swing	-28
Spares	★★★★
V.F.M.	★
S.R.	★★

SPECIFICATIONS

ENGINE: 1300cc – 1600cc (competition variations)	**SPEED:** 110mph–130mph (competitions higher)
BHP: 58 – 170	**SUSPENSION:** Ind wishbone/ coil – Swing axle/coil
FUEL: 24mpg (competitions lower)	**BODIES:** 2 door coupé
GEARBOX: 4 & 5 speed	**YEARS:** 1963-77
BRAKES: Disc	**PRODUCTION:** 7,914

DIEPPE FACTORY BUILT ALPINE–RENAULT
A110 BERLINETTES
(LIMITED PRODUCTION ALSO TOOK PLACE IN BRAZIL, BULGARIA, MEXICO & SPAIN)

1963–65 "1000" A110–950 (i) 956cc (55hp), 106mph, (Renault8/Floride S)

1963–65 "1000" A110–950 Mignotet (i) 956cc (70hp), mph n/a, (R8/Floride S)

1963–65 "1100" 80 (ii) 1108cc (55hp), 106mph, (Caravelle&R8)

1964–65 "1100" (ii)1108cc (66hp), 109mph, (R8) – later called "Standard"

1965–66 "85" (ii) 1108cc (85hp), 112mph, (Caravelle/R8)

1965–na "1100 Competition" (ii) 1108cc (90hp), 122mph, (R8Gordini)

1965–76 "100" (ii)–1108cc (95hp), 121mph, (R8Gordini)

1966–67 "Standard" (ii) 1108cc (66hp), 109mph, (R8)– was 1964/5 "1100"

1966–na "Standard Hautes Performance" (ii)1108cc (na), 116mph, (R8Gordini)

1966–71 "1300" (iii) 1296cc (115hp), 134mph, (R8) called Super after 1967

1967–69 "70" (ii) 1108cc (66hp), 109mph, (R8) – formally the "Standard"

1967–71 "1300 S" (iii) 1296cc (120hp), 138mph, (R8) called Super after 1967

1967–71 "1300 S Usine" (iii) 1296cc(na), 148mph, (R8) called Super after 1967

1967–na "1100GTH" (ii) 1147cc (110hp), mph n/a, (R8Gordini)

1967–70 "1300" (iii) 1255cc, (105hp), 134mph, (R8Gordini)

1970–71 "1300G" (iii) 1255cc (103hp), 134mph, (R8Gordini)

1970–74 "85" (iii) 1289cc (81hp), 113mph, (Renault 12TS)– became "1300" until 1976

1975–76 "1300" (iii) 1289cc, (81hp), 113mph, (Renault12TS) formally the "85"

1967–68 "1500" (iv) 1470cc (82hp), 116mph, (Renault16)

1969–70 "1600" (v) 1565cc (92hp), 122mph, (Renault16TS)

1970–70 "1600" (v) 1565cc (102hp), 122mph, (Renault16TS)

1970–73 "1600 S" (v) 1565cc, (138hp), 134mph, (Renault16TS)

1970–73 "1600 S" (v) Group IV, 1596cc (172hp), 141mph, (Renault16TS)

1973–74 "1600 S" (v) 1605cc, (140hp), 131mph, (Renault17TS)

1973–74 "1800 S Group IV Usine" (v) 1798cc, (185hp), 158mph, (Renault17TS)

1974–75 "1600 SC" – 1600Si (v) 1605cc, (140/145hp), 131mph, (Renault17TS)

1976–77 "1600 SX" (v) 1647cc (109hp), 122mph, (Renault16TX)

ALPINE–RENAULT GENERAL CLASSIFICATIONS

(i)	A110 "1000"
(ii)	A110 "Berlinette 1100"
(iii)	A110 "Berlinette 1300" VA–VB–VC
(iv)	A110 "Berlinette 1500"
(v)	A110 "Berlinette 1600" VA–VB–VC–VD–VH

N.B. All Power ratings are in S.A.E. HP
Prepared with the assistance of Club Alpine–Renault

BEST BUY

Engines sizes systematically grew from 956 to 1951 though the essential production models were around the 1300 & 1600 mark. Exclude the early 4-speed gearbox and be aware there were also Spanish-built examples. Almost inevitably, any A110 will have been driven hard, quite possibly in competition, and with most cars customized you should contact the Owners Club to help find one of these prized machines.

PORSCHE 911
WE'VE SAID NICE …

MANUFACTURER
PORSCHE

Which 911 is pictured above? Does it really matter? Well, of course it does. Turbo convertible, 1985-89 with the paint-work provided at source (originally offered as decoration on the 935). 300 bhp for the eighties winners. Whatever the author's misgivings, there must be a few nineties winners out there who are stiill enamoured: there is a seven-month waiting list for the latest £64,000 911 Targa.

I happily acknowledge the 911 as a very fine looking car and that, after the millions of Deutchmarks and hours of skilled German application, the machine is most beautifully engineered. However, we were saying that over 30 years ago, congratulating the company for effectively re-creating the same central design problem which existed on its predecessor. Hanging the engine at the very back and then adding more and more power over the years to compensate seems rather naïve. Yes, we should applaud their huge expenditure which off-set such mistakes, but more thought at the time might have left funds for genuinely new models. Porsche staggered and fell trying to make a 'People's Porsche' with the 914/16. They virtually apologised for the 924 and have never convinced anyone about the 928. Only the upgrade of the 924 to the 944 stands the test of time, and even that was left with borrowed bodywork. Design teams with such appalling track records wouldn't survive anywhere else. Indeed, if the 1980s consumer blitz hadn't connected with the excesses of Porsche fins and turbos, their management would have been transparently failing. The cars are truly exciting to drive, and generate lots of the correct noises from both the engine compartment and bystanders, but they are hugely expensive for something that is centrally flawed in its handling, with spartan basics for an interior, notchy, unattractive gear changes, excessive spares costs, poor ventilation and group 20 insurance. 'Great car, you've done your best, what's next?' should have been cried a decade or more ago. In the same time frame Jaguar created the Mk II, the E-Type, the Mk X, the 240/340/420 range, the XJ6, the XJS, the 220 and the new XK8. Even under-funded design teams like Lotus created the Lotus 7, the sports racers, the Formula Juniors, the FI cars, the Elite, the five Elans, the +2s, the Europa, the Elite SI, the Esprit range and the new Elise. It's praiseworthy to keep developing a single car, but we don't actually need too many 200mph, Carrera Turbos. Fine, keep stretching and learning on the race circuit, by why not give the public some really new models? The 911 has become like an obsessive body-builder pumping ever more irons and steroids to ensure continuing admiration – we've said nice. There must be employees in the Porsche design department with years of service who have never ever been involved in a genuinely new car launch.

The 911 itself was launched to an appreciate public in 1963 (as the 901) and has journeyed through endless incarnations, systematically improving until its fashion status became the core sales impetus. It is indeed a very exciting and exacting driver's car but 30 years on there are now a range of temptations for the knowledgable enthusiast and the 911 is becoming as

Cost	£16,500
(Carrera '73)	
% swing	2
Spares	★★
V.F.M.	★★
S.R.	★★

SPECIFICATIONS

ENGINE: 1582cc: 1971cc
BHP: 90 – 80
FUEL: 28mpg
GEARBOX: 4 & 5 speed
BRAKES: Disc
SPEED: 110mph

SUSPENSION: MacPherson Strut/Torsion bar & Semi trailing/Torsion bar
BODIES: 2 door Coupé: Targa
YEARS: 1965 – 69: 1975 – 76
PRODUCTION: 32,399

A CHRONOLOGY

1963 Launch at Frankfurt Motor Show – as the 901
1964 Initial production cars renamed 911 following
Peugeot objections
1965 1991cc model with 130bhp,130mph and Solex carbs
First right hand drives reach Britain
912 launch with 1,582cc, 90bhp and 122mph
1966 S version and Targa with 160bhp ventilated disc
brakes and Webers
1967 911L launch with 110bhp, Sportomatic gearbox
911T launch with 1991cc, 110bhp and 125mph
1968 911S receives fuel injection and 170bhp
911T rises to 140bhp
911E with 140bhp replaces 911L
Targa gets fixed glass window
912 ends production
1969 911S to 2195cc, fuel injection 170bhp and 136mph)
911E to 2195cc, fuel injection 155bhp and 137mph
911T to 2195cc, Zenith carbs 125bhp and 128mph)
911L to 1991, 130bhp – last year
911 wheelbase stretched to 2268mm
Enlarged 5.5 inch wheel rims
1970 New front air dam, galvanising undersides
1971 911S to 2341cc, 190bhp and 144mph
911T to 2341cc, 130bhp,and 129mph
911E to 2341cc, 165bhp and 140mph
New 915 gearbox
1972 911RS 2.7 Carrera launch with 2687cc
210bhp and 149mph
Enlarged rear wings and wheels for Carrera

1973 911T gets Bosch Kjetronic fuel injection
All models to 2687cc
911 replaces T and has 150bhp
911S replaces E and has 175bhp
1974 911 3.0 Carrera RSR Turbo launch at Paris Show with
260bhp and 153mph
1975 912E reintroduction with 1971cc, 80bhp and 110mph
1976 Bodies now zinc coated
1977 911 3.3 Turbo, 3299cc, 300bhp and 160mph
1980 911SC 3.0 with 204bhp
1982 Cabriolet body launched
1983 911 3.2 Carrera launched with 3164cc, 231bhp and
152mph
1984 3164 installed in non Turbo models with 231bhp
1987 959 launch with 2848cc, twin turbos, 4WD,
450bhp and 196mph
1988 911 3.6 Carrera 4 with 3600cc, 4wd, 250bhp and 155mph
Speedster begins short production run
1989 911 3.6 Carrera 2 with tiptronic gearbox and 159mph
1990 911 3.3 Turbo to 320bhp and 171mph
1991 911 3.6 Carrrera RS with 260bhp and 161 mph
911 Turbo servo steering and ABS introduced plus ABS
1992 911 3.3 Turbo S special with 355bhp
911 Carrera RS, essentially the Carrrera 2 with 260bhp
1993 911 3.6 Turbo with 360bhp and 175mph
911 Speedster limited edition version of Carrera 2

---

estranged from real drivers as the Range Rover has become from real offroad terrain. The 911 doesn't invite DIY restorations, costs large sums to have rebuilt and requires all your attention, all the time, when driving. Magazines sell extra copies flaunting state-of-the-art Porsche features but virtually none remember the 912, which is identical to its contemporary 911 sister but used the 4-cylinder engine from the final trusted 356C model. The 912 will still get you to 110mph, give brilliant fuel consumption and with the lighter engine over the tail, not behave as badly. So the interior trim is basic – so it is for virtually all the 911s. It does, however, enjoy the early and pure body styling, its own cachet; and remember you could buy a good looking example for the cost of a hard top for the present 911 Cabriolet.

RELATIONS

Designed by Dr Porsche's son Ferdinand it paralleled most of the preceding 356C model and has been developed in–house over the decades. Other economy minded 911s include the 911T and 911S..

BEST BUY

The 912 was launched in 1965 when the 356C was dropped. 1967 saw a Targa roof option and dual circuit braking, with longer wheelbase and five speeds following. It reappeared as the 912E (not the 911E) just for 1975 as an export using the larger fuel injected engine from the discontinued 914 model. If you get serious, check any Porsche obsessively for rust.

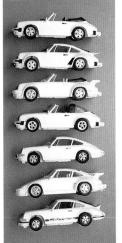

SAAB 900 TURBO

BRILLIANT – I JUST WISH IT HAD BEEN FOR SALE

MANUFACTURER

SAAB

Decades of enjoying press cars spoils you. It also destroys many day dreams as almost inevitably, fancied cars proved to have annoying traits, or didn't suit day-to-day life – something car buyers find out the hard way. It was an extraordinary shock when I found a SAAB fulfilling virtually all criteria for a perfect road car. The model concerned was one of the very last SAAB 900 Turbos before the current Vauxhall Cavalier cloned version. Called the Ruby, just 200 of these cars were imported as a final celebration of the 900's impressive 15 years in production. The range evolved out of the 99 through increased wheelbase and redesigned front end and has been offered in two, three, four and five door versions plus a convertible – all constantly improved in terms of safety and with regard to the environment: they were the first with asbestos free brakes pads. The 99 was the first mass production turbo. The engine remained the two litre but their policy of development took the power output from 100bhp up to the Ruby's 185bhp. The 900 had 16 valves from October 1984 and water-cooled turbos arrived in 1987 along with ABS; while in 1991 they introduced a 145bhp light turbocharged S engine option. Often as a car reaches old age the manufacturers add nothing but weight and badges, but with SAAB's constant evolution of a single range the final Ruby was a triumph. It came with their most powerful 1985cc full turbo engine, three door body, aero wheels, air conditioning and leather heated seats. With the turbo lag problems ironed out there was an endless stream of power; with near perfect steering (weighted 60% over the front axle) excellent brakes and firm suspension it drove like a fine sports car while offering saloon comfort, space and traditional Swedish build quality. It's a great road car and its qualities combined with long life expectancy ensure eventual classic status. A stunning combination – I wish it had been for sale.

RELATIONS

A naturally evolved model. First SAAB Turbo was the January 1978 99 model and the first 900 Turbo came in March 1979. The present day 900 is the GM based range introduced in 1993.

BEST BUY

If you can find a Ruby, all finished in dark red mica–metallic paint, it's a gem, but any post-1988 water cooled turbo is interesting though the 1989 go faster Carlsson version lacks class. Excellent build limits body troubles. Mechanical aspects are chiefly limited to clutch wear: see if it judders. Worn high mileage turbos expensive. Seek a good service record.

Spares	★★★★
V.F.M.	★★★★
S.R.	★★★

SPECIFICATIONS

ENGINE: 1985cc	**SUSPENSION:** Ind coil/wishbone – coil/trailing arms
BHP: 185	
FUEL: 27mpg	**BODIES:** 3 door Saloon
GEARBOX: 5 speed	**YEARS:** 1978 – 1993
BRAKES: Disc	**PRODUCTION:** 26,346
SPEED: 130mph	

MANUFACTURER
ALVIS

After the war the Alvis range was of 3 litre ladder framed chassis cars culminating in the TC21 Grey Lady. By the early 1950s sales were diminishing. In fact with considerable military work, car production all but ceased. However the Swiss coachbuilder Carrosserie Graber had been using the Alvis chassis since 1948 to build expensive commissions and so a deal was struck for a Graber-designed Alvis to be built in the UK under licence. Based on the Grey Lady just 17 examples of the TC108G were built as the costs were too high. Alvis negotiated a buy–out and asked Park Ward to build a more economical version, the 1958 104bhp TD21 with the 3 litre engine married to a BN4 Austin-Healey gearbox. Reaction was good and in 1959 enlarged carburation lifted power to 115bhp while the Series II added all-round disc braking, a German 5-speed ZF gearbox and an automatic option. Various body styling changes included new aluminium door panels and recessing secondary driving lights in place of the for-mer air intakes. The TD would prove to be Alvis'

best seller. Series III, the 1964 TE21, saw front end changes to allow double vertical headlights, improved suspension and steering and power up to 130bhp. By then opposition such as the 3.4 Mk I Jaguar was reaching 120mph and an increasingly dated Alvis was given a last facelift with the Series IV TF21 – redesigned facia, triple SU carbs, raised compression and a jump to 150bhp. In 1965 Rover bought Alvis, which meant British Leyland in 1967, and the end.

RELATIONS

Body styling by Swiss designer Graber, engine and most components from the preceding Alvis model range, gearboxes from Austin-Healey and Germany.

BEST BUY

Core decisions are saloon versus rarer drophead models and double headlights versus earlier TD treat-ment. Despite mixed materials bodywork has held up well, though check boot and interior floors for rust. Everything is under-stressed, including fine engine.

The last of the TE21s left production on 20th August 1967. Parts for the ZF gearbox are rare and equally coveted by Aston Martin owners. The exciting Alvis prototype (below left) was the mid-engined V8 replacement for the TF, which was cancelled under BL maagement.

SPECIFICATIONS	
ENGINE: 2993cc	**SUSPENSION:** Ind wishbone/
BHP: 104 – 150	coil – Live axle/semi-elliptic
FUEL: 17 – 25mpg	**BODIES:** 2 door saloon; drop-
GEARBOX: 4 & 5 speed	head coupé
BRAKES: Disc/drum; Disc/disc	**YEARS:** 1956 – 1967
SPEED: 105mph –120mph	**PRODUCTION:** 1,559

Cost	£14,600
(TE/TF21 Saloon)	
% swing	2
Spares	★★★
V.F.M.	★★★
S.R.	★★★

MANUFACTURER
DAIMLER

DAIMLER SP250

MORE DESIRABLE NOW THAN WHEN NEW

This is a car that deserves careful attention. Daimler's unexpected excursion into the 1960s sports car market, with unconventional body styling, had little chance of survival particularly as Jaguar took over the company and within two years were to unveil their world beating E-Type. However the low production figures, its glorious V8 engine and a strong fibreglass body have combined to give the Daimler a very collectable status. Informed observers feel that approximately two-thirds of the total production are still in existence – and that's Rolls-Royce survivability. The powerful and lightweight Edward Turner-designed V8 was the envy of the industry and many cynics wrote referring to a fine engine test rather than a road test – thus utterly dismissing the unconventional styling or the natural Daimler concerns for passenger comfort. The car wasn't trying to be an Austin-Healey or a TR – it was a Daimler boasting leather trim, adjustable bucket seating, wind up windows, detachable hard top, standard disc braking, an automatic option. Daimler's independence disappeared within a year of the SP250's 1959 New York launch and despite good orders and reviews, the new Jaguar masters hardly wanted in-house competition for their imminent E-Type.

Briefly named the Daimler Dart, the initial A specifications offered full 120mph performance but the chassis proved to flex under stress and shortly after Jaguar's takeover the 1961 B version added extra chassis and body strength, a full-width front bumper and detail refinements. Towards the end of its short life there was also a C spec, fitting as standard previous options such as a heater and even a cigar lighter. This unique car offers rapid and elegant touring with suspension and handling to suit: inevitably compromising finesse if driven in anger. Rare, comfortable, with wonderful engine and head turning retro style, it's more desirable now than when new.

RELATIONS

Daimler body concept and new V8 engine; Jaguar controlled after 1960. Daimler had also owned Hooper who coachbuilt a prototype SP250 Coupé for the 1959 Earls Court show. Aimed at the US market, it preempted much of the MGB GT concept but was still born…Jaguar's fixed head E-Type was coming.

BEST BUY

Sought after so choice is limited. Tap into the owners club network and try to find B or C versions. The engine wears well and the largely trouble-free fibreglass body is strong. Check rear sections of the chassis, around the steering box and front suspension.

Cost	£13,750
% swing	-5
Spares	★★★
V.F.M.	★★
S.R.	★★★★

SPECIFICATIONS

ENGINE: 2548cc
BHP: 140
FUEL: 27mpg
GEARBOX: 4 speed; 3 speed automatic
BRAKES: Disc
SPEED: 122mph

SUSPENSION: Ind wishbone/coil& live axle semi-elliptic
BODIES: 2 door sports
YEARS: 1959 – 64
PRODUCTION: 2,645

MANUFACTURER

GENERAL MOTORS

The 40 years of the Corvette is a story of competition – not motor sport, but pure commerce. Its catalyst was GM design chief and enthusiast Harley Earl's growing frustration at the European influx of sports cars such as the XK 120 and the Austin-Healey 100. Now, such is the UK/European love affair with '50s Americana that the era's body styling appears particularly attractive, but ironically the initial Corvette was a terrible compromise and only survived thanks to corporate pride in the face of Ford's new Thunderbird. It is the 1956–62 period that best represents the early cars. The Corvette first appeared as the 1953 Motorama show car. Fibreglass was used for development economy while the chassis and engine were ageing saloon items. A pre–war in–line 6 engine, negligible brakes and a two-speed automatic gearbox hardly amounted to a sports car. *Road and Track*, viewing it as a woman's car, drove the point home by suggesting a three-tone paint scheme and frilly curtains. Production staggered onward but unsold stock and mounting criticisms heralded a swift end: until Ford launched that Thunderbird, goading GM into competition. In 1955 the new V8 265 cubic inch saloon Chevrolet engine was squeezed into the Corvette adding 45bhp – and a 3-speed manual gearbox. Harley Earl and team then set about re–styling and in 1956 the car came of age. Deep elliptical grooves down the body sides appeared, a more aggressive front treatment with protruding headlights, a hardtop, winding or electric windows, upgraded tuning options and in best form a 120mph+ top speed. Each year it gained extra performance and the

styling actually became more Rock 'n' Roll – until the 1963 Sting Ray took over.

RELATIONS

General Motors body styling with the rest a GM parts bin extravaganza. Initial in-line 6 dated back to the Depression; subsequent V8s from saloon range.

BEST BUY

The 1953–55 car (see above) is interesting and collectable as a boulevard cruiser. The 1956–62 era is progressively more sporting until the Sting Ray. 4-speed manual from 1957 and from '58 quad headlights and a truly amazing cockpit worthy of any sports car. Basically trouble-free, but watch for accident damage beneath the (easily repairable) bodywork. With retrimming expensive and spares tricky, prioritise interior condition when choosing and join the club to tap into members' cars for sale.

The interior is as important as the running gear and bodywork when buying, maybe more so.

SPECIFICATIONS

ENGINE: 3861cc; 4344cc; 4639cc; 5359cc	arms/coil – Live axle/semi-elliptic
BHP: 150 –250 (360 bhp tuned)	**SPEED:** 106 – 120mph (135mph tuned)
FUEL: 13 – 25mpg	**BODIES:** 2 door Sport; Hard Top
GEARBOX: 2 speed auto; 3 & 4 Manual	**YEARS:** 1953 – 1962
BRAKES: Drum	**PRODUCTION:** 69,475
SUSPENSION: Unequal A	

Cost	£16,500
(Sting Ray '63-67)	
% swing	-5.5
Spares	★★★
V.F.M.	★★
S.R.	★★★★

MERCEDES 230–250–280 SL

HARD TO FAULT MIDDLE GROUND CLASSIC

MANUFACTURER

MERCEDES-BENZ

Mercedes–Benz entered the 1960s with some trepidation: while their once revered 300SL was dating fast, and the 190SL languished in the Gullwing's shadow, the competition was forging ahead, offering that all-important impressive top speed – once the Gullwing's domain – plus greatly improved creature comforts. In March 1963 they unveiled their answer, the 230SL. Inevitably there were mixed reactions and to many the title sports car was inappropriate. However as road testers and the public got behind the wheel, attitudes changed, for much of Mercedes' effort had gone into handling – never the Gullwing's strong suit. So much care in fact, that they even instigated the design of brand new tyres. The car was based on the floorpan, engine and equipment from the 220SE which some pointed to as an endorsement of the non sports car argument: forgetting a Works 220SE team came first, second and third in the 1960 Monte Carlo Rally. The engine was slightly bored out, with new camshaft, improved compression and fitted with fuel injection for 170bhp. Transmission was four speed with awkward gear ratios or the generally specified four speed automatic. Power steering was available, front disc brakes standard. Soft top was an option; or a solid five point fixing hardtop with extra tall door windows, which forced the hardtop roof sides to tilt upward – hence the famous Pagoda nickname. These finely built cars began to create a very wide customer base. In 1967 they answered lack of power criticism by putting their fuel-injected 2.5 into what was then called the 250SL. This also offered a choice of final drives, four and five speed boxes as

well as auto and disc brakes all round. Despite traditionally long runs, Mercedes took less than a year before eclipsing the 250SL with the 280SL. This was the last of the 6-cylinder SLs and the most popular, enjoying a power hike to 2778cc courtesy of the 280/300SE range. The 6-cylinder SLs make beautiful touring cars and basically safe investments.

RELATIONS

Substantially based on the 220SE saloons with subsequent versions taking engines from the 250SE and finally the 280/300SE. Bodystyling is original.

BEST BUY

The 230SL underpowered but actually more agile than the bigger engined cars which became increasingly heavy – and comfortable. Buy through recognised sources and with service history: mistakes are expensive. Rust limited to wings, sills, rear floor area.

Cost	£16,900
(280SL)	
% swing	-14
Spares	★★★
V.F.M.	★★
S.R.	★★★

SPECIFICATIONS

ENGINE: 2306cc; 2496cc; 2778cc	Disc/disc after '67
BHP: 150 – 170	**SUSPENSION:** Ind wishbone/ coil – swing axle/coil
FUEL: 17 – 25mpg	**BODIES:** 2 door roadster soft/hard tops
SPEED: 115 – 121mph	
GEARBOX: 4 speed; Automatic; 5 speed 280SL	**YEARS:** 1963–67; 1966–68; 1967–71
BRAKES: Disc/drum –	**PRODUCTION:** 19,831; 5,196; 23,885

MANUFACTURER
FIAT

FIAT ABARTH 850 TC

AN INDIVIDUALIST'S CLUB CAR

Whether it was a Ford Galaxy battling the Mk II racing Jaguars, three wheeling Lotus Cortinas, John Rhodes burning Cooper S tyres or the latest Mercedes/Alfa tussle in the DTM, racing production cars have always held real fascination. Just to see familiar models tuned to perfection and thrashed to within inches of destruction brings out the gladiatorial instincts. Naturally this type of classic competition appeals to amateurs and leads to the quest for something different, something affordable to run. John Cooper's magic transformed the humble Mini into a world beating competition car while in Italy a man specialising in exhaust pipes achieved the same with even more modest machinery – the tiny 500 and 600 Fiat saloons. Carlo Abarth's Fiat-tuning gifts are truly legendary. The basic 600 saloon developed just 28bhp yet such was his skills that in its extreme TCR state it yielded 130bhp. There were over 7,000 class wins! The tiny saloons were reliable, fun and millions were sold creating a good supply of both cars and parts. The actual Works cars were the pinnacle of development and frequently changed livery from season to season which, combined with so many Abarth conversion kits, makes establishing a genuine Works car extremely tricky. I tried out just such a rarity, the 1966 Works 850 TC Corsa – the TC is Turismo Competizione. Having driven BMC Works Cooper S's I approached the drive with more amusement than excitement but within minutes the acceleration, the glorious noise, the rock steady suspension and disc braking in each corner of the tiny thing commanded great respect. They really are the giant killers

you read about and exceptional fun – though reverse in the initial gear position and actual first where second should be does keep you concentrating. The historic machine pictured is prepared and raced by Tony Castle-Miller at Middle Barton Garage who is the UK's Abarth specialist and can restore or build you any grade of Fiat Abarth. These cars win events, need little space, create large crowds and make you smile a good deal – an ideal clubman's classic.

RELATIONS

The Fiat 500 and 600 were the replacements for the tiny Tipolino while Abarth's ideas blossomed under his own badge and as the tuning element for a wide range of manufacturers including Lancia and Ferrari.

BEST BUY

If your quest is just for a hot road car then all the usual warnings about that virile Italian rust applies. If however you are tempted to prepare a modest but competitive race or hill climb car, talk to Barton.

SPECIFICATIONS

ENGINE: 982cc	**SUSPENSION:** Wishbone/transverse leaf – Semi trailing/coil
BHP: 93	
FUEL: 4 gallon racing tank	**BODIES:** 2 door 4 seat saloon
GEARBOX: 5 speed	**YEARS:** 1968
BRAKES: Disc	**PRODUCTION:** NA
SPEED: 122mph	

Spares	★★★★
V.F.M.	★★★
S.R.	★★★★★

MAZDA MX–5

AN HONOURABLE HOMAGE TO THE 1960s

MANUFACTURER
MAZDA

There are curiously mixed feelings about Mazda's great success story. An enormous army of new fans have elevated this little two-seater to all-time greatness – most of them fresh to sports cars. Numbers of hardened individuals however dismiss it as a lightweight copy of a 1960s Lotus Elan. Such cynicism does not become the true enthusiast; some appear to turn a blind eye to a number of factors, not least that the Elans were always falling apart. Equally, the

MX–5 may not burn rubber in any macho way but no more did the incomparable Frogeye Sprite which was, after all, basically a Morris Minor. Mazda's little masterpiece is an honourable journey back to 1960s style using 1990s technology – thank heaven a manufacturer somewhere still recognises the `feel' of motoring. They openly studied the swinging decade and then used research from three continents to distil the essence into the MX–5. I've tested two now

Spares	★★★★
V.F.M.	★★★★★
S.R.	★★★★

SPECIFICATIONS

ENGINE: 1839cc	**SUSPENSION:** Ind wishbone/
BHP: 130	coil all round
FUEL: 25mpg	**BODIES:** 2 door sports:
GEARBOX: 5 speed	hardtop
BRAKES: Disc	**YEARS:** 1989 – to date
SPEED: 115mph	**PRODUCTION:** Current

Shades of Austin-Healey Frogeye: Mazda placed great importance on creating a friendly 'face' for their worldbeater. Just about the only complaint heard about the car is that the steering is perhaps a little over-assisted.

and it's only a matter of time before one joins the household. It has achieved its huge success on three counts – firstly it works well. The 1.8 litre engine is smooth, willing and deliberately tuned to rasp as you peak the revs, while the close ratio five-speed box is as good as you will find in any production car. You just flick it into place and the combination of engine response and beautifully weighted steering and suspension tempts you again and again. The interior is deliberately simple though not really that retro, luggage space reasonable, the heater superb and weather protection is great. The simple folding soft top needs one hand and seconds, plus there's provision for that sorely missed 1960s extra – a decent hard top. The car's second virtue is its aesthetics – fine design work with a grasp of period, great care with complimentary curves and subtle styling to add a sense of purpose. A dipping waistline profile accentuates the haunches, parallel bumper and boot lip hint at TVR urgency, a screen angle perfectly complimenting the shape of the soft top. Add such excellence to the third achievement – the development of

a car with genuine character – and you understand why it has won 60 major awards. To be dismissive of such a car ignores the main criterion for any classic – public affection.

RELATIONS

Original Mazda body styling with their B60 engine refined from the 323 block.

BEST BUY

Long warranty and high secondhand prices evens out the choice. Early cars were 1.6 but from May 1995 became 1.8 powered. Limited editions such as the all black SE and the Gleneagles are really just cosmetic, although the first anniversary edition does look wonderful in British Racing Green.

No retro styling here, which would look like trying too hard, no matter how clever. The 1.8i is great value for money. There is no owners' club in the UK at the moment, but there is in the US, where the car has been welcomed with open arms; no begrudging acceptance there.

BENTLEY MK VI

GREAT PERIOD COMFORT – AT A RISK

MANUFACTURER
ROLLS-ROYCE

Bentley Mk VI (above) with standard steel body. The four-door saloon was the first example of a Rolls-Royce 'factory' body; built by Pressed Steel and finished at Crewe.

Cost	£17,250
(Standard steel)	
% swing	5.5
Spares	★★★
V.F.M.	★★★
S.R.	★★

Immediately pre–war, Rolls-Royce was developing a 4257cc prototype called the Corniche but hostilities stopped work. However, they used the war years to appraise ideas by loaning the prototypes to leading military and political figures. The resulting 1946 launch of the Mark VI was something of a revolution for this famous manufacturer. Driven by the conviction that traditional bespoke construction had to be replaced by production line methods, they appointed Pressed Steel at Cowley to construct this new four-door saloon with its strong channel section chassis, independent front suspension and a reworked version of the pre–war B60, 6 cylinder, 4257cc engine fitted with twin SU carburation. An initial novelty which they later discontinued was to chrome plate the bores to reduce wear. During 1951 there was an increase in the engine capacity to 4556cc, and the original by–pass oil filter system was replaced by a more conventional full flow arrangement. Rolls-Royce themselves used the Mk VI platform to continue the tradition of coachbuilding all the Silver Wraith bodies – although, by 1949, the logic of a more accessible prestige car led them to use the Bentley VI in R Type form as the basis for their Silver Dawn model. Undoubtedly the Mk VI offers excellent entry level Bentley enjoyment, but is it practical? In the 1960s Maurice Wiggin of *The Sunday Times* evaluated running costs of a then new 1963 Mini and a 1951 Bentley Mk VI – both then costing around £500. There was just an old half penny per mile difference, (see box) yet they were a world apart in quality and safety. 18 coats of paint, acres of veneer and leather, tables, a drawer full of tools, a remote operated rear window blind, even slightly raised rear seating. Decades on it is telling that both cars are true classics yet the Bentley is now worth 30 times its 1960s value, while the Mk I Mini has risen just six-fold – neither figure takes currency or inflation factors into account.

RELATIONS

In-house body design with enhanced pre-war B60 engine. It gave birth to many coach-built examples, including desirable dropheads and to the later R Type, the famous Continental R (or more properly, the R-Type Continental, as 'Continental R' is the name given to the 1991 niche model) and the Rolls-Royce variants. The four-door saloon from Pressed Steel and finished at Crewe was later offered with a Rolls-Royce radiator as the Silver Dawn.

BEST BUY

Buy the best you can afford, for it will be much cheaper than hunting out a bargain and meeting

SPECIFICATIONS

ENGINE: 4257cc – 4556cc	**BRAKES:** Drum
BHP: Never released	**SPEED:** 95mph
FUEL: 16 – 18mpg	**BODIES:** 4 door saloon;
GEARBOX: 4 speed	Coachbuilt versions
SUSPENSION: Ind coil/wish-	**YEARS:** 1946–52
bone – live axle/half elliptic	**PRODUCTION:** 4964

1948 4¼ drophead with body from Mulliner; rarer and therefore, of course, far more expensive than the standard steel version.

1960s ANALYSIS OF COMPARATIVE RUNNING COSTS

	BENTLEY MK VI	MK I MINI
Depreciation:	£50.00	£100.00
Servicing:	£10.00	£ 10.00
Petrol:	£80.00	£ 40.00
Tyres:	£30.00	£ 20.00
Insurance:	£30.00	£ 15.00
	£200.00	£185.00
Cost per mile (Based upon 6,000 miles)	8d	7½d

Pounds, shillings and pence currency

post-1951 enlarged engine and changed oil flow is preferable. The enemy is rust and you need to check all the body mountings, the sills, the boot area, door bottoms and the wings. Ironically, the chassis generally escapes major troubles. The drophead coupé will cost you at least double the standard body version – multiply by five if you set your heart on an R-Type Continental with body from H.J.Mulliner (see pages 176-77). With the exception of the T-series saloons of the mid-1960s, the post-war Pressed Steel Mk VI is entry level for a classic flying wing. In 1930, Bentley had published a 'Resumé of Policy' as part of the celebration of victory at Le Mans: 'Participation in races {stamps] the Bentley ... as a racing car. Nothing could be further from the truth. On the conrrary, as our racing successes have increased our cars have become more silent, more docile, more refined.' The Mk VI is faithful to that promise.

painful restoration bills. A well maintained example will give enormous pride and pleasure to its owner. Mechanically there are no real problems though the

And even more exotic, a 1950 Mk VI once owned by the Indian Maharaja of Mysore. Before independence in 1947, India's ruling princes were among Rolls-Royce's best customers. Some continued to buy – 'in bulk!' – afterwards.

ASTON MARTIN DBS

MORE MISPLACED CLASS PREOCCUPATION THAN ANY OTHER MARQUE

MANUFACTURER

ASTON MARTIN

Until the mid-eighties it was quite possible to buy a reasonable Aston Martin for a few thousand pounds but then the madness of the boom years saw their prices in particular soar through the roof. These are rare cars and so naturally valuable, but the unprecedented price rise told most about the owners. The world of Aston is probably riddled with more misplaced class preoccupations than other classic marque, though ultimately we all benefit when enthusiasts invest in restoring examples of our motoring heritage. Unfortunately, Astons enjoy the same cachet as a good country address, making them the ultimate accoutrement for successful types – who in turn attempt to cast an exclusion zone around the marque. This isolationism no longer applies to other prestige marques, but ageing executives and showbusiness types have used cheque books to try colonising Aston Martin. The two models which missed their gaze were the DB2/4 which 'wasn't a DB4 darling', and the DBS which 'wasn't a V8'. The DB2/4 has now entered the investment stakes, but so far, the DBS remains just about affordable. A young Aston seat designer, William Towns, watched sports cars lose credibility as 2+2 versions got gradually longer. He sketched ideas for an initial 2+2 length car with an optional shortened sports version. His rare and ultra long Lagonda proved the starting point, with the DBS the derivative. With the DB4/5/6 range rapidly dating, Aston used the Towns DBS design to give birth to the whole new family of V8s. However, that engine would take two years more to refine and so the 1967 DBS launch revealed the powerful Towns body styling, and used the excellent Talek Marek six-cylinder engine within an adapted DB6 chassis. The emphasis was on fast touring, and it offered four seats, practical luggage space and considerable comfort, aided by advanced de Dion rear suspension and an adjustable ride control. Although the heavy chassis and comfortable trimmings turned it into a heavy car, the steering was a delight, while speeds of 140mph was attainable. It's a wide, luxurious car, with timeless body styling – and that endlessly evocative Aston badge.

RELATIONS

Towns designed the DBS and the 1970s Lagonda. The chassis, engine and other elements were taken

Cost	£18,000
% swing	14
Spares	★★★★
V.F.M.	★★★
S.R.	★★

SPECIFICATIONS

ENGINE: 3995cc
BHP: 282; 325
(Vantage version)
FUEL: 12mpg
GEARBOX: 5 speed: automatic
BRAKES: Disc
SPEED: 140mph: 150mph
(Vantage version)

SUSPENSION: Ind
wishbone/coil – de Dion
axle & coil
BODIES: 2 door, 4 seater
Coupé.
YEARS: 1967– 72
PRODUCTION: 899

from the DB6, while the famous V8 range followed afterwards, in September 1969. All those distinctively Aston coupés and convertibles are effectively related, from the DB4 which grew into the 4-litre DB5, DB6 and DBS.

BEST BUY

These are only an economic buy if you don't have to face very expensive restoration. The six-cylinder cars enjoyed a good reputation, but rust crept into all the lower sections. However, spares are excellent and good specialist firms are helpful. The last batch of cars reverted to single rather than quad headlights, a DB3S grille and were called AM Vantage – in preparation for the arrival of the V8. Remember that the whole point about this model is that it *isn't* a V8, which keeps prices down. (It isn't as if the company was profiteering at the time – Sir David Brown was forced to sell out in the DBS's last year.)

It's a DBS body (opposite, inset) but from 1978 and therefore has the V8. From 1969 to 1972 the DBS body with V8 engine was called the DBS V8, thereafter simply the V8, and had single headlights. The Aston two-door fastback coupé/convertible look had begun with the 3.7-litre DB4, which was launched in October 1958.

MANUFACTURER
MORGAN

MORGAN PLUS 8
TURNS LACK OF DEVELOPMENT INTO HIGH NOSTALGIA

As a classic for restoration it's not hugely attractive; as a brand new car only the Rover engine is truly worthwhile – if you remove its style and romance, that is. It would be unforgiveable not to include a Morgan in a list of classic cars, and dishonest not to warn of endless troubles. The two truly impressive elements are a beautiful, timeless body coupled with the sense of history which the marketing prowess of the Morgan family has fostered. With precious few changes to the car, and meagre resources, they have outshone even Porsche in maintaining perpetual motion for a single design. After all, the Porsche 911 has been endlessly regurgitated to hold enthusiasts' attention, while the very absence of change in Morgan design is what maintains the company's quite astonishingly long waiting lists.

Concepts of a V8 Morgan actually go back to the 1930s, when H.F.S. Morgan ran an experimental 4/4 car with a flat head 22hp V8, but it was not until the 1960s when supplies of the TR engine were diminishing that the search for new powerplants led Morgan to the Cortina GT engine for the 4/4, and produced the Plus 8 in 1968, which used the lightweight 161bhp Rover P6B 3500 engine. Until 1972 a quite demanding Moss gearbox was used, before the five-speed Rover unit was installed. Three years later an alu-

minium lightweight Sports option appeared; 1976 changes including an overdrive to help fuel economy. The radiator was enlarged in 1979, a high lift cam was added in 1982. Constant small improvements continued with rack and pinion steering in 1983, and a fuel injection option adding extra power from 1984. Straight line performance takes your breath away – as does the desperate suspension. Why such sales figures for a car that combines 1930s (sliding pillar) front suspension and a present day alloy V8 engine – configurations which were never intended to work together?

A trip around the craftsman-filled Morgan factory helps to illuminate what is going on: it's like a living motor museum – timeless traditions are used to create masterpieces apparently ill-equipped for our motoring world. Ash frames left to season for at least a year in the factory wood shed, power tools rarely used, snips, shears and mallets to the fore; Morgans have been built at the same Malvern Link site since 1923. Just as Paul Simon borrows ethnic roots to sell his contemporary records, so Morgan turn their lack of development since the 1930s into high nostalgia.

Cost	£17,500
% swing	7
Spares	★★★★
V.F.M.	★★★
S.R.	★★★

SPECIFICATIONS

ENGINE: 3528cc	**SUSPENSION:** Ind coil –
BHP: 157; 190	live axle leaf
FUEL: 20mpg	**BODIES:** 2 door Sports
GEARBOX: 4 & 5 speed	**YEARS:** 1968 – to date
BRAKES: Disc/drum	**PRODUCTION:** 4000+
SPEED: 124mph – 126mph	

They really are hand-built with an extraordinary selection of tools to create delicious curves in wood and metal. The whole factory feels like some painstakingly productive time warp.

RELATIONS

Born of the Morgan 4/4 which was first produced in the mid-1930s but powerered by Rover engines. The steering was modified with joints to clear the wider cylinder block. Dimensions slightly larger than the Plus 4, one inch wider and three inches longer.

BEST BUY

Brand new. The earlier the car the more likely structural grief. Rust is a problem for body and chassis, the aluminium alternative is vulnerable to knocks. More significant is the virtually invisible wooden framework which rots and can only be replaced by stripping down the car and through the work of skilled craftsman – even Morgan concede bodies need attention every five years. The archaic sliding pillar front suspension, like the passengers, wear out quickly but the engines are generally trouble-free. The Rover V8 3528cc engine was employed 1968-76, followed by the SDI to 1987; the SDI Vitesse was used from 1983-1990 – then came the big change, to the Range Rover 3946cc V8.

Men with enough time; the detailed final checks of every car add to the traditional wait for delivery of a new Morgan.

MANUFACTURER
PORSCHE

Some of the world's acknowledged masterpieces depict humble subjects such as bowls of fruit or views from the window – the artistry is in translating such simplicity through personal vision. Dr Ferdinand Porsche and his son Ferry achieved that transformation when they took the essence of the VW Beetle – another brainchild of Herr Doktor, and created the Porsche 356. The very first prototype used a space frame chassis, three abreast seating, and a mid engine. However, when production began in 1949 they used the VW floorpan and chassis, its suspension, gearbox and a modified version of the 1131cc flat-four engine – under a breathtaking aerodynamic coupé body. Over the following 18 years, it matured from a humble 40hp to the latest 2.0 litre Carrera offering 130hp, and more class, in the author's opinon, than a garage of 911s. Various changes occurred, including the 1954 launch of the stripped-down Speedster, before the next key upgrade to the 1955 356A. These retained the initial

jelly mould body style, but were mainly 1600s powered by the 60bhp or 75bhp engines, while the first Carrera appeared offering 125mph from a 1498cc twin cam engine. The A was replaced by the 356B model in 1960 with higher bumpers, changed headlights, improved rear seating, larger brakes and rear window, but the same engine options until the Super 90 version which boasted 115mph. The Carrera 2 followed in 1962 boasting disc braking and a 130bhp powerplant. Two years later, the final incarnation was the 356C using the 1582cc engine, except for the 356SC which raised the output to 95bhp – the fastest standard 354. The last Carrera, the 2000GS, was by then yielding an impressive 130bhp. Maturing the modest VW concept to a high performance sports car took great technical skill given the engine's position. It took a lack of foresight to then nurture the same problems with the 911. The 356 dash layout is supremely functional, even pure, while the gear lever movement is a precision tool compared to the heavy and notchy 911s. Porsche lived just long enough to see what a true masterpiece he had created.

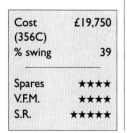

Cost	£19,750
(356C)	
% swing	39
Spares	★★★★
V.F.M.	★★★★
S.R.	★★★★★

SPECIFICATIONS

ENGINE: 1100cc – 1300cc – 1500cc – 1600cc – 2000cc
BHP: 40 – 130
FUEL: 35mpg
GEARBOX: 4 speed
SPEED: 84 – 125mph
BRAKES: Drum; Discs on C range cars & Carrera

SUSPENSION: Ind transverse torsion bars, swing axle
BODIES: 2 seater coupé, roadster, speedster, hard top
YEARS: 1949 – 65
PRODUCTION: 76,303 (all types)

The interior and dash went through several facelifts. The two-spoke steering wheel with the Porsche crest in the centre first appeared in 1953, replacing the three-spoke 'banjo' wheel.

MODEL GUIDE

PORSCHE 356 1949–55
Three engines sizes, split screen, original body style.

1100	1086cc
1300	1286cc
1300 Super	1290cc
1300A	1290cc
1500	1488cc – Rise to 55/60bhp
1500S	1488cc – Rise to 70bhp

PORSCHE 356A 1955–59
Smaller engines now overhead valves – while Carrera is double overhead

1300	1290cc
1300 Super	1290cc – Rise to 60bhp
1600	1582cc
1600 Super	1582cc – Rise to 75bhp
Carrera	1498cc
Carrera GT	1498cc – Rise to 110bhp
Carrera 1600	1588cc
Carrera 1600GS	1588cc – Rise to 115bhp

PORSCHE 356B 1959–63
Larger rear window, raised headlights, bumpers

1600	1585cc – 60bhp
1600 Super 75	1585cc – Rise to 75bhp
1600 Super 90	1582cc
Carrera 1600GT	1588cc
Carrera 2 2000 GS	1966cc

PORSCHE 356C 1963–65
Fastest standard 356 plus all round disc brakes

1600	1582cc
1600SC	1582cc – Rise to 95bhp
Carrera II 2000 GS	1966cc – Rise to 130bhp

RELATIONS

Apart from the original body styling, all the basic ingredients stemmed from the VW Beetle. It bred over 20 body variants and was followed by the conveyor belt of 911s.

BEST BUY

The car's addictive but be respectful of its handling. Excluding followers of the more specialist Carrera, Speedsters and the rare early 356s, there are three groups of enthusiasts: purists revere As, lovers of early style but more power like the Bs, while the refined C is the best all-rounder. (The subtle changes through the years make for great obsessional dating: the rear licence plate light went <u>underneath</u> in mid 1957!) Suspension and steering wear need watching, although the engine is long lasting. Rust is the traditional enemy, as are badly repaired cars. Buy from specialists or better still through the club and benefit from their knowledge of this great car.

The 'Continental' script was added to some coupés and cabriolets in 1955.

CATERHAM 7
THE PERFECT START

MANUFACTURER

CATERHAM CARS

The central flaw to competing for enjoyment, is that it means risking a cherished classic you've just spent years and too much money restoring. The alternative is to be rather more committed and invest in an outright competition machine. Colin Chapman's basic

1953 Mark 6 was a development of his early rough and ready trials models and provided a unique solution to the problem. With tax concessions favouring kit cars, he launched his street version – the famed Lotus Seven – with the Ford 100E engine in a lightweight tubular steel framed two seater.

Using various engines it flew, and was loved on and off the race track, but full-blooded competition cars, and his desire for sports car recognition, reduced Lotus' commitment to virtually nil. Their London sales agent Graham Nearn thought differently, however, and bought the manufacturing rights in order to expand the interest. Caterham Cars have shone in the task, continually refining and improving the cars mechanically without spoiling the traditional appearance. Lotus Sevens officially ran from 1957 to 1973, with Caterham then progressively improving models, introducing engines such as the JPE, which achieved a world record for production cars with 0–60 in 3.44 seconds. One mark race series were introduced and complete packages of car kit for road or track, includ-

ing race harness, fire equipment, everything. You are 70 hours' construction work from pure adrenaline. They're low, and fast, with pin-point precision handling and offer that overwhelming confidence of new machinery. A very rare instant of a true classic – with full pedigree, unspoilt lines and modern equipment.

RELATIONS

Pure breeding line back to that 1953 Lotus 6 with long list of engine suppliers.

BEST BUY

A period Lotus VI or Seven will have been kit-built and well used, so only buy if you can service and restore. Caterham continued the Lotus S4 briefly until reviving the previous classic – the S3 – which remains their production model. Unless you want a workshop exercise, simply buy new with all Mr Nearn's brilliant aids such as finance link-ups, and race starter packs, even Rent-a-Seven with refund if you go on to buy. Go.on, 2-litre 7HPC, 130mph …

Spares	★★★★
V.F.M.	★★
S.R.	★★★

SPECIFICATIONS

ENGINE: 1397cc	**SPEED:** 112mph
BHP: 103	**BRAKES:** Disc
FUEL: 40mpg	**BODIES:** Two seater sports
GEARBOX: 5 speed	**YEARS:** 1973 – to date
SUSPENSION: Ind coil/wishbone – coil/radius arms	**PRODUCTION:** Current

MANUFACTURER
JOHN COOPER

COOPER 500

THE ORIGINAL BEGINNER'S FORMULA

During the Second World War there was much talk about creating a new street level of competition and this bred many informal events. A group of West Country enthusiasts pressed on further and presented a set of rules for an official formula – Formula 500. These allowed up to 500cc, one gallon of fuel, four wheel braking, a handbrake and optional bodywork. Initial examples were powered by JAP and Vincent engines, and among the first enthusiasts was John Cooper, whose car took just five weeks to build. Gradually the 500 Club grew, with Cooper's machines gaining dominance. The 1948 British Grand Prix incorporated a 500 support race with 26 entrants. Europe followed, and such growth required sanctioning by the governing bodies, new rules and the status of F3. A motor racing version of go-karts the open cockpits and lightweight bodies (min. 500lbs) made their epic duels very appealing to watch and the cars very tempting to own. Many great drivers ventured up through this formula, and even the godfather of present-day Grand Prixs, Bernie Ecclestone, became an owner. Cooper's dominance continued, but always there was the search to improve, with engineer Francis Beart creating his own version of the 1953 Cooper VIII with differing handling and body profile. Racing grew in cost and status over the remainder of that decade before being squeezed out by the birth of Formula Junior. With the overall growth in historic racing there is renewed interest in any single seater, and while the numbers of cars are now reduced, prices are still held down until race classifications provide a competitive class

structure. I was invited to Goodwood to enjoy rare time with the newly restored and unique Beart VIIA special (above) recently bought by a knowledgable Peter Altenbach whose next task is to replace the current JAP engine with an original Norton. It's extraordinarily small and fragile looking, but actually beautifully light and responsive with braking to tempt you ever deeper into corners. Stirling Moss remembers his eight Beart car wins in 1954 and anyone who has ever watched 500s racing knows just how much excitement they generate.

RELATIONS

The formula's essence was anything goes, though inevitably they used motorcycle engines.

BEST BUY

Brilliant progression from motor bikes or small DIY restoration. Present absence of competitive race class helps prices and less threatening hill climbs always available as economical christening – exactly where the formula came in.

SPECIFICATIONS

ENGINE: 498cc	**SUSPENSION:** Transverse leaf
BHP: 75	**SPEED:** 95mph
FUEL: 15mpg (Methanol)	**BODIES:** Single seater
GEARBOX: 4 speed	**YEARS:** 1953
BRAKES: Drum	**PRODUCTION:** NA

Spares	★★★
V.F.M.	★★★★
S.R.	★★★

LAMBORGHINI ESPADA
A FORGOTTEN ITALIAN TREASURE

MANUFACTURER
LAMBORGHINI

The 1960s fashion for 2+2 seating caused manufacturers many headaches trying to adapt existing two seat sports cars to fit the famous pair of legless midgets. The rather sad sight of misshaped cars such as the E Type Jaguar 2 + 2 struggling to maintain original 2 seater imagery, has helped to cast a shadow over the concept. Lamborghini, however, managed to achieve a stunning 2 + 2 model. Indeed the Espada eventually turned into the second best selling Lamborghini of all time – behind the famed Countach. The original plan was to base the car upon the spectacular transverse-engined Miura and a Bertone prototype, called the Marzel, was displayed at the 1967 Geneva Motor Show. Space was created by halving the Miura's V12 and using large gullwinged doors. The car proved too heavy and too slow, and a semi monocoque design was used instead. Most of the mechanical parts came from the Lamborghini Islero, itself a development of the 400GT. This included their glorious V12 which must be one of the motoring world's finest engines.

Many of the prototype Marzel ideas were incorporated in the stunning 1968 Espada which turned heads around the world. I still remember my first sight of one, particularly from that overhead view. It looked long but was actually just four inches longer than other Lamborghinis and virtually the same as the present Honda Accord. It was wide, however, at just over 6 ft and extremely low, all exaggerating the feeling of interior space. Four leather bucket seats, extraordinary visibility, and good luggage space were complemented by a long list of items such as power

steering, optional automatic, air conditioning. The engine revs into the gods, creating sounds from an enthusiast's dreams and is silky smooth – all the way beyond 150mph. It underlined just how clumsy others were at approaching that 2 + 2 market.

RELATIONS

Earlier front-engined Lamborghini V12 engines and mechanics married to the development of Bertone's Marzel prototype.

BEST BUY

Well treated engines and gearboxes last well and all too common oil leaks actually preserve the chassis. Traditional Italian rust is a big worry so take an expert with you and steer clear of troublesome automatics. Good brightwork is valuable. Series I – III saw improving interior and power. Few true supercars will ever combine practical space, powerful, forgiving engines and awesome good looks as successfully as the Espada.

Cost	£21,000
% swing	-4
Spares	★★
V.F.M.	★★
S.R.	★★★

SPECIFICATIONS

ENGINE: 3929cc
BHP: 325 – 350
FUEL: 14–16mpg
GEARBOX: 5 speed
SUSPENSION: Ind wishbone & coil all round
BRAKES: Disc
SPEED: 155–160mph
BODIES: 2 door, 4 seater coupé.
YEARS: 1968– 78
PRODUCTION: 1217

MANUFACTURER

FERRARI

Enter the world of fantasy, the mythological state of Ferrari ownership, if not the possession of the 308 specifically. Period Italian cars rust furiously, quality varies widely, spares are expensive, and the existence of a great competition past is no guarantee of anything except status. Did the MG's sporting heritage bias your MG 1100 purchase, the troublesome Alfetta appear wise because of their legendary GP cars? If you are investing good money try balancing logic with your heartbeat. Ironically, the 308GT4 is interesting because its 1973 body styling followed fashion not tradition. The net result is the least-loved production Ferrari and consequently one of the very best for value. There is no doubt this solitary Bertone/Ferrari adventure lacked the visual grace and romance of Pininfarina cars, but the decision ought to be seen in context. The wedge form and slabbed panels were forward-thinking then – think of the fashionable Fiat X1/9 ('72), or Lotus Esprit ('76); with a brand new V8 engine Ferrari were looking to the future. The car itself followed in the shadow of the Dino 246 which was losing ground to the new US emission laws, but used its multi–tubed chassis, transverse mounted mid-ships engine position, and similar all independent suspension. The 308GT4 was badged as a Dino, although its 155mph performance truthfully lifted it above second division Ferrari status. Poor American reaction to the car led to Ferrari badges being added and by 1978 these were factory-fitted on all cars. The important change was the new all aluminium 255bhp, 3 litre, quad cam engine, actually a descendant of the 1964 Grand Prix Ferrari 158

which gave John Surtees the World Championship. Brilliantly flexible, this gem of an engine can pull in 5th from 25mph yet take 6.9 seconds to propel you from 0–60 in anger. It also used toothed cam belts rather than traditional chains, thereby reducing engine noise. It has a functional period dashboard, but the plus two seating has the standard limitations of the genre, and some customers had the area carpeted for additional storage.

RELATIONS

Ex-F1 engine, original Bertone bodywork, many other elements from the Dino 246.

BEST BUY

Always remember it's just a 1970s Italian car with huge rust potential, poor wiring and perhaps an abused engine. The difference isn't the badge – it's the restoration bills. If you find a decent one, then it's undoubtedly the perfect first Ferrari, excellent value and virtually a supercar mechanical package.

SPECIFICATIONS

ENGINE: 2926cc	**SUSPENSION:** Ind wishbone/
BHP: 255	coil – all round
FUEL: 19mpg	**BODIES:** 2 door coupé
GEARBOX: 5 speed	**YEARS:** 1973 – 80
BRAKES: Disc	**PRODUCTION:** 2,826
SPEED: 154mph	

Cost	£20,000
% swing	22.5
Spares	★
V.F.M.	★★★
S.R.	★★

GORDON-KEEBLE

WORLD-BEATING PROMISE – UNFULFILLED

MANUFACTURER
GORDON-KEEBLE

Sometimes a car appears which is intrinsically right. The E-Type Jaguar, or perhaps the new Aston Martin DB7, lay claim to classic status at first sight, because our visual senses are the first to make judgement. Even if subsequent handling proves tricky, the chances are we still view the car as a star. When in 1964 the first (production) Gordon-Keebles reached customers that same sense of authenticity prevailed. The two door Bertone-styled coupé was a masterpiece of glass, slender window frames and slippery bodywork housing four-seater luxury and good luggage space. And under the long sloping bonnet was a serious American Chevrolet V8 engine. It seems hard to imagine how such a model could fail – but fail it did.

John Gordon had previously been managing director of a company making the similar if smaller Peerless GTs (later briefly re–born as a Warwick). His vision for his own Gordon GT was Italian flair, British strength and American muscle. The complex space frame chassis was designed by Jim Keeble and the body by Giorgetto Giugiaro at Bertone. The initial steel prototype was shown at the 1960 Geneva Show causing great excitement, but a year past, the company folded and another formed, before the first Gordon-Keeble rolled from the new factory in Hampshire. The production cars used a fibreglass body, a 5356cc Chevrolet engine with four barrel progressive choke, Carter carb and Girling disc brakes all round. Suspension was fully independent and the package weighed just 28cwt. The 280bhp available gave startling acceleration figures and a top

speed just short of 140mph. Under-priced, and with demand outstripping production the company folded after a year. Two months later another company took over but just six cars were made, while 12 months on, a US relaunch also faltered. An enthusiasts' car, it failed only through missing business expertise.

RELATIONS

Original British chassis, Italian body styling and American Chevrolet V8. It also owed some concept origins to the much smaller TR engined Peerless GT.

BEST BUY

Clearly with a car as rare as this it's more a matter of finding one. There is a good UK club who have records of all the cars produced so even if you found one privately, much would be learned about its background by checking with them first. The fibreglass bodies have greatly helped the preservation of these beautiful cars. The initial suffix was GK1 and the later six car run used GK1 iT.

Cost	£21,500
% swing	-1.5
Spares	★★
V.F.M.	★★
S.R.	★★★★

SPECIFICATIONS

ENGINE: 5355cc
BHP: 300
FUEL: 15mpg
GEARBOX: 4 speed
BRAKES: Disc
SPEED: 138mph

SUSPENSION: Ind coil/wishbone – Watts linkage & De Dion axle
BODIES: 2 door grand touer
YEARS: 1964–67
PRODUCTION: 99

MANUFACTURER
FERRARI

We tend to think that the great marques, like movie stars, are immune from everyday commercial pressures, but this is not so. Rivals such as Aston Martin and Lamborghini secured good market shares of the 1960s GT trade, and Ferrari needed a seductive 2 + 2 to regain lost ground. In 1967 their 365GT 2 + 2 was launched at the Paris Motor Show and boasted fully independent suspension and considerable attention to interior silence and comfort. Sales were encouraging, although few reached the USA, and in 1972 it was followed by the four cam 356GT4 2 + 2 which was longer, wider and luxuriously appointed. By now Fiat had invested in Ferrari, easing design and production finances, but rival +2 cars such as the Espada and Maserati's Indy had joined the battle. Ferrari retaliated in 1976 by launching a further improved version of the 356GT4 called the 400GT with striking new bodystyling by Pininfarina successfully slimming a necessarily large Ferrari. Among the more controversial features was the American Cadillac automatic gearbox – an unthinkable addition in the minds of many purists. The fact four seat executive expresses were ideal candidates for such equipment and the fact that both Rolls Royce and Jaguar were using the box all missed the traditionalists. However, it sold surprisingly well, and in 1979 it became the 400i with the inclusion of Bosch fuel injection Revisions in 1982 improved the interior, power, self levelling rear suspension and even provided dual air conditioning – all added attractions to this 150mph dream. Finally, in 1985 it went to 4943cc, received another interior refit and a greater

luggage area as the 412. Although purists consider it unloved, the +2 range was actually the longest Ferrari production run, ending in 1989.

RELATIONS

It started with the 1964 500 Superfast, through the 365GT 2 + 2, the 365GTC/4 and the 365GT4 2 + 2 – the actual 400 range, like all the others, was Pininfarina-designed. The engine was the classic 60 degree V12 which powered all their masterpieces and optional automatic was from the Cadillac.

BEST BUY

Most examples have either found appreciative homes or are unloved, bargain Ferraris on some non-specialist forecourt. Don't even think about them, as restoration is painfully expensive. Contact a recognised Ferrari dealer or the excellent owners club and take your time. While some Ferraris belong on posters this is really usable – though its one disgrace is fuel consumption of around 10mpg.

SPECIFICATIONS

ENGINE: 4,23cc; 4943cc	**SUSPENSION:** Ind A arm/coil all round
BHP: 315 – 340	**SPEED:** 150mph
FUEL: 9 – 12mpg	**BODIES:** 2 door, 4 seat coupé
GEARBOX: 5 speed manual & 3 speed automatic	**YEARS:** 1976 – 89
BRAKES: Discs	**PRODUCTION:** 2,386

Cost	£23,000
% swing	5.5
Spares	★★
V.F.M.	★★★
S.R.	★★

ALFA SPIDER

IT'S ABOUT BECOMING AN INDIVIDUAL AGAIN

MANUFACTURER

ALFA ROMEO

I confess a bias. I think the new Spider and GTV models are wonderful and I celebrate a great sporting marque reclaiming its position in the motoring world. We have endured far too many instances of great names being reduced to badges on dismal cars. Fiat gave Lancia its head to take back the high ground in rallying, they left Ferrari free to chase the Grand Prix crowd, while Alfa has been encouraged to regain its sporting pedigree. After decades of their old Spider, this brand new car enters an increasingly competitive world. Rivals range from Mazda's MX–5, the MGF, the BMW Z3 and M Roadster to the Fiat Barchetta and forthcoming models such as the expensive Porsche Boxster and the first of Mercedes' SLK cars. There is no doubt this is to be the most publicized automotive battleground and although prices and technical specifications are relevant, glamour and class play a disproportionate role. This is the very area in which Alfa flourish and their intention to remain 'style kings' was clear when they showed their Proteo Project at the Geneva show. The wedge-like body with a tapered front is an approach that can be seen in the competition, but the upsweep towards the tail provides a strong identity. Based on the 164 V6 even the original drawings revealed advances – it read 'Alfa Romeo 164 Spider/Coupé 4WD 4WS'.

Though some aspects were dropped, or held back for future announcement, the production Spider and GTV have stuck boldly to the stunning Pininfarina styling (originally in collaboration with the manufacturer's Arese Style Centre) and win hearts and admiration at every sighting. Both these models have been launched with the two litre Twin Spark 16V engine which uses two spark plugs per cylinder and creates 150bhp, 130mph and comfortable 27mpg. Latest ABS, high ratio sports steering, new multi-link suspension, safety features – all the toys for combat with rivals. However, the car is sold when you climb into the cockpit, face a dashboard of individually cowled instruments, turn the key and drive.

This is one of the true classic engines, providing music and performance in equal measure, and with a flat torque curve, it's no trouble undertaking day-to-day city use.

Floor the pedal and listen to those twin cams as you dart between 4500 and 7000 revs and drink in the glories of everything streaming past that distinctive Alfa nose and its man-eating snake from the Visconti crest. There will be more expensive rivals,

Spares	★★★★
V.F.M.	★★★★
S.R.	★★★★

SPECIFICATIONS

ENGINE: 1970cc		**SUSPENSION:** Ind wishbone/	
BHP: 150		coil – Multi link/coil	
FUEL: 27mpg		**BODIES:** 2 door Spider: GTV	
GEARBOX: 5 speed		coupé	
BRAKES: Disc		**YEARS:** 1995 – to date	
SPEED: 122mph		**PRODUCTION:** Current	

Promise fulfilled; the final production model proved close to the Alfa concept car, (opposite, inset) though four-wheel drive and four-wheel steering have not appeared – yet.

faster ones, but probably none which make you feel so special. A sports car is about being an individual and no manufacturer in the world can better claim that title than Alfa.

RELATIONS

Pininfarina body styling, the 2 litre Twin Spark Alfa engine and 164 components. Is it claiming too much to list the '66 1600 Duetto, the '68 1750 Veloce, the '68 1300 Junior and the '71 2000 Veloce?

BEST BUY

It is too early as yet to assess, though in your eagerness don't get caught with poor lhd conversions impatiently created during the wait for the UK launch. The GTV Coupé, though less glamorous, is as stunning and by its very nature slightly more rigid. (It would be absurd to talk of a 'future classic' in terms of investment potential.) Interestingly, Alfa UK expected the majority of new orders to be for the Coupé, but in fact the Spider held its own.

N171YJH

AUSTIN-HEALEY 100/4

A SLICE OF MOTORING HISTORY

MANUFACTURER

AUSTIN-HEALEY

The Austin-Healey 100/4 is the epitome of a classic sports car, although its evolution owed much to chance. Donald Healey built sporting cars with Riley engines but knew they were due to be phased out. He also knew that there was a gap in the market, particularly the American market, with a niche between the Jaguar XK 120 and the MG waiting to be filled. Healey wanted to produce the first 100mph car that was affordable by the average motorist. His friend Leonard Lord, chairman of Austin, had produced a failure, the Austin Atlantic, and was left with an underused factory and components. That engine started life as a pre–war six cylinder range for light trucks, and re–appeared as a four cylinder for the Champ Jeep, before being enlarged for the abortive Atlantic. Donald Healey, his son Geoff and Barrie Bilbie worked secretly from home, combining new car ideas and the spare Austin engine. Healey insisted that the the frame had to be as rigid as possible, and the car had excellent roadholding for its time. The chief design problem was in building a car light enough to perform well, but strong enough to cope with the heavy mechanical components inherited from the Atlantic. Just two chassis and a single car

were in existence as the 1952 Earls Court International Motor Show approached, and the one car was so late being finished it missed the pre-publicity. However, it was an instant success. The New York Motor Show voted it Car of the Year, the Miami World's Fair gave it the Grand Premier Award, and over 3000 orders swamped their modest factory. An astute Leonard Lord stepped in and it became the Austin-Healey – the rest as they say is history. Lord's intervention instantly cut the car's price by £50 as a consequence of mass-production. In 1954 Healey developed 50 lightweight competition versions called the 100S (Sebring), and within a month the first examples scored a 1–2–3 in a Sebring Series littered with D Type Jaguars and Ferraris. The 100M (Le Mans) followed, with a modified engine, suspension and a louvred bonnet which maintained the sporting imagination until the BMC Competition department grasped the Healey 3000. The initial 100/4 examples were designated BN1, switching to BN2 in 1955 with the change to a four speed A90 Westminster box. In 1956 the six cylinder Westminster engine replacement became the BN4.

Cost	£17,250
% swing	-2.5
Spares	★★★★
V.F.M.	★★
S.R.	★★★

SPECIFICATIONS

ENGINE: 2660cc
BHP: 90
FUEL: 25mpg
GEARBOX: 3 speed + O/D on 2nd/3rd: 4 Speed
BRAKES: Drum
SUSPENSION: Ind wishbone/ coil – Live axle/half elliptic
SPEED: 102mph
BODIES: 2 door sports
YEARS: 1952 – 1956
PRODUCTION: 14,012

This car was slower, heavier, a 2 + 2 and not popular – so BMC reverted to two seats, a power increase and BN6 status.

The car I tried was Peter Banham's beautifully prepared Historic Rally 100/4 with S specifications, (this page and below left) although a partially opened bonnet dispersed the engine's incredible heat rather than the S's louvres. Driving such a classic is the height of motoring pleasure: the car drives beautifully and looks terrific..The engine torque is so great that virtually everything can be achieved in top gear. Change down, floor the throttle, and it stirs the latent beast in both car and driver. Healey's initial aim was to produce 'a very fast everyday car with genuine sporting characteristics, capable of 100mph, which would also be exceptionally cheap and easy to maintain'; he succeeded on every count.

RELATIONS

Original Healey bodywork, Austin Atlantic engine with the Westminster gearbox and the famed Healey 3000s to follow from 1959.

BEST BUY

Solid and well built, with long lasting mechanical parts, the main problem is rust generally around the floors and chassis areas. Replacement panels are tricky and any serious restoration work is likely to requiring expert hands. However, good ones last and last while giving enormous pleasure to driver and admirers. Watch out for claims of S or M Types – there are many conversions. The early BN1s are excellent value.

AC ACE
THE PUREST OF SPORTS CARS

MANUFACTURER
AC CARS

One of our panel of 'Car of the Year' judges, (above) Simon Taylor in his long-nosed Ace 2.6.

'The Great British Sportscar' is a phrase grossly overused by all the leading magazines. We are, however, blessed with both our pre-and post-war sports car legacies – the Morgans, Healeys, the value-for-money Jaguars and yet, for me, the purest celebration of the British sports car is the 1950s AC Ace. It may have grown up into a rough and ready supercar thanks to Carol Shelby, but the initial Ace captured a sense of agility, with its long sloping bonnet and haunched rear quarters, all the classic signals of a true sports car within a body of supreme grace. With the lowered nose of the 1961 Ford-powered version, the Ace was truly beautiful. However, a new AC was needed as both AC's boss, William Hurlock and the Buckland Tourer were nearing retirement. Next door to the body shop, a young racing engineer, John Tojeiro, was preparing cars which were regular winners in British sports car racing. One customer had commis-

sioned a two seater body based upon the 1949 Ferrari 166 Barchetta, and he was persuaded to show this example to AC who fell in love, bought the car and the licence to manufacture. Tojeiro immediately built the first example for the 1953 London Motor Show – using the 40-year-old AC two-litre engine. Reactions were excellent – the rare all-independent suspension and fine handing were thanks to Tojeiro's competition experience, and a simple ladder-type chassis saved sufficient weight to allow a well trimmed interior. The production version appeared in mid-1954, with a subtly strengthened chassis and minor body modifications. With superb roadholding and handling, it set new standards at a time when no other British sports car had all-independent suspension. It weighed only 16.5 cwt and could easily top 100mph. Experts agreed that the car's compact yet powerful body looked even better than the Ferrari which had inspired it. As its status grew, it needed a new engine, and so AC began fitting the two-litre Bristol engine developed from the BMW 328. This eased racing developments and one race driver was

Cost	£31,250
% swing	-15
Spares	★★★
V.F.M.	★★
S.R.	★★★★

ACLAND & TABOR LTD.
WELWYN BY-PASS
HERTS.
Tel : WELWYN 481-2-3

AC BRISTOL

A.C. "ACE BRISTOL" 2-Seater Sports

A.C. Cars Limited in cooperation with the Bristol Cars Limited offer the well-known 6-cylinder Bristol Engine, complete with Gearbox as an optional extra, both in the Ace and Aceca Classis.

A.C. CARS LTD   SURREY
THAMES DITTON   ENGLAND

SPECIFICATIONS

(Ace engine : Bristol engine : Ford engine)

ENGINE: 1991cc – 1971cc – 2553cc
BHP: 75; 125; 170
FUEL: 21–25mpg
GEARBOX: 4 speed
BRAKES: Drum: Front disc after 1957

SUSPENSION: Ind Transverse leaf/wishbone
SPEED: 103mph/ 120/ 130mph
BODIES: 2 door sports; coupés
YEARS: 1953–63 : 1956–63 : 1961–63
PRODUCTION: 223 : 463 : 37

Ken Rudd who drew the best from the Bristol unit, and then inspired the factory to install his tuned Ford Zephyr engine. Bristol switched production to an American V8 powerplant and AC turned to Rudd's idea thus creating the 2.6 litre Ace. Its short stroke permitted the lowering of the bonnet to the classic position, but very few of these supreme versions were made before Shelby squeezed in a 4.2 V8 and caused such excitement AC had to drop all cars to meet the Cobra demand.

RELATIONS

The body was Ferrari-inspired, and initially the 1919 AC-designed 2 litre engine was used. A BMW-influenced Bristol engine followed, ending up with the 2.5 Ford Zephyr unit, before the Ace gave birth to the powerful V8 Cobras.

BEST BUY

Styling remained constant, front discs came after 1957, and the last cars had the lowered noses; but the real deciding factor is the engine. The AC unit is desirable, the Bristol eager to work hard, while the fastest, the Ford, naturally has spares more readily

available. Coupé bodies were called Aceca and if you're tempted, a quarter of the Aces produced were right hand drive. Despite the age of the cars, many have only passed through a few owners, production numbers were so low, and most are known – so use the club or specialists to check histories.

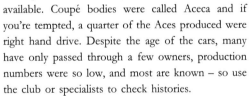

The traditional single cam six (above) was fitted to 223 of the Aces. Tony Bancroft's car, (left) with 1950s competition modifications – short exhaust, bonnet air scoop and wing vents – has the Bristol engine.

FORD SCORPIO WHY....?

MANUFACTURER

FORD

Ford's ability to create memorable small cars is legendary, with its distinctive 105E Anglia, the Capri, the Cortina, the Escort – even interim models such as the Consul Capri and Classic conceived and marketed with flair. However, for some extraordinary reason they appear incapable of creating a flagship model with any real style or class – surely de rigueur for the executive market. One can only assume the current Granada-based Scorpio remains in production thanks to car hire firms and major fleet deals where hapless executives are trapped into participation. The awesome Japanese car industry has undertaken major surveys of successful western body styling and takes very seriously the `facial' expression caused by frontal

SPECIFICATIONS

ENGINE: 1,998cc – 2,935cc – 2,500cc (D)
BHP: 115; 136; 150
FUEL: 18 – 27mpg
GEARBOX: 5 speed; 4 speed automatic
BRAKES: Disc

SUSPENSION: Ind Macpherson strut/wishbone – semi trailing/coil
SPEED: 120mph – 140mph
BODIES: 4 door saloon, Estate
YEARS: 1994 – in production
PRODUCTION: N/A

treatments. It is no accident Mazda analysed an Austin-Healey Frogeye before arriving at the contented MX–5 – both cars offer a friendly impression and both sold in huge numbers. The crude and

Vauxhall can do it, with the Vauxhall Carlton (right) Jaguar can of course do it, to the manor born. Why not the parent company, the mighty Ford? The Scorpio, despite its sad-eyed looks and smartend up trim, was a 1985 Granada. In its defence, Ford can point to its penetration of the depressed UK executive car market; and outstanding sales in Italy and elsewhere.

depressed Scorpio front end styling somehow reflects both the car's embarrassment and the potential customer's feelings – torn between Ford's legendary reliability and dreading onlookers' sympathies, a desperate rictus sets in. There are options to please virtually the entire population's taste and many praiseworthy technological advances. The dark and excessive luxuries of the interior remain just this side of poor taste and it's got leg room for the tallest would–be key executive. But none of it can ever spell personal prestige within a body looking like an overglazed model kit. In 1964 BMC thought top quality trimmings and a Rolls-Royce engine would move mountains – the Vanden Plas 4 litre R sold barely 7,000.

Vauxhall have delivered finned Cresta PA's to purposeful Senators, Jaguar/Daimler journeyed from glorious Mk II 3.8's to the XJ range, the BMW output, Mercedes too, even the much underrated Alfa 164 – all the major players appear to understand the need to balance appearance along with the individual manufactured ingredients. If you want to arrive at a prestige meeting who wouldn't rather appear from something like an XJ than from a car that looks as if it's suffering from a severe head cold? Ford's lack of flagship body styling isn't new, for the Mark III Zephyr, the slab sided Mk IV Executive and the earlier Granadas all lacked finesse.

I confess to a brilliant through–the–night journey in a 24v Scorpio and the Cosworth influences certainly bring out the best in Ford engineering … but fortunately it was dark and I could walk away. American imposed design ideals work no better in Europe than similar attempts from Japan. Successful

individuals wanting a car to reflect their position aren't going to be seduced by pairs of sagging head and tail lights – even if they do happen to be revolutionary poly–ellipsoidal projecting.

BRISTOL 404
A CONNOISSEUR'S DB4 GT

MANUFACTURER
BRISTOL

Pace SAAB, aerospace engineering works to tolerances beyond any mass production car's dreams, and the Bristol has a genuine aerospace background. In 1945 the Bristol Aeroplane Co. tried to retain their workforce and use redundant hangar space by building cars. The 1947 Bristol 400 was based upon the pre–war BMW 328. An airfield for testing and a private wind tunnel aided development, and in 1949 the 401 appeared, mechanically the same, but with a new lightweight alloy streamlined body, tube framing and little superfluous trim. Beautifully built, the 402 convertible version appeared later in the same year, followed in 1953 by the 403 looking much the same, but with increased power, braking and a new gearbox. The series became heavier with the four-door 405 and again with the 406 which used additional bhp to maintain pride. After this the Bristol range moved to the big 250bhp Chrysler V8 and the custom-built tourer reputation was established. However, between 1953 and 1955, Bristol's spirit of adventure led them to cut the wheelbase from 9ft 6in to 8ft and build a beautiful aluminium two-door body over an ash frame, incor-

porating a one-piece bonnet and a nose deliberately inspired by the Brabazon aircraft. The 404 was introduced at the '53 London Motor Show. This was Bristol's answer to the DB4GT six years before Aston produced it. With two true seats, a sloping roofline, and tiny tail fins, it was capable of 110mph in considerable luxury. It was powered by their excellent two litre engine with triple carbs and a delightful gearbox, and every part was manufactured by Bristol. This is a connoisseur's classic, rare, and finely made.

RELATIONS

The initial 400 was basically a rebodied 328 BMW, developing through to the 406 before turning to V8 Chrysler power from 407 to present day.

BEST BUY

Body rust is not a huge problem, although the concealed ash frame members need checking for rot. The chassis is hardy, and most aspects are reliable. Bristol know about most cars, and are very approachable.

Cost	£32,750
% swing	5.5
Spares	★★★★
V.F.M.	★★★
S.R.	★★★

SPECIFICATIONS

ENGINE: 1971cc	**SUSPENSION:** Ind Transerse
BHP: 105 – 125	leaf – Torsion Bar/Live axlel
FUEL: 20 – 25mpg	**BODIES:** 2 seater coupé
GEARBOX: 4 speed	**YEARS:** 1953 – 55
BRAKES: Drum	**PRODUCTION:** 52 (disputed)
SPEED: 105mph – 110mph	

MANUFACTURER
FERRARI

It turns heads, quickens hearts, prompts dreams and desires just outside your reach – well maybe. You sit in traffic staring down the bonnet of your Merc diesel estate and flirt with a straight swap for one of these stunning scarlet machines. The 308 GTB was in some ways inferior to the technically similar 308GT4, but the seduction of the near perfect Pininfarina body fuses with Ferrari legend. A Porsche is sold to us through advertising and style makers – Ferrari really is different, for when did you last see them advertising in your colour supplement?. They've made their business competition and sporting cars and they simply rely upon you climbing into a Ferrari cockpit and absorbing the decades of experience. The 308 has impeccable handling, responsive controls without ever feeling flimsy. The four cam alloy engine doesn't howl like some, but you know it's working and when you floor the pedal and grab the gear lever and the car feels ready for anything. The car was launched in 1975 in the shadow of the poorly received Bertone-bodied GT4, but the new version was immediately praised for its stunning bodywork. So critical is the combination of implied power and grace that the same car's two bodies caused completely different reactions.. The 308 GTB was joined two years later by a Targa topped GTS primarily to please the appreciative American market. The four Weber carbs were replaced by Bosch fuel injection between 1980–82, losing performance but in 1982 a four valve per cylinder 308GTB Qv model restored reputations with its 240bhp. An upgraded GTB/GTS – the 328, appeared for four years before Ferrari moved on. These are Ferraris to dream about; beaten up or unloved examples are affordable, but if you are ever going to give yourself that prancing horse key ring – this is the car.

RELATIONS

Spiritual descendant of the loved 248 Dino, and actual development of the 1973 Bertoned bodied 2 + 2 308 GT4. Matured into the 328 and then the V8 was used in the extremely rare and exciting 288GTO

BEST BUY

Fibreglass bodies were used in the first year – 150 for the UK. The 308 was in production for an entire decade, although there are only 2000 right hand drive cars. Avoid the fuel injection version and the Targa GTS are 20 per cent more expensive. Naturally there's rust and other important points, but really it's about budgets. Get experienced help and always, always remember the most important asset is a good service history.

SPECIFICATIONS

ENGINE: 2926cc	**SUSPENSION:** Ind double
BHP: 240 – 255	wishbone coil all round
FUEL: 20mpg	**BODIES:** 2 door coupé; targa
GEARBOX: 5 speed	**YEARS:** 1975 – 1985
BRAKES: Disc	**PRODUCTION:** 19,555
SPEED: 154mph	

Cost	£27,500
% swing	-0.5
Spares	★★
V.F.M.	★★
S.R.	★★★★

JAGUAR V12 E-TYPE

COMFORT AND PEDIGREE

MANUFACTURER
JAGUAR

The impact of the 1961 E-Type at the Geneva Motor show is hard to over-estimate. I was at art school and we all sat around in the common room just staring at the magazine pictures – it was stunning and probably fired more dreams than any other post-war car. An impressive competition tradition with the C- and D-Types, and a near-exhausted era of XK sports cars inevitably set the stage for something new, but the brilliance of the concept leant heavily upon an aviation man, Malcolm Sayer, who was inclined to sketch design ideas onto anything – even the walls. The monocoque construction of the D-Type was a starting point, while the need for increased power was resolved by the inspired decision to use the excellent V12 engine from the still-born prototype competition XJ13. Sayer's aircraft background drove his interest in aerodynamics and he was even known to stop en route to the MIRA test track to buy sticky tape and balls of wool to study wind movement from a tandem car. Thus the sleek E-Type cut through the air – urged forward by the 272bhp V12 at speeds virtually twice most equivalently priced road cars. The initial 3.8 litre engine came from the XK150S with a

SPECIFICATIONS

ENGINE: 5343cc	**SUSPENSION:** Ind wishbone/Torsion bar – Ind coil/wishbone
BHP: 272	
FUEL: 16mpg	
GEARBOX: 4 speed	**BODIES:** 2 door 2 + 2 roadster: coupé
BRAKES: Disc	
SPEED: 146mph	**YEARS:** 1971 – 75
	PRODUCTION: 15,290

period Moss gearbox and narrow wheel tracks. It leaked, didn't stop, but was agile and sparse – it's the purist's dream machine. As the 4.2 Series II it became compromised and middle-aged as it tried to accommodate US regulations. A 9 inch extended wheelbase offered the 2 + 2 configuration. For some, the Series III V12 was the model's dotage, while for others it became the most desirable of them all. Everyone agreed that a serious hike in performance and prestige was needed and the V12 was shoehorned into the extended +2 wheelbase, along with wider wheels, flared wings, power steering, automatic option, and a visual meanness to match the 145mph performance. From the pure sports car Series I, it crawled through Series II to emerge as a stunning Grand Tourer. It broke a pre-war tradition by making an accredited 'real sports car' comfortable.

RELATIONS

Spiritually born of the XK120, through C- and D-Types to the Series I E-Type, the V12 E-Type had a

Cost	£31,500
(V12 Roadster)	
% swing	-4
Spares	★★★★
V.F.M.	★★
S.R.	★★★★★

The E-Type was introduced in March 1961, replacing the XK150 which had been in production since May 1957. It is easy to forget that both cars were similarly powered.

The V12 was a quantunm leap forward from the original 3.8 and 4.2. The four cam V12-engined racing XJ13 of 1966 was a technically advanced design scotched by BMC amalgamtion.; but it provided the 5.3-litre ohc power for the 1971 III Series E-Type (and the XJ12 saloon in the following year).

perfect pedigree, with body styling from the E2A prototype and a legacy for the XJ.

BEST BUY

This is where the romance ends. Experts find diagnosing trouble within the complex body very hard, so don't even consider the solitary 'bargain' on a general dealer's forecourt. They probably look good, but opening the bonnet may reveal a can of mechanical worms. Use the strengths of the owners' club, or specialists such as XK Engineering who are ex–factory. Buy the best you can afford and remember coupés are cheaper than roadsters. All are expensive on fuel, parts and restoration, but owning a good one will make you feel pretty special.

MASERATI BORA
A FORGOTTEN VINTAGE

MANUFACTURER
MASERATI

During the 1960s, the fashion in fast cars became increasingly mid-engined. This presented difficult compromises for designers juggling lost luggage, seating and rear vision with desired high performance and handling. It also created some cars that looked seriously fast. The forgotten personification of this breed is the Maserati Bora. The company were main players in World Sports Car championships until withdrawing in 1957. Their Works car, the mighty V8 450S, was the spiritual ancestor of the Bora, although the intervening years saw action for the famous sports/racer the Birdcage Maserati and the F1 Cooper Maseratis. Citroën took control of Maserati in the mid-sixties, bringing fresh investment and requirements leading to the powerful and smooth V8 which was destined for the new mid-engined supercar. Giulio Alfier, who was involved with the classic F1 Maserati 250F, devised a complex monocoque two seater coupé with all the main elements mounted on an isolated frame. There was no pretence of 2 + 2 seating, but reasonable luggage storage up front, all independent suspension, disc braking and styling by Giugiaro who had created the classic front-engined Ghibli and the dramatic mid-engined De Tomaso Mangusta. The V8

engine had chain-driven twin cams per bank, alloy block, a bank of four carbs hurling 310bhp towards the tarmac via a five-speed gearbox. The advantage over rivals was the engine's forgiving nature, and thanks to impressive flexibility it can negotiate most conditions in a single intermediate gear. Understated, classy, but just waiting to fly, this 165mph supercar offers a great deal.

RELATIONS

Body by Giugiaro at Ital Design, with V8 engine rooted in the racing 450S, and some components such as the pressured braking system from Citroën. The 1975 V6 Merak SS was a Bora derivative.

BEST BUY

The car barely changed over its production life as the slight increase in engine capacity merely off set American emission control modifications. The chief enemy is rust, and apart from obvious body areas check suspension and engine mounts.

Cost	£35,500
% swing	63
Spares	★★
V.F.M.	★★★★★
S.R.	★★★

SPECIFICATIONS

ENGINE: 4719cc; 4930cc	**SUSPENSION:** Ind wishbone/coil all round
BHP: 310 – 320	
FUEL: 14mpg	**BODIES:** 2 seater coupé
GEARBOX: 5 speed	**YEARS:** 1971 – 78
BRAKES: Disc	**PRODUCTION:** 571
SPEED: 160–165mph	

MANUFACTURER
JAGUAR

8835 PX

JAGUAR XK150
THE DISCREET E-TYPE

During the post-war recovery period William Lyons needed a new engine to power a fresh range of family cars. Starting with XA, theory became trial engines by version XF, finally maturing into the XK design. The new cars would be the Mk IV through X, and the now revered Mk II saloons. As part of development 200 aluminum sports cars were built as test beds based upon a cut-down Mk V saloon chassis. Using the new 3447cc, 160bhp XK engine, a staggering 120mph was achieved, thus creating the XK 120's name. The impact of this car at the 1948 London Motor Show was colossal, and orders flooded in defying notions of only 200 cars. In 1950 a slightly altered steel production version emerged with further performance options for the Fixed Head, Drophead and Roadster bodywork. In 1953 the XK140 was unveiled with improved cabin space by moving the engine forward, rack and pinion steering, redesigned grille, an uprated engine and an automatic gearbox option. By 1957 the ultimate XK was ready. The 150 enjoyed sleek modern lines, a refined grille and light treatment, a single wraparound windscreen and, thanks to development in the competition C-Type, the XK150 became the first production car with disc brakes. Fixed and Dropheads initially matched the old 140 power, but in the second year came the Roadster and the S versions with new head, triple carbs, 250bhp and over 130mph which was approaching Ferrari performance for half the price. The final 1959 versions used a 3.8 engine developing 220bhp with 265bhp for the S option. It had wind-up windows, limited slip diff (S only) mohair hood

design and an air of high speed refinement which became the very hallmark of Jaguar's tradition. Driving a completely rebuilt 3.4 Drophead example was just wonderful. All the joys of that long bonnet, the period interior and yet virtually an E-Type performance was magical.

RELATIONS

Original Jaguar body styling wedded to one of the most important post-war engines which powered numerous successful saloons, the XK sports range and the awesome Le Mans-winning C- and D-Types.

BEST BUY

At this level it's largely about finances and aesthetics. The three body styles give choice, though the Fixed Head outsold the other two, and is half the Roadster's price. The S models provide the extra excitement but don't buy anything without guidance.

SPECIFICATIONS

ENGINE: 3442: 3781cc	**SUSPENSION:** Ind
BHP: 190 – 265	wishbone/torsion bars –
FUEL: 18mpg	Live axle/semi-elliptic
GEARBOX: 4 speed	**BODIES:** 2 door sports; fixed
BRAKES: Disc	and drophead
SPEED: 124mph – 136mph	**YEARS:** 1957 – 1960
	PRODUCTION: 9,395

Cost	£45,000
(150S 3.4 Roadster)	
% swing	4
Spares	★★★
V.F.M.	★★★
S.R.	★★★★

ROLLS-ROYCE CAMARGUE

A SERIOUS LOSS OF FACE

MANUFACTURER

ROLLS-ROYCE

As you grow up there are certain people you look up to, who seem to represent all the things you'd like to become. Innocence dies later when you discover they were just as flawed as the rest of us. A Rolls-Royce shone above everything. In time I came to understand the coachbuilders' contribution, but still I judged them as a Rolls. I'd see stars in convertible Silver Clouds, John Lennon with his painted Phantom: all sorts chased the same dream and little prepares you for the genuine pleasures of owning and driving one of these cars. My first was a Bentley S1, and although I've owned Shadows and Spirits, I can still remember those wraparound rear armchairs and the virtually silent in-line 6-cylinder engines. The Shadow developed into an excellent car, with its performance only hindered by the suspension compromises. It sold around 30,000 examples in comparison with approximately 7,500 of the three Silver Clouds, and its unitary body construction and modern looks successfully negotiated the change from coachbuilding to factory production. A waisted Mulliner Park Ward version was to become the successful Corniche, but huge financial problems had brought in the Receivers just as the Corniche was to be launched. Among their fighting plans was the idea of commissioning another full-blooded coachbuilt model of great prestige, pitched well above the Corniche and defiantly declaring Rolls Royce's continued presence. The Camargue was the eventual outcome and at least their pricing concept worked – it was the world's most expensive car. Everything else about the project reeked of poor decisions. The Pininfarina design

house has created great work, but the Camargue was an over-conscious effort which looked far better when it reappeared on the Fiat 130 Coupé. In fairness to Pininfarina, Rolls' economies required a totally new body be designed to fit over a standard Shadow floorpan complete with engine and the seating for five. The result is oversized, ugly and shattered Rolls' infallibility. The frontal treatment looks like a cheap toy, the wheels swamped by bodywork, the steep screen rake and narrow pillars out of all proportion. Its main claim to fame was the installation of an excellent bi-level air conditioning unit later to go into the standard models. Poor Rolls, one might think, a momentary slip while under financial pressure. No – ten years later having sold most examples to the US and Middle East, they announced a final commemorative US production of 12 cars.. In white acrylic with white Everflex roof, scarlet coachlines and an interior of red leather above the waist and white below with scarlet seating piped in white, inlaid silver on the veneers, a red and black steering wheel and central dash layout akin to a cheap stacking hi fi unit. A car to be ashamed of designing.

SPECIFICATIONS

ENGINE: 6750cc
BHP: Approx 220
FUEL: 14mpg
GEARBOX: 3 speed automatic
BRAKES: Disc
SUSPENSION: Ind

SPEED: 120mph wishbone/coil – semi–trailing arms/coil
BODIES: 2 door, 4 seater coupé
YEARS: 1975 – 85
PRODUCTION: 534

MANUFACTURER

ASTON MARTIN

NMY 486

ASTON MARTIN
DB MK III
PURE ASTON MOTORING DELIGHTS, PRE-DB4

Early in 1947 David Brown bought Aston Martin, and a few months later Lagonda Cars, and then set about building them up as *the* sporting and luxury British marques. The first post-war Motor Show in 1948 included Aston's DB1 – a tiny production of two-litre alloy-bodied Drophead Tourers, while Lagonda designer Frank Feeley was exploring shortened competition coupé versions. Using both the two-litre and the Bentley-designed Lagonda 6-cylinder engines, these cars carved a reputation on the international race circuits. Named the DB2 Mk I, the eventual production coupé was launched in the spring of 1950, rapidly followed by the faster Vantage version and the Drophead, creating capacity production for the factory. Occasional rear seating became the fashion and somehow Aston managed, within the same wheelbase, to deliver the 1955 DB 2/4 Mk II, (the 4 denotes seating) while establishing the often copied opening rear hatchback. During the early 1950s outright competition cars were the DB3s (never production road models) and much of that experience was poured into the final Aston Martin DB2 model – the DB Mk III launched at the Geneva Show. Produced between 1957–59 this model has, until more recent times, been largely overlooked – masked by the world-beating DB4 which followed. The Mk III had the final (and much revised) version of the Lagonda-based, originally W.O.Bentley-designed, engine, the DBA, which produced 162bhp; 180bhp versions were to be offered later. Frank Feeley re-styled the front of the car, using an enlarged version of his elegant DB3S grille and this shape was reprised in the dashboard layout. The DB2 two seater and the DB 2/4 Mk III represent pure classic Astons – before high fashion and show business coloured their personas.

RELATIONS

Born of the DB2 road car, with Lagonda designer Frank Feeley's body styling, this car led directly to the famed DB4, 5 and 6.

BEST BUY

Generally these are very sturdy cars. Rust does eat into traditional areas, while the suspensions needs expert checking. The spares position is excellent. It is important to check for horizontal cracks half way down the engine – particularly as the Mk III has its own unique block.

The DB2 from the beginning of the decade used the Lagonda engine. Beautiful bodywork from ex-Lagonda stylist Frank Feeley.

SPECIFICATIONS

ENGINE: 2922cc	**SUSPENSION:** Ind trailing
BHP: 162	links/coil – Live axle/Panhard
FUEL: 18 – 21mpg	rod/coil
GEARBOX: 4 speed	**BODIES:** 2 door, 2 + 2 Drop-
BRAKES: Disc/Drum	head: coupé: hatchback
SPEED: 120mph	**YEARS:** 1957– 59
	PRODUCTION: 551

Cost	£36,500
% swing	18.5
Spares	★★★★★
V.F.M.	★★★
S.R.	★★★★

LAMBORGHINI COUNTACH

THE WORLD'S MOST BEAUTIFUL MOTORING FOLLY

MANUFACTURER
LAMBORGHINI

In truth this is probably the most useless car in the book. It emulates competition machinery yet it's not a circuit machine, its excessive speed and fuel consumption have no place in our motoring world, and with neither wing mirrors, nor three-quarter vision negotiating public roads is a lottery – reversing simply unwise. Yet this car has become an icon among classic cars. It would be easy to leave it to the mercies of a *Top Gear* script were it not for the mechanical achievements beneath that 1mm thick aluminium bodywork. It was designed to follow in the footsteps of the celebrated, but imperfect transverse-engined Miura and the same basic team revealed their plan with the Countach prototype at the 1971 Geneva Motor Show. Its futuristic wedge shape and upwardly hinged doors caught everyone's attention, while the decision to place the V12 engine backwards, mounting the gearbox in the cockpit and devising an internal drive shaft through the sump to the final drive was an inspiration. This dismissed the need for long gear lever linkages, it brought all the weighted aspects of the car within the wheelbase, and greatly improved handling – a Miura failing. As significant as the prototype was the three year delay to production, during which every aspect was reviewed. Air intakes were installed over the rear haunches to increase cooling, and an enhanced Espada 4.0 litre was substituted for the unreliable 5.0 litre engine, marginally reducing top speed. Extraordinary discrepancies between manufacturer and different road testers' top speed figures abound in print, but all are agreed it was then the fastest road car. The Countach LP400 was unveiled

early in 1974 and four years later the 400S saw improved tyres, enlarged wheel aches and nose spoiler, a tail mounted wing, and improvements to suspension. In 1981 the LP500S introduced the 5.0 litre engine (actually 4754cc) and dashboard changes, while the 1985 Quattrovalvole offset sapping US emission laws with the enlarged 5167cc, four-valve-per-cylinder 455bhp unit, hurtling the car into the 180mph zone. It is one of great motor cars to test drive or to admire – if not live with on today's roads.

RELATIONS

The classic Miura/Espada V12 with unique space frame chassis and Bertone body.

BEST BUY

Don't. Buy the model, the poster, or CD Rom ride, but leave this unique car to show business and museums. The cognoscenti consider the simpler 400 lines superior to later cluttered models.

Cost (LP400)	£55,800
% swing	28
Spares	★★
V.F.M.	★★★
S.R.	★★★★

SPECIFICATIONS

ENGINE: 3929cc: 4754cc: 5167cc	**SUSPENSION:** Ind wishbone & coil all round
BHP: 375: 455	**BODIES:** 2 door coupé.
FUEL: 12mpg	**YEARS:** 1973–79: 1978–82 –
GEARBOX: 5 speed	400 models 1982–85:
BRAKES: Disc	1985–89 – 500 models
SPEED: 180 – 190mph	**PRODUCTION:** 2199

MANUFACTURER

BMW

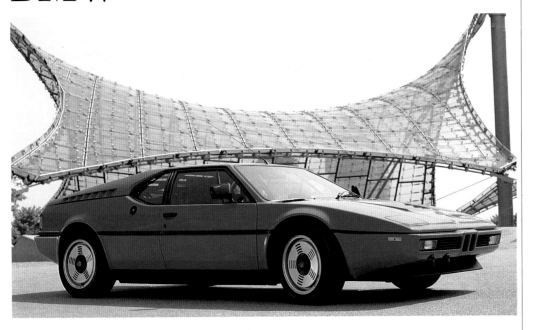

BMW M1

UNDERSTATED THOROUGHBRED

Comparisons between Lamborghini and the MI are interesting, not least because BMW commissioned the Italian company to construct their stunning Giugiaro breathtaker. The Countach and Miura were deliberately status symbols with imposing top speeds. In the 1970s, however, when BMW decided to build their one and only true supercar, the entire project was centred around designing an outright race car to challenge Porsche in the World Sports Car Championship. Others might sell cosmetic road stars, but building 400 customer MIs was purely to qualify for categorisation on Group 5 grids. However, fate took a hand as a regulation changed, edging the car into uncompetitive Group 6 — until the 400 cars were built. But Lamborghini were in financial trouble and weren't delivering, so production had to be brought back to Germany. To maintain a profile BMW created the ultimate one race series, the Procar, run for two years within European Grand Prix events with an entire field of these spectacular cars and some of the fastest FI drivers as competitors. Inevitably the long delay in direct competition lost them momentum, and eventually BMW slipped away from plans for a 700bhp turbo and a V12 version, electing to develop engines for Grand Prix cars. The subsequent BMW-engined McLaren FI road car was a natural outcome. Thus the MI is a unique celebration of total BMW skills and, with just 400 stunning road cars plus race machines in existence, they are extraordinarily rare and important classics. I was loaned the actual factory MI and could not have been more surprised. So often such cars are hard work to drive in all but perfect conditions, and festooned with wings and dams. Low, wide and free of all body clutter, it is beautifully understated. You sit low and a long way forward similar to a FI car, but this is primarily to give space for the 3.5 litre in–line 6 just behind your head. The cockpit would not be unfamiliar to a BMW owner, but fire that engine up and you enter another world.

RELATIONS

Original Giugiaro body style born of the 1972 BMW Turbo prototype. The MI engine is in essence also present in the M6, 635CSi and 735CSi.

BEST BUY

Parts back-up is good, and the road versions are actually useable, while race versions are highly specialist.

SPECIFICATIONS	
ENGINE: 3453cc	**SUSPENSION:** Ind wishbone/
BHP: 277 – 470 (racing)	coil/gas dampers all round
FUEL: 27mpg (claimed)	**BODIES:** 2 door Coupé
GEARBOX: 5 speed	**YEARS:** 1978 – 81
BRAKES: Disc	**PRODUCTION:** 454
SPEED: 162mph	

Cost	£65,000
% swing	-18
Spares	★★★★
V.F.M.	★
S.R.	★★★

MANUFACTURER
ROLLS-ROYCE

BENTLEY CONTINENTAL R

MASTERPIECE – THOUGH DONOR CAR IS THE POTENTIAL BARGAIN

The Bentley Mk VI was the first product of Rolls-Royce's post-war shift to building complete cars, and evolved between 1952 and 1955 with the more elegant R Type. This improved Mk VI featured an elongated rear section and boot, the bigger 4566cc engine, an optional automatic gearbox and some dashboard changes. Like its predecessor, it attracted a number of coachbuilt models – none more successful than the

Mulliner Continental R. Numerous legends exist about its design inspiration, though fastback models were hardly new. Having bravely entered the world of 'production' cars, Rolls needed to impose superiority anew. The competition was blossoming, with the first Jaguar XK; the first of the Porsche 356s; the initial road-going Aston Martin DB2 with its tubular framework; the alloy-panelled, tube frame, and

Of all the post-war Bentleys, surely the R-Type Continental is the one which would have received the nod of approval from W.O. Design work began in 1950 with the intention 'to exhibit those characterstics which appeal to the connoisseur of motoring.'

Cost (H.J.Mulliner)	£89,000
% swing	2
Spares	★★
V.F.M.	★★★
S.R.	★★★★

SPECIFICATIONS

ENGINE: 4556cc; 4887cc
BHP: Never released
FUEL: 16 – 20mpg
GEARBOX: 4 speed manual & automatic
BRAKES: Drum
SUSPENSION: Ind coil/wishbone – live axle/half elliptic
SPEED: 120mph
BODIES: 2 door, 4 seat coupé; coachbuilt versions
YEARS: 1952–55 (a few later)
PRODUCTION: 208

Italian-designed Bristol 401. In this context, a streamlined, aluminium-bodied, R-Type, constructed around a tubular frame, was intelligent rather than inspired. It was the style and detail, however, which made this car stand apart from virtually all others in motoring history. They sent engineers to Italy to study coachbuilding practices and went to considerable lengths to create a truly aerodynamic shape while retaining the vital dignity of the marque. Less than two inches height reduction was permitted on the famed grille, and yet they managed to created a supremely quiet 120mph four seater, taking hills in top gear. All but a handful were the same Mulliner design, though Farina, Graber, Park Ward and Franay all built examples. The four years of production were discreetly divided into classifications but only a compression increase in 1953 and the move to the larger bore 4887cc engine in 1954 were significant. It's a hard task to explain exactly what justifies the car's status without experiencing the feel of the car from behind the wheel. What makes the difference between an off-the-peg suit and a tailor-made one? Subtle qualities, details, a feeling. Couple these with Bentley engineering, 20mpg and four hand-made leather armchairs, and the car was a rare motoring achievement: owners had to agree not to compete in them.

RELATIONS

Essentially a 1952–55 R-Type Bentley and engine, the Continental had a lightweight framework and streamlined body from Mulliner and other coachbuilders. Of the 208 built, 193 had the Mulliner sports Saloon body. Farina's interpretation was perhaps one of the most successful of the other 15 with thick C-pillars and 'straighter' lines nose to tail.

BEST BUY

With so few built and astonishing price tags, the condition of a Continental R is likely to be excellent. Pure driving bliss and rarity value will continue to keep them highly collectable. The donor car – the saloon R-Type, is a far more accessible classic, with a longer, more elegant rear section than the Mk VI, but there are the same concerns over rust. Later Continental S-Types are humble, rebodied saloons by comparison. As the years passed, the original intentions of producing a lightweight sporting saloon were traduced: customers demanded too many extras! Radios, automatic transmission, bigger seats …

MANUFACTURER
LOTUS

LOTUS 21

ENTRY TO F1 – FOR THE PRICE OF A PORSCHE

The sreamlined shape first seen with the 1960 Lotus 20 was a winner, and continued to reappear almost unchanged in the 21 (F1), 22 (FJ), 24 and 25 (F1), 27 (FJ), 29 (Indy) and 33 (F1).

Spares	★★
V.F.M.	★★★
S.R.	★★★

There is a very special place reserved for F1. The World Championship is a roller coaster of events creating mythological status for man and machine, with a TV audience recently quoted as 589,808,000. Depending on age, certain teams or drivers fire the imagination, while a string of superheroes transcend everything: Ascari, Fangio, Moss, Clark, Prost and Senna. Cars, too, attain the same status – the Mercedes W196, the Maserati 250 F, the shark-nosed Ferrari 156, the Lotus 25 and even the team managers such as Enzo Ferrari, Frank Williams, and Colin Chapman become household names. The unimaginable costs of building and racing a competitive Grand Prix team is outside our understanding, but relentless racecar development and changing rules actually produce a stream of retired cars. Now, with the huge growth in historic competition, grids of ex–F1 cars are filled with enthusiasts savouring the excitement at a fraction of the original cost. It's still not cheap, but for the cost of a Porsche Carrera you could own the genuine article and drive a motoring legend.

Each specific car represents a precise window of time for the marque. This beautiful Lotus 21, restored by Alan Baillie, is a fine example. The first F1 Lotus was the Coventry Climax 16 looking not unlike the old Vanwall and performing double duty for F1 and F2. The same dual Formula design operated for the Lotus 18 which was based on a space frame chassis with the 237bhp 2.5 F1 Coventry Climax engine set behind the driver. It appeared at the Brands Hatch Boxing Day meet just five weeks from the drawing board, and during 1959 Moss, Clark, Surtees and Ireland brought the car on – even delivering GP victories. At season's end rules changed, limiting engines to 1.5 litres, and while teams protested, Ferrari employed their Formula II V6 engine and developed the 129 degree V6 1.5. Lotus' new V8 was not yet ready and an interim car using Mk II version of the 4-cylinder FPF Climax engine was married to a new ZF gearbox. Though the FI Lotus 21 shared much with its Formula Junior

SPECIFICATIONS

ENGINE: 1498cc
BHP: 151
FUEL: 5mpg (approx)
GEARBOX: 5 speed
BRAKES: Disc
BODIES: Single seater

SUSPENSION: Ind coil/wishbone – coil/radius arms
SPEED: 150mph (varied with gearing)
YEARS: 1961
PRODUCTION: 11

sister, the 20, it was wider, with 30 gallon fuel storage including a third tank doubling as the driver's seat. The space frame was smaller gauge, oil pipes actually ran within each other, but terminated through separate outlets, oil and water cooling ran through the internal monocoque skin with supply pick-ups at each end. A car full of ideas which would later blossom into the mould-breaking full monocoque V8 Lotus 25. Early GPs saw misfortunes for Ireland and Clark, though Moss, still in the underpowered interim 18–21, won an impressive Monaco GP and again at a rainsoaked Nurburgring. The full Lotus 21 saw him at Monza along with five Ferraris sitting on the front three rows, but two laps in Von Trip's Ferrari and Clarke's Lotus touched, and Von Trip, along with 14 spectators, died in the ensuing accident. The season ended with the combined efforts of 18–21s and full 21s becoming runners up in the Constructors' Championship, with further successes in the winter's South African events before Lotus turned to what would be next season's V8 Lotus 24. Seven cars were built for the Works team plus just four others. One for Rob Walker/Stirling Moss, one for Jack Brabham and one for South African Syd van der Vyver which was written off and

eventually replaced in 1964 by the factory for privateer Aldo Scribante, which makes the car we feature a later chassis number than the 1963 Type 24s.

RELATIONS

Lotus operated a constant development programme with this car directly descended from the Lotus 18 and bodywork shared with the Formula Junior 20.

BEST BUY

Obviously with limited productions all FI cars are highly collectable – particularly with good histories. Owning a Grand Prix car isn't difficult, – but you do need knowledgable mechanical help. However, for the price of a luxury road car you could buy a 4-cylinder example, join the world's most exclusive club – and enjoy the real excitement of historic competition.

The fuel tank was immense in relation to the rest of the 21, running along the left hand side and crossing under the seat. It was a nightmare to make leakproof, wrapping itself around each chassis tube. A secondary tank was squeezed in behind the right hand front wheel.

The 21 had the four cylinder Coventry Climax engine; the imminent V8 was not yet ready.

ASTON MARTIN DB7

A BEAUTIFUL BALANCE OF NOSTALGIA AND TECHNOLOGY

MANUFACTURER
ASTON MARTIN

From a 1947 advert in *The Times,* David Brown bought a bomb-damaged factory and the Aston Martin name. He leant his initials to one of the most prized series of sporting cars ever produced, but in 1972 the DB prefix was replaced by the initially irksome V8 series and Brown sold up. A decade and a half of troubles and changing ownership led to Ford buying the company. With both Jaguar and Aston Martin owned by Ford, cynics saw a grim future.

Under the new team, however, a series of inspired decisions were made to reposition the marque without loss of credibility. Ex-Ford designer Ian Callum crafted a stunning new coupé body, incorporating strong shadows of former DB4 glories, while ensuring four seats, a good boot and the powerful elegance synonymous with Aston Martins. TWR used the 3.2-litre straight 6, twin cam engine similar to the Jaguar XJR, but incorporating a unique 24 valve head, Zytec electronic management and an Eaton supercharger combining to produce 335bhp and 165mph. Sat upon the same sized chassis as the XJS, the finished car incorporated weight-saving panels where practical, and used the Rolls-Royce paint shop to complete the task. The quality of the interior, and the introduction for the first time of a veneered Aston dashboard,

combined to offer relative exclusivity for a fraction of a custom-built Aston's price. They also sought the blessing of David Brown himself, and then re-established the distinguished line with the DB7 name. The striking convertible Volante model followed and with record production under way, (the first DB7 to reach the vital US market is pictured left) the factory now talks confidently of further DBs, even racing versions. Ford have been shrewd, and there is little doubt that the DB7 has firmly re-established Aston Martin and created a future classic model.

RELATIONS

TWR Design styling, primarily Jaguar XJ parts, including basic chassis and engine.

BEST BUY

It's too early to discuss second-hand models. Such is the delight at the DB7, a number of teething troubles have not been reported by the press – so perhaps the early models ought to be viewed with caution.

Spares	★★★★
V.F.M.	★★★★
S.R.	★★★★

SPECIFICATIONS

ENGINE: 3239cc	**SUSPENSION:** Ind wishbone
BHP: 335	& coil all round
FUEL: 25mpg	**BODIES:** 2 door coupé: twin
GEARBOX: 5 speed	turbo coupé: convertible
BRAKES: Disc	**YEARS:** 1994 – to date
SPEED: 165mph	**PRODUCTION:** Current

MANUFACTURER

MERCEDES-BENZ

The 300SL Roadster isn't so much the sister car to the legendary Gullwing, as its progeny. The Roadster may not boast those top-hinged doors, it but did enjoy important improvements over the Gullwing. Just ten 300SLs started out as competition cars as Mercedes wanted to wave the sporting flag again, but with little development funding, they had to take the engine, gearbox, suspension etc,. from their then current saloon, the 300 Series. Naturally the engine was refined with a new dry sump, triple carburation, competition camshaft, new valves, and manifolds but its 160bhp+ wasn't enough alone. So they designed a complicated tubed space frame chassis, and tilted the engine through 45 degrees to reduce height. Keeping the car this low, however, meant extra strengthening along the chassis sides, creating huge door sills and not enough room above them for conventional doors – hence the half-height gullwings. The result of this body and chassis combined, along with the engine developments, gave Mercedes an instant competition winner. An enterprising American tried to order 1000 road versions, and this was enough to tempt the factory into production in 1954, with a largely steel bodied version which was successful, if hugely expensive. However, critics questioned the door design – escape in a road accident would be impossible, the windows did not open, and it was difficult getting in and out with any decorum. Gullwing production ended in 1957, and was replaced by the 300SL Roadster which looked identical, (roofline apart) but was substantially reworked. The space frame chassis was redesigned to permit conventional full height doors, fuel injec-

tion was added, there were important rear suspension improvements; a hard top and enhanced interior all contributed to an increasing GT role. Blisteringly fast in their day, it's their original design which promotes status, not their sophistication. Yes, it is one of the world's supercars, but it's a considerable sum of money to invest in a model with that much power and unstable handling. Attractive styling, flawed manners – buy a house instead.

RELATIONS

New body styling over engine, gearboxes and other components from the 300 range.

BEST BUY

If you are seriously considering this level of investment, first join the Owners' Club and draw on their knowledge and contacts. Repairs and restoration are very expensive. If you are not seduced by those Gullwings, then the later Roadster is technically improved and 20 per cent cheaper.

SPECIFICATIONS

ENGINE: 2996cc
BHP: 250
FUEL: 16mpg
GEARBOX: 4 speed
BRAKES: Drum – Discs from 1961
SPEED: 155mph

SUSPENSION: Ind double wishbone/coil – high pivot swing axle (low pivot after 1961)
BODIES: 2 door sports: hardtop
YEARS: 1957– 63
PRODUCTION: 1858

Cost (Roadster)	£103,000
% swing	22.5

Spares	★★★
V.F.M.	★★★
S.R.	★★★★

MANUFACTURER
FERRARI

Ferrari's position in the motoring world is unique. Whether it's millions willing them to win a Grand Prix, or informal crowds around a parked road car, they command and receive the utmost respect. Much of this has been earned through competition and Ferrari ownership is partly about buying closer association with that magical world. As a consequence, the few dual-purpose Ferraris represent the supreme personal transport. The F40 is such an example, and so too, was the beautiful 275 GTB. Whereas the F40 was strictly limited, the 275 managed skilfully to ful-

fil every Ferrari obligation. It had the virtually impossible task of following in the footsteps of the legendary SWB 250 GT, sharing its short wheelbase as well as the classic V12 Colombo engine. This would be pedigree enough, but Ferrari also brought all the lessons from the racing P 275 and introduced independent rear suspension and a new five speed gearbox developed from the Le Mans-winning mid-engined V12 250LM. With direct family ties to the 250 GTO, the stunning P3 and P4, and the Daytona, this was a union of everything sacred. The GTB was

Cost	£205,000
% swing	0.5
Spares	does it matter?
V.F.M.	★★★
S.R.	★★★★★

launched in October 1964 as both a Berlinetta Coupé and the GTS Spyder with the sublime Pininfarina body over a new multi-tube chassis and a rear-mounted gearbox linked to the V12 in 260bhp/280bhp form. In 1966 an improved Mk II version revealed the new longer nose, which prevented the steering from going light at high speed. However, the finite 300bhp version was announced in spring of 1967 – the 275GTB/4, which introduced four camshafts and created an incredible power curve soaring relentlessly to 8000 revs. This twin cam was a direct development from the famed P racing cars. Most of the 275GTB/4s were of lightweight construction, though many remained road cars. The Americans naturally sought an open version, and Ferrari supplied a limited number which have since become priceless classics. The 250LM, the Prototype racers, and the 275 GTB/4s are all a lot smaller than you may imagine, and driving the GTB/4 quickly reminds you it's still a competition car. Nothing can prepare you for the sensations such a world-beating car provides, but like riding a thoroughbred race horse, it demands skills of you as well. You have to take control and drive it with authority – yet never forget the car's ability to take its own course.

RELATIONS

Pure race-bred, and a road car lineage with 250GTO, 250GT and Daytona

BEST BUY

Remaining objective, and assuming the funds, ignore the early short nosed GTBs, as the Mk IIs were an improvement, the GTB/4 the very best. A good history and original specifications are vital to the investment, though upgraded braking is well worthwhile. The curious choice of chassis tubing means accident damage is expensive to fix.

SPECIFICATIONS

ENGINE: 3285cc	**SUSPENSION:** Ind wishbone &
BHP: 300	coil all round
FUEL: 17mpg	**BODIES:** 2 door coupé: Spyder
GEARBOX: 5 speed	**YEARS:** 1966 – 68
BRAKES: Disc	**PRODUCTION:** 360
SPEED: 167mph	

As a fitting tail piece to the Stanley 100 and introduction to the next chapter, we assembled a lineup of Ferraris some of which are so rare that this picture could never be taken 'for real.' The 275 GTB/4 (see previous page), which shared its V12 power plant and often its chassis and running gear with these family members, is in the centre, (29).

From left to right: 142, the Trintignant/Cavrois 1961 Tour de France swb 250 GT; 27, the Spoerry/Boler 1965 Le Mans 250 LM; 11, the 1963 Graham Hill Tourist Trophy 250 GTO; 26, the Andretti/Rodriguez 1966 Sebring 330 P2; 17, the Piper/Bonnier 1965 Le Mans 365 P2; 9, the Piper/Attwood 1967 Brands Hatch 412P; 27, the Ginther/Rodriguez 1966 Le Mans 330 P3 Spider; 23, the 1967 Chris Amon/Bandini Daytona 330 P4 Spider.

The collection of ⅟₄₃rd scale models comes courtesy of the companies Best, Bang and Brumm.

SMALL WONDERS

Model Car of the Year

Model car collectors are just as much classic car buffs as anyone owning the odd couple of full sized versions. The chances are their knowledge of their chosen marques minutiae could even be greater, plus they have the added delight of being able to own whole collections of '50s saloons, American convertibles or Grand Prix grids. To the casual observer this is seen as just a group of hobbyists with a handful of old toys they remember once having themselves. But owning £3,000's-worth of classic Morris Minor doesn't necessarily make you the big fish. A small promotional model van for Bentalls, for instance, fetched a staggering £12,650 at Christies – which is four full-sized Morris Minors, while a later auction of a second example didn't even reach its reserve of £3,000. It's a very complex and sophisticated world, with all the same criteria about grades of condition and price premiums for rare examples, plus the added hazards and delights of Limited Editions.

In essence the model fraternity breaks into two distinct worlds with various offshoots of each. With considerable skill, the *Model Collector* magazine somehow manages to bridge these two interests and within the pages of its annual bible – The Model Price Guide, you can look up the current values of vast numbers of Dinkies, Corgi, Matchbox – turning you grey at the

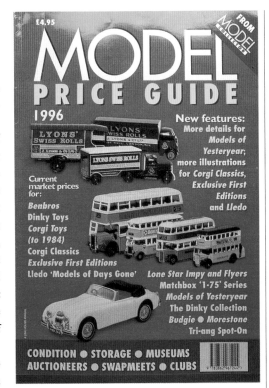

The circulation figures for model magazines have never been healthier.

memories of toys you once owned!. Through regular local indoor gatherings it is possible to buy and sell generally well-worn examples while pristine and still boxed examples are the joy of dealers and auction

houses. Military, commercial, public transport and all forms of cars have armies of focussed collectors. A Guy Weetabix van is currently fetching between £1,200 and £1,600, a mid-green Morris Oxford is around £80 while a mid-blue version is seriously rare. It all sounds a bit silly unless you love motor cars, it becomes almost compulsive if you hunt or find something rare. Find an undervalued blue and tan Dinky Lincoln Zephyr Coupé and you've just gained enough potential cash for a serious overseas holiday, a prime trophy for your collection, or indeed a future investment as the prices continue to swell.

The other side of the coin involves the increasing avalanche of modern ⅓rd scale products. The collector of period models is concerned with gathering in specific families of models in near perfect condition, even though mouldings themselves were inevitably fairly crude. The modern collector however is focussed on the sheer quality of manufacturer and detailing; although both worlds still tend to narrow their personal interests, be it '60s Le Mans cars or different liveried bus companies from a specific region. Resin and white metal kits have been the traditional source of the more sophisticated modern miniatures, but such is the growth of interest that companies such as Corgi Classics, Matchbox and Lledo are now producing huge ranges of budget priced collectors' models, trying to fill the position once held by the legendary Dinky range.

Recently Corgi, who staged a management buy-out from their multinational owners, have been building up a complete range of all the differing Morris Minor models. These are not high quality models and optional stick-on chrome wing mirrors fail to add

anything, but the proportions and colours have genuinely captured the mood of these loved cars and make excellent starter models – or indeed gifts to Minor owners! Also from Corgi is a new range of British sports cars including the XK Jaguar, the TR, the Austin-Healey 3000 and a very pleasing version of the classic MGA. Detail Cars of Milan have now become more visible through links with the newly independent Corgi and their handsome open '58 Alfa Giulietta typifies a range that even includes domestic stars such as the 3000GT Capri and VW Golf.

Beautiful German saloons and race cars may be powerfully promoted by Minichamps, but two Italian manufacturers, Bang and Best, fly their national flag high with endless celebrations of the fabled Ferrari marque. These two fine examples (below left) are nearing the end of production and will rapidly slip from stock to become targets at swap meet events – that's how the invest market begins. Only mass production allows a price of under £20.00 and so just as these two cars slip towards collectable status others arrive in the shops with fresh driver and race livery.

Hand built collector's ranges such as Pathfinder or Brooklin's Lansdowne range with cars such as its '57 Cresta, Austin Somerset, Triumph Renown actually sell without need for advertising; but this growth of general interest now affects some mass production models too. Recently, the 30,000 Model Collector readership voted a modest Lledo VW Beetle as their 'Best Family Saloon' model. Yet all our attempts to buy an example failed – production had ceased to make way for an upgraded model, thus creating yet another potential classic.

STANLEY CLASSIC MODEL OF THE YEAR

Although I sought expert opinions before nominating this magnificent model it is primarily a subjective decision. Lots of good-looking models loosely qualified, but I set out deliberately (with some expert advice) to find a miniature of an authentic classic subject, a high quality of detailing, having considered value for money and the overall level of period charm it conveyed.

On all these counts the stunningly pretty Vitesse-produced 1956 Morgan Series IF 4/4 is a clear winner. It is currently available in four versions with further cars to follow, including a 1952 Le Mans model, maybe others. They are destined to become a fabulous mini collection in their own right.

KHL 606

Our Model Car of the Year. The Vitesse Morgan 4/4 Series II from 1956, complete with bonnet strap, club badges and GB plates.

Wire wheels for the British Racing Green version.

The full line-up of Vitesse Morgans currently available.

The £60 to £150 hand-built model market used to be the only way to enjoy any serious detail until the German company Minichamps began mass production of competitive quality for just a third of the price. Their lead has encouraged others to improve quality and nowhere is this more apparent than with the Portuguese organisation Vitesse. Started in Oporto in September 1982, they are now a successful group of companies creating Vitesse, Victoria, Trofeu, Onyx and Quartzo; providing ranges of '50s US models, '50s–70s European favourites, '60s sports cars, modern rally cars, present-day F1, plus military. Their staff of 250 supply regular orders to 34 countries across five continents with a factory output of 8,000 models each working day.

It is the sheer scale of the operation which has kept the prices down to under £20 and it is a major part of their achievement that modelling detail is still virtually the equal of their hand-built rivals. Each of the Morgans is given a different character. The navy blue model for instance is a French touring example complete with national plates, a luggage rack and is of course left hand drive, while the ivory example enjoys a partially fitted tonneau. The British Racing

The French lhd model, with luggage rack.

filled with fully coloured badges. It is these details coupled with an overall Morgan authenticity which stands the car apart from its rivals. It is a miniature deserving pride of place on anyone's shelf and reflects well on its British distributor, Modeltime. Run by Harry Lewin who became a Vitesse distributor just two months after their formation all those years ago, his faith through the earlier years is now fully repaid with their new models such as these Morgans. As if to underline the very closeness between motoring enthusiast and model collector, even Modeltime's owner eagerly recalls his interest being awoken by watching the likes of Fangio and Gonzales racing in the 1950s; while his own youthful modelling involved Keilkraft aircraft.

There is something reassuring about a classic model being built with such detailed sympathy for the marque and being sold by a man immersed in historic motor sport. Vitesse, Modeltime and especially these most splendid of Morgans deserve the recognition for so sympathetically celebrating the classic car world in miniature.

Green car has side screens, flaps and tiny chrome door handles as well as Morgan's optional wire wheels. In the case of the stunning scarlet version GB plates and bonnet strap join with a tiny badge bar

A reminder of the real thing. Rowan Isaac's picture of Roger and Celia Pollington's 4/4 Series IV (201 built between 1961 and 1963) keeps company with an immaculate Morgan three-wheeler: surely a challenge to any modeller.

RESTORATION

Stern admonitions from expert Jim Tyler

Few restored cars have a market value reflecting the combined costs of purchase and even an amateur (let alone a professional) restoration. Many are worth only a fraction of these costs. Home car restoration is NOT a viable method of owning a classic car at low cost. Restore a car if you enjoy hard work and do not mind paying for the privilege; if not, then buy a completed or nearly-restored car – and save yourself a lot of money, hard work and frustration in the process!

The true costs of an amateur or semi-professional restoration are – sadly – often realised only at the end of the project or (often) part-way through when the restorer runs out of money, and yet another part-restored car comes on the market! Just take a look at all those advertisements for '90% restored' cars, for part-restored cars with 'all the hard work done' – if completing the restoration was as cheap and easy as the adverts suggest, ask yourself why the sellers do not complete them and sell at top value. The truth behind the advertisements is that completing the cars will still take considerable time, effort and money.

The problem is that few first-time restorers appreciate how costs are distributed through the project. Most people who have not experienced restoration at first-hand will assume that the bodywork repair is the most expensive part. But, in the vast majority of cases, it is in fact the combined costs of mechanical/electrical/trim replacement or reconditioning, re-chroming and tyres which ends up making the larger part of the budget.

Generally speaking, the older a car is, the more likely you are to be able to repair or recondition rather than replace mechanical and other components; older cars were built with a greater proportion of repairable components (in addition to containing fewer than more recent cars). This is, to a great extent, due to the materials used in the car's construction – wood, metals and leather are more easily repairable than plastics – and the components

on older cars were, in general, designed to be taken apart and repaired. Progressively more recent cars contain more and more sealed 'for life' units.

Thus an older and rarer car, from the 1930s, can in some instances be easier and cheaper to restore than a 1970s car – even though the full range of body and mechanical components may be available for the latter. What is more, the older car when restored will usually be worth a higher percentage of its restoration costs than will the more recent vehicle. However, repairing components on older cars requires a range of skills: you cannot hope to be able to strip, repair and rebuild most of the mechanical components unless you possess some engineering knowledge and also have suitable equipment.

Although car manufacturers have made great improvements in quality control during recent years, where classic cars are concerned, the general rule is that the earlier the car, the better the build quality. For instance, many (not all) 1950s cars are better built than those of the 1960s which, in turn, can prove to be vastly better built than some of the poorly designed vehicles of the 1970s and early 1980s. The better the original build quality, the easier the restoration.

REBUILDING OR RENOVATION?

The term 'restoration' is commonly used to describe two quite different processes; the renovation and the rebuilding of classic cars. Those who set out to restore fairly recent (monocoque-bodied) cars for which a full range of spares is widely available often end up not so much renovating the car as rebuilding it, substituting new or factory reconditioned components for old. There is an important distinction to be made between rebuilding a car and renovating it, because the major difference between the two is the amount of expense involved.

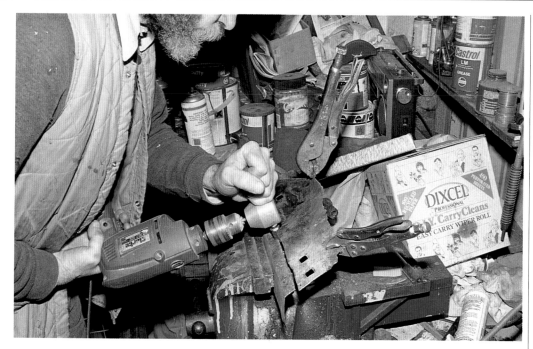

For instance, a renovator might spend hours freeing seized brake-cylinder pistons, honing the bores, cleaning the pistons (tappets) and renewing only the seals. The rebuilder, on the other hand, might be tempted to either scrap the salvageable brake-cylinder and buy a new one outright, or simply exchange the old part for a factory reconditioned part, in the process, spending perhaps five or six times as much money, but less time and effort, than the renovator.

The most extreme case of cost differences between classic car rebuilding and renovation, concerns cars for which new bodyshells are available – MGB, Sprite/Midget, TR6, VW Beetle and more recent Minis. The author will use his favourite – the MGB – as an example, although the following could equally apply to any car for which new bodyshells are still manufactured or can sometimes be found. The prices quoted all relate to 1996 unless otherwise stated.

If the new bodyshell costs £3,000, then the rebuilder is hardly likely to jeopardise that outlay by accepting anything other than a first-class (which usually means a professional) paint finish. This could add another £1,000 to the costs. Now possessing a superb-looking and structurally perfect bodyshell, the rebuilder may look with some disdain at the shabby collection of spares taken from the 'donor' car. Having invested so much time and money in the project to date, the rebuilder could decide that there is no question of spoiling the finished car and fit only new (factory reconditioned or, where available, re-manufactured) components.

Now the cost of the rebuilding really starts to escalate. Back in the early 1990s, I listed and priced those components, counting only items which cost £10 or more, which might typically be used rebuilding an MGB. I gave up – and most people will find the figure unbelievable unless they go to the trouble of costing it for themselves – when I reached £8,000. The spares catalogue and price list which I used for this exercise was dated 1989! Add that figure to the costs of buying and painting the bodyshell are you are looking at a minimum cost of £12,000. You might at this stage suspect me of manipulating these figures to prove a point; so how do my calculations relate to actual practice?

The actuality is even more alarming – in 1994, I learned of no less than three MGB GTs which were restored (using new bodyshells) at total costs of over £20,000 each – one cost a staggering £25,000, of which

around £10,000 would have been labour charges. To carry out a home rebuild to the same standard, therefore, would have cost around £15,000. If any of the owners of these cars had to sell them, they would be lucky to recoup half of their expenditure.

The difference in cost between rebuilding a car with a new bodyshell and mainly re-manufactured and factory reconditioned components at home, and having the same work carried out professionally can be surprisingly small. In fact, you could discover that you have to spend virtually as much on your own rebuild as some companies would charge to supply and assemble the same car for you! Many of those

Sill asemblies and many other box sections rot from the inside: this Minor sill assembly has been badly bodged - the horizontal section is a welded-on cover plate. Always anticipate the worst when you start stripping car - that way, you won't be too disappointed if the innards turn out to be a mess.

businesses which sell spares also restore cars and most buy their spares at the best trade discounts and may – for a complete build – pass some of those savings on to the customer. Usually they will be pleased to quote for the supply of a rebuilt car so, before launching into your project, cost it carefully compare the final figure with that quoted for a professional rebuild.

Now consider the case of the economy-minded MGB renovator. He accepts that the repaired bodyshell is not perfect – but its condition is entirely in keeping with a car of its age – and he is not afraid to tackle the paint spraying at home. Typically, he might spend around £800 on new panels, £200 on paint and another £100 on sundries to get to the finished bodyshell stage, at which point, the rebuilder could have spent four times as much. Furthermore, if he accepts that components and trim which may be less than perfect but can be made reasonably tidy further savings can be made. Examples might include a renovated radiator grille (£100 saved), cleaned and repaired seat covers (over £250 saved), to repaired, cleaned and repainted lower wishbone assemblies (£80 saved) and so on. The list is endless.

What is the difference between both projects? The renovator has a car which is in excellent condition for its age but which is, perhaps more importantly, authentic. The rebuilder has a superb almost 'factory fresh' car which is probably no different to drive than the renovated vehicle. Perhaps more pleasure which comes from driving an authentic period car?

There is another consideration. A car which is renovated should retain as many of its original components as possible. Originality is not only an important characteristic from the aesthetic viewpoint, it is reflected in the prices realised in sales of classic cars. As more and more modern classics are rebuilt using a large number of re-manufactured components, the more original car will probably become rarer, making it more collectable and possibly more valuable.

The other great difference between renovating and rebuilding a car is the time requirement. A car like the MGB can be rebuilt in weeks (maybe 500 hours for building from a new shell) even if the majority of the work is carried out by the owner. Complete renovations can take many months and some may take years of spare time working. Were the renovator to cost their own time, even at a modest labour rate, add on the overheads which might be incurred by a professional restorer, the total prices would probably be very close indeed.

Most amateur and many professional restorers have engines and transmissions reconditioned professionally. This for most people is the sensible option. It would be heartbreaking to finish the car only to discover later that your engine or gearbox reconditioning was less than perfect and that the unit has to be removed again with the risk of damaging freshly-painted bodywork. Unless you have a motor engineering background, access to engineers' measuring equipment and specialist tools it is more sensible to have this work carried out professionally (you will not know what work is required until the engine/transmission has been stripped and examined). Depending on the condition of the unit, it could be less expensive to purchase an exchange unit.

TYPES OF RESTORATION

There are two distinct types of restoration; the complete stripdown and rebuild, and the 'on the road' restoration. In the former the car is taken off the road and stripped – usually to a bare shell – then repaired and rebuilt. In the latter, work is done as and when funds and time permit, the car being generally used throughout.

The complete stripdown has numerous drawbacks. It takes the car off the road for a long time and, because most restorations usually take several times

Many small repair sections can be fabricated at home, but some are just oh so complicated that it makes more sense to buy the appropriate, professionlly made repair section.

longer than the estimated. This can run into many months or more often into years. Secondly, the stripping of many otherwise functional components and fastenings from the car could result in some being lost or damaged and replacing these increases the cost. Thirdly, it involves a tremendous amount of work, much of which is very dirty. Lastly, the period between the mechanical stripdown and rebuild can be so long that home restorers may have very real problems remembering where various components and fixings are stored.

In favour of the complete stripdown restoration is its thoroughness, because every component comes in for attention and, more importantly, all the bodywork can be properly rust-proofed.

The greatest disadvantage with 'on the road' restoration (the main problem appears at the end of this section) is that the car does not receive a one-off, comprehensive overhaul. Mechanical and electrical components will require attention as they wear out and become unreliable. Small areas of bodywork which are missed in the de-rusting and paint treatment will continue to rust away. In its favour is that jobs can be tackled as and when money and spare time allow, and that the car can provide the owner both with transport and driving enjoyment. The 'on the road' restoration is usually – but need not be – fairly random. However, it is better to approach this type of restoration by examining the car thoroughly, making priorities for the various tasks and setting a work timetable.

The first step, in an 'on the road' restoration is to make the car's bodywork sound and ensure that none of the mechanical and electrical components are in a dangerous condition. Begin by inspecting the car thoroughly (to MOT standard) then carry out a full service, replacing faulty or worn components as necessary. Next examine the bodywork, and list those

areas which are in need of repairs, giving priority to structural panels (the most important parts for attention) with outer panels being attended to later. Thus, sill replacement is more important than – and should be tackled before – wing replacement: make the body sound, THEN worry about its looks!

As well as making the bodyshell sound, it is also important to take any measures necessary to prevent rusted but salvageable non-structural body panels from further deterioration. Prevention is not only better, but also much cheaper than cure. The earlier in the rusting process you can act, the better. Flat down any paintwork which is starting to blister and clean the underlying metal thoroughly before applying any paint, thus salvaging an expensive panel.

On the majority of monocoque-bodied cars, equal importance should be attached to the condition of the chassis legs (chassis rails) which are the strongest sections of the bodywork. On to these are bolted sub-frames – assemblies on which the engine and transmission are mounted. The sills – which connect the chassis legs front and back – all cross-members, the heelboard and toeboard are also important areas.

However, a feature of monocoque construction is the utilisation of the greatest possible number of body panels to spread stress loading. Some panels which, at first sight, might not appear to have a structural function can in fact be contributing to the strength of the bodyshell. For instance, on many cars the assembly of pressings which connect the front end of the sill to the chassis leg, (including the scuttle and flitch panels), are debatably almost as important as the sills and chassis legs.

The importance of such panels varies between cars and, if you are unable to find a restoration guide which designates them, an examination of the chassis construction should reveal which are structurally important.

Once the structural repairs have been completed and the car made mechanically sound, the bulk of the remaining work will comprise removing individual components, cleaning and/or renovating and replacing them – jobs which can be carried out in a day or over the course of a week-end. In the case of more complicated tasks, such as wiring loom replacement, these could be timed to coincide with holidays.

An 'on the road' restoration can go on for years, by which time, some of the tasks completed early in the project will very likely have to be done again. The awful truth of 'on the road' restoration, is that the car is never truly completed.

'EASY' RESTORATIONS

It is not uncommon to read that the restoration of a particular model or type of car is somehow 'easier' than most and probably a good prospect for the novice restorer. Those, however, with practical first-hand experience of restoration – rather than book-learned or observation-based knowledge – will know this to be a complete fallacy. No particular model or type of car is an 'easy' restoration project. Anyone who has carried out the full restoration of any classic car will tell you that it is very hard work, always difficult, sometimes hazardous and often completely disheartening.

Proof of this can be easy to find. The classified advertisement columns in magazines often contain an assortment of part-restored classic cars – their vendors having abandoned the project at the cost of having to sometimes lose vast amounts of money. The most common reason for an uncompleted restoration is that the owner ran out of money.

The most important aspect of survival is not to get into trouble in the first place. Start by helping with the restoration of a car belonging to a fellow enthusiast, though a second choice would be to enrol on a college course in vehicle restoration.

ANATOMY OF THE MOTOR CAR

When on the move the chassis of a car is subjected to enormous forces. Apart from shocks transmitted from bumps and holes in the road – which are absorbed initially by the tyres and suspension – the axle (on acceleration) and brakes generate powerful forces. The suspension, axle and engine have to be mounted on something sturdy enough to withstand these forces, and the earliest solution was to bolt them to a chassis.

A chassis is a very strong 'ladder-type' framework which, in classic cars, is usually manufactured from a heavy gauge steel section. In addition to taking the forces already mentioned, it has to provide sufficient rigidity to control twisting between the front and rear axles.

There are essentially four distinct types of classic car construction. Most earlier cars consisted of a steel section chassis on which was mounted an ash-framed body tub covered with cloth, aluminium or steel sheet. Other 'separate chassis cars' have a body tub constructed of welded steel panels; examples include the majority of immediate pre-World War Two cars and more recent vehicles such as the MGA, Triumph (Spitfire, GT6, and TR except the TR7 and 8) and saloon – Herald – ranges.

Most cars manufactured from the 1950s onwards do not have a chassis as such but instead incorporate strong, chassis-like members (rails) onto their welded steel bodyshells. These are known as 'monocoque', 'unitary' or 'integral construction' bodyshells. Lastly, since the introduction of the quite revolutionary Mini, cars have appeared in semi-monocoque construction, having in effect separate chassis called subframes.

The range of skills, equipment and facilities required for bodywork restoration varies according to the construction of the car in question; chassis-based cars with ash-framed bodies obviously require good carpentry skills. Ash is a very hard wood, difficult to work, especially to saw – a band saw is almost a necessity. With the sole exception of the Morgan, new body parts will have to be made, this will require panel beating skills and equipment. Any repairs to the separate chassis usually demand that the body tub is removed, so that a large workshop becomes essential. Most people will, for these types of repair, employ the services of a skilled person.

A full range of steel replacement panels are available for the more popular cars, alleviating the need for the restorer to be a skilled sheetmetal worker – although, as seasoned restorers know, few new panels fit without a degree of tailoring and in many instances re-shaping.

Most of the steel body tubs fitted to these cars do incorporate certain structurally important assemblies – most notably the sills and lower sections of the A and B posts. Lift off a steel body tub – especially from a convertible – with rotten sills and it will bend in the middle just like a monocoque in the same

condition! Because of this, the restoration of such cars usually commences with making the body tub structurally sound, then lifting it from the chassis so that the chassis can be cleaned and repaired. The problem with this – the 'text book' method – is that a chassis can subsequently be found to be bent or to be the most appalling mess, made-up from sections of two or sometimes more chassis.

It is often erroneously believed that cars with a separate chassis are in some way simpler to restore than monocoques – in fact, restorers of these cars require all of the facilities and skills of the monocoque restorer.

Despite not having to separate a chassis and body shell, monocoque restoration is far from easy: cutting out rotted structural and semi-structural panels always brings a risk of distorting other panels. As a result, this could distort the complete shell.

Restoration of the Mini, despite it having sub-frames, is essentially the same as the restoration of any other monocoque. All the sub-frames are used for is the initial absorption of road stresses, which are still transmitted to the body shell.

THE PROJECT CAR

It sounds too obvious, but the most important foundation of economical restoration is to begin with a car which can be restored at low cost. Many people unthinkingly launch into what could become a hugely expensive restoration of a car which is really only fit for scrap or as a source of spare parts. Only experienced restorers can tell a cheap-to-restore car from one for which you will need a second mortgage. An experienced restorer might not be able to estimate the true costs of the work until the car has been par-

This 'A' post assembly turned out to be thoroughly rotten and, in such cases, it is worth considering obtaining full replacement rather than repair panels.

It's easy to see how body-filler came by its dubious reputation when bodgers slap half an inch (or greater) thickness of it into deep dents! In fact, there's nothing 'wrong' with body-filler if it is used sensibly. Beat or lever the dent as shallow as possible, clean off all surface rust, use the thinnest of skims of filler and it will be there for the life of the car.

tially stripped down. Even two cars of the same make, model and year which, at first glance, might appear to be in almost similar condition can in fact vary greatly in restoration costs.

For those who already own a car in need of restoration, the first step is to cost the work and, if the figure passes the bounds of reason, to find another example of the same model which can be restored more cheaply.

Costing a restoration is an exacting process, but very worthwhile if it saves you wasting a small fortune on an uneconomic project. Firstly, examine the car and itemise all those components and body panels which will have to be replaced. Be methodical – start at one end of the car and work your way slowly to the other, listing body panels, mechanical, electrical and trim components separately.

Next acquire a good spares catalogue with a current price list, and itemise the prices of all the components you will need. Because spares catalogues tend to come with separate price lists and because they tend to use the manufacturer's original and usually confusing part numbers, this process can take some time but, again, the result is worth the effort. You do not necessarily have to complete your list – when you have priced half of the items, make a total of the cost so far, the resultant figure may astound you and convince you to seek a project car in better condition.

Before you begin travelling about viewing potential project cars it is as well firstly to establish exactly what you are looking for. Economic restoration being the priority, the first important item to check is that can the majority of mechanical, hydraulic, electrical

and trim components be cleaned and/or repaired as necessary and re-used. Paradoxically, the vast majority of these components tend to deteriorate more quickly on a car which has been left idle than they do on a car which is in continual use.

Second in importance comes the state of the bodywork. While areas of body rot should be quite apparent and hold no special fears for the restorer, collision damage and camouflaged rot is another matter altogether. Collision damage can – and frequently does – move suspension mounting points, with the effect that the suspension is misaligned making the car's handling and roadholding dangerous. Straightening a distorted bodyshell or chassis is a job for a professional bodyshop, equipped with a jig. Even after straightening there can be some concern that structural members might have been weakened during the straightening work.

Camouflaged body rot may lie undetected through the initial stages of restoration, and not become apparent until the shell is stripped of paint. If camouflaged body rot is discovered prior to welded repairs being carried out then it is annoying. But to discover that a heelboard is made up mostly from cardboard and GRP after you thought you had finished welding, can be devastating.

Having set priorities for the importance of the condition of various mechanical, electrical and bodywork components, it is recommended that you then seek information specific to the vehicle you wish to buy. Classic car magazines often publish quite thorough buyers' guides to various classics, and any back issues of interest are normally available from the publishers. Where a back issue is out of print, the staff will usually photocopy the article for you at a reasonable cost. Alternatively, most restoration books include buyers' guides which can be very thorough and the only drawback is that some of the information included might not be current. For instance, a buyers' guide in a book might advise that a certain spare is unobtainable, but since the book was published the component has been re-manufactured.

When assessing buyers' guides, try to ascertain whether they have been written by a practising restorer or a journalist. The more valuable guides are those written by people with extensive experience of restoring your particular car.

When you read a buyers' guide, make a list as you go along of various points of interest such as areas of bodywork which commonly rust or which are normally dealt with using bodyfiller, mechanical components which are prone to fail and expensive to replace – and so on. Write the page and paragraph numbers next to each entry. Then organise the list into what seems like the most logical order, and read the text which refers to that until you understand exactly what you should be looking for when appraising the car.

Always take an experienced companion with you when you go to assess a car. There is so much detail to absorb that no matter however comprehensive you believe your appraisal to be, you are bound to miss something if you are on your own.

THE NATURE OF RESTORATION

Thousands of words have been written on the subject of home classic car restoration, most of which is informative and very creditable but, irrespective of how comprehensive the coverage appears, it is somehow incomplete. Not that the contents are in any way wrong – the works are usually scrupulously researched – but they fail to impart the true flavour of restoration.

So what is it like to undertake a home car restoration? Mainly, it is a tremendous amount of hard work and few first-time restorers appreciate beforehand just how much work has to be done. An experienced home restorer can expect to take many hundreds (sometimes thousands) of hours to complete a project and a novice may have to spend much more time than this in the workshop.

Of course, the time requirement will vary greatly dependent on the car concerned and its original con-

Keeping the car as 'original' as possible is a very worthy aim, but some components will prove beyond any reasonable repair. These MGB seat covers are not only approaching the limits of 'repairability', they're the wrong colour for the car. The solution ….

… A local upholsterer made these covers up from a single hide; they cost about the same as a set of 'off-the-peg' MGB seat covers. Never be too proud to call in professional assistance, especially for skilled work like upholstery.

dition. A car for which new panels and reconditioned mechanical components are available should take less time to restore than one where panels have to be fabricated from sheet metal, and damaged mechanical components have to be repaired or searched for at autojumbles. But to merely establish that car restoration is hard work fails to impart the real flavour of what is involved.

Restoration consists largely of countless hours of tedious scraping and cleaning. To do the job properly paint, underseal and rust have to be removed from the chassis/bodyshell; burnt oil deposits and other substances have to be scraped from the mechanical and electrical components.

Experience suggests that comparatively few people (other than those with previous professional motor trade experience) carry out complete classic car restorations. This should not be so surprising. The most basic elements of restoration such as producing consistently strong and neat welds, shaping a replacement panel so that it fits properly, or fabricating new panels from sheet metal, for example, can take years of practice. If anything, painting a car

There is a world of difference between restoring a car to good 'useable' condition and concours. Decide what standard of car you really want before starting the restoration.

requires even more experience and, given that the most skilled of paint sprayers, welders and panel beaters still have occasional disasters, it is little wonder that the sensible home restorer should seek professional assistance.

Strangely, although there is no disgrace attached to the admission that elements of a restoration were carried out by a professional, it seems that some people who claim to have fully restored their cars are happy to bask in the reflected glory of someone else's work. A friend of the author once proudly claimed to have restored a car but, on closer questioning, admitted that he had not done the actual welding, nor the actual paintwork, nor the actual mechanical repair – the list went on. In the end it became apparent that his experience of car restoration probably extended to some cleaning and polishing – but was mainly concerned with writing out cheques!

STRIPDOWN

This is the easiest aspect of a restoration; even first-timers usually make it through the stripdown and – vitally – remain in good spirits. Because the work is relatively easy, it seems to go quickly – so quickly, in fact, that the novice can in all the excitement overlook the all-important issue of labelling the components, sorting and storing them according to where they fit on the car.

The importance of this will not be apparent until the time comes to build the stored components back in to the bodyshell, when countless hours will be wasted trying to find the right fastening, or in quiet contemplation as to what fitted into that hole in the bulkhead.

However, not all stripdowns go as smoothly as they should, particularly with cars which have been standing idle for some years. Fastenings can become so completely seized that they cannot be shifted by lubricating or force. This fact does not deter many restorers from using ever-increasing force on the fastening with not only the inevitable result that the fastening eventually shears but also that the associated component is often damaged. Even worse, a weak bodyshell can be distorted if too much force is directed at something such as a damper mounting bolt.

Workshop manuals – invaluable for anyone repairing a car which is in generally good condition – do not cater for the typical restoration project and consequently do not warn the restorer of the problem of dealing with old, rusted and often seized-up components and fastenings.

The stripdown can be a time for the thinking novice restorer's spirits to plummet and the restoration to come to a premature end; first, it is the realisation that the petrol tank is leaking and in need of replacement, added to which the seized suspension and braking components are totally unserviceable and must be replaced, plus the wiring loom has also to be replaced, plus the …

Sitting down with a spares catalogue and price list, listing and pricing the components which will have to be renewed can give a total outlay figure to bring the most optimistic restorer to earth with a bump. No wonder so many cars make it to the classified advertisements as part-completed restorations.

It might seem fatuous to repeat this, but what you are about to undertake is dirty and dangerous, involving poisons as well as lethal equipment. If you do not protect yourself, you are heading for disaster.

INSPECTION

After the mechanical components have been stripped from the bodyshell, a full inspection usually takes place to try and establish the true extent of bodyrot. This means firstly removing the old paint and underseal and discovering (A) that your beautiful Ferrari-esque red sports car was originally painted a disgusting and very 1970s mustard, and (B) that underseal is the most stubborn substance known to man (scrape off what you can with an old chisel, remove the last vestiges with a paraffin-soaked rag).

Unfortunately, most monocoque cars seem to possess pressings which are hidden from view until other panels are cut away. So, you efficiently order all of the repair panels you think you'll need, then cut away the first rotten panel only to discover that the joker who designed the car hid another panel underneath – which will of course have rotted.

Then there's the problem of recognising the work of the talented sculptor who constructed a new inner wing from chicken wire and body filler, which you don't discover until you try to weld a new outer wing onto it. Upsetting though it may be to discover such horrors, you cannot help but admire the sheer artistry which goes into such bodges.

Then you find evidence of the art of the patcher - he who welds patches over areas of rotten steel, then welds patches over patches when the originals rot through, which never takes long. The author has seen evidence of no less than seven overlapping layers of patches on one inner wing, and this car he mischievously dubbed 'Apache'.

Those who survive the inspection without having a nervous breakdown then have to support the shell so that it cannot distort before the rotten metal is cut away. But when a shell is badly rotted you cannot help but wonder whether it's already distorted and, being short of a jig to check it, you have to resort to jacking, chocking, endless measuring and creative use of a spirit level. When you're satisfied that the shell is true you can move on to the glamorous work – cutting and welding.

BODYWORK

There appears to be a tradition amongst some of the manufacturers of spurious body repair panels that no panel should fit without some degree of cutting, shaping or more usually both. The very worst examples of pressings and sub-assemblies can be so wildly inaccurate that you may wonder whether you could have fabricated a better version at home, and the answer is probably yes - you could have. Even worse, the author has encountered some repair panels which, under their standard issue black primer, had both light surface rusting and evidence of oil contamination. Since then, he has made a point of taking all repair panels back to bright steel and re-priming them himself.

Before you can fit repair panels, however, there comes the problem of how to cut out the unwanted steel from the bodyshell. More specifically, the problem is finding a method to cut out the rotten steel without your neighbours complaining to the Environmental Health Officer about the din. In residential areas, the use of air chisels is often ruled out simply on noise grounds, and the cacophony created by an air hacksaw being used on resonant panels is no better. The quiet tool for cutting steel is the tin snip, but if you do much cutting with this then a repetitive strain injury is most likely, and aviation shears are little better. A drill-powered nibbler is thus an indispensable tool.

You should, of course, wear the fabled 'stout leather gloves' when cutting metal (as advised by all written works on restoration) but those who have actually attempted to work while wearing gloves will understand just how much more awkward the process becomes, and most appear to take their chances with the razor-edged steel. Bodywork repair is usually summarised as offering up repair panels and marking the edges, cutting out the rotten metal, clamping and finally welding in the new. In fact, the process should be described as follows. Clean the steel around the repair bright, cut out the rotten parts and somehow clean the back of the adjacent steel where the weld will be made (paint, oil or rust on the reverse side of a Mig weld will weaken the joint). Spend half an hour truing up the repair panel so that it bears a passing resemblance to that which it is to replace, and cut it down to the smallest practical size, not only to reduce the amount of welding which will be needed but also to enable you to use a full repair panel if the repair ever has to be repeated.

Offer the tailored repair panel into position, smile wryly and spend a further fifteen minutes shaping it. Clean off the original primer and apply a rust retarding primer to within half an inch of the edges which are to be welded, and allow this to dry. Spray all remaining bare metal with weldable zinc paint (which not only helps prevent future rusting but also makes weld splatter removal that much easier). Clamp or tack the repair panel into position, then begin welding it up a short length at a time, stopping to hammer the next bit of the edge down before continuing. Extinguish fires as and where they occur. Finally, fill the holes which you have blown into the panel, grind the weld flush and clean the panel of ALL weld residue. Get some primer on it before it rusts. Put out the flags and throw a party.

Repair panels are actually straightforward to fit in comparison with replacement whole panels; the problems of poor fit are exacerbated in relation to the size of the panel, the larger areas concerned are more prone to heat distortion during welding and the chances of the shell distorting when a whole panel is cut out are increased.

PAINTING

This is where the strongest men have been known to break down and weep. The process is long and not a little uncomplicated, and one small error or a quirk of fate can ruin countless hours of hard work. To make matters worse, paint spraying is like learned manual skill; you can read the text books until you're blue in the face, but the only way to learn is to experience it - and to make mistakes.

Preparation - as the scribes all tell us - is the secret

Two of the favourite cars for restoration projects flank another. A '66 MGB GT and a 1970 1500 Beetle. But the one in the middle is a 1993 Limited Edition – the easiest way to get some of the feeling of classic car ownership, with none of the heartache.

of good paintwork. You begin by beating out and filling all of the visible dents. A few stalwarts still use near-molten lead for filling dents, but the user-friendliness of modern body fillers has won over the majority of us. Then you flat the filler, which fills the atmosphere with millions of particles of dust (hardly ideal conditions for spraying) if you flat it dry with a random orbital sander, or – if you flat it wet (and remember that body filler is porous) – this creates rivers of milky liquid which run down the car for the sediment to settle out and leave traces of a dry, chalky substance in the most inaccessible crannies.

Then you spray on the primer, and the car looks fabulous. Smarter people leave the primer to harden properly (a couple of weeks is the minimum) before spraying on a thin guide coat which can be flatted to reveal a myriad of surface scratches, dents and bumps which were not visible when the car was in primer but which stand out like the proverbial sore thumb at this stage or (if the guide coat stage is omitted) only after the topcoats have been applied.

Body stopper (cellulose putty) takes care of surface blemishes, though don't allow it to harden fully before blocking it down, or the effort required will probably result in your going right through adjacent areas of primer. Then you can prime it again, leave the primer to harden (another two weeks) and finally flat it with 1000 grit or finer wet 'n dry ready for the topcoats. Most classic cars were originally finished in cellulose, which is a good paint for the DIY restorer due to its rapid air-dry time, cutting the time during which sundry airborne substances can fall on and adhere to the surface. Cellulose also has drawbacks, not least of which is its shrinkage, which shows up every minor imperfection – however tiny – in the underlying primer. The greatest problem is that the amateur restorer is unlikely to possess an expensive face mask with a filtered air supply and, consequently breathing in copious amounts of thinner fumes, ends up completely spaced-out and not giving a tinker's cuss what the finish looks like.

The shrinkage of cellulose coupled with the scroll marks liable to be left in the primer surface after the most careful flatting mean that many thickness' of paint are required to get sufficient depth in order that the surface can be cut back to give the legendary 'mirror' finish. Most people let each coat flash off (the thinners evaporate) before applying the next some twenty to thirty minutes later. Fanatics – sorry, concours restorers – wet flat in between coats, use a lot of paint and spend a lot of time.

But there's more which can go wrong when topcoats are being sprayed - much more, and the only way to get to understand the right way to go about spraying is to learn from your own mistakes.

THE REBUILD

The rebuild should be the most pleasurable part of a restoration, simply because the end of the restoration grows ever closer. However, if you're dealing with anything but a prolific car (for which every conceivable spare is available) then unavoidable delays while hard to find spares are acquired can drag the process out and make it anything but enjoyable.

The temptation to rush to get the car assembled and running must be resisted for fear of damaging the paintwork. The engine and gearbox must be carefully guided over the bonnet slam panel and under the scuttle without touching the shiny new paint, chrome trim must be oh-so-carefully popped into position to avoid scratching the cellulose.

Assuming that you are able to remember where everything goes, the time comes to bite the bullet and fill the fuel tank, connect the battery and try to fire the engine up. If the engine runs, you have a few seconds to listen to a deep rumbling noise and deeply regret not having first spun the engine with the spark plugs removed to get the oil pressure up.

Anticipate having to sort out electrical faults; most non-functioning components will be suffering nothing more than poor earth connections, so check these first. Blowing fuses can be a nightmare to diagnose, and if you are one of those people to whom a wiring diagram is as comprehensible as a treatise on nuclear physics, bring in help.

THE MOT

In most published accounts of restorations, the fairytale ending is normally a first-attempt MOT pass, but the reality can be very different. A friend of the author once had to fail a freshly and seemingly beautifully restored Aston Martin on a maladjusted hand brake – the fact that the restorer was not competent enough to adjust drum brakes should bring into question his competence in other aspects of the restoration, such as whether the welds are going to pop open the first time the car is driven over a pothole. A newly-restored car belonging to the author waited until late evening the day prior to its MOT to suddenly develop a complex electrical fault which was only traced and rectified after burning the midnight oil. But that's the nature of classic car restoration.

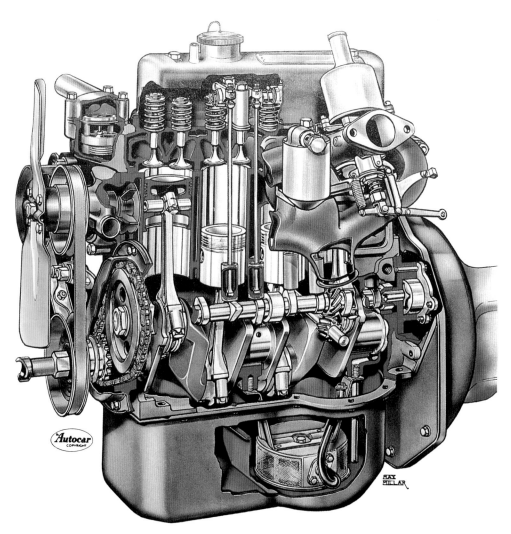

CENTRES OF POWER
The politics and impact of a great engine

The vast range of classic cars in guide books and price listings reflect an industry brimming with novel ideas and styling. However the reality is that a large proportion of these different models are actually the same family under the skin. This common dependence on shared engines is completely logical in terms of cost saving but does serve to underline that the success of a large number of cars depends on the right development teams and decisions. Landmark engines such as the Ferrari Colombo V12 provided the very heartbeat to a collection of vital road and competition cars, while other engines such as Ford's Kent and the incredible Jaguar XK120 power plant can be highlighted as the golden nuggets which helped reap rewards for the factories over time. In terms of day-to-day classics, one of the most significant of these is the BMC A-series power plant (*Autocar* cutaway by Max Miller, above) and the politics and tension surrounding its birth make interesting reading.

To try and place its significance into perspective we really have to look back to the early days of

1937 Austin Seven; the car which which had seen Austin through the difficult period that followed the First World War, the car that had done more, according to Sir Herbert, to 'bring about the realization of [his] ambitions to motorize the masses.' But it was old even then, and would continue in production post-war. The Motor caught the mood in 1949, reporting from the Earls Court show: 'There are not many pennies about ... A latter-day Austin Seven is what many people yammer for.'

Austin. The Austin Motor Company was founded by one Herbert Austin, the son of a Buckingham farmer, who gained initial engineering experience working for his uncle's Wolseley Sheep Shearing Company in Australia. Back in Britain Herbert Austin started building Wolseley tri-cars which Vickers acquired but they then fell out over engine design and Austin soon walked. That was in 1905 and led to Herbert Austin forming his own company, buying land on the outskirts of Birmingham and embarking on a 10-year expansion which was helped (as were so many other manufacturers) by wartime production activity.

By the cessation of hostilities he had a factory complex on over 200 acres of ground but unwisely had limited his car production to a single model, which gave him no safety net as the post-war recession bit.

A receiver was brought in and Austin had to temporarily step down. However he refocused on new cars and by the mid thirties had surpassed the annual production figures of even his arch rival Morris, with whom he had held unsuccessful merger talks. To further militate against any professional liaison, Morris had succeeded in buying Wolseley cars from Vickers – something Austin had been seeking to achieve. As the Second World War approached, the 70-year-old Morris – by then Lord Nuffield – made the unexpected choice of Leonard Lord as his replacement. Lord had been successful at Wolseley and moved to be Managing Director of Morris Motors where he skilfully integrated both Wolseley and MG into the organisation. However, he suffered

a volatile relationship with the meddlesome Nuffield and eventually stormed out, having been excluded from enjoying a share in the increased profits he had generated. This created a virtual vendetta which would ultimately fuel the development of the A-series engine. While Lord took a long holiday to consider his future, Nuffield went on to acquire another marque – this time Riley.

On his return from a round-the-world trip Lord took up the position of Works Director for Nuffield's arch rival Austin. Within just four weeks Lord had evolved a vision for the company's future and presented it to an appreciative board. There would be a new range of OHV engines rated at 14hp, 18hp and 25hp, scrapping a planned truck and instead creating a new range which were nicknamed the Birmingham Bedfords. These would use the 6-cylinder 3.3 litre engine to be known as the D-series and which would eventually provide post-war 4-cylinder variations for Austin's road cars. Also within Lord's vision was a smaller range of side-valve engines yielding 8hp, 10hp and 12hp, but these failed to materialize before the onset of the war. Leonard Lord's position with Austin was already very secure when in 1941 Lord Austin died, followed by the early retirement through ill health of the then chairman and managing director Payton – catapulting Lord into a powerful position to focus company growth. The factory's production output during the war years was impressive and was helped by their own airfield from which to release finished aircraft. Immediately following the restoration of peace the old models were

All the testing of the new Austin Seven took place in great secrecy; one newspaper even tried a light aircraft in its search for a scoop, a measure of the interest generated. At Earls Court in 1951 it stole the show. Austin's first attempt at unitary construction was a hit with the press and public alike.

Its Sensibly *designed*

The Austin A30 Seven is a masterpiece of design and skilful production. Its dimensions are limited yet it is roomy and accessible; it is inexpensive to buy yet fully equipped and lustrously finished; it occupies little space on the road and can be parked in places that drivers of other cars have rejected as impossible, yet it is no less competent than models of far greater bulk. It is practical in every way and without equal as a value-for-money investment.

The top-opening bonnet of the Seven combines with the low build of the body to afford excellent engine accessibility for routine inspection and maintenance.

Good rearward visibility is an important safety feature of the A30, for manoeuvring in reverse and keeping following traffic in view.

A front view of the car shows that forward vision through the windscreen has been well provided. The outlook is further enhanced by a short sloping bonnet.

The A30 door hinges were external to reduce the thickness of the doors.

returned to productions together with the addition of the Austin Princess. By then there was a 1,200cc, 4-cylinder version of the truck engine to power both their new A70 Hampshire and unsuccessful US targeted A90 Atlantic model. The now redundant airfield acreage was also turned into factory facilities to house the critical new economy family saloon – the A30. The immediate post-war drive was to favour making larger, exportable models and this having already been undertaken, cheap and practical British cars were now needed.

While all these production stepping stones were being put in place Lord – convinced of the commercial logic of combining forces in order to facilitate the regrowth of the car industry, continued to try to achieve a merger with BMC. Unfortunately, Lord's treatment under Nuffield remained a very personal sore and neither man actually enjoyed the other's company. In 1948 a tentative working arrangement was struck but it fell apart within the year. Again in 1950, Lord made overtures, gained agreement in principle but this time the BMC board, aware they were losing commercial ground to Austin, blocked further progress.

This was the key moment: having been denied proper rewards for his initial work with Nuffield in the '30s, then repeatedly thwarted in merger negotiations, he struck out immediately, ordering the go ahead to create tooling for the production line for the planned AS3 – the Austin A30 – and its hugely important engine. Nuffield's commercial mainstay was the 1948-launched Morris Minor but it was powered by a 1930s side valve engine while Lord's Austin A30 would boast a brand new, ohv engine. The gloves were off and what Lord had initially seen as a logical commercial union of two equals rapidly became a battle for corporate supremacy. The strategy worked and on the 31st March 1952, Leonard Lord achieved his goal, creating B.M.C.

The first design notes for the project were recorded in the spring of 1949 and the eventual A30 was unveiled to the public in October 1951. The initial 4-door, then 2-door, Countryman, the pick–up and the van all entered the marketplace; but with only 48 inches of shoulder width and very basic trim levels it was in reality poor competition for the new Morris Minor – that is, had it not been for that new ohc 803cc engine. The importance of this engine to Lord, to BMC and later British Leyland, is underlined that by the fact an amazing nine variations on its cubic capacity would exist by the end of the sixties and that by the early eighties over 20,000,000 cars would be fitted with derivatives of that basic 803cc unit.

Strictly speaking its roots lay in that 1939 ohv so-called Birmingham Bedford truck engine which was enhanced for military use in 1940 to the 4-litre `High Speed' using Zenith carburation and known as K-series. Its later use, along with a further High Speed 100hp version on Stromberg carbs, was in the Princess saloons and A110 Sheerlines by then designated as D-series. The 1949–57 Jensen Interceptor also employed the same power supply linked this time to triple SU carburettors.

Because of military production, engine development continued throughout the war and in 1944 a 2.2-litre 4-cylinder version appeared for both military use, and domestic in the Austin 16, the Gypsy and the taxi chassis. From this developed the 1948 2.6-litre unit which went into the Austin A90 Atlantic, the roadgoing Austin Champ and the Austin-Healey 100. Parallel with this 2.6 engine existed the old 1932 Austin 10 side-valve engine which remained in production until 1947. Elements of this ageing 10/4 engine and the D-series unit amalgamated to create the 1200cc A40 Devon engine. It was this 1.2-litre engine that was effectively the parent to the new and important BMC series A and B ranges. This wartime evolution of future civil engines was thanks to Austin's work for the military and caused even more tension and resetnment within the Nuffield camp.

One of Lord's main achievements in the industry was the creation of a complete family of versatile engines suitable for use in ever-changing body styles and with different market requirements. The A-series engine was in no way revolutionary, but it *was* post-war; and it was built on brand new production lines. All the BMC series engines utilized cast iron blocks and cast iron cylinder heads with the cam driven by chain from its mounting on the side of the cylinder block. There were three main bearings, a single down

The A90 Atlantic was a star of the '48 London show, but it failed in the US.

Two recipients of the A-series; the 1100 and the Mini are pictured here by the author in the Silverstone pits in 1968. That's the paddock behind!

A reminder of another string to Leonard Lord's bow; the Riley company had originally been acquired by Lord Nuffield in 1938. 'The One-Point-Five is brilliantly modern from stem to stem ... The interior has a striking contemporary smartness.' The 1957-65 car was one BMC product that didn't have the A-series engine!

You'll take your hat off to the **NEW** *Riley* *One-Point-Five*

powered for thrilling performance

recapture true motoring pleasure with the *Riley* *One-Point-Five*

draft Zenith carburettor and an output of 30bhp – hence the initial cars being called A30.

Though this little car may be viewed as the launching pad for an extremely famous engine it ought not to be at the expense of admiring the construction of the vehicle itself, which was in many ways more modern than the engine. Leonard Lord listened to his instincts and when in the late forties

an Ian Duncan emerged in Birmingham trying to convince any manufacturer that would listen that his tiny two-seater Duncan Dragonfly prototype was the way forward, Lord saw the talent and acquired both the man and his design. It was a tiny two-seater coupé built using unitary construction, employing front wheel drive and a cross-mounted engine but it was sadly under-developed. Lord put Duncan and Ken Garrett together and their pooled skills helped devise the basic construction plans for the all-new Austin A30. Unlike the rival Morris Minor which required internal armatures and support for the body, the A30 was truly a unit construction. The body panelling itself was designed and built to maintain strength and this compact yet quite complex body shape was a testament to those two men both with aeronautical backgrounds. Genuinely chassisless, this was a modern car. It is ironic that its main rival – the Morris Minor – became its stablemate after the eventual takeover and creation of BMC. Eventually with all Leonard's logic the Minor, like so many cars in the group, would end up being powered by this incredible engine. The man's leadership played a significant role in the general reconstruction of a healthy British car industry.

The amalgamating of standard production elements – along with fresh styling and construction thinking,

stood him apart from competitors. Consider how from this initial car/engine package the cards were shuffled. How the A30 grew into the 948cc A35 and donated its engine to finally transform the Morris Minor into a real post-war winner, how that Minor floor pan was then the platform for the Riley 1.5 and Wolseley 1500 combined with the BMC Series B engine. How the A35 was recreated to attract exports by giving it an Italian body and calling it the Farina A40. Consider the sheer brilliance of mounting the engine sideways in Alex Issigonis' famous Mini, remember the world-beating competition Cooper S versions, the strange American-styled Nash Metropolitans powered by this engine, the distinctive Elfs and Hornets, the whole range of 1100/1300s, the much later Metros and Turbos. It is a list of great distinction and reminds us just how easily commerce and originality could work hand in hand back then.

Perhaps one of the finest examples of this fusion of production parts and fresh thinking was the 1958 Austin-Healey Frogeye. This world beating little car was the direct result of a meeting in the winter of 1956 between Donald Healey and Leonard Lord. It had been Lord's quick thinking that turned the 1952 Healey 100 début motor show into a commercial partnership forging Austin-Healey while simulta-neously filling the production hole left by their

unsuccessful Atlantic. During that 1956 meeting Lord explained he was looking for a cheap, practical two-seater to replace the old Austin Seven Nippy and Ulster and is reputed to have said what he wanted was 'a bug'. The talented Healey team under Donald and Geoffrey Healey set about meeting his brief.

The chassis design was extremely advanced, bor-rowing the same monocoque construction ideas

The Sprite fulfilled Lord's brief, 'sports car performance, small car economy,' as the copy boasted.

207

Minis old and new. For a car to last so long, its original power plant had to be something special.

which had helped the famous racing Jaguar D-Types to their historic Le Mans victories. Great care had been taken so that most of it was constructed with flat surfaces for easy, economical manufacture with the entire rear section of the body shell as one piece – boot storage was accessed from the seat area. In the best of Lord traditions, the Austin A35 engine and gearbox were installed and parts such as steering were taken from the Morris Minor. The initially planned pop-up headlights proved to be too expensive and so the now famed Frogeye headlights were installed – the resultant two-seater was unveiled to much praise and instant commercial success.

Naturally, the Morris Minor was in existence when Lord took over, but the systematic improvements to the car and the use of the A35 engine turned it into an undisputed classic generating a further 1,3000,000 sales for his BMC. Alex Issigonis who had designed the Minor was obviously closely affiliated with Austin over the secret plans for the birth of the Mini. The series A engine was the obvious choice for this project but even in its crudest form – little more than planks of wood, wheels and an engine, the design team were astonished at the outright performance from a transverse mounting. Indeed, the 848cc engine size chosen for the first Minis was actually a decrease on the then current BMC series A engines such as 948cc for the Sprite. While ideas were being evolved on how best to use the A engine in the Mini it is not widely known that Issigonis was actually using his Morris Minor as a test bed for his experiments. For a while we saw Issigonis and his mother

fairly regularly within Oxford and at that time the Morris Minor he used had the BMC A engine removed and then re-installed, this time in the transverse position, thus simulating the eventual Mini. It was kept a secret and clearly provided a lot of active research towards the Mini.

The eventual raw power of the great Works Mini Cooper S team was a far cry from the modest 30bhp, 803cc first engines; but actually the development had further still to go, for in the 1980s that basically similar engine – now called the `A Series – A Plus' range, was proved capable of delivering 93bhp from the Metro Turbo.

Interestingly the progression of both the A30 to A35 and A40 to Mk II form actually incorporated more development and power than the visibly obvious larger rear windows or added tailgates suggested. The initial A30 offered just 62mph and a 0–50mph of around 29 seconds. With its low gearing it was not a fast car but did present the attraction of 42mpg. Five years into production its replacement by the A35 saw significant improvements and numbers of young racing drivers learned their skills with modified versions of the little A35. The top speed rose to 72mph and it could now reach 0–60 in a fraction over the previous 0–50 times. A brand new set of close ratio gears married to a higher axle ratio and the increase to a 948cc sized engine meant a full 25% increase in the torque performance – all this with the loss of just 2 mpg. In that five years the quality of roads had improved and petrol itself was now available in higher octane grades so that greater compression ratios were desirable. However, the existing A30 white metal bearings were close to their limit so the A35 adopted lead–indium ones along with full flow oil filtration to protect the crankshaft from the harder bearings.

These valued and real improvements would see the baby Austin remain in good shape until its inevitable fall from grace in the shadow of the revolutionary new Mini.

It was this revamped and faster A35 which was the platform for the Farina A40 which may have first appeared as a saloon but was really designed as a semi-estate. Within a year of its launch it gained the illusive tailgate while mechanically remaining virtually identical to its sister, the A35. However, two years later in 1961 the Mk II version was announced with 3.5 extra inches of wheelbase, improved suspension and a slight increase in horse power through

A-Series Engine
THE INCREASE IN HORSPOWER 1951 TO 1982

Year	Engine size (cc)	Model first to use	Max horse power	
1951	803	Austin	30bhp (gross) @ 4800 rpm	Original
1956	948	Austin A35/Minor 1000	35bhp (net) @ 4800 rpm	
1958	948	Austin-Healey Sprite	43bhp (net) @ 5000 rpm	First twin-SU installation
1959	848	Austin/Morris Mini	34bhp (net) @ 5500 rpm	
1961	997	Austin/Morris Cooper	55bhp (net) @ 6000 rpm	High-tune Mini-Cooper, first twin-SU *saloon* installation
1962	1098	MG1100	56bhp (net) @ 5750 rpm	Twin-SU installation
1963	1071(S)	Austin/Morris Cooper S	70bhp (net) @ 6200 rpm	
1964	1275(S)	Austin/Morris Cooper S	76bhp (net) @ 5800 rpm	Most powerful non-turbo
1966	1275	Sprite/Midget	65bhp (net) @ 6000 rpm	production A-series
1967	1275	MG/Riley/Kestrel/Wolseley 1300	58bhp (net) @ 5250 rmp	
1982	1275	MG Metro Turbo	93bhp (DIN) @ 6130 rpm	Most powerful A/A-Plus engine ever

Plus many minor variations down through the years

Would you like a chronology of engine changes through the years? We would need another book. Here's just one: the 1275GT Mini engine does not have tappet chest covers, the 998cc does. Use it in polite conversation.

The A40 MkI was produced between June 1958 and September 1961, the Countryman arrived a little later and disappeared at the same time. Farina's styling was superb – but the Mini was at the same show for the first time.

A-SERIES POWERED CARS PERFORMANCE EXAMPLES

BL Model	Engine size (cc)	Max power (bhp)	Overall fuel consumption (mpg)	Maximum speed (mph)
Austin A30	803	30	42	63
Austin A40	948	34	38	72
Minor 1000	948	37	39	73
Minor 1000	1098	48	31	73
Morris 1100	1098	48	33	78
MG 1100	1098	56	29	85
MG 1300 Mk2	1275	70	27	97
Mini 850	848	34	40	73
Mini 1000	998	38	34	82
Mini-Cooper	997	55	27	85
Mini-Cooper 1071S	1071	70	29	90
Mini-Cooper 1275S	1275	76	28	96
Sprite 'Frogeye'	948	43	34	80
Spridget 1100	1098	59	30	92
Spridget 1275	1275	65	28	94
Metro 1.0	998	45 (DIN)	35	84
MG Metro	1275	72 (DIN)	39	100
MG Metro Turbo	1275	93 (DIN)	30	110

This is not an exhaustive list! Many other BMC and BL cars, of course, have been fitted with derivatives of the A-Series/A-Plus engine.

changing carburation to the Morris Minor 1000 SU. Like the A30, the Mk I A40 enjoyed competition success both on the race circuits and in rallies. As a result, much of the real improvement to the Mk II A40 wasn't the valued, if cosmetic, body trimmings but in areas such as the suspension set-up. Telescopic rear dampers instead of lever arm rear ones, a front anti roll bar and a switch to full hydraulic Girling brakes. The horsepower might have only risen by a fraction, but the car became more sure-footed, leaving the way clear for yet another moment of Lord/BMC integration.

In the summer of 1962 the Morris version of the new 1100 range was unveiled – from the same Italian design house as the A40, and this enlarged 1098cc offering of that trusted series A unit instantly became the finite version of both the Morris Minor and the Farina A40, along with creating the MG Midget and Mk III Sprite. This final transformation of the A40 gave it a greatly improved gearbox as well as a top speed of 80mph. Needless to say, while these initial carriers of the incredibly versatile series A engine

were edging towards retirement, the full impact on the next generation was being felt with the 1100/1300 range and the irrepressible Mini. The A30, A35 and A40 collectively sold just under a million units for Lord and his teams, pulling both the company and the motoring public out of the doldrums of the post-war years.

Their simplicity, their ease of maintenance, their individuality of styling, have carved out a special place for them with the classic car enthusiast. The later front wheel drive A-series cars brought great performance and considerable fun, but construction had begun to make DIY maintenance less and less attractive and it would not be long before the grey shadows of Lord Stokes' British Leyland gathered. All the emphasis moved towards literal badge engineering with common bodies and diminishing pride in individual marques.

Terminal signs for many makes – though the inimitable family of engines conceived by Leonard Lord would remain the solid basis even of British Leyland for many years.

STARS AND CARS
Making Impressions

S tars and their cars have long held a curiosity value. More often than not the celebrity enjoys the pleasures of a Rolls-Royce or Bentley, or sometimes an expensive sports coupé. Such cars are part of the spoils of victory within their professional world. Less frequently chronicled is their earlier transport. In the mid-1960s I spent some of my time working with such people and this led, inevitably, to a great many 'Stars and Cars' features. Sometimes cars were just transport, for others they were a very real interest, while occasionally professional image-making played its part, too.

Just for fun I have returned to my own notebooks and pictures to revisit some of those earlier encounters.

ROGER MOORE

The encounter with Roger Moore was on the clinical side. I was invited to visit him at Elstree Film Studios where he was engaged in the making of an episode of *The Saint*. His rather supercilious air as Simon Templar didn't much appeal to me, but there was no denying he was criss-crossing our screens with panache in the pretty Volvo coupé. The day hadn't started well. I had just plucked up the courage to tell my Mini it was being replaced by a shiny new white and black 1275 Cooper S and it instantly went into a sulk. Having been the epitome of reliability, it suddenly split a by-pass hose between block and head and having scrambled to make repairs to get to Elstree, a front tyre went within just a few miles of my destination. I should just have waited until the forecourt handover and simple announced 'goodbye'.

The studios seemed vast, with a veritable army of technicians and actors scurrying to and fro. I was met by a PR who ushered me into Studio Three where we stood respectfully just outside the pool of film lights until the introductions were effected. With crisp efficiency we were almost immediately marched down successive corridors towards Mr Moore's reserved parking place to admire the familiar cream P1800 Sports, complete with magnesium wheels. He explained that there were, in fact, two identical cars which provided both on-camera and private transport, but was anxious to point out that when *The Saint* started production, it proved very difficult to persuade British motor manufacturers to co-operate. 'I learnt to drive in the army', he explained, 'with three-ton trucks, Jeeps, motorcycles. They would give us a track test and then let us on to the roads'. Riding a Matchless on one occasion, he arrived at the bottom of a London hill to notice a policeman halting traffic. It was all too late for Mr Moore who continued on into a branch of Woolworths, coming to rest on a counter. One of his first career opportunities was acting in an AA

promotional film standing by an AA box on the Hogs Back road in Surrey. He marched back towards the set to be descended on by mirrors and make-up. 'My first car was a Jaguar SS, then a Standard Vanguard which I actually swapped for a friend's Alvis.' He slips into a waistcoat and checks himself again in the mirror. 'I've had two- and four-seater Thunderbirds, Chevrolet Impalas, a Jaguar XK150 and a Sunbeam Alpine'. A PA gets restless waiting for him to step into the set of a cellar/dungeon containing a captive. 'Oh yes and all three types of Volvo'. What, I asked, was he currently driving apart from the Volvo? A Hillman Imp and a Princess 1100, drifted back the reply as he was moved into place. The place fell silent. A thug walked on set with the prisoner's food, Simon Templar appears from nowhere, kicks him over, releases the man, picks up a sandwich and exits. '… Sooooper', burbles the producer. 'Print it'.

BRITT EKLAND

There were certain attractions to this encounter. Not only was the actress the idol of every picture desk in Europe, but she and Peter Sellers were enthusiasts. Indeed, Sellers was actually running a racing team and my previous meeting with her had been at undoubtedly the wettest meeting ever held at the Crystal Palace race track. Their London

apartment was tucked round behind London's Park Lane and was suitably impressive. The long mirrored hall was graced by a stunning portrait of Britt by Lord Snowdon, and the L-shaped lounge was finished in muted turquoise. It had a white dining table and egg shaped chairs, while coloured sofas and chairs were designated white for women, black leather for the men. This was the 1960s incarnate and the Beatles *Revolver* album was playing as the stunning Ekland joined me. She was wearing an ochre sweater and mini kilt, and curled up on a coloured sofa. Fortunately, talking cars was effortless. 'Once it was my biggest dream to have an open sports car. Flashing by with my hair flying in the wind, waving at everyone – you know.' She giggled. 'Three days after meeting Peter, when he had that Lincoln, the E-Type and the 330 Ferrari, he offered me a chance to drive the gold Jaguar and we ended

up in a ditch with this lorry driver trying to help Peter get it out. He never said anything, but it was a long time before I drove his cars again. I've had a Bristol for a year, a Lotus Elan for three weeks and two Mercedes.' The current model proved to be a navy and white 230SL with manual gearbox – the previous black and white version was automatic and failed the fun factor. 'They are quite fast', she insisted 'and I've only had one accident when I was changing lanes and scraped a VW … Oh, and when I was stationary in Chelsea a school bus ran into the back. You should have seen the mess it made of the bus' she added, perching on the armrest of another sofa. 'I suppose I've been quite lucky because I pay the first £800 of damage. I really think the Mercedes is a woman's car, it suits me, though I know David Bailey has one like mine. Another woman's car is the Rover 2000 and the new Alfa. The Mini and the E-Type are universal, but cars like the Aston Martin and the Ferrari – there are really men's cars.' She continues to fidget and play with strands of her hair. 'You aren't married are you … Then I imagine you must have something like a Cooper S: am I right? I love playing these games.'

DAVID FROST

Frost was at the height of his work for Rediffusion Television when I met him, during his famous period commuting to American TV. He had just moved into his new home in an exclusive Knightsbridge crescent and I had arrived at breakfast time which, according to his housekeeper, he was notorious for allowing to get cold. Amidst partly installed kitchen fittings, I sipped coffee and listened to stories of her devotion to him. Eventually, clutching briefcase and mail, he appeared, announcing we had just four minutes to cross town to the studios. We scrambled into his car and forced all crescent foot and road traffic into submission with our getaway. The car was the Mercedes 220SE Automatic and his second Mercedes in less than a year, following his driving test. 'I had one hour's lesson the morning of the test', Frost explained, as he creatively engineered a gap in the traffic queue. 'The 70mph limit is a Luddite law'. A Wolseley owner eyed his threatened bodywork. 'I drive within the car's limits. If it didn't have good brakes I wouldn't travel at these speeds.' An irritating traffic light provides a perfect opportunity to display the Merc's stopping power. 'A Rolls would have been too institutional for me' he explains, as we hurtle away from the line. We make a series of unsuccessful

attempts at short cuts, to the bewilderment of bystanders, and are eventually confronted with multiple lanes of stationary rush hour traffic. We arc in a single sweep across three lanes of startled traffic and head down towards the river. Frost explained his vision of the British motorist as someone who perceived themselves in an ivory tower, safe within their car, able to confront anything or anyone who obstructs them – ideal material for his satire. The journey was, by any standard, eventful, but we arrived at the television station intact and he was instantly escorted direct to the studio. It was an era when David Frost did a lot of rushing.

SUSANNAH YORKE

I was very much a fan of this actress and eagerly drove down to her 19th century Sussex mansion looking forward to the prospect of photographing her. We sat for ages in front of a log fire before she remembered a missing ingredient for the evening meal. 'We'll have to take the Alfa, my Fiat's out of petrol' she explained. The navy blue Italian machine waited in the formal courtyard. She turns the key and we lurch forward. 'Oh dear, we are in reverse or something'. This time it behaves and we weave through the Sussex lanes to the village. 'I hope you don't mind going shopping' she apologises, 'I must just get the petrol first'. We pull up at the local petrol station – 'Oh good Lord, it's the wrong car. Never mind, we'll fill up anyway'. She shrugs and giggles at her own confusion. This was clearly not a woman who considered what she drove as an extension of her 'star' image.

We ended up sitting on the study floor by the open fire drinking tea. Conversation tumbled from her on a huge range of topics often unrelated to each other but always interesting, personal to her. She introduced topics clearly close to her and moments passed in silence, her fingers tracing carpet patterns. You knew to say nothing but felt an overwhelming sense of her vulnerability. It was an experience that haunted me for some time.

The telephone interrupted and she then returned to the basic interview. Her driving test had been a great success – until, that is, she went the wrong side of one of those 'keep left things' and faced an oncoming lorry driver who wasn't too polite to the examiner – assuming him to be her instructor. Subsequently faced with a film role driving around London in a 1925 Lagonda, she practised with wooden chocks on the pedals and used a Mini for the actual test. 'I love holidays in cars' she declared, shrugging her shoulders, 'you can stop whenever you want. One time we took the Coventry Climax-engined Turner to France but it even used up the spare torsion bars and overheated in towns.' The telephone rang again and she was lost to transatlantic scripts.

JIMMY SAVILLE

I travelled to a rain-soaked Manchester for an 11.30pm rendezvous at the Belle Vue Club where he appeared regularly – it was a 4000 capacity ballroom nestled in between the silent fun fairs and a Zoo. Dressed in deep blue doubled breasted suit and permanently equipping himself with vast cigars from a leather case, he was instantly the performer you expected. The arm around my shoulder, the 'pleased to meet you my friend', the pacey delivery of every sentence, he was the consummate professional DJ – without any signs of the private man. We sat for a while in the now virtually deserted ballroom and talked cars, his cars. More a businessman than enthusiast, his choice of transport was early evidence of his long proven skills to be all things to all people. 'Right now' he proclaimed igniting another Churchillian-sized cigar, 'I have a new Rolls-Royce Phantom Five here in Manchester, a 4.2 E-Type at Scarborough and my bubble. I travel about 1000 miles a week – half by road, which means I live out of suitcases between seven houses, flats and caravans across the country. My first car was a 2.4 Jaguar, but now I keep a steady stream of three cars. In the last five years I've owned seven Rolls-Royces and the bubble is my seventh.' He draws breath and we step out into the damp Mancunian night to admire his

bright yellow BMW Isetta. 'I only ever keep them for 4000 miles then get another.' He adopts a sequence of familiar poses for my camera. 'I've had eight in her' he proclaims with a broad grin. Why the Isetta I asked? 'It's the two seats my friend – side by side.' His eyes twinkle and he re-lights the cigar.

SUSAN MAUGHAN

When I met Susan Maughan she was a 24-year old with nine years experience in show business, including a year with Ray Ellington and a recording contract with Philips. Her popularity crystallized when she recorded the hit record Bobby's Girl reaching number three in the charts during 1962. Four years later I sat in a Bournemouth Winter Gardens café and waited for the singer to arrive. On cue she appeared, complete with a white poodle called Bobby suitably dressed in a jewelled collar. From her lap it eyed me constantly, refusing chocolate throughout its vigil. Susan's first car was a Zodiac but without a licence she had to use a driver. Next came the 2.5 litre Daimler, then the driving licence, but seven months later she and her partner were involved in a crash which wrote the car off. However, they had been using seat belts and she was naturally anxious to reinforce the difference belts had made to their chances. As a result of this scare they took considerable trouble selecting a new car and eventually chose the Jensen CV8 after a visit to the factory. They took delivery of an entirely black version including special matt black dashboard and matching luggage and within the year they had already covered 38,000 miles. The car's safety and comfort perfectly suited her work and her stage clothes could be accommodated within the boot. The dog's eyes remained fixed, but Susan, enjoying a solid meal, explained the only criticism of the car was tyre wear. The original Dunlop RS5's lasted just 15,000 miles while the Firestone 130S's replacements were already 23,000 miles in and still looking excellent. Final titbits refused, the tea drunk, Susan and Bobby prepared for the evening's performance. We strolled out to the shining Jensen parked up under the pine trees and Susan adopted a series of poses against the bonnet, in the boot, the driving seat – all with the ease of a professional who had performed an eight-month season at the London Palladium and walked onto the stage at the famed Royal Command Show. The entertainer in her bell bottomed trousers and pink sweater was as much part of the 1960s as Jensen itself. The dog on the other hand, was not such a memorable icon.

DEJA VU
Modern Manufacturers find our weakness

The font end styling of the Jaguar XK8 (above) echoes unmistakably that of the E-Type (opposite).

One of the less publicised victims of the Second World War was individuality. It was perhaps an inevitable casualty with the need to combine both resources and thinking to begin the economic recovery. Building design for instance lost much of its sense of style and began a depressing phase in architectural history of uniform construction, culminating in those infamous tower blocks which we have now begun to demolish. The motor industry too suffered the same fate, with many of the proud pre-war marques being closed, sold or merged. Fortunately though, re-stabilizing meant an urgent need to capture overseas orders which at least kept these swelling motor giants focussed on fashionable cars. The '50s models made way for the likes of the Mini and the E-Types and during this avalanche of motoring activity matured perhaps the most powerful

consumer group of this century – the immediate post-war Baby Boomers. It is their ingrained motoring dreams and memories of their youth which have carried the present classic car movement to such unexpected heights.

The effect of industrialists like Lord Stokes who systematically destroyed the traditions of individual marques is a separate and lengthy topic – though rationalising of some kind was undoubtedly valuable in the light of the subsequently tough seventies. What is truly fascinating is the vision of the more far-sighted manufacturers who now target this same powerful army of enthusiasts whose interest and spending power is defined by this nostalgia for the cars of their youth. Occasional magazine features cite retro styling but utterly miss the more subtle visions of certain manufacturers. Sympathetic styling and the resurrection of period names/badges has the potential to bring enlightened companies considerable success.

The undoubted visionary is Mazda. They not only recognized that the re-birth of an affordable period-inspired two seater was timely, they also invested heavily to ensure it triggered the dormant affection of the post-war children. Even during the pre-drawing board stages someone persuaded the Mazda Managing Director Keniche Yamamoto to take a company-owned Triumph Spitfire for a journey into the tranquility of the Japanese mountains – to savour the enjoyment of that era's open motoring. The resultant MX-5 has virtually singlehandedly led Mercedes, Porsche, MG, Alfa, Fiat, and BMW to look afresh at the affordable two seater. The fact it reminds us of various former classics while performing as a mid-1990s machine is utterly to their credit. Even specialist cars such as the Rochdale Olympic and the little GSM Delta were part of the design team's homework. In fact, the early prototype was secretly tested and compared alongside a Toyota MR2, a Fiat X1/9 and a Reliant Scimitar – they knew what they were doing and the world has not surprisingly been seduced.

European companies may have been slower to spot the opportunities but we are now entering an era of considerable activity. Perhaps such a perfect car as the Mazda does not come along too often but familiar and much loved period trading names are certainly winging themselves at us, hoping to strike a pocket of loyalty in our hearts. After a lapse of virtually 30 years since the last Spider launch there is now a stunning new Alfa two seater. There is a brand new two seater MG continuing the traditional alphabetic suffix and the new Jaguar XK8 featuring a powerful nose with more than a passing resemblance to the classic E-Type. More subtle but equally appealing are the clusters of period styling details emerging. Take, for instance, the extremely promising Fiat Barchetta which is currently only lhd. It's clean and simple lines have incorporated new high tech lighting behind good old fashioned streamline glass protectors, while you can check the health of the 130bhp 16-valve 1747cc engine on white background instruments tucked into their own binnacle – a period fashion item also used in the MGF. Interestingly the Barchetta employs slender flush door handles which emerge at the press of the button and will certainly appear extremely familiar if you just happen to own a 300SL Mercedes! Another of the present Fiat range, the highly individual 16V Coupé, boasts a Pininfarina styled dashboard painted in the actual body colour – just as

we used to see on cars such as the MGA What's more it looks good alongside contemporary controls.

In France there are repeated rumours of a future `replacement' for the unique and much-loved Citroën 2CV and although it's unlikely to be as stunningly original as the first, just the link with the old jalopy will draw custom. At the 1995 Geneva Motor Show Renault were anxious to celebrate the fiftieth anniversary of their classic 1940s, million-selling 4CV. To honour the occasion they unveiled a concept car named the Fiftie which was a two-seater, mid-engined coupé based on the Spider basics and housing their new 60hp DF7 engine. Concept cars have a habit of turning up a year or two later as production models and this tiny car brilliantly captured the free and easy spirit of the 4CV while boasting the brand new engine, a roll back roof, light but strong carbon fibre bodywork and interior gems such as wicker-work clad door trim, seats in linen and cotton

The Fiat Barchetta, one of the many two seaters chasing some of the MX-5 pot of gold.

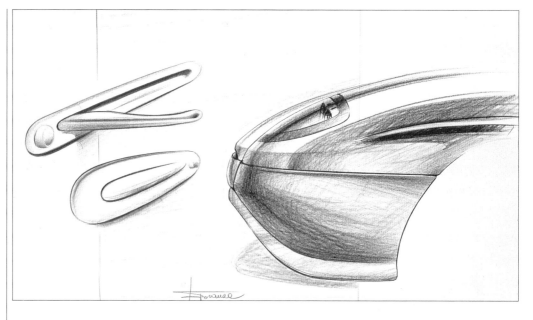

Original sketches for the Fiat Barchetta door handles (left). Which is the Barchetta, which is the Mercedes 300SL (below and below right)? Mercedes on the right.

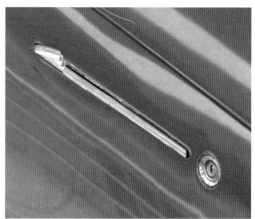

and a tailored picnic basket. A bit too cute perhaps but the basic car offers enormous period character with genuinely modern equipment.

This vogue of mixing past and present offers new commercial opportunities to smaller marques who have managed to continue trading and thus not lose credibility. Marcos are a fine example, so too are TVR while Lotus despite numerous problems over the years have now just presented us with the brand new Elise. Interestingly, as part of Mazda's comprehensive research for the MX-5 they polled Americans for their immediate list of real sports cars. The result was Ferrari, Alfa Romeo, Lamborghini, Corvette,

Any excuse to contemplate that marvellous Mercedes body: so here is another angle on the door handle.

Pininfarina dash on the Fiat
16V Coupé, painted in body
colour – just like the MGA.

Porsche and Lotus. Such valuable customer awareness should stand this Norfolk firm in good stead with the Elise which utilizes the responsive Rover K-series engine within a lightweight body involving a structural frame of aluminium dressed in advanced plastic body panels. This gives it a weight much the same as a Mini and linked to all independent suspension offers performance figures to embarrass many rivals – particularly at around £20,000. It may present a very hi tech, modern image but even here there are the little styling signals from the past. The small flying buttresses from the rear of the roll bar reminiscent of numerous '70s supercars,

Project leader Tony Shute
looks justifiably proud of the
Lotus Elise and its relaxed
driving position, obtained via
moderately angled seating.
Shute has a broad pedigree
includiing Esprit variants
and a spell as a Goodyear
tyre development engineer.

The full-size 'clay' model of the Elise is very close to the final shape in 1995. Much thought was given to those little F1-style 'winglets' to remind customers of a glorious Grand Prix pedigree.

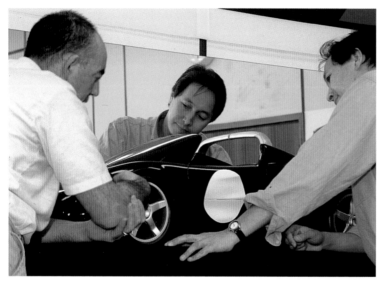

the fluted side panels and intakes seen on Dinos and even the nice turned-up tail looked just as good on a 1960s Prototype P4 racing Ferrari. These are all the little details that seduced on the original cars and now hold considerable appeal to us who remember.

Another example is the new BMW Z3 Sports which is the German company's entry in the race for a slice of the Mazda-exposed nostalgia market. James Bond's transport in *Golden Eye*, this pretty car is really based on the conventional 3-Series saloon but like the rivals it encodes body styling with shadows of former glories. The subtle indentation of the waistline and the more blatant copy of the side intakes cannot help but trigger recall of the classic 1950s BMW 507. In fact, although this two seater may not in itself suggest BMW are at the forefront

This early model is actually half a car and half mirror reflection. A trio of such scale masterpieces preceded the first full-size work. Another is pictured above, with Lotus design boss Julian Thomson (centre) and his skilled staff. The car's unique aluminium construction, featuring adhesive bonding, meant substantial weight savings.

It is only a concept car of course, but Renault's Fiftie points to the preoccupation of many of the big manufacturers with historical styling cues.

of the commercial adventure, they are probably the best equipped of all manufacturers and the present hierarchy suggests it intends to make full use of what they possess. By spending 800 million pounds on buying the Rover organisation they have not only acquired a going concern but also the rights to forgotten marques. With considerable understanding of the market they have already let it be known that they are considering a re-launch of the Riley marque rekindling the status of the Pathfinder and the smaller 1.5. It's gone further, with plans to turn the eventual replacement for the present Rover 800 series into the first new Riley model since the twilight days of the Elf and Kestrel under British Leyland. Not content, there is talk that Wolseley too might reappear and that Austin-Healey also is being considered as the home for a possible big sports car.

There were fears that British model identities would disappear if BMW bought Rover. As it turns out they are proving to have a greater understanding of the present-day power of the classic car appeal than most. One thing is certain: a new Riley model range parented by BMW is likely to generate renewed pride in this once famous marque.

The 1956 BMW 507 never surpassed 100 cars a year, was built at a time when the company was practically bankrupt, but its presence was memorable enough to see the intakes echoed on the new Z3.

A DRIVE IN THE COUNTRY

Private time in the last Works Healey

At any significant gathering there are usually one or two guests possessing that certain something, people who either deliberately or without trying become the centre of attention. Inevitably their appearance, their clothing, their manner, colour our judgements – their personality and character having little bearing. So too with cars. Scan a race meeting car park and hundreds and hundreds of perfectly decent cars become metallic wallpaper alongside the handful of shimmering E-Types, Aston Martins or even domestic '50s two seaters. It is this charisma that creates star cars but as every motoring journalist discovers, the existence of eye catching bodywork is no guarantee the car has any real character or personality. Neither Pininfarina bodywork nor Armani wardrobes ensure membership of the true Super League – real characters – human or automotive, are very rare items.

In the late spring of 1967 I was invited to drive a car already internationally famous and which would go on to become historically significant. This truly was a supercar, a personality so strong that just a handful of gifted drivers ever fully harnessed its potential. This was the glorious Works Healey 3000. Not one of the endless replicas which now exist, not even one of that rarefied collection of real BMC Works cars but the actual last one, the car the competition chief himself bought. Peter Browning had just replaced the brilliant Stuart Turner as the BMC Competition Manager. An ex music scholar and one-time designer of church organs, he had stepped into this powerful position at a difficult time with both the dominating Mini Cooper S and Healey 3000 machines nearing the end of their competitive lives while BMC's own future remained confused for a further nine months until Lord Stokes achieved control, creating British Leyland.

Shortly after his appointment I spent time with Peter publishing an interview introducing him and listening to his mixed feelings about the task ahead. We enjoyed each other's company, shared common interests in both music and naturally cars, leading to an unexpected invitation to sample the delights of finite big Healey.

It was a hot day and even as I drove through the gates to Abingdon's Competition Dept headquarters this scarlet and white machine dominated the landscape – simply parked in the courtyard. Trade plates were needed and Peter disappeared to hunt out a set. The car and I just stood there in silence. The famous body panels felt warm in the sun and I remember watching white clouds distorting across the paint work. It sat rugged, dignified, wearing its full battle dress of lamps and trimmings like a virile Chelsea Pensioner. Indeed, Peter later underlined the reluctance to retire it: "The age of the ralliest' hairy sports car is passing, yet the incredible Healey won't die." Often we read about rare competition cars and are left with a sense of some glamorised production model, easily replaced if it leaves the road. This however was still in the era when world-beating giants were very much the product of gifted craftsmen. As Peter attached the plates, figures appeared around the big workshop doors. Faces such as Nobby Hall who

had conceived and hand-built those famous side exhaust pipes and Cliff Humphries who would later go on to become Chief Development engineer. They were part of the Healey's family, who lived and breathed just to bring the car success, hand-built and nurtured it into its global status. Like proud and anxious parents they watch over even our private outing. These completely unsung heroes were part of

Competition chief Peter Browning hoped a victory in the RAC might halt plans to end Healey production.

Proud parents (below). Four of the Works team of craftsmen who built the car. From left to right: Nobby Hall, an old Abingdon road tester who went on to create the special chassis and bodywork; Den Green, ex-Oxford Garage, who became Competitions Deputy Foreman; Gerald Wiffen, one of the most talented and long serving Competition Department mechanics; and Cliff Humphries, gifted with power units and tuning, he became Chief Development Engineer.

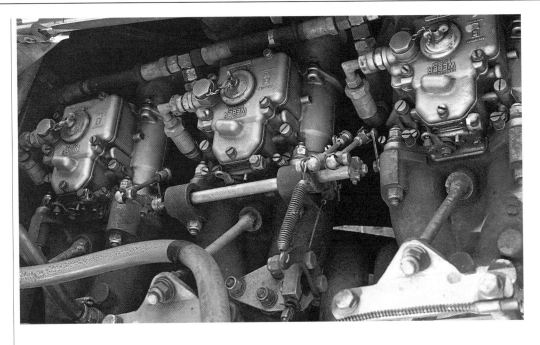

a small team who helped the Morely brothers chalk up two outright wins in the Alpine Rally, Pat Moss and Rauno Aaltonen to first places in the Liege and Timo Makinen so close to success in the 1966 RAC International Rally. That Makinen effort in fact proved to be the last official Works entry for this all-time thoroughbred, thanks to the newly introduced Appendix J regulations. The Healey 3000 production line was known to be ending and a decision was taken to try and do everything possible to build a Works car capable of winning the next RAC Rally – the one rally which had eluded the factory team. The unspoken hope was that if it could achieve this mission the publicity might just prevent the production line closing. Peter Browning had previously bought the triumphant 1964 ex–Morely's Alpine car – then ARX 92B, and under his leadership the Abingdon Competition team set about rebuilding his car as the absolute Healey.

The car I was about to sample was bored out from 2912cc to 2982cc and fitted with a gas flowed aluminium head which raised the compression to 11.1. There was a nitrided crankshaft, nimonic valves and a six-branch manifold linked to Nobby's modified side exhaust system to improve ground clearance. A bank of triple 45DCOE Weber carburettors completed the cocktail which produced 173bhp at the wheels. By the end of preparation this was raised to an astonishing 200bhp. The standard Healey box was not its finesr point and to cope with these extremes of power a set of straight cut gears with overdrive on third and top provided six evenly spaced options. The suspension too was strengthened with 14 leaf springs and fresh shockers installed helping to raise the ground clearance from 5 to 7.5ins. Braking was via a twin system with tandem master cylinders and twin servos with DS 11 disc pads all round. Traditionally the competition cars were something of a handful and so the steering was changed, with smaller leather wheel and lower ratio providing something closer to a Cooper S feel.

All this equipment was concealed beneath that famous Healey bodywork largely constructed of aluminium with bolt on steel guards for the sump, gearbox and the 20-gallon fuel tank. With the seven powerful driving lights and all the interior fitments

this lightweight bodied car was actually 1.25cwt heavier than the standard roadgoing Mark III. Statistically it offered 135mph with a standing quarter in 15.5 seconds consuming 8mpg. On ordinary roads the consumption did raise to around 15mph depending on how you behaved.

"We'll go somewhere private so you can squirt it about as you want" offered Peter as we hook up our full harnesses. He turns the key, instantly filling the cramped cockpit with a thunderous sound of heavy machinery. "I'm afraid" he shouted, "this is where conversation has to end." He studies the gauges very intently, appears satisfied and we curve round the Competition Dept tarmac and out through the Works gates to a crisp salute from the uniformed guard. "We'll take it quietly until she warms up" comes the message over the thrashing of moving parts. It's strange, but even now the most vivid recall of that buildup drive was the smell of the rapidly hot engine, the worn carpets and the relatively minor sounds of bodywork chattering and protesting at the near solid suspension settings. Surprisingly, it was quite prepared to behave itself through Abingdon town running as low as 800 revs while the temperature rose quickly to 160 and remained solid.

My subsequent drive in this famous car was memorable and instantly underlined the more aggressive

This Healey didn't stay at home; the Morely brothers won the Alpine Rally outright in it.

side to its character. As I mentioned earlier, not too many cars really possess the personality to match their outward appearance. This however, was certainly one of them. It had but one purpose in life and everything about the car gave you the impression it was awaiting any opportunity to cut loose. Even the journey to our 'somewhere private' illustrated the sensation. It would be easy to parallel the situation to a race horse wanting to break into a gallop, challenging the rider for authority. That's fatuous cry the cynics, a car is inanimate; and I'd be happy to concede that the battle is largely between two sides of a driver's psyche, but still the appearance, the sound, the willingness of such

Peter Browning's car was originally plated ARX 92B.

Another Works car:
Timo Makinen in the 1963
RAC Rally. This glorious car
was written off in the fol-
lowing year.

an incredible car is a critical part of the seduction and invites such a comparison.

As we edged away from built-up areas and towards our destination the long road ahead was an open invitation to the Healey. Peter reflected on the temptation and in a flurry of feet and wrist movements dived into lower gears. There is a roar quite beyond description, the long powerful bonnet lifted and set its sights upon the stretching tarmac. The tail snaked, the wheels kicked and the body pitched while Peter's face remained gaunt and intent, his hands twitching around the steering wheel and darting momentarily to the gears to satisfy the beast's insatiable hunger for tarmac. There was little doubt he was in control and no question that the situation was permanent. The car was heading due north by mutual agreement, any small slip by a lesser driver and the car would have dominated. A well known S bend passed to the

accompaniment of briefly whistling disc brakes and again the road opened out. England passed by in much the same way as that famous period short film of a compressed three-minute train ride between London and Brighton.

As the awesome beast catapulted us down the long, straight road an Oxford Mail Mini van pulled out from a side lane. Instantly we dropped down two cogs, the car moved out, lifted its distinguished nose and stretched out. We advanced at unpublished speed with the most incredible sound, rushed the modest Mini van, the air horns screaming a fanfare to this truly great sports car. Experiencing this car's urge for long open forest tracks or Alpine passes on English byways was like watching a lion pacing up and down its cage pining for the open plains of Africa.

Tragically the private dreams of postponing production line closure through a final rally triumph for

Rauno Aaltonen and Henry Liddon were dashed when at the last moment the 1967 RAC Rally had to be cancelled because of a national outbreak of Foot and Mouth disease. So the ultimate Works Healey never flexed its considerable muscles in anger.

However, I had enjoyed this unique occasion and, as Peter put it, this incredible car was "Probably the most developed car ever to come out of the Competition Department."

There is a roar like you've never heard, as the long, powerful bonnet lifts and takes aim at the tarmac.

HOUSES OF PLENTY
What do Auctions Offer?

There really are no firm rules on how to research the purchase of your first classic other than to yet again recommend liaison with the appropriate owners' club. Their specialist advice is invaluable and there is always the chance a suitable member's car will answer all your prayers. However, in all probability you will gain vital information but still have to turn somewhere to find your future motor car. Who do you trust? Only a handful of one-marque specialists make themselves known through the magazines and though these are an obvious route you are still left with the nagging thought that in your obvious innocence – and with the distinct lack of commercial alternative sources – you are still vulnerable while buying what is essentially an elderly second-hand car. Clearly, classified

adverts are another source but you are still wholly at the mercy of others. This makes most of us feel uneasy and even when a car is found and priced, you wonder: for that price plus all the restoration, would a slightly more expensive, but less wrecked, car be preferable? It's a debate raging in a great many households every year. It is ironic that one of the best moves is to visit a reputable classic car auction – a traditional seat of anxiety to most laymen.

Sadly, we generally view the auction houses with too much circumspection. Certainly, unless you are an expert, the sense of danger in buying an unknown car is very real, but these events can also be of huge value in themselves. They are really fascinating for a spectator, not just as entertainment, but also for offering highly concentrated information on what cars attract interest, what prices are actually paid, how to actually participate. It's also a rare opportunity to spend time openly examining a large array of classics – treating the gathering as a huge classic car showroom. In many ways visits to auctions are a perfect starting point to classic ownership allowing you a chance to build up knowledge – maybe even change your mind a few times on models – before finally attending one as a buyer; only this time, accompanied by an expert friend.

A respected motoring colleague, Richard Hudson-Evans, has become one of this country's leading auction experts. He not only provides valuable weekly insight into cars and prices at each event through the pages of *Classic Car Weekly* but also performs precise valuations for individuals and organisations based upon his deep knowledge. He is adamant that the only true way to compile classic car price guides is from the performance of each model at auction. In pure terms he is correct, but only certain cars appear at auction; and ultimately a red Austin 1100 may have a known auction price, but to someone looking for just that car its value may well be greater – if only they had attended that sale. His column will certainly give you insight into current figures but there is so much more value in attending sales and being able to assess differing classics and their conditions.

There are many regional sales throughout the year which may well be fairly simply staged events, but with only local attendance there are opportunities to catch a car which might draw far more attention at one of the more fashionable venues. Again, it pays to either research your chosen model well beforehand or take someone with you who is experienced. Above this regional spread of sales there are five national organisations who cater from time to time for the classic market. Defining the differences between what they offer is extremely difficult.

A 1952 book entitled *British Motor Cars* displayed details of the production cars available during that year and was heavily endorsed by the Society Of Motor Manufacturers. In a clear attempt to support the British industry, it also invited the big players to offer a brief statement giving a sense of their company's position and the key products for the year. Leonard Lord (Chairman of Austin), David Brown (Chairman of Aston Martin Lagonda). Sir Rowland Smith (Chairman of Ford UK) and others all defined their company's position and discussed immediate plans. In the 1990s the increasingly powerful classic car market has a similar peer group of leading figures – this time it is the principals of the big auction

houses. So we invited the five big organisations to provide something akin to those much earlier statements and also provide us with definitions of their houses.

The first to respond is probably the most genuinely aligned house to the day-to-day classic market – ADT – while Brooks and Sotheby's quickly followed with their own view points. Coys made calls to us but never followed through, while Christie's remained silent. It is of course important to remember cars are not the only, nor even the major, element to their trading, but Brook's and Sotheby's enthusiasm to engage with the classic car enthusiast does stand in contrast. Being associated with high visibility race meetings under one's own name clearly raises a company profile; but as our price guide underlines, the widening trade base for relatively humble classic cars is far removed from the entertainment value of a day out watching expensive period race cars compete. When looking for a 1960s Rover do you go to the company with the most prestigious classic car event, or the one that lists good examples for sale?

ADT AUCTIONS STATEMENT

Tom Gibson. Chairman and Chief Executive

There is a very positive trend that we have noticed at our classic and historic sales, as enthusiasts and collectors have returned to supporting the market in strength. It is this knowledgeable group of people who are maintaining the momentum in classic car sales, having reclaimed the initiative from the institutional investment houses, who had such influence in 1988–89. While there is undoubtedly a select, niche market for the most glamorous vehicles worth hundreds of thousands, the reality is that the enthusiast wants a practical, affordable and usable classic for weekend driving, rallies, hill climbing or whatever his or her passion may be.

Price, therefore, is a strong factor and initiatives such as the abolition of Road Tax on vehicles aged 25 years and over have a very noticeable effect on the market. In our sales subsequent to that announcement it has been very apparent that pre-

1970 vehicles are very much in demand. Of course, at ADT Auctions our customers get the added benefit of our low 5% premiums and unique drive-through auction facilities.

In our experience of selling in the classic market – whether it is £200,000 worth of Ferrari or a £2,000 Ford Popular – there is a classic car for everyone. While purists may not agree, it is often the ordinary, everyday vehicles that attract the most attention at classic auctions. Good, usable classics with a solid club following, for example, and a plentiful supply of parts and spares.

And this is a market where the beauty is very much in the eye of the beholder. We have had enthusiasts buy cars because their family owned one when they were growing up. Or the man who always wanted a Jaguar E-Type in his youth and now, some 30 years later, is in a position to afford such a car. As a case in point, ADT Auctions recently sold a 1961 Jaguar E-Type S1 Roadster, finished in red with tan leather trim for £17,800 to a private buyer, while a similar model, but dating from 1953 and finished in gun metal grey, was purchased by another enthusiast for £16,000.

When you look at the list of affordable and available classic cars in the market place, from MGB's to Austin 7s, there's little wonder that the enthusiast is back in numbers and buying with confidence – and for pleasure, not for profit.

SOTHEBY'S STATEMENT

Martin Chisholm
Deputy Director and Head of Car Department

"Are they really worth all that?" asked an American dealer at Sotheby's first sale of Veteran & Vintage vehicles in 1965. Sotheby's was the first fine auction house to conduct specialist sales of collectors' cars and a full house at the opening auction saw a Rolls-Royce Silver Ghost, formerly owned by the Maharajah of Mysore, sold for the princely sum of £9,800, the highest figure ever achieved for a collector's car. *The Autocar* described the price as a `shattering sum' and the Times reported that the auction of `old metal and ancient engines' was so popular and the prices so keen that it was bound to become a regular event. The Daily Telegraph delivered itself of the opinion that some of the real enthusiasts were as `picturesque as the lots on view'. Historically, the enthusiasts, alongside the connoisseurs and dealers, have provided the motivating force for the market.

Since the first sale Sotheby's have set the standard with spectacular record prices realised in the sporting market, for luxury bespoke motor cars and, of special interest, with sought after `barn discoveries'. Sotheby's have sold more museum and one-owner collections than any other auction house, conducting major car sales in London, Monaco, Zurich, Geneva, Monza, New York, Cleveland, Palm Beach, Santa Barbara, Melbourne, Canberra, Sydney, Perth, Auckland, Johannesburg and various other locations around the globe as well as nationally. Sotheby's team of specialist staff offer an unrivalled network of contacts through its international offices, providing expert confidential advice in all matters relating to dating, valuation and sale of collections, individual vehicles, motorcycles and automobilia worldwide.

Collectors' motor cars have unique qualities to recommend them and, by their use, provide a dividend denied conventional investments. For the prospective buyer, the specialist auction reduces time spent on research and travel and if the car is bought well, the purchaser's chances of appreciation are much better than ever. Apparently sensible assumptions about forecasts remain vulnerable but notwithstanding, a well considered investment can prove the most rewarding of allegiances for the owner.

bracket is also healthy. The larger Austin Healeys are consistently achieving £15–£17,000, a good Jaguar XK-type roadster will make £25–£28,000 and MGAs in concours condition are selling for £12–£15,000. Aston Martins have made a modest recovery with good DB4s and DB6s selling for figures in excess of £20,000 – a far cry from the days when £180,000 could be asked – but generally the market has adjusted to `Enthusiast' rather than `Investment' prices, and levels are now back to those of 1986/7.

There has been a very definite resurgence in interest in Ferraris, particularly those requiring some work, and therefore at the cheaper end of the market, and this is difficult to explain because generally cars requiring restoration work are the hardest to sell at present. The exceptions are invariably important cars where the finished value will exceed restoration costs.

The average age of drivers on the Formula Ford grid is now 40+, and there is therefore increasing demand for single seater racing cars from those who can afford them. The market for high value competition cars, however remains unpredictable. Market confidence across the board is now returning, however, and this is evidenced by the increasing number of sales currently being held in the UK – a large proportion of which are organised by Brooks.

BROOKS STATEMENT

Malcolm Barber - Managing Director

While the early 1990s witnessed a dramatic decline in the market for post–war classic cars – compared perhaps with the fall in value of modern impressionist paintings during the same period – there have been clear indications of a steady recovery since 1993. Doubtless this is due in no small measure to the establishment of the single market in January 1993, which has encouraged European buyers throughout the EU to buy classic cars in Britain. While levels at the top end of the market are nowhere near those achieved in the heady days of the late 1980s, we are seeing some good prices. Witness the £464,800 paid for the ex-Carroll Shelby 1960 2-litre Maserati Tip 61 Birdcage at Brooks's sale in Monaco in May 1996.

By far the most buoyant sector of the market, however, in terms of sales volume, is that for cars costing up to £10,000 while the £10,000–£25,000

PRICE GUIDE
1993–Present-day Fluctuations

In the following list of cars and prices, we decided to compare values in 1993 with those today, in order to produce a percentage swing entry. The reasoning was two-fold: firstly, by 1993, the volatility of the classic car market caused by the entry of the speculators at the end of the 1980s had stablised. Secondly, having adjusted the figures for the currency fluctuation across the years, the percentage swing provides a comparative review, car on car. This is in fact in some ways more revealing than absolute values, which of course change continuously and can never represent the market position for the incredible variety of model years and state of repair of individual cars, except with a broad brush stroke. In the end of course, you will set the price of any car, face-to-face with the vendor: ultimately, the only price that really means anything.

Open leading price guide pages and discover, for instance, Ford Capri prices two years *before* the announcement of the car, compare rival publications and find during the same month that the matching grade of Rover 75 is astonishingly valued at both £2,200 and £6,500, that a concours condition Lamborghini Miura would cost you £30,000 more in one publication, a DB6 50% extra, if you happen to rely upon one guide and reject another.

Another problem is dates: is a car dated from its announcement, from its motor show debut, from its first showroom appearance? Likewise, the end of production doesn't mean the end of stocks.

Given these problems and the inherent difficulty of prices being set by *individual* sales of older, more exotic cars, we approached the task of providing an informative guide using the following bases.

* We averaged values given for 1993 – safely beyond the price distortions of the late 1980s.

* We took the contemporary valuations and produced the same computerised mean figures for each car.

* With professional assistance, we introduced the exact Bank of England change in the value of the pound during the intervening years into the assessment.

* Finally, we added a precise percentage swing based upon the initial averaged value compared with the present figures after the sterling adjustments.

What can be learned from this year's published listings? Certainly it has not been a good period for some of the larger engined models. The domestic family cars have seen the greatest improvement – with significant exceptions to the rule! The Morris Marina for example, showed a 92% loss, while the Morris Minor 1800 enjoyed a 115% increase in value for the period. Now, more and more individuals are looking with affection on their early motoring, thus lifting the values of quite humble machinery. It may mean more restoration work, but at least the cars were simple and in plentiful supply.

MANUFACTURER	ACTUAL CAR	YEAR FROM	YEAR TO	1993 VALUE	PRESENT VALUE	VALUE SWING
A.C.	2 LITRE DROPHEAD	1947	1956	£8,500	£9,000	−2.91%
A.C.	2 LITRE SALOON	1947	1956	£5,500	£5,500	−8.30%
A.C.	3000ME	1979	1984	£15,000	£14,333	−12.38%
A.C.	428V8	1965	1973	£23,500	£22,375	−12.69%
A.C.	428V8 dhc	1965	1973	£32,500	£29,000	−18.18%
A.C.	ACE AC	1953	1963	£33,750	£31,250	−15.10%
A.C.	ACE BRISTOL	1956	1963	£40,250	£41,500	−5.46%
A.C.	ACE FORD RUDDSPEED	1961	1963	£38,750	£38,250	−9.49%
A.C.	ACECA AC	1955	1963	£18,750	£24,125	17.98%
A.C.	ACECA BRISTOL	1955	1963	£23,750	£27,250	5.21%
A.C.	BUCKLAND TOURER	1949	1954	£6,750	£9,000	22.27%
A.C.	COBRA 289V8	1962	1968	£82,500	£92,500	2.81%
A.C.	COBRA 427V8	1965	1968	£110,000	£132,500	10.45%
A.C.	COBRA MkIV	1981	1987	£40,000	£44,000	0.87%
A.C.	GREYHOUND	1959	1963	£17,000	£16,625	−10.33%
ALFA ROMEO	1300 GT JUNIOR fhc	1966	1976	£5,000	£6,000	10.03%
ALFA ROMEO	1600 GT JUNIOR	1974	1977	£5,000	£7,000	28.37%
ALFA ROMEO	1750 BERLINA SALOON	1967	1972	£2,500	£3,313	21.53%
ALFA ROMEO	1750 GTV	1967	1972	£6,250	£7,250	6.37%
ALFA ROMEO	1750 SPIDER VELOCE	1967	1971	£7,250	£9,625	21.73%
ALFA ROMEO	2000 SPIDER	1958	1961	£11,000	£9,625	−19.76%
ALFA ROMEO	2000 SPIDER VELOCE dhc	1971	1978	£7,500	£9,333	14.11%
ALFA ROMEO	2000 SPRINT COUPE	1960	1962	£6,500	£8,667	22.26%
ALFA ROMEO	2000GTV	1970	1977	£6,250	£4,350	−36.18%
ALFA ROMEO	2600 BERLINA SALOON	1962	1968	£3,500	£7,000	83.39%
ALFA ROMEO	2600 SPIDER	1962	1965	£10,750	£12,125	3.42%
ALFA ROMEO	2600 SPRINT COUPE	1962	1966	£7,000	£8,375	9.71%
ALFA ROMEO	2600 SZ ZAGATO	1965	1966	£25,000	£30,000	10.04%
ALFA ROMEO	ALFASUD SPRINT	1976	1983	£1,500	£2,608	59.41%
ALFA ROMEO	ALFASUD Ti SALOON	1974	1979	£1,500	£2,625	60.45%
ALFA ROMEO	ALFETTA 1.6 GT	1976	1979	£1,500	£1,867	14.12%
ALFA ROMEO	ALFETTA GT/GTV/GTV6	1976	1987	£5,500	£3,667	−38.86%
ALFA ROMEO	GIULIA GTA	1965	1969	£25,000	£26,667	−2.19%
ALFA ROMEO	GIULIA GTV	1965	1968	£8,500	£6,833	−26.29%
ALFA ROMEO	GIULIA SS	1963	1966	£25,000	£21,000	−22.98%
ALFA ROMEO	GIULIA TZ ZAGATO	1963	1967	£75,000	£80,000	−2.19%
ALFA ROMEO	GIULIA SPIDER	1962	1965	£10,000	£10,250	−6.02%
ALFA ROMEO	GIULIA SPRINT/GT JUNIOR	1962	1972	£5,250	£6,875	20.09%
ALFA ROMEO	GIULIA Ti/SUPER	1962	1973	£3,750	£5,094	24.55%
ALFA ROMEO	GIULIETTA BERLINA	1955	1963	£4,000	£6,250	43.28%
ALFA ROMEO	GIULIETTA SPIDER	1955	1962	£10,000	£11,500	5.45%
ALFA ROMEO	GIULIETTA SRINT COUPE	1954	1965	£8,000	£9,750	11.76%
ALFA ROMEO	GIULIETTA SS	1957	1962	£22,500	£18,500	−24.61%
ALFA ROMEO	MONTREAL	1971	1977	£15,500	£11,000	−34.93%
ALFA ROMEO	SPIDER DUETTO	1966	1977	£7,500	£11,250	37.55%
ALLARD	J2	1950	1952	£42,500	£58,333	25.86%
ALLARD	J2X	1951	1952	£85,000	£58,333	−37.07%
ALLARD	K1/K2/K3	1946	1953	£16,500	£20,125	11.84%
ALLARD	L/P	1946	1953	£12,500	£19,500	43.05%
ALLARD	M/M2X	1947	1953	£17,500	£25,000	30.99%
ALLARD	P1/P2	1949	1954	£10,250	£19,500	74.45%
ALLARD	PALM BEACH 21c/21z	1952	1956	£10,000	£20,000	83.39%
ALLARD	PALM BEACH MK11	1956	1960	£18,000	£25,000	27.36%
ALPINE–RENAULT	A108 BERLINA	1961	1964	£17,500	£15,333	−19.66%
ALPINE–RENAULT	A110 1300	1966	1971	£15,500	£12,333	−27.04%
ALPINE–RENAULT	A110 1500/1600	1967	1977	£21,000	£16,500	−27.95%

MANUFACTURER	ACTUAL CAR	YEAR FROM	YEAR TO	1993 VALUE	PRESENT VALUE	VALUE SWING
ALPINE–RENAULT	A110 956	1959	1968	£8,500	£10,000	7.87%
ALPINE–RENAULT	A110 BERLINA	1964	1967	£12,500	£12,000	–11.97%
ALPINE–RENAULT	A110 GT4 1108	1963	1968	£7,000	£8,833	15.71%
ALPINE–RENAULT	A310 1600	1972	1976	£7,000	£6,000	–21.40%
ALPINE–RENAULT	A310 V6	1976	1985	£11,000	£7,833	–34.70%
ALVIS	TA14 dhc	1946	1950	£13,500	£16,833	14.33%
ALVIS	TA14 SALOON	1946	1950	£10,000	£10,000	–8.31%
ALVIS	TA21 dhc	1950	1955	£15,000	£16,500	0.87%
ALVIS	TA21 SALOON	1951	1955	£8,000	£9,750	11.76%
ALVIS	TC21/100	1950	1955	£15,000	£10,500	–35.81%
ALVIS	TC21/100 dhc	1950	1955	£17,500	£17,750	–7.00%
ALVIS	TD21	1956	1963	£14,750	£13,250	–17.63%
ALVIS	TD21 dhc	1956	1963	£21,500	£22,000	–6.17%
ALVIS	TE/TF21 dhc	1963	1967	£23,750	£25,375	–2.03%
ALVIS	TE/TF21 SALOON	1963	1967	£13,125	£14,625	2.17%
AMPHICAR	AMPHICAR	1961	1967	£6,000	£9,000	37.55%
A. SIDDELEY	HURRICANE	1946	1953	£7,500	£10,875	32.96%
A. SIDDELEY	LANCASTER	1946	1952	£6,000	£8,750	33.73%
A. SIDDELEY	SAPPHIRE 234/236	1956	1958	£4,000	£7,375	69.07%
A. SIDDELEY	SAPPHIRE 346	1953	1959	£6,000	£10,388	58.77%
A. SIDDELEY	STAR SAPPHIRE	1959	1960	£7,000	£11,188	46.55%
A. SIDDELEY	WHITLEY	1950	1953	£4,250	£8,688	87.44%
ASTON MARTIN	DB1 dhc	1948	1950	£25,000	£50,000	83.39%
ASTON MARTIN	DB2	1950	1953	£26,250	£29,500	3.05%
ASTON MARTIN	DB2 dhc	1951	1953	£35,000	£43,750	14.62%
ASTON MARTIN	DB2/4 MK I	1953	1955	£22,250	£28,500	17.45%
ASTON MARTIN	DB2/4 MK I dhc	1953	1955	£35,000	£40,000	4.79%
ASTON MARTIN	DB2/4 MK II	1955	1957	£26,250	£28,500	–0.44%
ASTON MARTIN	DB2/4 MK II dhc	1955	1957	£35,000	£40,000	4.79%
ASTON MARTIN	DB2/4 MK III	1957	1959	£28,250	£36,500	18.48%
ASTON MARTIN	DB2/4 MK III dhc	1957	1959	£33,750	£47,250	28.38%
ASTON MARTIN	DB4	1958	1963	£31,250	£39,000	14.44%
ASTON MARTIN	DB4 dhc	1961	1963	£42,500	£70,500	52.11%
ASTON MARTIN	DB4GT	1959	1963	£95,000	£112,500	8.59%
ASTON MARTIN	DB5	1963	1965	£27,250	£43,750	47.22%
ASTON MARTIN	DB5 dhc	1963	1965	£38,500	£57,000	35.76%
ASTON MARTIN	DB6 MK I	1965	1969	£22,250	£32,600	34.35%
ASTON MARTIN	DB6 MK II	1969	1970	£26,250	£33,250	16.15%
ASTON MARTIN	DB6 VOLANTE MK I CONVERTIBLE	1967	1969	£45,000	£57,000	16.15%
ASTON MARTIN	DB6 VOLANTE MK II CONVERTIBLE	1969	1971	£57,500	£57,000	–9.10%
ASTON MARTIN	DBS	1967	1972	£14,500	£18,000	13.83%
ASTON MARTIN	DBS V8	1969	1972	£17,750	£20,250	4.61%
ASTON MARTIN	DBS V8 SALOON	1972	1991	£23,250	£21,000	–17.18%
ASTON MARTIN	V8 OSCAR INDIA	1979	1985	£32,500	£28,000	–21.00%
ASTON MARTIN	V8 VANTAGE	1978	1985	£37,500	£34,500	–15.64%
ASTON MARTIN	V8 VOLANTE	1978	1985	£45,000	£44,875	–8.56%
AUDI	60/70/80/90/100	1965	1976	£1,475	£1,550	–3.67%
AUDI	GT COUPE	1981	1984	£3,500	£2,500	–34.50%
AUDI	QUATRO TURBO	1980	1989	£6,750	£5,000	–32.07%
AUSTIN	1100	1963	1974	£925	£1,150	13.97%
AUSTIN	1300 MKI–III	1967	1974	£1,075	£1,188	1.37%
AUSTIN	1300GT	1969	1974	£1,225	£1,463	9.51%
AUSTIN	1800/2200	1964	1975	£817	£1,413	58.59%
AUSTIN	3 LITRE	1967	1971	£1,875	£2,175	6.36%
AUSTIN	A125 SHEERLINE	1947	1954	£4,250	£7,025	51.56%
AUSTIN	A135 PRINCESS	1947	1958	£5,250	£7,650	33.62%

MANUFACTURER	ACTUAL CAR	YEAR FROM	YEAR TO	1993 VALUE	PRESENT VALUE	VALUE SWING
AUSTIN	A30	1953	1956	£1,425	£2,138	37.58%
AUSTIN	A30 COUNTRYMAN	1956	1959	£1,650	£2,425	34.80%
AUSTIN	A35	1956	1959	£1,525	£2,300	38.30%
AUSTIN	A40 DEVON/DORSET	1947	1952	£1,650	£2,600	44.52%
AUSTIN	A40 FARINA MKI	1958	1967	£1,625	£1,750	−1.24%
AUSTIN	A40 SOMERSET	1952	1954	£1,875	£2,750	34.47%
AUSTIN	A40 SOMERSET CONVERTIBLE	1952	1954	£4,000	£4,900	12.33%
AUSTIN	A40 SPORTS	1950	1953	£4,500	£5,125	4.42%
AUSTIN	A55/A60 CAMBRIDGE	1959	1969	£1,633	£2,763	55.14%
AUSTIN	A70 HAMPSHIRE	1948	1950	£1,925	£4,025	91.76%
AUSTIN	A70 HEREFORD	1951	1954	£1,925	£3,125	48.88%
AUSTIN	A90 ATLANTIC	1947	1952	£5,250	£8,500	48.47%
AUSTIN	A90 ATLANTIC dhc	1949	1952	£7,250	£3,250	−58.90%
AUSTIN	A90/95/105 WESTMINSTER	1954	1959	£1,600	£3,063	75.53%
AUSTIN	A99/A110 WESTMINSTER	1959	1968	£1,725	£3,113	65.50%
AUSTIN	GIPSY	1958	1967	£1,750	£1,750	−8.30%
AUSTIN	MINI 1275GT	1969	1980	£2,000	£1,650	−24.35%
AUSTIN	MINI COOPER	1961	1964	£4,500	£4,750	−3.22%
AUSTIN	MINI COOPER 1071S	1963	1964	£5,750	£6,625	5.65%
AUSTIN	MINI COOPER 1275S	1964	1971	£6,250	£6,275	−7.94%
AUSTIN	MINI COOPER 970S	1964	1965	£5,500	£6,625	10.45%
AUSTIN	MINI COOPER MKII	1964	1969	£3,500	£4,200	10.03%
AUSTIN	MINI MKI	1962	1967	£2,500	£2,100	−22.96%
AUSTIN	MINI MKI COUNTRYMAN	1960	1967	£1,800	£2,525	28.63%
AUSTIN	MINI MKII	1967	1969	£1,000	£1,500	37.49%
AUSTIN	MINI SEVEN	1959	1961	£2,500	£3,075	12.80%
AUSTIN	NASH METROPOLITAN	1954	1961	£4,000	£4,000	−8.30%
AUSTIN	NASH METROPOLITAN dhc	1954	1961	£4,750	£5,500	6.18%
AUSTIN-HEALEY	100/4 BN1/BN2	1952	1956	£16,250	£17,250	−2.66%
AUSTIN-HEALEY	100/6 BN4/BN6	1956	1959	£12,750	£15,250	9.67%
AUSTIN-HEALEY	100M	1954	1956	£20,250	£22,125	0.19%
AUSTIN-HEALEY	3000 MKI	1959	1961	£15,000	£16,500	0.87%
AUSTIN-HEALEY	3000 MKII	1961	1963	£16,750	£18,250	−0.09%
AUSTIN-HEALEY	3000 MKIII	1963	1968	£19,500	£22,188	4.34%
AUSTIN-HEALEY	3000 MKIIA	1962	1963	£17,000	£18,875	1.81%
AUSTIN-HEALEY	AUSTIN SPRITE	1970	1971	£4,500	£4,150	−15.44%
AUSTIN-HEALEY	SPRITE MKI 'FROGEYE'	1958	1961	£5,500	£6,425	7.12%
AUSTIN-HEALEY	SPRITE MKII	1962	1964	£3,850	£4,013	−4.43%
AUSTIN-HEALEY	SPRITE MKIII	1964	1966	£3,750	£4,013	−1.88%
AUSTIN-HEALEY	SPRITE MKIV	1966	1970	£3,600	£4,350	10.80%
BENTLEY	CORNICHE	1971	1981	£28,750	£31,500	0.47%
BENTLEY	CORNICHE dhc	1971	1984	£33,750	£39,000	5.96%
BENTLEY	MK6 dhc	1951	1952	£35,000	£39,333	3.05%
BENTLEY	MK6 STANDARD STEEL	1946	1952	£15,000	£17,250	5.45%
BENTLEY	PARK WARD dhc	1959	1962	£40,000	£52,000	19.21%
BENTLEY	R TYPE 4.5 LITRE dhc PW	1952	1955	£38,500	£46,667	11.15%
BENTLEY	R TYPE 4.5 LITRE SALOON	1952	1955	£12,500	£13,675	0.32%
BENTLEY	R TYPE CONTINENTAL HJM	1952	1955	£80,000	£89,000	2.01%
BENTLEY	S SERIES SALOON	1955	1959	£16,000	£19,750	13.19%
BENTLEY	S1 CONTINENTAL dhc	1955	1959	£47,500	£110,000	112.35%
BENTLEY	S1 CONTINENTAL PW dhc	1955	1959	£80,000	£110,000	26.08%
BENTLEY	S1 CONTINENTAL PW fhc	1955	1959	£80,000	£50,000	−42.69%
BENTLEY	S2 CONTINENTAL PW dhc	1959	1962	£45,000	£46,667	−4.91%
BENTLEY	S2 FLYING SPUR HJM	1959	1962	£40,000	£50,500	15.77%
BENTLEY	S2 STANDARD STEEL	1959	1962	£15,500	£17,000	0.57%
BENTLEY	S3 CONTINENTAL FLYING SPUR	1962	1965	£47,500	£59,000	13.90%

MANUFACTURER	ACTUAL CAR	YEAR FROM	YEAR TO	1993 VALUE	PRESENT VALUE	VALUE SWING
BENTLEY	S3 CONTINENTAL MPW	1962	1965	£55,000	£40,167	−33.03%
BENTLEY	S3 CONTINENTAL MPW dhc	1962	1965	£55,000	£58,667	−2.19%
BENTLEY	S3 STANDARD STEEL	1962	1965	£21,500	£21,750	−7.24%
BENTLEY	T SERIES CORNICHE MPW	1965	1977	£19,750	£22,500	4.46%
BENTLEY	T SERIES CORNICHE MPW dhc	1965	1977	£30,000	£30,000	−8.30%
BENTLEY	T SERIES SALOON	1965	1967	£10,000	£11,375	4.30%
BENTLEY	T2 SERIES SALOON	1977	1981	£15,250	£16,500	−0.79%
BERKELEY	B60/B65	1956	1957	£2,000	£2,200	0.87%
BERKELEY	B90	1957	1959	£2,375	£2,225	−14.09%
BERKELEY	B90 dhc	1957	1959	£2,500	£2,550	−6.46%
BERKELEY	B95/105 SPORTS	1959	1961	£2,500	£2,738	0.44%
BERKELEY	T60	1959	1961	£1,500	£2,000	22.25%
BMW	1500/1800	1962	1972	£2,500	£2,675	−1.87%
BMW	1502/1600−2/1602	1966	1977	£2,600	£2,600	−8.29%
BMW	1502/1602 TOURING	1966	1977	£2,400	£2,875	9.86%
BMW	2000	1966	1972	£2,625	£2,875	0.42%
BMW	2000CS	1965	1969	£4,500	£4,833	−1.53%
BMW	2002 CABRIO	1971	1973	£6,500	£6,688	−5.66%
BMW	2002 TURBO	1973	1974	£11,250	£10,625	−13.40%
BMW	2002/2002Ti	1968	1975	£3,563	£3,438	−11.53%
BMW	2500/2800	1969	1977	£2,500	£2,767	1.50%
BMW	2800CS	1968	1971	£5,750	£5,083	−18.94%
BMW	3 SERIES	1975	1982	£N/A	£2,000	N/A%
BMW	3.0CS/CSi	1971	1975	£6,750	£7,375	0.19%
BMW	3.0CSL	1972	1975	£7,100	£10,625	37.22%
BMW	3.3L SALOON	1971	1977	£3,000	£3,850	17.67%
BMW	501	1952	1956	£6,500	£12,500	76.33%
BMW	501 V8/502	1955	1963	£8,000	£16,000	83.40%
BMW	503 COUPE	1956	1959	£9,250	£32,000	217.21%
BMW	503 dhc	1956	1959	£14,250	£40,000	157.40%
BMW	507	1957	1959	£90,000	£75,000	−23.59%
BMW	600	1958	1959	£1,000	£2,000	83.32%
BMW	628CSi	1979	1990	£5,000	£3,500	−35.82%
BMW	633CS	1976	1990	£5,000	£4,725	−13.35%
BMW	635CSi	1976	1990	£5,250	£6,250	9.17%
BMW	700	1960	1965	£1,625	£1,667	−5.93%
BMW	ISETTA	1955	1962	£5,000	£4,667	−14.41%
BMW	M1	1978	1981	£72,500	£65,000	−17.79%
BOND	875	1966	1970	£1,000	£1,033	−5.32%
BOND	BUG	1970	1974	£1,500	£1,863	13.88%
BOND	EQUIPE 2 LITRE	1967	1970	£2,250	£2,925	19.19%
BOND	EQUIPE 2 LITRE dhc	1967	1970	£3,250	£3,625	2.29%
BOND	EQUIPE GT4/GT4S	1963	1970	£1,775	£2,125	9.76%
BORGWARD	BIG SIX	1959	1961	£4,500	£7,750	57.91%
BORGWARD	ISABELLA COUPE	1955	1961	£5,000	£7,250	32.95%
BORGWARD	ISABELLA TS	1954	1961	£4,000	£3,500	−19.76%
BRISTOL	400	1947	1950	£21,250	£20,500	−11.54%
BRISTOL	401	1948	1953	£9,500	£19,500	88.22%
BRISTOL	403	1953	1955	£13,750	£19,400	29.38%
BRISTOL	404	1953	1955	£28,500	£32,750	5.37%
BRISTOL	405	1954	1958	£13,250	£18,875	30.62%
BRISTOL	406	1958	1961	£12,250	£16,125	20.71%
BRISTOL	407	1962	1963	£15,000	£14,775	−9.68%
BRISTOL	408	1964	1965	£15,500	£14,775	−12.59%
BRISTOL	409	1966	1967	£16,000	£15,050	−13.75%
BRISTOL	410	1968	1969	£16,500	£16,750	−6.91%

MANUFACTURER	ACTUAL CAR	YEAR FROM	YEAR TO	1993 VALUE	PRESENT VALUE	VALUE SWING
BRISTOL	411	1969	1976	£14,750	£19,500	21.22%
BRISTOL	412	1975	1982	£13,250	£17,125	18.51%
BRISTOL	603	1976	1982	£20,000	£15,750	−27.79%
CATERHAM	SEVEN	1974	1982	£10,000	£9,857	−9.62%
CHEVROLET	CORVETTE	1953	1954	£23,750	£21,250	−17.96%
CHEVROLET	CORVETTE	1955	1957	£15,500	£13,750	−18.66%
CHEVROLET	CORVETTE	1958	1962	£13,250	£13,500	−6.57%
CHEVROLET	CORVETTE	1963	1967	£16,000	£16,500	−5.44%
CHEVROLET	CORVETTE	1968	1972	£13,250	£11,750	−18.69%
CHEVROLET	CORVETTE	1973	1976	£8,250	£7,500	−16.64%
CHEVROLET	CORVETTE	1976	1982	£9,250	£7,875	−21.94%
CITROEN	AMI 6	1961	1969	£1,750	£1,825	−4.35%
CITROEN	2CV	1948	1971	£2,000	£2,313	6.05%
CITROEN	2CV	1971	1991	£1,000	£1,250	14.57%
CITROEN	AMI 8	1969	1979	£1,125	£1,019	−16.95%
CITROEN	AMI SUPER	1973	1976	£1,350	£1,900	29.08%
CITROEN	BIG 15/LIGHT 15	1935	1957	£7,750	£10,063	19.06%
CITROEN	BIG 6	1939	1955	£8,000	£12,750	46.15%
CITROEN	BIJOU	1959	1964	£2,125	£2,188	−5.57%
CITROEN	CX	1974	1989	£2,200	£2,500	4.21%
CITROEN	DS CONVERTIBLE	1963	1971	£10,000	£18,500	69.63%
CITROEN	DS19/ID19/DW19	1956	1965	£4,438	£6,525	34.81%
CITROEN	DS20/21/23 PALLAS	1966	1975	£6,000	£7,313	11.77%
CITROEN	DYANE 4	1967	1974	£900	£900	−8.35%
CITROEN	DYANE 6	1968	1984	£1,000	£1,150	5.41%
CITROEN	GS	1970	1986	£1,000	£1,075	−1.47%
CITROEN	SAFARI ESTATE	1957	1975	£4,000	£5,833	33.72%
CITROEN	SM lhd	1970	1975	£11,750	£14,250	11.21%
CLAN	CRUSADER	1972	1974	£2,500	£2,800	2.71%
DAF	44	1966	1975	£1,200	£800	−38.88%
DAF	46	1974	1976	£1,000	£925	−15.22%
DAF	55	1968	1972	£925	£1,067	5.75%
DAF	55 COUPE	1968	1972	£1,800	£1,500	−23.59%
DAF	66	1972	1975	£925	£1,067	5.75%
DAF	750/33	1962	1975	£1,125	£1,000	−18.50%
DAIHATSU	CAMPAGNO	1964	1970	£1,000	£1,500	37.49%
DAIMLER	2.5 LITRE V8 SALOON	1963	1969	£8,000	£10,650	22.08%
DAIMLER	250 V8	1968	1969	£6,000	£7,475	14.24%
DAIMLER	CONQUEST CENTURY	1954	1958	£4,000	£4,175	−4.29%
DAIMLER	CONQUEST ROADSTER	1954	1956	£11,250	£13,250	8.00%
DAIMLER	DB18 CONSORT	1950	1953	£6,000	£5,500	−15.94%
DAIMLER	DB18 SPORTS	1949	1953	£15,250	£13,000	−21.83%
DAIMLER	DOUBLE SIX	1972	1973	£3,375	£4,250	15.46%
DAIMLER	DOUBLE SIX 2	1973	1978	£3,375	£3,675	−0.16%
DAIMLER	DOUBLE SIX COUPE	1975	1977	£8,833	£8,875	−7.87%
DAIMLER	DOUBLE SIX VP	1972	1973	£3,500	£7,500	96.49%
DAIMLER	MAJESTIC 3.8	1958	1962	£4,500	£4,750	−3.22%
DAIMLER	MAJESTIC MAYOR DR450 LIMOUSINE 4.5	1959	1968	£5,333	£7,000	20.36%
DAIMLER	REGENCY MK1	1951	1952	£3,500	£6,000	57.19%
DAIMLER	REGENCY MK11/111	1954	1956	£4,500	£5,750	17.16%
DAIMLER	SOVEREIGN 1 2.8	1969	1973	£2,500	£4,188	53.63%
DAIMLER	SOVEREIGN 1 4.2	1969	1973	£2,500	£4,917	80.37%
DAIMLER	SOVEREIGN 2 3.4/4.2	1975	1978	£2,500	£4,630	69.85%
DAIMLER	SOVEREIGN 2 4.2 COUPE	1975	1977	£5,000	£8,125	49.00%
DAIMLER	SOVEREIGN 420	1966	1970	£6,000	£7,955	21.58%
DAIMLER	SP250 DART	1959	1964	£13,250	£13,750	−4.84%

MANUFACTURER	ACTUAL CAR	YEAR FROM	YEAR TO	1993 VALUE	PRESENT VALUE	VALUE SWING
DATSUN	240Z	1969	1971	£6,000	£7,875	20.36%
DATSUN	240Z	1971	1974	£4,750	£5,375	3.76%
DATSUN	260Z	1973	1978	£3,500	£3,833	0.42%
DATSUN	260Z 2+2	1974	1979	£2,250	£3,333	35.82%
DATSUN	280ZX	1978	1981	£3,000	£3,000	−8.31%
DATSUN	280ZX 2+2	1978	1981	£2,500	£2,563	−5.98%
DE LOREAN	DE LOREAN	1980	1981	£12,500	£14,333	5.14%
DE TOMASO	DEAUVILLE	1970	1988	£8,000	£10,000	14.63%
DE TOMASO	LONGCHAMP	1972	1990	£8,000	£12,333	41.37%
DE TOMASO	MAGUSTA COUPE	1967	1972	£27,500	£31,750	5.87%
DE TOMASO	PANTERA COUPE	1970	1989	£20,000	£24,500	12.33%
DELLOW	MKI/II/III	1949	1957	£7,000	£8,667	13.53%
DKW	1000S	1958	1963	£5,000	£2,000	−63.32%
DKW	F102	1964	1966	£1,500	£1,600	−2.20%
DKW	JUNIOR	1959	1965	£5,000	£2,000	−63.32%
DODGE	CHARGER 440	1967	1972	£11,250	£9,250	−24.61%
ELVA	COURIER MKI/MKII	1951	1961	£2,000	£6,750	209.49%
ELVA	COURIER MKIII/MKIV	1962	1969	£3,500	£7,250	89.94%
FACEL VEGA	EXCELLENCE	1957	1964	£18,750	£23,500	14.93%
FACEL VEGA	FACEL 2	1962	1964	£28,750	£45,000	43.52%
FACEL VEGA	FACEL 3	1963	1964	£10,000	£8,000	−26.65%
FACEL VEGA	FACEL 3 CONVERTIBLE	1963	1964	£10,000	£12,000	10.03%
FACEL VEGA	FACELLIA	1961	1963	£8,750	£8,917	−6.55%
FACEL VEGA	FACELLIA dhc	1960	1963	£13,000	£14,000	−1.25%
FACEL VEGA	FVS	1954	1959	£17,500	£17,000	−10.92%
FACEL VEGA	HK500	1958	1961	£25,000	£22,667	−16.86%
FAIRTHORPE	ELECTRON MINOR	1957	1973	£2,750	£3,575	19.21%
FAIRTHORPE	TX GT/S/Ss	1967	1973	£3,500	£3,950	3.48%
FALCON	CARIBBEAN	1957	1963	£2,000	£2,833	29.89%
FERRARI	212	1951	1953	£110,000	£150,000	25.04%
FERRARI	250 CALIFORNIA SPIDER lhd	1959	1963	£200,000	£375,000	71.93%
FERRARI	250 GT LUSSO	1962	1964	£120,000	£105,000	−19.77%
FERRARI	250 GTE 2+2	1956	1964	£35,000	£40,000	4.79%
FERRARI	250 SWB LIGHTWEIGHT	1959	1963	£250,000	£415,000	52.22%
FERRARI	275 GTS SPIDER lhd	1965	1966	£115,000	£113,333	−9.63%
FERRARI	275 GTB	1965	1966	£112,500	£136,667	11.39%
FERRARI	275 GTB/4	1966	1968	£187,500	£205,000	0.25%
FERRARI	275 GTB/4 SPIDER lhd	1966	1968	£400,000	£800,000	83.39%
FERRARI	308 GTB	1975	1981	£25,500	£27,667	−0.51%
FERRARI	308 GTB SC fibreglass	1975	1977	£32,500	£29,167	−17.71%
FERRARI	308 GTS qv SPIDER	1983	1985	£32,500	£32,500	−8.30%
FERRARI	308 GTS SPIDER	1975	1981	£31,000	£30,833	−8.80%
FERRARI	328 GTB	1981	1988	£37,000	£37,000	−8.30%
FERRARI	330 GT	1964	1967	£29,000	£27,500	−13.05%
FERRARI	330 GTC	1966	1968	£67,500	£60,000	−18.49%
FERRARI	365 GT4 2+2	1972	1976	£25,000	£25,500	−6.47%
FERRARI	365 GTC/4	1968	1974	£57,500	£48,750	−22.26%
FERRARI	365 GTS SPIDER lhd	1968	1969	£117,500	£150,000	17.06%
FERRARI	365 GT 2+2	1967	1971	£30,000	£35,167	7.49%
FERRARI	365 GTB/4 DAYTONA	1968	1974	£85,000	£89,000	−3.99%
FERRARI	365 GTB/4 DAYTONA SPIDER	1968	1974	£250,000	£250,000	−8.30%
FERRARI	365 GTC	1967	1970	£72,500	£60,000	−24.11%
FERRARI	400 GT	1976	1985	£20,000	£23,000	5.45%
FERRARI	410 SUPERAMERICA	1955	1960	£120,000	£133,333	1.88%
FERRARI	500 SUPERFAST	1964	1966	£100,000	£115,000	5.45%
FERRARI	512 BB BOXER COUPE	1973	1984	£77,500	£68,500	−18.95%

MANUFACTURER	ACTUAL CAR	YEAR FROM	YEAR TO	1993 VALUE	PRESENT VALUE	VALUE SWING
FERRARI	DINO 206GT	1968	1969	£65,000	£50,333	−28.99%
FERRARI	DINO 246GT	1969	1974	£35,000	£46,333	21.39%
FERRARI	DINO 246GTS SPIDER	1972	1974	£45,000	£50,333	2.56%
FERRARI	DINO 308GT4 2+2	1973	1980	£15,000	£20,000	22.26%
FERRARI	MONDIAL	1981	1986	£22,500	£20,000	−18.49%
FERRARI	MONDIAL CABRIO	1984	1986	£32,500	£30,000	−15.36%
FIAT	124 COUPE	1966	1972	£2,750	£3,775	25.88%
FIAT	124 SPIDER lhd	1966	1982	£4,600	£5,925	18.10%
FIAT	128 3P	1975	1978	£2,875	£2,750	−12.28%
FIAT	130	1969	1976	£3,000	£2,667	−18.49%
FIAT	130 COUPE	1971	1970	£6,500	£7,125	0.51%
FIAT	131 MIRAFIORI	1974	1984	£1,000	£1,475	35.20%
FIAT	1500 CABRIO	1963	1967	£3,500	£6,667	74.67%
FIAT	1500S/1600S	1959	1975	£4,500	£6,188	26.08%
FIAT	2300S	1961	1968	£4,000	£6,875	57.61%
FIAT	500 TOPOLINO	1948	1955	£6,000	£5,425	−17.09%
FIAT	500/500D/500F	1957	1975	£2,500	£2,500	−8.29%
FIAT	600/600D	1955	1970	£2,000	£3,025	38.70%
FIAT	850 COUPE	1965	1972	£1,750	£1,983	3.93%
FIAT	850 SPIDER	1965	1973	£2,850	£4,300	38.35%
FIAT	DINO 2000/2400 lhd	1967	1973	£9,000	£9,500	−3.21%
FIAT	DINO 2000/2400 SPIDER	1967	1973	£14,500	£15,000	−5.14%
FIAT	MULTIPLA	1955	1966	£2,250	£4,000	63.00%
FIAT	X 1/9	1972	1989	£2,750	£2,733	−8.87%
FIAT	X 1/9 1500	1979	1985	£3,500	£3,500	−8.30%
FIAT ABARTH	595	1963	1971	£1,200	£4,667	256.53%
FIAT ABARTH	595/695SS	1963	1971	£1,500	£5,000	205.62%
FORD	500 SKYLINER	1957	1958	£15,000	£13,000	−20.53%
FORD	ANGLIA 100E	1953	1959	£1,125	£1,638	33.50%
FORD	ANGLIA 105E	1959	1967	£1,733	£1,738	−8.04%
FORD	CAPRI 109E/116E	1961	1963	£2,625	£4,025	40.59%
FORD	CAPRI 1600/2000	1969	1974	£1,000	£1,688	54.72%
FORD	CAPRI 2.8iV6	1981	1987	£4,000	£3,400	−22.05%
FORD	CAPRI 2000GT	1969	1974	£1,500	£1,775	8.50%
FORD	CAPRI 3000E	1970	1974	£3,500	£3,000	−21.40%
FORD	CAPRI 3000GT	1969	1974	£2,500	£2,000	−26.63%
FORD	CAPRI 3000V6	1969	1974	£1,000	£2,375	117.69%
FORD	CAPRI GT	1962	1964	£2,750	£4,167	38.95%
FORD	CAPRI RS3100V6	1973	1974	£5,000	£6,167	13.09%
FORD	CLASSIC 109E/116E	1961	1962	£1,575	£2,456	42.96%
FORD	CONSUL MKI	1951	1956	£2,125	£2,500	7.90%
FORD	CONSUL MKI CONVERTIBLE	1952	1956	£5,750	£7,250	15.61%
FORD	CONSUL MKII	1956	1962	£2,750	£3,038	1.30%
FORD	CONSUL MKII CONVERTIBLE	1956	1962	£6,250	£7,200	5.63%
FORD	CONSUL/GRANADA MKI	1972	1977	£1,350	£1,767	20.04%
FORD	CORSAIR	1964	1965	£1,450	£1,638	3.61%
FORD	CORSAIR 2000E	1967	1970	£1,375	£1,875	25.00%
FORD	CORSAIR GT	1964	1965	£1,500	£2,225	36.00%
FORD	CORSAIR V4 GT	1966	1967	£1,400	£1,583	3.67%
FORD	CORTINA 1600E	1968	1970	£2,750	£3,875	29.21%
FORD	CORTINA GT MKI	1963	1966	£5,250	£3,075	−46.29%
FORD	CORTINA GT MKII	1966	1970	£1,450	£1,975	24.92%
FORD	CORTINA MKI	1962	1966	£1,400	£1,475	−3.41%
FORD	CORTINA MKII	1966	1970	£1,150	£1,213	−3.27%
FORD	CORTINA MKIII	1970	1976	£825	£867	−3.67%
FORD	CORTINA MKIV	1976	1979	£1,000	£800	−26.67%

MANUFACTURER	ACTUAL CAR	YEAR FROM	YEAR TO	1993 VALUE	PRESENT VALUE	VALUE SWING
FORD	CORTINA MKV	1979	1982	£1,200	£800	−38.88%
FORD	CORTINA SAVAGE	1968	1970	£6,750	£9,000	22.27%
FORD	ESCORT GT	1968	1973	£1,700	£2,050	10.57%
FORD	ESCORT MEXICO	1970	1974	£3,000	£4,833	47.71%
FORD	ESCORT RS1600	1970	1974	£4,250	£7,250	56.42%
FORD	ESCORT RS1800	1975	1977	£8,000	£9,667	10.81%
FORD	ESCORT RS2000 MKI	1970	1974	£4,500	£4,175	−14.93%
FORD	ESCORT RS2000 MKII	1976	1980	£5,750	£4,238	−32.42%
FORD	ESCORT SPORT	1971	1975	£2,175	£2,375	0.13%
FORD	ESCORT TWIN CAM	1968	1971	£4,500	£6,125	24.80%
FORD	ESCORT/ESQUIRE/100E ESTATE	1956	1960	£1,250	£1,975	44.90%
FORD	GRANADA COUPE	1974	1977	£2,000	£2,433	11.55%
FORD	GRANADA GHIA	1972	1977	£1,500	£1,933	18.15%
FORD	LOTUS CORTINA MKI	1963	1966	£9,500	£12,000	15.83%
FORD	LOTUS CORTINA MKII	1967	1970	£4,500	£6,250	27.34%
FORD	MUSTANG 289	1964	1966	£6,000	£7,500	14.63%
FORD	MUSTANG 289 CONVERTIBLE	1964	1966	£8,000	£13,000	49.01%
FORD	MUSTANG 289 FASTBACK	1964	1966	£7,000	£8,000	4.79%
FORD	PREFECT 107E	1959	1961	£1,250	£1,763	29.35%
FORD	PREFECT/ANGLIA	1940	1953	£2,000	£2,500	14.63%
FORD	PILOT	1947	1951	£6,250	£6,625	−2.80%
FORD	POPULAR 100E	1960	1962	£800	£1,533	75.80%
FORD	POPULAR 103E	1953	1959	£1,750	£2,250	17.92%
FORD	SHELBY MUSTANG GT350	1966	1967	£20,000	£18,500	−15.18%
FORD	SHELBY MUSTANG GT500	1966	1967	£28,500	£27,000	−13.13%
FORD	ZEPHYR 4 MKIII	1962	1966	£2,000	£2,700	23.80%
FORD	ZEPHYR 4 MKIV	1966	1972	£1,125	£1,438	17.20%
FORD	ZEPHYR 6 MKIII	1962	1966	£2,500	£2,600	−4.62%
FORD	ZEPHYR 6 MKIV	1966	1972	£1,675	£1,925	5.36%
FORD	ZEPHYR MKI	1951	1956	£2,625	£3,300	15.26%
FORD	ZEPHYR MKI CONVERTIBLE	1952	1956	£7,000	£8,075	5.78%
FORD	ZEPHYR MKII	1956	1962	£3,417	£4,025	8.02%
FORD	ZEPHYR MKII CONVERTIBLE	1956	1962	£6,667	£7,688	5.74%
FORD	ZODIAC EXECUTIVE	1966	1972	£2,100	£2,275	−0.66%
FORD	ZODIAC MKII	1956	1962	£3,650	£4,200	5.50%
FORD	ZODIAC MKII CONVERTIBLE	1956	1962	£6,583	£4,200	−41.50%
FORD	ZODIAC MKIII	1962	1966	£2,875	£2,725	−13.08%
FRAZER NASH	LE MANS REPLICA/REPLICA 2	1948	1953	£77,500	£95,000	12.40%
GILBERN	GENIE	1966	1970	£4,500	£4,225	−13.92%
GILBERN	GT COUPE/1800	1959	1967	£3,125	£4,300	26.17%
GILBERN	INVADER	1969	1974	£4,750	£5,425	4.73%
GINETTA	G15	1968	1974	£4,000	£6,625	51.88%
GINETTA	G21 1800/1800S	1971	1978	£4,500	£6,750	37.53%
GINETTA	G21 3LITRE	1971	1975	£5,250	£6,750	17.90%
GINETTA	G4 1498	1967	1968	£7,500	£13,750	68.11%
GINETTA	G4 997	1961	1968	£7,750	£15,750	86.35%
GORDON KEEBLE	GKI/II	1964	1967	£20,000	£21,500	−1.43%
HEALEY	ABBOTT dhc	1950	1954	£13,250	£20,000	38.41%
HEALEY	ELLIOTT	1946	1950	£15,000	£14,333	−12.38%
HEALEY	NASH-HEALEY	1951	1954	£15,000	£21,500	31.43%
HEALEY	SILVERSTONE	1949	1950	£25,000	£35,167	28.99%
HEALEY	TICKFORD	1950	1954	£7,250	£14,000	77.06%
HEINKEL	CRUISER TROJAN	1956	1965	£4,000	£3,633	−16.71%
HILLMAN	AVENGER	1970	1976	£750	£875	6.97%
HILLMAN	AVENGER TIGER	1972	1973	£3,000	£2,500	−23.59%
HILLMAN	CALIFORNIAN	1953	1956	£2,000	£2,663	22.10%

MANUFACTURER	ACTUAL CAR	YEAR FROM	YEAR TO	1993 VALUE	PRESENT VALUE	VALUE SWING
HILLMAN	CALIFORNIAN dhc	1953	1956	£5,000	£3,717	−31.84%
HILLMAN	HUNTER	1966	1967	£1,000	£950	−12.92%
HILLMAN	HUNTER GLS	1972	1976	£2,000	£1,800	−17.47%
HILLMAN	HUNTER GT	1970	1973	£1,500	£1,300	−20.54%
HILLMAN	HUSKY MKI/2 ESTATE	1954	1960	£1,250	£1,950	43.07%
HILLMAN	IMP CALIFORNIAN	1968	1970	£1,150	£1,550	23.60%
HILLMAN	IMP/SUPER IMP	1963	1976	£975	£1,088	2.35%
HILLMAN	MINX MKI–VIII	1940	1956	£1,500	£1,663	1.65%
HILLMAN	MINX SI–IIIC	1954	1963	£1,375	£1,475	−1.67%
HILLMAN	MINX SI–IIIC CONVERTIBLE	1954	1962	£4,000	£3,238	−25.77%
HILLMAN	MINX SV/VI	1963	1967	£925	£1,138	12.78%
HILLMAN	NEW MINX	1967	1977	£850	£913	−1.51%
HILLMAN	SUPER MINX SI–IV	1962	1966	£875	£1,225	28.41%
HILLMAN	SUPER MINX SI–IV CONVERTIBLE	1962	1964	£2,750	£3,300	10.04%
HONDA	S600/S800	1966	1970	£2,500	£3,750	37.56%
HONDA	S600/S800 CONVERTIBLE	1967	1970	£4,250	£6,250	34.84%
HONDA	Z COUPE	1970	1975	£700	£1,400	83.49%
HRG	1100/1500	1939	1955	£35,000	£20,000	−47.60%
HUMBER	HAWK I–IV	1957	1968	£3,250	£3,350	−5.47%
HUMBER	HAWK III–VIA	1947	1957	£3,500	£3,488	−8.62%
HUMBER	PULLMAN	1945	1953	£4,000	£6,075	39.27%
HUMBER	PULLMAN/IMPERIAL	1953	1954	£5,000	£6,933	27.14%
HUMBER	SCEPTRE I/II	1963	1967	£1,783	£1,975	1.59%
HUMBER	SCEPTRE III	1968	1976	£1,300	£1,400	−1.27%
HUMBER	SNIPE	1945	1946	£3,600	£3,550	−9.58%
HUMBER	SUPER SNIPE	1947	1952	£4,000	£4,000	−8.30%
HUMBER	SUPER SNIPE I	1958	1959	£4,000	£3,883	−10.98%
HUMBER	SUPER SNIPE II–III	1960	1964	£2,375	£2,900	11.97%
HUMBER	SUPER SNIPE IV	1953	1956	£4,000	£4,125	−5.43%
HUMBER	SUPER SNIPE CONVERTIBLE	1949	1952	£8,500	£11,500	24.06%
HUMBER	SUPER SNIPE IMPERIAL	1965	1967	£2,125	£3,317	43.16%
ISO	FIDIA	1967	1974	£12,000	£9,000	−31.23%
ISO	GRIFO	1969	1974	£34,000	£36,667	−1.11%
ISO	LELE	1969	1974	£14,000	£14,333	−6.12%
ISO	RIVOLTA	1962	1970	£15,000	£16,333	−0.15%
JAGUAR	1.5	1945	1949	£12,500	£13,083	−4.03%
JAGUAR	2.5	1946	1949	£15,000	£14,833	−9.32%
JAGUAR	240	1968	1969	£6,250	£9,025	32.41%
JAGUAR	3.5	1946	1949	£20,000	£20,250	−7.16%
JAGUAR	340	1967	1968	£8,000	£11,875	36.12%
JAGUAR	420	1966	1968	£5,750	£7,400	18.00%
JAGUAR	E TYPE 3.8 ROADSTER	1961	1964	£32,500	£33,000	−6.89%
JAGUAR	E TYPE fhc 3.8	1961	1964	£21,250	£22,000	−5.07%
JAGUAR	E TYPE SI 4.2 2+2	1966	1968	£13,000	£15,500	9.33%
JAGUAR	E TYPE SI 4.2 fhc	1965	1968	£17,500	£20,375	6.76%
JAGUAR	E TYPE SI 4.2 ROADSTER	1965	1968	£24,000	£28,625	9.37%
JAGUAR	E TYPE SI/SII 2+2	1967	1968	£12,500	£15,500	13.70%
JAGUAR	E TYPE SI/SII fhc	1967	1968	£17,500	£21,250	11.34%
JAGUAR	E TYPE SI/SII ROADSTER	1967	1968	£27,500	£30,500	1.70%
JAGUAR	E TYPE SII 2+2	1968	1970	£11,250	£14,750	20.22%
JAGUAR	E TYPE SII fhc	1968	1970	£12,500	£18,250	33.88%
JAGUAR	E TYPE SII ROADSTER	1968	1970	£20,000	£25,750	18.06%
JAGUAR	E TYPE V12 fhc	1971	1975	£16,500	£17,500	−2.75%
JAGUAR	E TYPE V12 ROADSTER	1971	1975	£30,000	£31,333	−4.23%
JAGUAR	MK V 3.5 CONVERTIBLE	1949	1951	£24,750	£29,688	9.99%
JAGUAR	MK V 2.5	1949	1951	£11,500	£17,625	40.54%

MANUFACTURER	ACTUAL CAR	YEAR FROM	YEAR TO	1993 VALUE	PRESENT VALUE	VALUE SWING
JAGUAR	MK V 2.5 CONVERTIBLE	1949	1951	£21,250	£25,875	11.66%
JAGUAR	MK V 3.5	1949	1951	£16,000	£20,438	17.13%
JAGUAR	MK VII/VIIM	1951	1956	£11,250	£12,063	−1.68%
JAGUAR	MK VIII	1956	1959	£9,000	£10,750	9.53%
JAGUAR	MK X 3.8	1961	1964	£5,750	£7,750	23.58%
JAGUAR	MK X 4.2/420G	1964	1970	£5,750	£4,838	−22.85%
JAGUAR	MK I 2.4	1955	1959	£8,000	£8,650	−0.85%
JAGUAR	MK I 3.4	1957	1959	£9,750	£12,125	14.03%
JAGUAR	MK II 2.4	1959	1967	£7,750	£10,963	29.71%
JAGUAR	MK II 3.4	1959	1967	£10,250	£16,550	48.06%
JAGUAR	MK II 3.8	1959	1967	£15,750	£19,625	14.26%
JAGUAR	MK IX	1958	1961	£6,250	£13,313	95.32%
JAGUAR	S TYPE 3.4	1964	1968	£6,250	£10,275	50.75%
JAGUAR	S TYPE 3.8	1964	1968	£7,000	£13,625	78.48%
JAGUAR	XJ12 COUPE 5.3	1975	1978	£8,000	£8,500	−2.57%
JAGUAR	XJ12 SII	1973	1979	£3,750	£4,925	20.42%
JAGUAR	XJ12 SIII	1979	1986	£12,500	£9,000	−33.98%
JAGUAR	XJ12 SI 5.3	1972	1973	£4,000	£4,233	−2.96%
JAGUAR	XJ6 4.2 SI	1968	1973	£2,500	£4,450	63.24%
JAGUAR	XJ6 COUPE 4.2	1975	1978	£5,750	£19,000	202.98%
JAGUAR	XJ6 SI 2.8	1968	1973	£2,500	£3,750	37.56%
JAGUAR	XJ6 SII 3.4	1973	1979	£3,250	£3,938	11.12%
JAGUAR	XJ6 SII 4.2	1973	1979	£3,533	£4,363	13.24%
JAGUAR	XJ6 SIII 3.4/4.2	1979	1986	£10,000	£4,250	−61.03%
JAGUAR	XJ6 SI 2.8	1968	1973	£2,500	£3,750	37.56%
JAGUAR	XJS	1975	1986	£7,750	£5,708	−32.47%
JAGUAR	XJS 3.6 CABRIO	1984	1987	£10,000	£8,000	−26.65%
JAGUAR	XJS V12	1981	1987	£7,500	£5,500	−32.75%
JAGUAR	XJS V12 CABRIO	1985	1986	£12,500	£9,000	−33.98%
JAGUAR	XK 120 dhc	1953	1954	£25,000	£34,833	27.76%
JAGUAR	XK 150 3.4 ROADSTER	1958	1960	£35,000	£41,000	7.41%
JAGUAR	XK 150 dhc	1957	1960	£21,250	£34,750	49.95%
JAGUAR	XK 150S 3.4 ROADSTER	1958	1959	£40,000	£45,333	3.92%
JAGUAR	XK 150S 3.4 dhc	1959	1960	£36,250	£41,000	3.71%
JAGUAR	XK 150S 3.4 fhc	1959	1960	£23,500	£26,333	2.75%
JAGUAR	XK 150S 3.4 ROADSTER	1959	1960	£40,000	£45,333	3.92%
JAGUAR	XK 150 3.8 dhc	1959	1960	£30,000	£39,625	21.11%
JAGUAR	XK 150 3.8 fhc	1959	1960	£19,750	£23,113	7.31%
JAGUAR	XK 150 3.8 ROADSTER	1959	1960	£46,500	£52,600	3.73%
JAGUAR	XK 120 ALLOY	1949	1950	£50,000	£63,333	16.15%
JAGUAR	XK 120 fhc	1951	1954	£20,250	£35,000	58.49%
JAGUAR	XK 120 ROADSTER	1950	1954	£30,000	£40,333	23.28%
JAGUAR	XK 140 dhc	1954	1957	£22,250	£33,000	36.00%
JAGUAR	XK 140 fhc	1954	1957	£17,250	£23,375	24.26%
JAGUAR	XK 140 ROADSTER	1954	1957	£31,250	£40,333	18.35%
JAGUAR	XK 150 3.4 fhc	1957	1960	£16,250	£21,813	23.08%
JAGUAR	XK 150S 3.8 dhc	1959	1960	£38,500	£47,067	12.10%
JAGUAR	XK 150S 3.8 fhc	1959	1960	£26,250	£26,667	−6.85%
JAGUAR	XK 150S 3.8 ROADSTER	1959	1960	£46,500	£52,600	3.73%
JENSEN	541	1953	1959	£11,250	£14,250	16.15%
JENSEN	541R	1957	1960	£9,750	£15,000	41.07%
JENSEN	541S	1961	1963	£11,750	£12,250	−4.40%
JENSEN	CV8 MKI/II/III	1962	1966	£14,750	£16,500	2.57%
JENSEN	FF MKI/II/III	1967	1971	£16,000	£24,333	39.45%
JENSEN	INTERCEPTOR 1	1967	1969	£6,000	£13,125	100.60%
JENSEN	INTERCEPTOR 2	1970	1972	£7,000	£12,375	62.10%

MANUFACTURER	ACTUAL CAR	YEAR FROM	YEAR TO	1993 VALUE	PRESENT VALUE	VALUE SWING
JENSEN	INTERCEPTOR 3	1972	1976	£8,000	£12,875	47.58%
JENSEN	INTERCEPTOR CONVERTIBLE	1974	1976	£22,500	£29,333	19.54%
JENSEN	INTERCEPTOR COUPE	1975	1976	£12,000	£31,500	140.70%
JENSEN	INTERCEPTOR SP	1971	1976	£10,000	£16,500	51.29%
JENSEN-HEALEY	JENSON HEALEY CONVERTIBLE	1972	1976	£4,500	£5,000	1.87%
JENSEN-HEALEY	JENSON HEALEY GT	1975	1976	£5,750	£6,000	−4.32%
JOWETT	JAVELIN	1947	1953	£6,250	£6,250	−8.30%
JOWETT	JUPITER dhc	1950	1954	£11,000	£14,250	18.79%
LAGONDA	2.6/2.9	1947	1958	£10,750	£14,875	26.88%
LAGONDA	2.6/2.9 CONVERTIBLE	1951	1956	£19,000	£21,000	1.35%
LAGONDA	RAPIDE	1961	1964	£23,500	£24,833	−3.10%
LAGONDA	SALOON V8	1976	1987	£22,500	£22,167	−9.66%
LAMBORGHINI	350 GT	1964	1966	£62,500	£63,750	−6.47%
LAMBORGHINI	400 GT	1966	1968	£45,000	£56,667	15.47%
LAMBORGHINI	COUNTACH LP400	1973	1982	£40,000	£55,833	27.99%
LAMBORGHINI	COUNTACH LP400S	1974	1989	£45,000	£55,000	12.07%
LAMBORGHINI	ESPADA I/II	1968	1973	£15,000	£20,333	24.30%
LAMBORGHINI	ESPADA III	1973	1978	£20,000	£21,000	−3.72%
LAMBORGHINI	ISLERO	1968	1969	£20,000	£31,667	45.19%
LAMBORGHINI	JALPA	1982	1986	£27,500	£24,000	−19.97%
LAMBORGHINI	JARAMA	1970	1978	£12,000	£29,333	124.14%
LAMBORGHINI	MIURA SV	1971	1975	£125,000	£90,000	−33.98%
LAMBORGHINI	MIURA/MIURA S	1966	1971	£75,000	£76,667	−6.27%
LAMBORGHINI	URRACO P250 COUPE	1970	1979	£16,000	£16,167	−7.35%
LAMBORGHINI	URRACO P300 COUPE	1970	1979	£27,500	£26,667	−11.08%
LANCHESTER	14	1951	1954	£3,000	£5,000	52.81%
LANCHESTER	10	1946	1951	£2,250	£4,167	69.80%
LANCIA	APPIA	1953	1963	£7,000	£5,917	−22.49%
LANCIA	APPIA ZAGATO	1957	1961	£27,500	£27,500	−8.30%
LANCIA	APRILIA	1937	1949	£15,000	£14,000	−14.41%
LANCIA	AURELIA B10	1950	1951	£8,500	£9,333	3.63%
LANCIA	AURELIA B12	1954	1955	£12,500	£11,333	−16.86%
LANCIA	AURELIA B20	1951	1958	£17,500	£24,500	28.37%
LANCIA	AURELIA B21/22	1951	1954	£10,000	£10,000	−8.31%
LANCIA	B24 CONVERTIBLE	1955	1958	£30,000	£40,000	22.26%
LANCIA	B24 SPIDER	1955	1958	£45,000	£55,000	12.07%
LANCIA	BETA COUPE	1973	1984	£3,000	£2,033	−37.87%
LANCIA	BETA HPE	1975	1984	£2,500	£2,407	−11.70%
LANCIA	BETA SPIDER	1977	1982	£3,750	£3,583	−12.40%
LANCIA	FLAMINIA	1957	1970	£8,250	£6,333	−29.61%
LANCIA	FLAMINIA CONVERTIBLE	1959	1967	£12,000	£36,500	178.90%
LANCIA	FLAMINIA COUPE	1959	1967	£12,500	£11,000	−19.31%
LANCIA	FLAMINIA GT	1959	1967	£20,000	£19,667	−9.83%
LANCIA	FLAMINIA GT/GTL	1959	1967	£20,000	£19,667	−9.83%
LANCIA	FLAVIA	1961	1966	£3,167	£2,750	−20.38%
LANCIA	FLAVIA 2000	1970	1974	£2,750	£3,250	8.37%
LANCIA	FLAVIA 2000 COUPE	1969	1975	£3,500	£4,800	25.75%
LANCIA	FLAVIA COUPE	1962	1968	£6,000	£4,917	−24.85%
LANCIA	FLAVIA ZAGATO	1963	1967	£25,000	£22,500	−17.47%
LANCIA	FULVIA COUPE SI/SII	1965	1976	£4,083	£4,500	1.06%
LANCIA	FULVIA HF	1966	1972	£5,000	£4,750	−12.89%
LANCIA	FULVIA HF SI	1968	1970	£20,000	£17,667	−19.00%
LANCIA	FULVIA HF SII	1971	1972	£7,500	£9,000	10.04%
LANCIA	FULVIA ZAGATO	1968	1972	£10,625	£10,400	−10.24%
LANCIA	GAMMA	1977	1984	£1,500	£1,667	1.89%

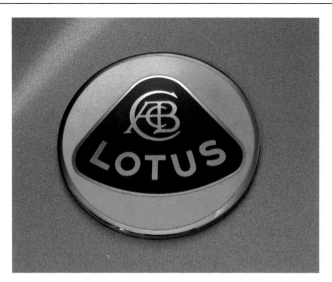

MANUFACTURER	ACTUAL CAR	YEAR FROM	YEAR TO	1993 VALUE	PRESENT VALUE	VALUE SWING
LANCIA	GAMMA COUPE	1977	1984	£3,250	£2,917	−17.69%
LANCIA	MONTE CARLO	1975	1984	£4,900	£6,563	22.81%
LANCIA	STRATOS	1974	1975	£50,000	£65,333	19.82%
LAND ROVER	SI	1948	1958	£2,000	£3,000	37.55%
LAND ROVER	SI/IIA	1958	1971	£2,500	£2,875	5.47%
LEA FRANCIS	12/14 hp	1946	1954	£6,500	£10,000	41.06%
LEA FRANCIS	12/14 hp COUPE	1947	1948	£7,500	£7,500	−8.30%
LEA FRANCIS	14 hp SPORTS	1947	1949	£15,000	£13,000	−20.53%
LEA FRANCIS	14/70	1949	1953	£10,000	£10,333	−5.25%
LEA FRANCIS	2.5 dhc	1950	1954	£14,500	£19,000	20.15%
LOTUS	ECLAT SI COUPE	1975	1980	£4,500	£3,500	−28.69%
LOTUS	ECLAT S2.2	1980	1982	£6,000	£4,833	−26.13%
LOTUS	ECLAT SPRINT	1975	1975	£5,500	£3,917	−34.69%
LOTUS	ELAN PLUS 2	1967	1969	£6,750	£6,613	−10.16%
LOTUS	ELAN PLUS 2	1969	1971	£8,500	£8,400	−9.39%
LOTUS	ELAN PLUS 2S 130	1971	1974	£9,000	£8,750	−10.85%
LOTUS	ELAN SI dhc	1962	1964	£14,000	£12,500	−18.13%
LOTUS	ELAN SII fhc	1964	1966	£11,500	£12,500	−0.33%
LOTUS	ELAN SIII dhc	1966	1969	£11,750	£11,250	−12.21%
LOTUS	ELAN SIII fhc	1966	1969	£11,750	£10,833	−15.46%
LOTUS	ELAN SII dhc	1964	1966	£11,250	£11,750	−4.23%
LOTUS	ELAN SIV dhc	1968	1971	£12,750	£12,875	−7.41%
LOTUS	ELAN SIV fhc	1968	1971	£10,250	£11,125	−0.47%
LOTUS	ELAN SPRINT dhc	1971	1973	£14,000	£14,000	−8.30%
LOTUS	ELAN SPRINT fhc	1971	1973	£11,750	£13,750	7.30%
LOTUS	ELITE	1958	1963	£22,500	£28,125	14.62%
LOTUS	ELITE SI	1974	1980	£4,000	£3,750	−14.03%
LOTUS	ELITE S2.2	1980	1982	£5,000	£3,750	−31.23%
LOTUS	ESPRIT SI	1976	1978	£6,500	£5,500	−22.42%
LOTUS	ESPRIT SII	1978	1980	£7,000	£5,917	−22.49%
LOTUS	ESPRIT TURBO	1980	1981	£9,250	£7,833	−22.35%
LOTUS	EUROPA SI/IA	1966	1969	£4,125	£5,500	22.25%
LOTUS	EUROPA SII	1969	1971	£5,250	£6,083	6.25%
LOTUS	EUROPA TWIN CAM/SPECIAL	1971	1975	£10,125	£10,833	−1.89%
LOTUS	LOTUS CORTINA MKI	1963	1966	£9,500	£12,000	15.83%
LOTUS	LOTUS CORTINA MKII	1967	1970	£4,500	£6,250	27.34%
LOTUS	SEVEN SI	1957	1961	£16,000	£13,250	−24.06%
LOTUS	SEVEN SII/III	1961	1969	£11,750	£12,125	−5.38%

MANUFACTURER	ACTUAL CAR	YEAR FROM	YEAR TO	1993 VALUE	PRESENT VALUE	VALUE SWING
LOTUS	SEVEN S4 SPORTS	1969	1972	£5,000	£6,625	21.49%
LOTUS	SIX	1953	1956	£13,750	£15,000	0.03%
MARCOS	1500/1600/1800 GT	1964	1968	£7,000	£7,625	−0.12%
MARCOS	2 LITRE	1969	1972	£5,000	£7,000	28.37%
MARCOS	3 LITRE	1969	1972	£8,250	£8,875	−1.36%
MARCOS	MANTIS	1970	1971	£5,000	£4,917	−9.83%
MARCOS	MINI MARCOS	1965	1972	£2,650	£2,950	2.08%
MASERATI	3500 GT lhd	1958	1964	£17,500	£29,500	54.57%
MASERATI	3500 GT SPIDER	1958	1964	£35,000	£41,667	9.16%
MASERATI	BORA	1971	1978	£20,000	£35,667	63.53%
MASERATI	GHIBLI	1967	1973	£30,500	£27,000	−18.83%
MASERATI	GHIBLI SPIDER dhc	1967	1973	£50,000	£43,333	−20.53%
MASERATI	INDY	1969	1974	£17,500	£22,667	18.77%
MASERATI	KHAMSIN lhd	1973	1982	£16,750	£23,667	29.56%
MASERATI	KYALAMI lhd	1976	1983	£10,000	£12,333	13.08%
MASERATI	MERAK/MERAK SS	1972	1983	£16,500	£19,333	7.44%
MASERATI	MEXICO	1967	1972	£18,500	£25,333	25.57%
MASERATI	MISTRALE	1964	1970	£30,000	£31,667	−3.21%
MASERATI	MISTRALE SPIDER lhd	1964	1970	£37,500	£42,000	2.70%
MASERATI	QUATTROPORTE	1967	1971	£12,250	£9,833	−26.39%
MASERATI	QUATTROPORTE II	1975	1977	£15,000	£14,000	−14.41%
MASERATI	SEBRING SERIES SI/II	1962	1966	£15,500	£25,000	47.89%
MATRA	BAGHERA	1973	1979	£3,250	£3,938	11.12%
MATRA	MURENA/MURENA S	1980	1984	£5,250	£7,267	26.93%
MATRA	RANCHO	1977	1984	£3,750	£3,200	−21.76%
MAZDA	RX2	1970	1978	£2,200	£2,750	14.63%
MAZDA	RX3	1971	1978	£2,000	£2,800	28.38%
MAZDA	RX7	1978	1985	£4,500	£5,125	4.42%
MERCEDES BENZ	190/190D	1961	1965	£3,000	£4,500	37.53%
MERCEDES BENZ	190/200	1956	1968	£3,500	£4,088	7.10%
MERCEDES BENZ	190SL	1955	1963	£16,250	£20,250	14.26%
MERCEDES BENZ	200/200D	1965	1968	£3,000	£4,500	37.53%
MERCEDES BENZ	220	1951	1954	£12,000	£11,167	−14.67%
MERCEDES BENZ	220	1968	1976	£5,000	£4,750	−12.89%
MERCEDES BENZ	220 CABRIO	1951	1954	£20,000	£23,000	5.45%
MERCEDES BENZ	220A	1956	1959	£7,500	£7,500	−8.30%
MERCEDES BENZ	220A CABRIO	1956	1959	£12,500	£10,500	−22.98%
MERCEDES BENZ	220S	1956	1959	£10,000	£9,000	−17.48%
MERCEDES BENZ	220S CABRIO	1956	1959	£17,500	£16,500	−13.54%
MERCEDES BENZ	220S COUPE	1956	1959	£11,500	£16,250	29.57%
MERCEDES BENZ	220S/SE	1959	1965	£10,000	£9,500	−12.89%

MANUFACTURER	ACTUAL CAR	YEAR FROM	YEAR TO	1993 VALUE	PRESENT VALUE	VALUE SWING
MERCEDES BENZ	220SE	1958	1959	£11,500	£11,750	−6.31%
MERCEDES BENZ	220SE CABRIO	1958	1959	£20,000	£20,833	−4.48%
MERCEDES BENZ	220SE COUPE	1958	1959	£17,500	£17,083	−10.49%
MERCEDES BENZ	220SEB	1960	1965	£12,500	£13,500	−0.97%
MERCEDES BENZ	220SEB CONVERTIBLE	1960	1965	£19,500	£26,000	22.26%
MERCEDES BENZ	220SEC	1959	1965	£15,000	£16,000	−2.19%
MERCEDES BENZ	230/230S	1965	1968	£10,000	£9,000	−17.48%
MERCEDES BENZ	230SL/250SL	1963	1967	£14,500	£15,938	0.79%
MERCEDES BENZ	250	1968	1972	£6,500	£5,500	−22.42%
MERCEDES BENZ	250CE/280CE	1968	1973	£5,750	£6,833	8.96%
MERCEDES BENZ	250S/250SE	1965	1969	£10,000	£6,050	−44.53%
MERCEDES BENZ	250SE/280SE CABRIO	1965	1971	£18,625	£21,667	6.67%
MERCEDES BENZ	250SEC/280SEC	1965	1971	£11,500	£13,500	7.65%
MERCEDES BENZ	280S/SE	1968	1972	£4,500	£4,688	−4.48%
MERCEDES BENZ	280SEC	1968	1972	£12,250	£16,000	19.77%
MERCEDES BENZ	280SL	1968	1971	£18,000	£16,875	−14.03%
MERCEDES BENZ	300 CABRIO D	1951	1957	£40,000	£43,500	−0.28%
MERCEDES BENZ	300A/B/C	1951	1957	£15,000	£15,167	−7.28%
MERCEDES BENZ	300D	1957	1962	£20,000	£22,000	0.87%
MERCEDES BENZ	300S CABRIO	1952	1958	£100,000	£80,000	−26.64%
MERCEDES BENZ	300S COUPE	1952	1958	£85,000	£80,000	−13.70%
MERCEDES BENZ	300S ROADSTER	1952	1958	£135,000	£80,000	−45.66%
MERCEDES BENZ	300SE/SEL	1961	1965	£10,250	£9,333	−16.51%
MERCEDES BENZ	300SE/SEL	1965	1967	£10,000	£7,750	−28.94%
MERCEDES BENZ	300SEC	1961	1965	£14,750	£18,000	11.90%
MERCEDES BENZ	300SEL	1971	1972	£7,500	£7,875	−3.72%
MERCEDES BENZ	300SEL 6.3	1967	1972	£12,500	£10,750	−21.14%
MERCEDES BENZ	300SL GULLWING	1954	1957	£125,000	£138,333	1.48%
MERCEDES BENZ	300SL ROADSTER	1957	1963	£77,500	£103,333	22.26%
MERCEDES BENZ	350SL	1970	1980	£11,000	£12,167	1.43%
MERCEDES BENZ	350SLC	1971	1980	£8,500	£9,500	2.48%
MERCEDES BENZ	450SE/SEL	1973	1980	£7,500	£6,333	−22.57%
MERCEDES BENZ	450SEL	1976	1980	£11,250	£10,000	−18.49%
MERCEDES BENZ	450SL	1971	1981	£11,000	£11,667	−2.74%
MERCEDES BENZ	450SLC	1972	1981	£9,000	£9,500	−3.21%
MERCEDES BENZ	500SL ROADSTER	1981	1984	£15,000	£15,000	−8.30%
MERCEDES BENZ	500SLC	1981	1984	£13,000	£12,000	−15.36%
MERCEDES BENZ	600	1964	1981	£23,500	£32,500	26.81%
MESSERSCHMITT	KR200	1955	1962	£5,000	£4,833	−11.37%
MG	1100	1962	1965	£2,500	£2,200	−19.30%
MG	1100	1966	1968	£1,500	£2,000	22.25%
MG	1300	1967	1971	£1,750	£2,267	18.82%
MG	MAGNETTE III/IV	1959	1968	£2,000	£2,390	9.58%
MG	MAGNETTE ZA/ZB	1953	1958	£3,750	£5,000	22.25%
MG	MGA 1500 fhc	1956	1959	£8,500	£7,875	−15.05%
MG	MGA 1500 ROADSTER	1955	1959	£10,750	£11,625	−0.84%
MG	MGA 1600 DELUXE ROADSTER	1960	1961	£11,250	£16,500	34.49%
MG	MGA 1600 fhc	1959	1961	£8,000	£8,625	−1.13%
MG	MGA 1600 fhc DELUXE	1960	1961	£8,000	£9,500	8.90%
MG	MGA 1600 MKII fhc	1961	1962	£8,500	£10,500	13.27%
MG	MGA 1600 MKII ROADSTER	1960	1962	£10,000	£12,500	14.62%
MG	MGA 1600 ROADSTER	1959	1961	£11,000	£13,000	8.37%
MG	MGA TC fhc	1958	1960	£13,500	£13,125	−10.85%
MG	MGA TC ROADSTER	1958	1960	£16,250	£16,500	−6.90%
MG	MGB GT	1965	1974	£5,500	£5,200	−13.30%
MG	MGB GT	1975	1980	£6,000	£3,675	−43.83%

MANUFACTURER	ACTUAL CAR	YEAR FROM	YEAR TO	1993 VALUE	PRESENT VALUE	VALUE SWING
MG	MGB GT V8	1973	1974	£9,000	£8,250	−15.94%
MG	MGB GT V8	1974	1976	£7,500	£8,000	−2.19%
MG	MGB ROADSTER	1962	1974	£10,000	£8,167	−25.11%
MG	MGB ROADSTER	1975	1980	£8,000	£6,100	−30.08%
MG	MGC GT	1967	1969	£6,500	£6,333	−10.66%
MG	MGC ROADSTER	1967	1969	£9,500	£8,875	−14.33%
MG	MIDGET 1500	1974	1979	£4,250	£3,967	−14.41%
MG	MIDGET MK I/II	1961	1966	£4,000	£4,117	−5.62%
MG	MIDGET MK III/IV	1966	1974	£4,500	£4,117	−16.12%
MG	TA	1936	1939	£15,000	£15,000	−8.30%
MG	TB	1939	1945	£20,000	£16,500	−24.35%
MG	TC	1945	1949	£17,500	£16,333	−14.42%
MG	TD	1949	1953	£13,000	£13,125	−7.42%
MG	TF1250	1953	1954	£17,500	£16,375	−14.20%
MG	TF1500	1954	1955	£16,500	£18,250	1.42%
MG	YA/YB	1947	1953	£5,250	£6,125	6.99%
MONTEVERDI	375 CABRIO lhd	1967	1977	£40,000	£70,000	60.47%
MONTEVERDI	375 lhd	1967	1977	£30,000	£35,000	6.98%
MONTEVERDI	375/4 LIMOUSINE lhd	1972	1977	£17,000	£25,000	34.84%
MORGAN	4/4 1600 SPORTS	1968	1981	£9,000	£13,000	32.45%
MORGAN	4/4 SI	1936	1950	£15,000	£14,750	−9.83%
MORGAN	PLUS 4 PLUS	1964	1966	£8,000	£16,500	89.13%
MORGAN	PLUS 4 SII–V	1954	1968	£9,400	£10,125	−1.23%
MORGAN	PLUS 4 TR	1954	1969	£11,500	£15,000	19.61%
MORGAN	PLUS 4 VANGUARD	1950	1958	£9,000	£11,000	12.07%
MORGAN	PLUS 8	1968	1997	£15,000	£17,500	6.98%
MORRIS	EIGHT SERIES E	1939	1945	£2,500	£3,000	10.05%
MORRIS	EIGHT SERIES E CONVERTIBLE	1939	1945	£3,500	£4,500	17.89%
MORRIS	1100/1300	1962	1973	£700	£1,256	64.61%
MORRIS	1800/2200	1966	1975	£625	£1,463	114.52%
MORRIS	COWLEY 1200	1954	1956	£2,250	£1,625	−33.78%
MORRIS	COWLEY 1500	1956	1957	£2,250	£1,675	−31.74%
MORRIS	ISIS	1955	1958	£2,250	£2,650	7.99%
MORRIS	ISIS I/II ESTATE	1956	1957	£1,300	£4,000	182.09%
MORRIS	ITAL	1981	1984	£950	£700	−32.43%
MORRIS	MARINA 1.3/1.8	1971	1976	£8,000	£700	−91.98%
MORRIS	MARINA 1.8TC	1971	1975	£900	£975	−0.71%
MORRIS	MARINA II	1976	1980	£850	£650	−29.88%
MORRIS	MINOR 100 CONVERTIBLE	1956	1970	£3,500	£3,713	−2.72%
MORRIS	MINOR 1000	1956	1970	£2,500	£2,350	−13.79%
MORRIS	MINOR 1000 ESTATE	1956	1971	£2,750	£3,038	1.30%
MORRIS	MINOR MM	1948	1952	£2,625	£2,888	0.87%
MORRIS	MINOR MM CONVERTIBLE	1948	1952	£3,875	£3,900	−7.71%
MORRIS	MINOR SII	1952	1956	£1,875	£2,175	6.36%
MORRIS	MINOR SII CONVERTIBLE	1952	1956	£3,750	£3,525	−13.81%
MORRIS	MINOR SII ESTATE	1952	1956	£2,500	£2,863	5.03%
MORRIS	MORRIS MINOR 1000	1962	1970	£2,000	£2,333	6.97%
MORRIS	MORRIS MINOR 1000 ESTATE	1962	1971	£3,000	£3,017	−7.79%
MORRIS	MORRIS MINOR CONVERTIBLE	1962	1969	£3,500	£3,600	−5.69%
MORRIS	OXFORD II–IV	1954	1959	£2,000	£1,513	−30.63%
MORRIS	OXFORD MO	1948	1954	£1,500	£2,125	29.89%
MORRIS	OXFORD V/VI	1959	1971	£1,517	£1,825	10.34%
MORRIS	SIX	1949	1954	£1,750	£2,275	19.23%
MORRIS	TEN SERIES M	1939	1948	£2,000	£2,200	0.87%
NSU	Ro80	1967	1977	£3,500	£3,375	−11.58%
NSU	SPORT PRINZ	1959	1967	£1,600	£2,167	24.18%

MANUFACTURER	ACTUAL CAR	YEAR FROM	YEAR TO	1993 VALUE	PRESENT VALUE	VALUE SWING
NSU	TT/TTS	1965	1967	£1,500	£3,100	89.49%
NSU	WANKEL SPYDER	1964	1967	£3,500	£3,667	-3.93%
OGLE	SX1000	1962	1964	£3,700	£4,100	1.61%
OPEL	GT1900 lhd	1968	1973	£4,000	£4,313	-1.12%
OPEL	KADETT RALLYE COUPE	1966	1973	£2,200	£2,250	-6.21%
OPEL	MANTA SERIES A	1970	1975	£2,000	£2,125	-2.57%
OPEL	MANTA SERIES B	1975	1988	£2,200	£2,267	-5.50%
OPEL	MONZA	1978	1987	£3,000	£2,375	-27.41%
PANHARD	24CT	1964	1967	£3,000	£4,233	29.37%
PANHARD	DYNA 120/130	1950	1953	£2,750	£3,750	25.04%
PANHARD	DYNA JUNIOR	1952	1955	£2,500	£3,867	41.86%
PANHARD	PL17	1959	1964	£3,250	£3,700	4.40%
PANTHER	DE VILLE/ROYALE	1974	1985	£7,000	£27,500	260.23%
PANTHER	J72	1972	1981	£9,000	£14,333	46.03%
PANTHER	LIMA SPORTS	1976	1982	£5,000	£5,333	-2.20%
PANTHER	RIO	1975	1977	£4,000	£5,000	14.63%
PEERLESS	GT	1957	1960	£7,500	£7,500	-8.30%
PEUGEOT	203	1948	1960	£2,000	£2,650	21.50%
PEUGEOT	204 CABRIO	1966	1970	£2,500	£5,000	83.42%
PEUGEOT	204/304	1965	1980	£1,000	£1,250	14.57%
PEUGEOT	205 GTi	1983	1994	£2,500	£4,750	74.25%
PEUGEOT	304 CABRIO	1970	1975	£3,500	£6,500	70.29%
PEUGEOT	403	1955	1967	£1,900	£2,025	-2.27%
PEUGEOT	403 CABRIO	1956	1961	£3,750	£14,000	242.30%
PEUGEOT	404	1960	1975	£1,500	£1,600	-2.20%
PEUGEOT	404 CABRIO	1962	1969	£6,500	£7,850	10.73%
PEUGEOT	504	1969	1982	£2,000	£1,133	-48.05%
PEUGEOT	504 CABRIO lhd	1970	1974	£6,250	£8,250	21.04%
PEUGEOT	504 COUPE lhd	1970	1974	£3,000	£4,000	22.25%
PEUGEOT	504 V6 CABRIO lhd	1974	1983	£8,000	£10,000	14.63%
PEUGEOT	604	1975	1986	£700	£1,250	63.83%
PORSCHE	356C CABRIO	1963	1965	£20,250	£32,700	48.07%
PORSCHE	356	1949	1951	£20,000	£18,333	-15.95%
PORSCHE	356	1951	1953	£17,500	£17,667	-7.43%
PORSCHE	356	1954	1955	£30,000	£15,667	-52.11%
PORSCHE	356 CABRIO	1951	1953	£27,500	£28,333	-5.53%
PORSCHE	356 CABRIO	1954	1955	£15,000	£24,667	50.79%
PORSCHE	356 SPEEDSTER	1954	1958	£39,000	£37,500	-11.83%
PORSCHE	356A CARRERA	1955	1959	£35,000	£44,250	15.93%
PORSCHE	356A/B	1955	1963	£12,250	£16,167	21.02%
PORSCHE	356A/B CABRIO	1955	1959	£19,000	£24,167	16.63%
PORSCHE	356C	1963	1965	£13,000	£19,767	39.43%
PORSCHE	911 3.0 TURBO	1975	1977	£15,500	£20,500	21.27%
PORSCHE	911 3.3 TURBO	1977	1986	£26,000	£25,667	-9.48%
PORSCHE	911 2.0	1964	1969	£10,750	£12,667	8.04%
PORSCHE	911 CARRERA	1973	1975	£15,000	£16,667	1.89%
PORSCHE	911 CARRERA 3.2	1983	1986	£17,500	£17,000	-10.92%
PORSCHE	911 CARRERA CABRIO	1983	1986	£25,000	£21,000	-22.98%
PORSCHE	911 RSL CARRERA	1972	1973	£35,000	£42,500	11.34%
PORSCHE	911 RST CARRERA	1972	1973	£30,000	£35,000	6.98%
PORSCHE	911E 2.4	1971	1973	£16,500	£16,500	-8.30%
PORSCHE	911E 2.0	1968	1969	£9,500	£12,750	23.07%
PORSCHE	911L/T 2.0	1967	1971	£9,000	£12,250	24.81%
PORSCHE	911S 2.2	1969	1971	£13,000	£15,000	5.81%
PORSCHE	911S 2.4	1971	1973	£18,500	£18,000	-10.78%
PORSCHE	911S 2.7	1973	1975	£9,750	£9,000	-15.36%

MANUFACTURER	ACTUAL CAR	YEAR FROM	YEAR TO	1993 VALUE	PRESENT VALUE	VALUE SWING
PORSCHE	911S 2.0	1966	1969	£14,250	£15,000	−3.47%
PORSCHE	911SC (180bhp)	1977	1983	£12,750	£12,000	−13.70%
PORSCHE	911SC (204bhp)	1980	1983	£15,000	£11,000	−32.75%
PORSCHE	911SC CABRIO	1982	1883	£17,500	£12,000	−37.12%
PORSCHE	911T 2.4	1971	1973	£14,000	£16,000	4.79%
PORSCHE	911T/E 2.2	1969	1971	£10,500	£13,750	20.08%
PORSCHE	912	1965	1969	£6,500	£5,250	−25.94%
PORSCHE	914–4	1969	1975	£4,750	£5,750	11.00%
PORSCHE	914–6	1969	1971	£5,500	£9,000	50.05%
PORSCHE	924	1976	1985	£5,000	£5,000	−8.31%
PORSCHE	924 CARRERA GT	1979	1980	£17,500	£14,250	−25.33%
PORSCHE	924 TURBO	1978	1982	£55,000	£5,667	−90.55%
PORSCHE	928/928S	1977	1982	£9,500	£10,000	−3.47%
PORSCHE	944	1981	1990	£7,500	£6,000	−26.64%
PORSCHE	CARRERA 2 B/C	1960	1964	£60,000	£64,667	−1.17%
PORSCHE	CARRERA 3	1975	1977	£12,500	£14,667	7.59%
RELIANT	REGAL I–VI	1952	1962	£650	£1,283	80.96%
RELIANT	REGAL 3/25 3/30	1962	1973	£600	£900	37.61%
RELIANT	SABRE 4	1961	1963	£4,000	£5,500	26.09%
RELIANT	SABRE 5	1962	1964	£6,000	£7,167	9.54%
RELIANT	SCIMITAR GTC	1980	1986	£6,250	£9,500	39.38%
RELIANT	SCIMITAR GTE SE5 ESTATE	1968	1975	£4,000	£4,575	4.88%
RELIANT	SCIMITAR GTE SE6 ESTATE	1975	1982	£5,125	£5,625	0.64%
RELIANT	SCIMITAR SE4A	1964	1966	£4,000	£4,575	4.88%
RELIANT	SCIMITAR SE4B	1966	1970	£3,625	£4,625	17.00%
RELIANT	SCIMITAR SE4C	1967	1970	£3,500	£4,625	21.17%
RENAULT	16	1966	1978	£1,200	£1,553	18.64%
RENAULT	4	1961	1986	£1,375	£1,100	−26.67%
RENAULT	4CV	1947	1961	£3,000	£3,100	−5.26%
RENAULT	4CV SPORTS	1952	1956	£5,000	£4,767	−12.58%
RENAULT	5 GORDINI	1976	1981	£2,500	£2,333	−14.42%
RENAULT	5 GT TURBO	1985	1989	£3,000	£3,000	−8.31%
RENAULT	5 TURBO 1	1980	1982	£12,500	£11,750	−13.81%
RENAULT	5 TURBO 2	1983	1985	£8,500	£10,000	7.87%
RENAULT	CARAVELLE 1100	1963	1968	£3,000	£3,375	3.15%
RENAULT	CARAVELLE 956	1962	1968	£2,600	£3,375	19.05%
RENAULT	CARAVELLE 956 CONVERTIBLE	1962	1968	£4,000	£4,375	0.30%
RENAULT	CARAVELLE CONVERTIBLE	1963	1968	£4,500	£4,000	−18.50%
RENAULT	DAUPHINE	1954	1963	£1,625	£1,725	−2.65%
RENAULT	DAUPHINE GORDINI	1957	1968	£2,125	£2,250	−2.89%
RENAULT	FLORIDE	1959	1962	£2,125	£2,950	27.32%
RENAULT	FLORIDE CONVERTIBLE	1959	1962	£3,750	£4,167	1.88%
RENAULT	FUEGO	1980	1988	£1,675	£1,550	−15.16%
RENAULT	R10	1970	1971	£2,000	£1,367	−37.32%
RENAULT	R8	1962	1971	£1,425	£1,875	20.66%
RENAULT	R8 GORDINI 1100	1964	1967	£2,750	£3,875	29.21%
RENAULT	R8 GORDINI 1250	1967	1970	£3,250	£4,500	26.98%
RENAULT	R8 1100	1964	1972	£2,000	£1,950	−10.59%
RILEY	1.5	1957	1965	£2,875	£2,788	−11.07%
RILEY	4/68,4/72	1959	1969	£1,900	£2,700	30.31%
RILEY	ELF 1/2/3	1961	1969	£2,125	£1,963	−15.28%
RILEY	KESTREL 1100/1300	1965	1969	£1,425	£2,225	43.18%
RILEY	PATHFINDER/2.6	1953	1959	£2,375	£3,250	25.48%
RILEY	RMA/RME 1.5	1945	1955	£5,750	£7,313	16.62%
RILEY	RMB/RMF 2.5	1946	1953	£9,500	£8,813	−14.93%
RILEY	RMC ROADSTER	1948	1950	£15,750	£17,250	0.43%

MANUFACTURER	ACTUAL CAR	YEAR FROM	YEAR TO	1993 VALUE	PRESENT VALUE	VALUE SWING
RILEY	RMD dhc	1948	1951	£14,000	£15,250	-0.12%
ROCHDALE	GT	1957	1961	£2,500	£2,200	-19.30%
ROCHDALE	OLYMPIC SERIES 1/2	1960	1968	£3,000	£3,188	-2.57%
ROLLS-ROYCE	CAMARGUE	1975	1985	£35,000	£46,667	22.26%
ROLLS-ROYCE	CORNICHE	1971	1977	£19,750	£23,333	8.33%
ROLLS-ROYCE	CORNICHE dhc	1971	1977	£33,750	£31,000	-15.77%
ROLLS-ROYCE	MPW CORNICHE	1966	1970	£22,500	£21,000	-14.42%
ROLLS-ROYCE	MPW CORNICHE dhc	1966	1970	£35,000	£30,000	-21.40%
ROLLS-ROYCE	PHANTOM V YOUNG SEDANCA	1960	1968	£95,000	£62,500	-39.67%
ROLLS-ROYCE	PHANTOM V JAMES YOUNG	1959	1968	£50,000	£72,500	32.96%
ROLLS-ROYCE	PHANTOM V MPW LIMOUSINE	1959	1968	£65,000	£65,000	-8.30%
ROLLS-ROYCE	PHANTOM VI LIMOUSINE	1968	1977	£100,000	£85,000	-22.06%
ROLLS-ROYCE	SILVER CLOUD I dhc	1955	1959	£70,000	£85,000	11.35%
ROLLS-ROYCE	SILVER CLOUD I	1955	1959	£17,250	£25,000	32.89%
ROLLS-ROYCE	SILVER CLOUD II	1959	1962	£18,000	£24,000	22.26%
ROLLS-ROYCE	SILVER CLOUD II dhc	1959	1962	£50,000	£84,083	54.20%
ROLLS-ROYCE	SILVER CLOUD III	1962	1965	£22,500	£28,000	14.11%
ROLLS-ROYCE	SILVER CLOUD III dhc	1962	1966	£50,000	£55,000	0.87%
ROLLS-ROYCE	SILVER CLOUD III FLYING SPUR	1962	1966	£40,000	£57,500	31.81%
ROLLS-ROYCE	SILVER CLOUD III MPW	1962	1966	£40,000	£37,500	-14.03%
ROLLS-ROYCE	SILVER CLOUD III YOUNG lwb LIMO	1962	1966	£60,000	£45,000	-31.23%
ROLLS-ROYCE	SILVER DAWN	1949	1955	£20,000	£27,667	26.85%
ROLLS-ROYCE	SILVER DAWN dhc	1952	1955	£55,000	£50,000	-16.64%
ROLLS-ROYCE	SILVER SHADOW I	1965	1970	£11,750	£12,125	-5.38%
ROLLS-ROYCE	SILVER SHADOW II	1977	1980	£15,750	£14,250	-17.04%
ROLLS-ROYCE	SILVER WRAITH HOOPER	1955	1959	£45,000	£50,000	1.88%
ROLLS-ROYCE	SILVER WRAITH II	1977	1980	£15,000	£15,000	-8.30%
ROLLS-ROYCE	SILVER WRAITH MULLINER LIMO	1955	1959	£85,000	£60,000	-35.27%
ROVER	P2 FOURTEEN/SIXTEEN	1946	1948	£6,000	£4,000	-38.87%
ROVER	P2 TEN/TWELVE	1946	1948	£5,000	£5,000	-8.31%
ROVER	P2 TOURER	1947	1947	£8,500	£14,000	51.02%
ROVER	P3 60/75	1948	1949	£5,000	£4,375	-19.77%
ROVER	P4 100	1959	1962	£3,750	£4,500	10.02%
ROVER	P4 105R	1956	1958	£3,375	£4,000	8.67%
ROVER	P4 105S	1956	1959	£4,500	£4,000	-18.50%
ROVER	P4 60	1954	1959	£3,250	£3,500	-1.24%
ROVER	P4 75	1950	1954	£4,350	£4,000	-15.68%
ROVER	P4 75	1955	1959	£3,250	£4,000	12.87%
ROVER	P4 80	1959	1962	£3,125	£3,100	-9.04%
ROVER	P4 90	1954	1959	£3,500	£4,000	4.79%
ROVER	P4 95/110	1962	1964	£3,625	£4,600	16.37%
ROVER	P5 3.0	1958	1967	£3,500	£5,300	38.85%
ROVER	P5 COUPE	1963	1967	£4,000	£5,500	26.09%
ROVER	P5B 3.5	1967	1973	£4,350	£5,850	23.31%
ROVER	P5B 3.5 COUPE	1968	1975	£4,600	£5,550	10.62%
ROVER	P6 2000/2000SC	1963	1972	£1,983	£2,075	-4.07%
ROVER	P6 2000TC	1966	1972	£2,125	£2,675	15.45%
ROVER	P6 2200/TC	1973	1976	£2,300	£2,175	-13.28%
ROVER	P6 3500/3500S	1968	1975	£3,425	£3,250	-12.99%
ROVER	SDI 2000/2300/2600	1977	1986	£900	£900	-8.35%
ROVER	SDI 3500	1976	1986	£4,500	£2,033	-58.58%
ROVER	SDI 3500 VITESSE	1982	1986	£4,250	£3,467	-25.20%
ROVER	SDI VDP	1980	1986	£2,200	£2,000	-16.63%
SAAB	95 BULLNOSE	1960	1965	£4,000	£3,975	-8.87%
SAAB	95 ESTATE	1960	1968	£3,500	£3,675	-3.72%
SAAB	95 LONGNOSE	1965	1968	£3,000	£3,175	-2.96%

MANUFACTURER	ACTUAL CAR	YEAR FROM	YEAR TO	1993 VALUE	PRESENT VALUE	VALUE SWING
SAAB	95 V4	1967	1970	£3,750	£3,000	−26.65%
SAAB	96 TS BULLNOSE	1960	1965	£5,000	£4,638	−14.95%
SAAB	96 TS LONGNOSE	1965	1968	£4,000	£3,650	−16.32%
SAAB	96 V4	1967	1979	£3,750	£3,050	−25.43%
SAAB	99 TURBO	1978	1983	£2,875	£2,600	−17.07%
SAAB	SONNET lhd	1966	1974	£5,000	£6,750	23.79%
SAAB	SPORT/MONTE CARLO	1962	1966	£4,500	£5,100	3.91%
SIMCA	1000	1962	1968	£1,000	£967	−11.37%
SIMCA	1000 BERTONE	1962	1967	£2,500	£2,100	−22.96%
SIMCA	1000 GLS/SPECIAL	1969	1978	£1,350	£1,400	−4.89%
SIMCA	1200S	1967	1971	£1,750	£2,375	24.48%
SIMCA	1300/1500	1963	1966	£1,000	£1,300	19.16%
SIMCA	1301/1501	1967	1976	£1,500	£1,067	−34.78%
SIMCA	9 ARONDE	1951	1955	£1,500	£1,725	5.44%
SIMCA	ARONDE	1956	1963	£1,250	£2,000	46.74%
SIMCA	OCEANE/PLEIN CEIL	1957	1962	£2,500	£3,150	15.55%
SINGER	11A/111 CONVERTIBLE	1958	1962	£3,000	£3,567	9.02%
SINGER	CHAMOIS SPORT	1966	1970	£1,350	£1,463	−0.61%
SINGER	GAZELLE I–V	1955	1965	£1,750	£1,925	0.89%
SINGER	GAZELLE CONVERTIBLE	1956	1958	£2,500	£3,500	28.39%
SINGER	GAZELLE VI	1966	1967	£850	£1,325	42.93%
SINGER	HUNTER	1954	1956	£2,250	£2,500	1.87%
SINGER	NEW GAZELLE	1967	1970	£850	£1,250	34.84%
SINGER	NEW VOGUE	1966	1971	£950	£1,400	35.14%
SINGER	ROADSTER	1939	1949	£6,500	£8,000	12.85%
SINGER	ROADSTER 4A/4B	1949	1952	£7,000	£8,000	4.79%
SINGER	SM ROADSTER	1951	1955	£8,000	£9,000	3.16%
SINGER	SM1500	1949	1954	£1,750	£2,500	31.03%
SINGER	SUPER TEN	1938	1949	£3,000	£3,500	6.97%
SINGER	SUPER TWELVE	1947	1949	£2,750	£3,750	25.04%
STANDARD	12/14 TOURER	1945	1948	£3,000	£4,800	46.70%
STANDARD	EIGHT/TEN	1953	1960	£1,150	£1,825	45.53%
STANDARD	ENSIGN	1957	1963	£1,875	£2,075	1.47%
STANDARD	FLYING 12	1945	1948	£2,000	£3,000	37.55%
STANDARD	FLYING 14	1945	1948	£2,250	£3,250	32.44%
STANDARD	FLYING 8	1945	1948	£1,500	£2,250	37.53%
STANDARD	FLYING 8 TOURER	1945	1948	£2,500	£3,650	33.90%
STANDARD	LUXURY SIX	1961	1963	£1,950	£2,550	19.89%
STANDARD	PENNANT	1957	1960	£1,500	£2,025	23.78%
STANDARD	SPORTSMAN	1956	1958	£2,300	£2,763	10.17%
STANDARD	VANGUARD I	1947	1952	£2,750	£3,125	4.20%
STANDARD	VANGUARD II	1953	1955	£2,000	£2,850	30.67%
STANDARD	VANGUARD III	1956	1958	£2,250	£2,150	−12.39%
STANDARD	VIGNALE	1958	1961	£2,250	£2,525	2.89%
SUNBEAM	ALPINE	1969	1975	£1,000	£1,300	19.16%
SUNBEAM	ALPINE I/II/III	1959	1964	£6,000	£6,875	5.07%
SUNBEAM	ALPINE IV/V	1964	1968	£5,500	£6,700	11.70%
SUNBEAM	ALPINE ROADSTER	1953	1955	£10,250	£12,875	15.18%
SUNBEAM	HARRINGTON GT	1961	1963	£7,500	£8,850	8.20%
SUNBEAM	IMP SPORT	1966	1976	£1,250	£1,583	16.14%
SUNBEAM	IMP STILETTO	1967	1972	£1,575	£1,688	−1.75%
SUNBEAM	RAPIER	1967	1976	£1,850	£1,550	−23.19%
SUNBEAM	RAPIER I–V	1955	1967	£1,933	£2,650	25.71%
SUNBEAM	RAPIER II/IIIA CONVERTIBLE	1958	1963	£4,250	£5,463	17.86%
SUNBEAM	RAPIER H120	1969	1976	£1,750	£1,975	3.51%
SUNBEAM	TIGER I	1964	1966	£10,250	£11,750	5.12%

MANUFACTURER	ACTUAL CAR	YEAR FROM	YEAR TO	1993 VALUE	PRESENT VALUE	VALUE SWING
SUNBEAM	TIGER 11	1967	1968	£12,500	£14,875	9.12%
SUNBEAM	VENEZIA	1963	1964	£5,000	£5,500	0.86%
SUNBEAM–TALBOT	2 LITRE	1945	1948	£4,000	£3,600	−17.47%
SUNBEAM–TALBOT	2 LITRE TOURER	1945	1948	£6,500	£7,250	2.27%
SUNBEAM–TALBOT	90 MK11/111S	1950	1957	£5,000	£4,500	−17.48%
SUNBEAM–TALBOT	90 MK11/111S CONVERTIBLE	1950	1957	£8,500	£8,250	−11.00%
SUNBEAM–TALBOT	TALBOT 80	1948	1950	£2,750	£3,625	20.87%
SUNBEAM–TALBOT	TALBOT 80 dhc	1948	1950	£5,000	£6,925	26.99%
SUNBEAM–TALBOT	TALBOT 90	1948	1950	£3,500	£4,125	8.07%
SUNBEAM–TALBOT	TALBOT 90 dhc	1948	1950	£6,500	£7,500	5.80%
SUNBEAM–TALBOT	TEN	1939	1948	£3,500	£3,475	−8.96%
SUNBEAM–TALBOT	TEN TOURER	1939	1948	£4,500	£6,500	32.44%
SWALLOW	DORETTI	1954	1955	£9,500	£15,333	48.00%
TALBOT	SUNBEAM LOTUS	1979	1981	£4,250	£4,500	−2.91%
TOYOTA	CELICA	1970	1977	£1,800	£2,500	27.36%
TOYOTA	CELICA	1977	1982	£1,500	£2,100	28.36%
TOYOTA	CROWN DELUXE	1969	1971	£2,000	£1,500	−31.22%
TOYOTA	MR2	1985	1988	£3,250	£4,000	12.87%
TRABANT	P600/601	1963	1989	£1,000	£800	−26.67%
TRIDENT	CLIPPER	1967	1978	£10,000	£11,500	5.45%
TRIUMPH	HERALD 13/60 dhc	1967	1971	£2,450	£2,850	6.66%
TRIUMPH	1300/TC/1500	1965	1973	£850	£1,117	20.50%
TRIUMPH	1500TC	1973	1976	£750	£1,038	26.89%
TRIUMPH	1800	1946	1948	£5,000	£6,575	20.58%
TRIUMPH	1850HL	1972	1981	£750	£1,563	91.08%
TRIUMPH	2000/RENOWN	1949	1954	£5,000	£6,250	14.62%
TRIUMPH	2000MK1	1963	1969	£1,750	£1,950	2.20%
TRIUMPH	2000MK1/11	1963	1977	£2,125	£2,125	−8.29%
TRIUMPH	2500/2.5Pi	1968	1977	£2,375	£2,188	−15.52%
TRIUMPH	DOLOMITE 1300/1500	1976	1981	£1,250	£1,000	−26.63%
TRIUMPH	DOLOMITE SPRINT	1973	1980	£2,625	£3,150	10.02%
TRIUMPH	DOVE GTR4 2+2	1961	1964	£9,000	£10,000	1.88%
TRIUMPH	GT6 MK1/11	1966	1967	£4,250	£4,050	−12.62%
TRIUMPH	GT6 MK111	1970	1973	£4,500	£4,775	−2.71%
TRIUMPH	HERALD 1200 & 12/50	1961	1970	£1,500	£1,625	−0.67%
TRIUMPH	HERALD 13/60	1967	1970	£1,500	£1,725	5.44%
TRIUMPH	HERALD COUPE	1959	1964	£1,750	£1,925	0.89%
TRIUMPH	HERALD/HERALD S	1959	1964	£1,350	£1,513	2.79%
TRIUMPH	MAYFLOWER	1950	1953	£2,625	£2,600	−9.19%
TRIUMPH	ROADSTER	1946	1949	£17,500	£12,625	−33.85%
TRIUMPH	SPITFIRE 1500	1974	1981	£2,963	£3,913	21.11%
TRIUMPH	SPITFIRE 4	1962	1965	£3,375	£3,400	−7.63%
TRIUMPH	SPITFIRE MK11	1965	1967	£3,000	£3,650	11.55%
TRIUMPH	SPITFIRE MK111/IV	1967	1974	£2,625	£3,500	22.25%
TRIUMPH	STAG	1970	1977	£7,500	£8,450	3.31%
TRIUMPH	TOLEDO	1970	1976	£600	£913	39.60%
TRIUMPH	TR2	1953	1956	£10,500	£11,088	−3.17%
TRIUMPH	TR250	1967	1968	£12,000	£7,167	−45.24%
TRIUMPH	TR3/TR3A	1955	1961	£11,000	£11,088	−7.57%
TRIUMPH	TR3B	1961	1962	£9,500	£10,250	−1.06%
TRIUMPH	TR4	1961	1965	£8,500	£8,350	−9.92%
TRIUMPH	TR4A	1965	1967	£8,500	£8,475	−8.58%
TRIUMPH	TR5Pi	1967	1968	£10,500	£11,238	−1.86%
TRIUMPH	TR6	1968	1976	£8,500	£9,375	1.13%
TRIUMPH	TR7	1976	1981	£1,900	£2,100	1.35%
TRIUMPH	TR7 CONVERTIBLE	1980	1982	£2,625	£3,813	33.18%

MANUFACTURER	ACTUAL CAR	YEAR FROM	YEAR TO	1993 VALUE	PRESENT VALUE	VALUE SWING
TRIUMPH	TR8 lhd	1978	1980	£8,000	£8,417	−3.52%
TRIUMPH	VITESSE 1600/2.0	1962	1968	£2,500	£2,525	−7.37%
TRIUMPH	VITESSE CONVERTIBLE	1962	1968	£3,250	£3,488	−1.58%
TRIUMPH	VITESSE MKII	1968	1971	£2,900	£3,088	−2.37%
TRIUMPH	VITESSE MKII CONVERTIBLE	1968	1971	£4,000	£4,213	−3.42%
TURNER	950 SPORTS	1957	1959	£6,250	£6,250	−8.30%
TURNER	A30 SPORTS	1955	1957	£4,000	£5,250	20.36%
TURNER	CLIMAX SPORTS	1957	1966	£7,500	£9,000	10.04%
TURNER	GT 2+2	1961	1965	£6,000	£7,000	6.98%
TURNER	MKII/III SPORTS	1960	1966	£5,500	£5,500	−8.30%
TVR	1300	1971	1972	£3,500	£3,900	2.17%
TVR	3000M	1972	1979	£6,750	£5,938	−19.33%
TVR	3000S	1978	1979	£10,000	£9,000	−17.48%
TVR	350i	1983	1988	£10,000	£8,000	−26.65%
TVR	GRANTURA I/II/IIA/III	1957	1964	£6,000	£4,550	−30.46%
TVR	GRANTURA 1800S	1966	1967	£5,500	£4,675	−22.06%
TVR	GRIFFITH 200/400	1963	1965	£25,000	£20,083	−26.34%
TVR	TAIMAR	1976	1979	£6,750	£7,125	−3.21%
TVR	TASMIN	1979	1983	£7,000	£7,000	−8.30%
TVR	TUSCAN V6	1969	1971	£6,250	£6,833	0.25%
TVR	TUSCAN V8 /V8 SE	1967	1970	£15,000	£18,333	12.07%
TVR	VIXEN SI–III	1967	1972	£5,750	£5,175	−17.48%
TVR	VIXEN SIV/1600M	1972	1977	£5,500	£5,075	−15.39%
UNIPOWER	UNIPOWER GT	1966	1970	£4,000	£4,000	−8.30%
VANDEN PLAS	4 LITRE	1959	1968	£4,500	£4,000	−18.50%
VANDEN PLAS	3 LITRE I/II	1959	1964	£2,250	£3,338	36.02%
VANDEN PLAS	4 LITRE R	1964	1968	£4,000	£4,000	−8.30%
VANDEN PLAS	PRINCESS 1100	1963	1968	£1,750	£3,163	65.78%
VANDEN PLAS	PRINCESS 1300	1967	1974	£1,875	£4,075	99.27%
VANDEN PLAS	PRINCESS 1500/1750	1975	1980	£1,750	£1,475	−22.69%
VAUXHALL	10/12/14	1939	1948	£2,375	£2,200	−15.06%
VAUXHALL	CHEVETTE HS 2300	1978	1980	£2,850	£3,500	12.61%
VAUXHALL	CRESTA E	1954	1957	£3,000	£3,350	2.38%
VAUXHALL	CRESTA PC	1965	1972	£1,250	£1,538	12.84%
VAUXHALL	DROOPSNOOT	1974	1975	£3,750	£3,500	−14.43%
VAUXHALL	FIRENZA SPORT	1971	1976	£1,575	£1,425	−17.05%
VAUXHALL	MAGNUM COUPE	1973	1978	£900	£1,413	43.89%
VAUXHALL	ROYALE COUPE	1978	1982	£1,500	£2,850	74.21%
VAUXHALL	VELOX	1948	1951	£2,250	£2,513	2.40%
VAUXHALL	VELOX E	1951	1957	£2,750	£3,188	6.30%
VAUXHALL	VELOX/CRESTA PA	1957	1962	£3,250	£4,075	14.98%
VAUXHALL	VELOX/CRESTA PA	1962	1965	£3,250	£4,075	14.98%
VAUXHALL	VENTORA/VICTOR 3300	1968	1972	£1,200	£1,500	14.59%
VAUXHALL	VICTOR 101FC	1964	1967	£1,125	£1,483	20.86%
VAUXHALL	VICTOR 1600FD	1967	1972	£500	£867	59.08%
VAUXHALL	VICTOR F	1957	1961	£2,150	£2,150	−8.32%
VAUXHALL	VICTOR FB	1961	1964	£1,450	£1,475	−6.70%
VAUXHALL	VICTOR/VENTORA FE	1972	1976	£1,400	£988	−35.30%
VAUXHALL	VISCOUNT	1966	1972	£1,500	£1,625	−0.67%
VAUXHALL	VIVA BRABHAM	1967	1968	£2,000	£2,850	30.67%
VAUXHALL	VIVA GT	1968	1970	£1,500	£1,825	11.55%
VAUXHALL	VIVA HA	1963	1966	£925	£1,088	7.83%
VAUXHALL	VIVA HB	1966	1970	£750	£1,000	22.25%
VAUXHALL	VX 4/90FD	1967	1972	£750	£1,188	45.23%
VAUXHALL	VX 4/90FB	1961	1964	£2,250	£1,850	−24.61%
VAUXHALL	VX 4/90FC	1964	1967	£1,500	£1,900	16.14%

MANUFACTURER	ACTUAL CAR	YEAR FROM	YEAR TO	1993 VALUE	PRESENT VALUE	VALUE SWING
VAUXHALL	WYVERN	1948	1951	£2,000	£2,050	−6.01%
VAUXHALL	WYVERN E	1951	1957	£2,250	£2,325	−5.26%
VOLKSWAGEN	1302/1302S	1970	1972	£2,450	£3,188	19.31%
VOLKSWAGEN	1303/1303S	1972	1975	£2,717	£3,363	13.50%
VOLKSWAGEN	BEETLE	1954	1960	£3,500	£4,075	6.76%
VOLKSWAGEN	BEETLE	1960	1965	£3,250	£3,338	−5.81%
VOLKSWAGEN	BEETLE 1100	1945	1954	£4,500	£6,675	36.00%
VOLKSWAGEN	BEETLE 1200	1966	1978	£2,750	£3,238	7.97%
VOLKSWAGEN	BEETLE 1200L	1979	1985	£3,500	£3,550	−7.00%
VOLKSWAGEN	BEETLE 1300	1965	1973	£2,750	£3,213	7.14%
VOLKSWAGEN	BEETLE 1500	1966	1973	£3,000	£3,275	0.09%
VOLKSWAGEN	CABRIO	1949	1954	£8,500	£8,250	−11.00%
VOLKSWAGEN	CABRIO	1954	1960	£7,000	£7,750	1.52%
VOLKSWAGEN	CABRIO 1302/1303 L/S	1970	1972	£10,125	£8,813	−20.19%
VOLKSWAGEN	CABRIO 1500	1966	1973	£9,500	£7,667	−25.99%
VOLKSWAGEN	GOLF MK1 GTi	1978	1984	£3,250	£2,583	−27.12%
VOLKSWAGEN	KARMANN GHIA	1955	1974	£7,500	£6,400	−21.75%
VOLKSWAGEN	KARMANN GHIA dhc	1958	1974	£9,500	£8,625	−16.75%
VOLKSWAGEN	SCIROCCO	1974	1992	£2,000	£1,700	−22.05%
VOLVO	121/122	1956	1967	£2,500	£3,213	17.87%
VOLVO	122S/B18	1961	1967	£4,000	£3,275	−24.92%
VOLVO	123GT	1966	1967	£4,000	£3,950	−9.45%
VOLVO	144	1967	1974	£900	£1,100	12.02%
VOLVO	164	1968	1973	£4,000	£1,950	−55.30%
VOLVO	200	1974	1980	£1,800	£1,700	−13.40%
VOLVO	P1800/P1800S	1961	1969	£6,750	£5,163	−29.86%
VOLVO	P1800E	1967	1972	£4,750	£4,283	−17.32%
VOLVO	P1800ES ESTATE	1971	1973	£5,050	£4,863	−11.69%
VOLVO	PV544	1958	1965	£4,000	£3,875	−11.16%
WARTBURG	312	1962	1966	£1,000	£1,150	5.41%
WARTBURG	353 KNIGHT	1966	1988	£1,000	£950	−12.92%
WARTBURG	TOURIST ESTATE	1966	1988	£1,200	£950	−27.43%
WOLSELEY	1100	1962	1968	£1,500	£1,850	13.08%
WOLSELEY	12/48	1938	1948	£2,000	£3,250	49.01%
WOLSELEY	1300	1967	1971	£1,375	£1,863	24.20%
WOLSELEY	14/60	1939	1948	£2,500	£4,500	65.08%
WOLSELEY	15/50	1956	1958	£2,750	£2,863	−4.53%
WOLSELEY	15/60 16/60	1958	1971	£1,625	£2,438	37.58%
WOLSELEY	1500	1957	1965	£2,500	£2,450	−10.12%
WOLSELEY	18/85	1967	1972	£1,200	£1,625	24.14%
WOLSELEY	18/85	1939	1948	£2,500	£4,500	65.08%
WOLSELEY	2200 WEDGE/SIX	1975	1972	£1,400	£1,825	19.52%
WOLSELEY	4/44	1952	1956	£2,500	£2,625	−3.71%
WOLSELEY	4/50	1952	1954	£1,350	£2,700	83.42%
WOLSELEY	6/80	1948	1954	£2,500	£3,825	40.32%
WOLSELEY	6/90	1954	1956	£2,000	£2,883	32.19%
WOLSELEY	6/90	1956	1959	£2,500	£2,933	7.59%
WOLSELEY	6/99 6/110	1959	1968	£1,925	£2,588	23.30%
WOLSELEY	EIGHT	1939	1948	£2,500	£2,500	−8.29%
WOLSELEY	HORNET	1963	1969	£1,900	£2,100	1.35%
WOLSELEY	TEN	1939	1948	£2,000	£2,850	30.67%

Miller's Collectors Cars Price Guide 1997-1998

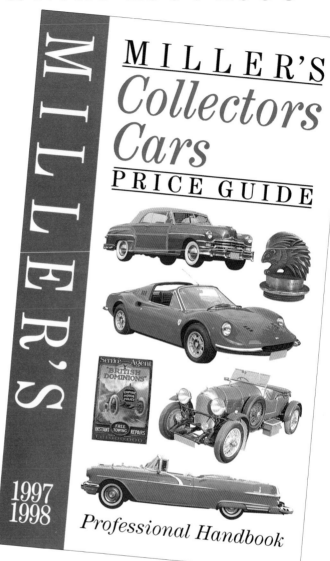

£19.99

For anyone interested in classic cars, this is a must!

With over 4,000 new photographs the guide reviews all aspects of collecting from veteran and vintage to today's collectable cars. Special attention is given to racing cars, American cars and the Morris marques; automobilia is not forgotten, with a wealth of badges, dashboard accessories, mascots and luggage. Marques are presented alphabetically and each picture is accompanied by a detailed caption listing year of manufacture, condition, degree of originality and a price range. An indispensable authority among car experts, dealers and enthusiasts. The only illustrated classic car price guide available.

Available from all good bookshops and specialist wholesalers. In case of difficulty please phone 0171 225 9244

Miller's Publications is part of Reed Books Limited
Registered Office: Michelin House, 81 Fulham Road, London, SW3 6RB
Registered in England No: 1527729

New edition available from October 1996

CLASSIC EVENTS DIARY
April to December 1997

It must be stressed that these dates are provisional, and should be checked with the relevant organisers. Nor, of course, is it exhaustive.

APRIL

3-6 EAST AFRICAN HISTORIC SAFARI RALLY: An event held over the less arduous stages of this famous rally. Nairobi, Kenya. *Details: 0171 586 3931*

4-7 CIRCUIT OF IRELAND HISTORIC RALLY: Bangor-Limerick-Bangor. *Details: 01232 426262*

11-13 CONCOURS D'ELEGANCE VILLA D'ESTE: Held in the beautiful garden of the Villa Olmo, Lake Como, Italy. *Details: Angelo Tito Anselmi, via Matteo Bandello 18, 20123 Milan, Italy; fax: 0039 2 4817351*

12-13 LOTUS FESTIVAL AND EXHIBITION: Donington Exhibition Centre, Donington Park, Leics. *Details: 01362 691144/694459*

15-19 HISTORIC TULPENRALLYE: The Tulip Rally for historic cars held on road stages in Holland. *Details: 0031 33 722747*

15-20 TARGA TASMANIA: Australian road event for classic cars. *Details: 01483 225120*

19-20 HAYNES PUBLISHING RACMSA TWO-DAY CLASSIC: An event for cars, of all types, over 20 years old. The route is through the Welsh borders in to the Cotswolds and includes secondary roads on Salisbury Plain. The rally includes three timed hillclimbs and timed laps at the Castle Combe circuit. *Details: 01753 681736*

19-23 COPPERSTATE 1000: Road event over 1000 miles in Arizona, USA. *Details 001 602 252 8382*

23-26 TOUR DE FRANCE AUTO: Paris-Le Mans-Vichy-Avignon-Nice. *Details: 0033 1 42 59 73 40*

27 BMW FAMILIES DAY: Billing Aquadrome, near Northampton. *Details: 01362 691144*

27 April – 1 May MINI MONTE: Dover to Monte Carlo over parts, including mountain stages, of the Monte Carlo rally route. *Details: 01235 851291*

29-22 LUXEMBOURG-ST. PETERSBURG RALLY. *Details: 0033 1 48 75 13 54*

MAY

2-3 CLASSIC HASPENGOUW RALLY: Belgium. *Details: 0032 11 882542*

3 VSCC NORTHERN RALLY: near Chipping, Lancashire. *Details: 01635 44411*

3-5 CLASSIC AND SPORTSCAR SHOW: NEC, Birmingham. Now firmly established as Britain's biggest and best show for classic enthusiasts. *Details 0171 402 2555*

4 VOLKSWAGEN CLASSIC EVENT: Stanford Hall, Leics. THE BIG RUN '97: A classic car run to the Classic and Sportscar Show at the NEC, from six starting points in Britain. *Details: 01304 380244*

4-5 LUTON HOO CLASSIC CAR SHOW: Luton, Bedfordshire. In 1996 over 1300 classic cars were on show in the grounds of this historic house. *Details: 01296 631181*

5-6 FIA INTERNATIONAL RACE MEETING: Historic and Classic racing and sportscars in action at the Donington Park Circuit. *Details: 01327 858400*

5-9 ECURIE ECOSSE TOUR 1997: Timed regularity runs are the feature of this event which passes through the stunning scenery of Scotland. *Details: 01334 839218*

7-8 HMSA WINE COUNTRY CLASSIC HISTORIC races: Sears Point, California, USA. *Details: 001 805 966 9151*

8-11 MILLE MIGLIA: Famous event which starts and finishes at Brescia, Italy. *Details: 0039 030 280036*

9-10 LEIPZIG OLDTIMER SHOW: This large and important show is now in its 3rd year. Leipzig, Germany. *Details: 0049 2405 71974*

9-11 TROPHÉE DES ARDENNES, SPA, BELGIUM: Roads are closed to allow this event for historic racing cars to take place on the original famous circuit. *Details: 0032 41 58 63 18*

10-11 JUBILÉ AUTOMOBILE MARSEILLE-PROVENCE: A show which features an auction, autojumble, and a concours; also includes the Retrospective Grand Prix de Marseille. *Details: 0033 9178 83 00*

OULTON PARK CLASSIC CAR SHOW: The tenth year for this event features an autojumble, a cavalcade, concours and a swapmeet. *Details: 0161 442 3048*

WEST CORK CLASSIC RALLY: An event held on the roads of the Irish Republic. *Details: 00353 21 883532*

10-17 IRISH FERRIES CLASSIC TOUR OF IRELAND: This event takes place over 7 days and is open to all pre-1975 cars. *Details: 01734 885206*

11 SOUTH WALES CLASSIC CAR CLUB SHOW AND AUTOJUMBLE: Pencoed College of Agriculture. *Details: 01222 890234*

AUSTIN MAXI OWNERS' CLUB MAXIMEET AND AGM: The Shuttleworth Collection, Biggleswade, Bedfordshire. *Details: 01526 398377*

16-17 EUROPEAN RALLY OF VINTAGE CARS: Le Chateu D'O, Normandy, France. *Details: 0033 1 48 80 89 15; Fax: 0033 1 48 80 33 35*

17 LES PASSE MONTAGNE: show and concours in Aix-les-Bains. *Details: J-F Barret, La Tour, 73800 Myans, France; tel: 0033 79 28 13 18*

17-18 FOURTH OLDIERAMA: Lörrach, Germany, near Basle. Autojumble for classic vehicle spares. *Details: 0041 32581810; Fax: 32581910*

LOTUS DRIVERS' CLUB LAND'S END TO JOHN O'GROATS CHARITY RELAY: This event is open to non-members. *Details: 01283 761972*

CLASSIC PRESCOTT HILLCLIMB: Nr. Bishop's Cleeve, Gloucestershire. *Details: Bugatti Owners' Club, 01242 673136*

18 VSCC SCOTTISH TRIAL: Biggar, Lanarkshire. *Details: 01635 44411*

BRITISH CAR SHOW: The event for owners of British built cars. The Continent, Columbus, Ohio, USA. *Details: 001 614 363 2203*

19-24 California Mille: 1000-mile run starting in San Francisco, CA, USA. *Details: 001 415 292 2700*

19-28 JAGUAR TOUR INTERNACIONAL PORTUGAL 1997: A tour of Portugal starting in the north and finishing in the south of the country. *Details: 00351 8592020; fax: 00351 8481709* PROVISIONAL

23-24 RALLYE DES LEGENDES: Belgium. *Details: 0032 87 230151*

NATIONAL TRUST VINTAGE TRIAL: A vintage car road rally over a distance of 300 miles in Northern Ireland includes driving tests in the grounds of some of the finest properties in Ulster. *Details: 01238 562436*

23-25 NORWICH UNION RALLY CLASSIC: Starts at 14 locations in England, Ireland, Wales and France, finishing at Silverstone Circuit, Northants. *Details: 01753 681736; fax: 01753 682938*

23-26 1997 INTERNATIONAL SAAB RALLY: Bilund, Denmark. *Details: 0181 598 8440*

24-25 CAPRI NATIONAL: The event for owners of all marks of Ford Capri. Badgers Hill Country Estate, Vale of Evesham. *Details: 01527 502066*

24-26 ENFIELD PAGEANT OF MOTORING: Whitewebbs Museum, Enfield, Middlesex. Usually attended by around 2000 cars and supported with 650 autojumble stands. *Details: 0181 367 1698*

25 THE CATS TRAIL: This Jaguar-only event starts at Jaguar Cars Ltd in Coventry and finishes at the Heritage Museum of Gaydon, Warwickshire. *Details: 0113 285 4057*

31 MGCC INTERNATIONAL RACE MEETING: Silverstone Circuit, Northants. *Details: 01235 555552*

31-1 June HSCC INTERNATIONAL RACE MEETING: Donington Park, Leicestershire. *Details: 01327 858400*

THIRD FERRARA CLASSIC CARS AND MOTORCYCLE SHOW: Italy. Held in the Ferrara Exhibition Centre this event, held in four halls, features stands from the important clubs, many dealers featuring restored vehicles. There is also a large autojumble. *Details: 0039 425 21266; fax: 0039 425 22473/30134*

MG CAR CLUB SILVERSTONE INTERNATIONAL: Silverstone Circuit, Northants. *Details: 01235 555552*

JUNE

7-8 MG OWNERS' CLUB MG '97: The main rally for all types of this marque takes place at the Imperial War Museum, Duxford. *Details: 01954 231125*

7-15 NORTH CAPE CHALLENGE: Rally from Oslo to North Cape, Norway. *Details: 0047 67 12 34 80*

8 LONDON-BRIGHTON CLASSIC CAR RUN: This event is open to all pre-1979 cars. Starts from Syon Park, Brentford, Middlesex also from Norman Park, Bromley, Kent, to finish at Madeira Drive, Brighton, Sussex. *Details: 01296 631181*

NATIONAL ALFA DAY AND CONCOURS: Open to all types of Alfa-Romeo and located at Stanford Hall, near Lutterworth, Leicestershire. *Details: 01223 894300*

AMOC ST. JOHN HORSFALL HISTORIC RACE MEETING: Annual event open to historic racing and sports cars. Silverstone, Northants. *Details: 01353 777353*

CLUB TRIUMPH SUMMER PICNIC: Highclere Castle, Newbury, Berks. *Details: 01663 74474*

8-9 NIGHT HAWK HISTORIC ROAD RALLY: Navigational rally over a distance of 100 miles. *Details: 01900 825642*

13 MINI MAD LAKELAND TOUR: Ony 250 are allowed in the entry for this tour of the nothern lakes. *Details: 0370 454545*

13-22 FIVA WORLD RALLY 1997: A touring trial with an entry limited to 400 cars. 1996 route was from Edinburgh, Scotland to Gaydon, Warwickshire. *Details: 01926 643048* PROVISIONAL

14-15 BLACKHAWK VINTAGE CLASSIC: Blackhawk Farms Raceway, Rockton, Illinois, USA. *Details: Vintage Sports Car Drivers' Association, PO Box 1451, Chicago, Illinois 60690, USA. Tel: 001 708 385 8899; fax: 001 708 385 8911*

ROLLS-ROYCE ENTHUSIASTS' CLUB ANNUAL NATIONAL RALLY: All models of this famous marque are displayed at this event, including many fitted with special coachbuilt bodies. Althorp Park, Northants. *Details: 01327 811489*

20-22 GOODWOOD FESTIVAL OF SPEED: Held in the grounds of Goodwood House this event is now a firm fixture in the historic and classic motor sport calendar. The event is a time trial and is open to racing and sports cars, also historic motor cycles. There are also static displays of racing and sports cars of all types. Goodwood House, Chichester, West Sussex. *Details: 01243 774107*

21-22 L'AGE D'OR HISTORIC RACES: Golden Age of motor racing event for historic cars at the famous Montlhéry track near Paris. *Details: 0033 1 42 59 73 40*

24-27 10TH ANNUAL Z CAR CONVENTION: hosted by the Z Car Club of Colorado in Denver. *Details: 001 303 526 2262*

YPRES HISTORIC RALLY: Belgium. *Details: 0032 57422157*

Althorp Park visitor, (left) one of the 2,000-plus examples of the coachmaker's art that make the trip to the annual Rolls-Royce National Rally. Stirling Moss and Denis Jenkinson (below), forty years after victory in the Mille Miglia, same 300SLR, Goodwood.

Line-up of historic Porsche racers at the Goodwood Festival of Speed; two 917s and the 1000-bhp 917/30 Can Am.

CITROËN TRACTION OWNERS' CLUB ANNUAL RALLY: Snowdonia National Park. *Details: 01286 674748*

28 BENTLEY DRIVERS' CLUB CONCOURS: Open to all types of Bentley and sited at Broughton Castle, Nr. Banbury, Oxon. *Details: 01844 208233*

28-29 SANDOWN PARK INTERNATIONAL COLLECTORS' CAR FAIR: Sandown Park, Esher, Surrey. This event, supported by Classic and Sportscar magazine, is the place to buy a classic car with hundreds for sale on display. *Details: 01594 232332*

LANCIA MOTOR CLUB NATIONAL RALLY: The event for Lancia owners of all types. *Details: 01633 895466*

MG ECOSSE '97: Annual event for MG owners in Scotland and located at the beautiful Doune Castle, Perthshire, Scotland. *Details: 01313 313057*

28-4 July CLARET AND CLASSICS: starts Bordeaux, France. Rally for veteran, vintage, post-vintage and cars built up until 1965. *Details: 01934 626136*

29 BROOKLANDS SOCIETY REUNION: Located in the grounds of Brooklands Museum, Weybridge, Surrey, this event allows owners to drive their cars on the surviving part of this famous banked circuit. *Details: 01932 857381*

JULY

4-6 CIRCUITO DI PESCARA: Italy. *Details: 0039 85 8991157*

4-11 RALLYE DES ALPES: Switzerland.
Details: 0041 22 849 85 05

5 BÅSTAD CLASSIC CAR SHOW: Båstad on southern Sweden. There are usually more than 900 cars exhibited at this event.
Details: 0046 44 21 00 50, fax: 0046 44 21 55 25

5-6 EUROPEAN CONCOURS D'ELEGANCE: Schloss Schwetzingen, nr. Heidleberg, Germany.
Details: 01398 361378

6 NATIONAL MINI DAY: Open to owners of Mini's and Mini-based specials. Coombe Abbey, near Coventry, Warwickshire. *Details: 01543 257956*

11-26 TURKEY RALLYE: Mediterranean-Black Sea.
Details: 0033 1 48 75 13 54

13 CLUB PEUGEOT UK NATIONAL RALLY: The event for all Peugeot owners is held at Burghley House, Stamford, Lincs. *Details: 01424 224238*

18-20 Chicago Historic Races: Road America, Elkhart Lake, WI. *Details: 001 312 593 0495*

19-20 TR REGISTER INTERNATIONAL WEEKEND: Several hundred TR1 to TR8's are displayed at this meeting making it the biggest event in Britain for all Triumph TR enthusiasts. Bath & West Showground, Shepton Mallet, Somerset. *Details: 01235 818866*

PORSCHE CLUB GB NATIONAL WEEKEND: All models from 356 to the latest 911 are on show at this event. Althorp Park, Northants. *Details: 01608 652911*

19-27 2000km Durch Deutschland rally: Germany.
Details: 0049 2434 5156

20 18TH ANNUAL CORVETTE NATIONALS: The event for this fabulous car, organised by the Classic Corvette Club UK, takes place at Knebworth Park, Hertfordshire. *Details: 01604 34478*

HIGHCLERE CASTLE CLASSIC CAR SHOW: A superb location for this event with around 1000 cars on display. Highclere Castle, Newbury, Berks. *Details: 01296 631181*

5th ANNUAL 'TEA AT THE VICARAGE' BRITISH CAR RALLY: Concours and fun event held at the Howe Military School, LaGrange County, USA.
Details: 001 219 562 2703

25-27 COYS INTERNATIONAL HISTORIC FESTIVAL: The chance to see historic Grand Prix cars, also classic sports cars and Can-Am cars in actions. Exhibition area includes stands for classic car traders and others where you can buy items from memorabilia to paintings. A fun fair is also in attendance making it a great day out for all the family. Silverstone Circuit, Northants. *Details: 01327 857271*

AUGUST

1-2 ULSTER HISTORIC RALLY: Northern Ireland.
Details: 01868 738318

2-3 23RD EUROPEAN HISTORIC GRAND PRIX: Historic racing cars competing on the famous Zolder Circuit, Belgium. *Details: 0032 10 32 1125 6569*

3 FORD FAIR '97: Cornbury Park, near Charlbury, Oxfordshire. Europe's biggest all-Ford show.
Details: 01452 307181

8-10 AVD OLDTIMER GRAND PRIX: The famous circuit is the location for this now annual event featuring historic racing and sports cars. Nürburgring, Germany.
Details: 0049 2691 302174

9-10 FOOTMAN JAMES RETRO FESTIVAL: Event for Veteran and Vintage Cars, Commercials, Buses and even Vintage boats. NEC Birmingham. *Details: 0121 767 3536*

9-10 YEOVIL FESTIVAL OF TRANSPORT: The largest classic car show, for all marques, in the west of England. Yeovil Showground, Barwick Park, Yeovil, Somerset. *Details: 01935 22319*

10 RALLY OF THE GIANTS: Knebworth, Herts. Concours and show for all classic American cars. *Details: 01277 372735*

13-17 PROFESSIONAL CAR SOCIETY 21ST ANNUAL INTERNATIONAL MEET: Holiday Inn, Arden Hills, Saint Paul, MI, USA. *Details: 001 612 638 9295*

15 CONCOURS ITALIANA: Open to all US owners of Italian marques. Quail Lodge Resort, Carmel, California.
Details: 001 206 688 1903

15-17 MONTEREY HISTORIC RACES: Leading event in the USA for historic racing and sports cars. Laguna Seca, California. *Details: 001 805 966 9151*

17 PEBBLE BEACH CONCOURS: The Lodge, Pebble Beach, California. The ultimate car restoration show.
Details: 001 408 659 0663

22-24 VEHIKEL CLASSIC CAR AND BIKE SHOW: Koninklijke Nederlandse Jaarbeurs, Utrecht, Holland.
Details: 0031 30 2328808

SCHEVENINGEN-LUXEMBOURG-SCHEVENINGEN RALLY: Open to all classic cars. Holland.
Details: 0031 17 20 21 068

23-25 HEALEY INTERNATIONAL SPORTSCAR WEEKEND: Although organised by the Austin-Healy Club this event is open to all marques of sports car. Royal Agricultural College, Cirencester. *Details: 01869 277618*

24-25 KNEBWORTH '97 CLASSIC CAR SHOW: An enormous event with over 2000 classic cars on show. Knebworth Park, Stevenage, Herts. *Details: 01296 631181*

29-31 FIA INTERNATIONAL RACE MEETING: Historic and classic racing and sports cars race at the famous Donington Park circuit. Donington, Leics. *Details: 01327 858400*

DODGE VINTAGE FESTIVAL: Lime Rock, CT, USA. *Details: 001 516 248 6237*

30-31 TARGA RUSTICANA: Forest tracks event for historic and classic rally cars. Llandrindod Wells, Wales. *Details: 01792 655562*

31 DONINGTON '97: This run starts at five locations in Britain and finishes at the famous Donington Circuit in Leicestershire. *Details: 0113 285 4057*

SEPTEMBER

7 SIX HOURS OF SPA-FRANCORCHAMPS: Spa, Belgium. The famous circuit to the main event an endurance race for pre-'66 Touring and GT cars. There are also other races for historic cars. *Details: 01767 677031 (UK) or 0032 41 54 19 50 (Belgium)*

7 NATIONAL MINI DAY: Stanford Hall, near Lutterworth, Leicestershire. *Details: 01543 257956*

LOUIS VUITTON CONCOURS D'ELEGANCE: The very best of European cars and coachbuilding on display. Parc de Bagatelle, Paris, France. *Details: 0171 493 6547*

11-13 MANX HISTORIC RALLY: Historic rally car event on various road sections. Isle of Man. *Details: 01624 852440*

11-17 26TH PHILPA INTERNATIONAL JUBILEE RALLY: Greece. *Details: 0030 1777 5931*

12-13 IMPARTS/PENRITE RALLY: Holland. *Details: 0031 25 442 9937*

13 LES DOUZE HEURES DE L'EST: Belgium. *Details: 0032 85 314782*

13-14 BEAULIEU AUTOJUMBLE: Now in it's 31st year this event is an important date in the motor enthusiasts diary. There are over 2000 stands where everything from spares to memorabilia can be purchased. National Motor Museum, Beaulieu, Hants. *Details: 01590 653151*

13-14 CIRCUITS DES RAMPARTS: Angouleme. *Details: 0033 1 45 11 11 11*

13-18 TARGA ESPANA: northern Spain. The 10th year of this classic marathon-style event. *Details: 01235 851291*

13-20 RALLYE MONTE CARLO DE VOITURES ANCIENNES: *Details: 0033 93 15 26 00*

14 WROUGHTON FESTIVAL OF TRANSPORT AND MUSEUM OPEN DAY: Transport and vehicles of all types on display and a chance to see what is stored at Wroughton by the Science Museum. Wroughton Airfield, Nr. Swindon, Wiltshire. *Details: 0121 502 3713*

18-21 MANX CLASSIC: This event, now in its 8th year, is open to all classic cars. Events include hillclimb, pursuit sprints and track racing. Douglas, Isle of Man. *Details: 01624 670150*

20-23 RACMSA EURO CLASSIC: A four day event run through Europe includes a visit to the Nürburgring, the French National Motor Museum and the CERAM test circuit. *Details: 01753 681736*

27-28 INTERNATIONAL CLASSIC SPORTS AND PERFORMANCE CAR SHOW: Tabley House, Knutsford, Cheshire. *Details: 0161 431 8191*

Plenty of GT6s and Spitfires on the Triumph Round Britain Run.

OCTOBER

3-5 CLUB TRIUMPH ROUND BRITAIN RELIABILITY RUN: The 31st running of this event with proceeds being donated to charity. *Details: 0181 440 9000*

EIFEL-KLASSIK: Nürburgring. *Details: 0049 22 075044*

5 VSCC BROOKLANDS SPRINT: Annual event which features racing on the famous Brooklands banking. Brooklands, Weybridge, Surrey. *Details: 01635 44411*

8-11 HERSHEY '97: USA. Classic car show during the week of the Antique Automobile Club of America's annual fall meet. *Details: 001 510 736 3444*

10-12 CIRCUIT OF IRELAND RETROSPECTIVE: Historic and classic rally cars run over some of this events original stages. Ireland. *Details: 01232 426262*

12 GIANT MIDLANDS INTERNATIONAL AUTOJUMBLE: A must for all Midlands-based enthusiasts. Newark & Notts Showground. *Details: 01629 534888*

24-30 CARRERA PANAMERICANA: Historic sports racing cars take part in this now famous road event. Mexico. *Details: 0171 938 4983*

31 OCT-3 NOV EURO HISTORIC MARATHON RALLY: Belgium. *Details: 0032 87 772060*

NOVEMBER

2 LONDON TO BRIGHTON VETERAN CAR RUN: Open to all cars manufactured before 1914. *Details: 01753 681736*

10-11 and 17-18 13TH AUTO MOTO D'ESPOCA: Padova, Italy. *Details: 0039 49 8076714; fax: 0039 49 8073771*

15-16 NATIONAL CLASSIC MOTOR SHOW: NEC, Birmingham. *Details: 0121 767 3536*

22 RALLY BRITANNIA: Historic cars rally on roads and stages through Yorkshire. Event starts and finishes in Leeds. *Details: 01452 790648*

22-23 RAC INTERNATIONAL HISTORIC RALLY: Starts from Leeds and runs through road and forest stages in advance of the main RAC event. *Details: 01452 790648*

DECEMBER

6 ARDENNES CLASSIC RALLY: Belgium. *Details: 0032 41 54 19 50*

6-9 LE JOG: Land's End to John O'Groats Rally. *Details: 01886 833505*

13-14 SCORPION RALLY: Peak District. *Details: 01709 894518*

27 CORONATION RALLY: Eppynt. *Details: 01222 569785*

Stanley 100 Directory
Addresses and Contact Numbers

Listed below are the addresses, contact names, and telephone/fax numbers of clubs and associations specializing in the marques detailed in the Stanley Hundred. Each has a secretary and spares register specialist who can help with the locating of parts and restoration companies.

2CVGB (Citroën)
15 Pinewood Close, Bourne,
Lincolnshire, PE10 9RL
Tel/Fax: 01778 394785
Membership Administration,
PO Box 602, Crick,
Northamptonshire, NN6 7UW

A40 Farina Club
75 Tennal Road,
Harborne, Birmingham,
West Midlands, B32 2JB

Abarth Club Great Britain
Juniper House, 42 Middle Barton
Road, Duns Tew, Bicester,
Oxfordshire, OX6 4JN
Tel: 01869 340289/340470
Fax: 01869 340110

AC Owners Club Ltd (America)
11955 SW Faircrest Street, Portland,
OR 97225-4615, USA
Tel: 503 643 3225
Fax: 503 646 4009

AC Owners Club Ltd (UK)
8 Nether Way, Upper Poppleton,
York, North Yorkshire, YO2 6JQ
Tel: 01904 793563

Alfa Romeo Owners Club
97 High Street, Linton,
Cambridgeshire, CB1 6JT
Tel: 01223 894300

Club Alpine Renault
1 Bloomfield Close, Wombourne,
West Midlands, WV5 8HQ
Tel: 01902 895590

Alvis Owners Club
1 Forge Cottage, Lower Bayham,
nr Lamberhurst, Kent, TN3 8BB
Tel: 01892 890043

American Auto Club UK
2 Cumbers Cottage,
Sandy Lane, Hanmer, Whitchurch,
Shropshire, SY13 3DL
Tel: 01948 74754
Fax: 01948 74754

**Association of Rootes
Vehicle Owners**
Kingfisher Court, East Molesey,
Surrey, KT8 9HL
Tel: 0181 941 0604
Fax: 0181 941 0604

Aston Martin Owners Club
1A High Street, Sutton, Ely,
Cambridgeshire, CB6 2RB
Tel: 01353 777353
Fax: 01353 777648

Audi Quattro Owners Club
Tel: 01886 884475

**Austin Cambridge/Westminster
Car Club**
4 Russel Close, East Budleigh,
Budleigh Salterton,
Devon, EX9 7EH

Austin Counties Car Club
Post Office Cottage, Church Road,
Pettaugh, Stowmarket, Suffolk,
IP14 6DW
Tel: 01473 890353

Austin Landcrab Owners Club
PO Box 218, Cardiff, South
Glamorgan, CF3 9HZ

Austin-Healey Club Ltd
4 Saxby Street, Leicester,
Leicestershire, LE2 0ND
Tel: 01162 544111

Bentley Drivers Club Ltd
16 Chearlsley Road, Long Crendon,
Aylesbury, Buckinghamshire,
HP18 9AW
Tel: 01844 208233
Fax: 01844 208923

BMW Car Club
PO Box 328, Andover, Hampshire,
SP10 1YN
Tel: 01264 337833

BMW Drivers Club
Bavaria House, 32a High Street,
Dereham, Norfolk, NR19 1DR
Tel: 01362 694459
Fax: 01362 695522

Bristol Owners Club
Vesutor, Marringdean Road,
Billingshurst, West Sussex, RH14
9RH
Tel: 01403 784028

British Racing & Sports Car Club
Brands Hatch, Fawkham,
Dartford, Kent, DA3 8NH
Tel: 01474 874445

British SAAB Enthusiasts
75 Upper Road, Parkstone, Poole,
Dorset, BH 3EN
Tel: 01202 721625

Cambridge-Oxford Owners Club
32 Reservoir Road, Southgate,
London, N14 4BG

Capri Club International
Field House, Redditch,
Worcestershire, B98 0AN
Tel: 01527 502066
Fax: 01527 520745

Citroën Car Club
Membership Administration, PO Box
348, Bromley, Kent, BR2 8QT

Classic Car Restoration Club
2 Salisbury Avenue, Barking, Essex,
IG11 9XW Tel: 0181 507 3915

Classic Corvette Club UK
Pencroft, Butchers Lane, Preston,
Hertfordshire
Tel: 01462 452111

Cooper Car Club (USA)
14 Biscane Drive, Ramsey, NJ 07446,
USA
Tel: 001 210-825 4548

Ferrari Club of Great Britain
7 Swan Close, Blackedown,
Worcestershire, DY10 3JT
Tel: 01562 700009
Fax: 01562 700009

Ferrari Owners Club
35 Market Place, Snettisham,
Norfolk, PE31 7LR
Tel: 01485 544500
Fax: 01485 544515

Fiat Motor Club (GB)
118 Brookland Road, Langport,
Somerset, BA6 8BD
Tel: 01458 831443
Fax: 01458 253225

Fiat X1/9 Owners Club
30 Kendal Court, Congletown,
Cheshire
Tel: 01428 805877

Ford Anglia 10SE Owners Club
81 Compton Road, North End,
Portsmouth, Hants. PO2 0SR

Ford Capri Enthusiasts Register
46 Manningtree Road, South Ruislip,
Middlesex, HA8 7EG

Ford Classic Capri Owners Club
58 Dewey Road,
Dagenham, Essex, RM10 8AR
Tel: 0181 595 2564

**Ford MKII Consul, Zephyr
& Zodiac Owners Club**
72 Fairway North, Bromborough,
Wirral, Merseyside, L62 3NA
Tel: 0151 334 8749

Ford Cortina MKI Owners Club
51 Studley Rise, Trowbridge,
Wiltshire, BA14 0PD
Tel: 01225 76388

Ford Sidevalve Owners Club
30 Earls Close, Bishopstoke,
Eastleigh, Hampshire, SO5 6HY
Tel: 01703 692359

Ginetta Owners Club
1 Furse Avenue, St. Albans,
Hertfordshire, AL4 9NQ
Tel: 01727 842776

Gordon-Keeble Owners Club
Westminster Road, Brackley,
Northamptonshire, NN13 6BY
Tel: 01280 702311

Historic Lotus Register
Badgers Farm, Short Green,
Winfarthing, Norfolk, IP22 2EE
Tel: 01953 860508

Historic Specials Register
18 Church Row, Hilton, Blandford,
Dorset, DT11 0DD
Tel: 01258 881051

Historic Sports Car Club
Swindon Road, Kington Langley,
nr Chippenham, Wiltshire, SN15 5LY
Tel: 01249 758175
Fax: 01249 758188

Honda S800 Sports Car Club
23A High Street, Steeton, Keighley,
West Yorkshire, BD20 6NT
Tel: 01535 653845

The Imp Club
215 Green Moor, Nuneaton,
Warwickshire, CV10 7EL
Tel: 01203 342095

**International Honda Sports
Car Club**
1 Wales Street, Watersheddings,
Oldham, Lancashire, OL1 4ET
Tel: 0161 620 7884

Isetta Owners Club of GB
72 Regent Drive, Skipton, North
Yorkshire, BD23 1BB
Tel: 01756 793935
Fax: 01924 870061

Italian Car Club (UK)
40 Belle Vue,
Wordsley, Stourbridge,
West Midlands, DY8 5BT
Tel: 01384 833730

Jaguar Car Club
Barbary, Chobham Road,
Horsell, Woking, Surrey
Tel: 01483 763811

Jaguar & Daimler Owners Club
130-132 Bordesley Green,
Birmingham, B9 4SU
Tel: 0121 773 1861

Jaguar Drivers Club Ltd
18 Stuart Street, Luton, Bedfordshire,
LU1 2SL
Tel: 01582 419332
Fax: 01582 455412

Jaguar Enthusiasts Club Ltd
Sherborne, Mead Road, Stoke
Gifford, Bristol, Avon, BS12 6PS
Tel: 0117 969 8186

Lancia Motor Club Ltd
Mount Pleasant, Penhros, Brymbo,
Wrexham, Clwyd, LL11 5LY
Tel: 01978 750631

Club Lotus
PO Box 8, Dereham,
Norfolk, NR19 1TF
Tel: 01362 694459
Fax: 01362 695522

Lotus Cortina Register
Nethermore Farm, Naish Hill,
Laycock, Chippenham, Wiltshire,
SN15 2QH
Tel: 01249 730294

Lotus Drivers Club
9 Boyleston Road,
Hall Green, Birmingham,
West Midlands, B28 9JN
Tel: 0121 745 5017
Fax: 0121 733 6831

Maserati Car Club
Travellers Rest, Old Church,
Cobbaton, Umberleigh, N. Devon,
EX37 9SD

Maserati Club
Tywarne Lodge, Silverwell,
Blackwater, Truro, Cornwall,
TR4 8JJ
Tel: 01872 560554

Maserati Club International
PO Box 1015, Mercer Island,
WA 98040, USA
Tel: 206 455 4707
Fax: 206 646 5458

Mercedes-Benz Club
Brighstone, Over Old Road,
Hartpury, Gloucestershire, GL19 3BJ
Tel: 01204 309219

MG Car Club
Kimber House, PO Box 251,
Abingdon, Oxfordshire, OX14 1FF
Tel: 01235 555552
Fax: 01235 533755

MG Owners Club
Octagon House, Station Road,
Swavesey, Cambridgeshire, CB4 5QZ
Tel: 01954 231125
Fax: 01954 232106

Mini Cooper Club
38 Arbour House, Arbour Square,
London, E1 0PP
Tel: 0171 790 7060

Mini Cooper Register
6 Willows Road, Bourne End,
Buckinghamshire, SL8 5HG
Tel: 01795 479397

Mini Owners Club
15 Birchwood Road, Lichfield,
Staffordshire, WS14 9UN
Tel: 01543 257956
Fax: 01543 416727

**Morgan Car Club of
Washington DC**
Bob Hanson, PO Box #3504,
Alexandria, VA, 22302-0504 USA
Tel: 703 351 8281 w/voice mail

Morgan Sports Car Club
41 Cordwell Close, Castle Donington,
Derby, Leicestershire, DE74 2JL
Tel: 01332 811644
Fax: 01332 853412

Morris Minor Owners Club
127-129 Green Lane, Derby,
Derbyshire, DE1 1RZ

Mustang Owners Club
187 Valance Wood Road,
Dagenham, Essex, RM8 3AJ

Club Peugeot UK
Pelham, Chideock, Bridport,
Dorset, DT6 6JW
Tel: 01297 489360
Fax: 01297 489152

A bottle of champagne to the first person to identify the car, the year, and the drivers!

Porsche 924-944 Club
PO BOX 3000, Woodford, Salisbury,
Wiltshire, SP5 4UF
Tel/Fax: 01722 424400

Porsche Club GB
Ayton House, West End, Northleach,
Gloucestershire, GL54 3HG
Tel: 01451 860792/01608 652911
Fax: 01451 860011/01608 652944

The Rapier Register
The Smithy, Newtown, Powys,
SY16 3EH
Tel: 01686 650396

Rear Engine Renault Club
Birch Farm, Cobbs Lane, Hough,
Crewe, Cheshire, CW2 5JJ

**Reliant Sabre/Scimitar
Owners Club**
PO Box 67, Teddington, Middlesex,
TW11 8QR
Tel: 0181 977 6625
Fax: 0181 943 4373

Renault Owners Club
11 Fernhurst Crescent, Southborough,
Tunbridge Wells, Kent, TN4 0TD

Riley Motor Club
127 Penn Road, Wolverhampton,
W. Midlands, WV3 0DU
Tel: 01902 773197

Rolls-Royce Enthusiasts Club
The Hunt House, Paulerspury,
Northamptonshire, NN12 7NA
Tel: 01327 811489

Rootes Easidrive Register
35 Glenesk Road, London, SE9 1AG

Rover P5 Owners Club
13 Glen Avenue, Ashford, Middlesex,
TW15 2JE
Tel: 01784 258166

Rover SD1 Owners Club
PO Box 10, Camberley,
Surrey, GU17 7XQ

SAAB Enthusiasts Club
PO Box 96, Harrow, Middlesex,
HA3 7DW
Tel: 0181 598 8440

SAAB Owners Club GB
16 Denewood Close, Watford,
Hertfordshire, WD1 3SZ
Tel: 01923 229945

Standard Motor Club
57 Main Road, Meriden, Coventry,
West Midlands, CV7 7LP
Tel: 01676 22181

Sunbeam Alpine Owners Club
PO Box 93, Reigate, Surrey, RH2 7FJ

Sunbeam Rapier Owners Club
12 Greenacres, Downton, Salisbury,
Wiltshire, SP5 3NG
Tel: 01725 511140

TR Register
1B Hawksworth, Southmead
Industrial Park, Didcot,
Oxfordshire, OX11 7HR
Tel: 01235 818866
Fax: 01235 818867

Club Triumph
86 Waggon Road, Hadley Wood,
Hertfordshire, EN4 0PP
Tel: 0181 440 9000
Fax: 0181 440 4694

TVR Car Club Ltd
21 Hawkswood Road,
The Woodlands, Cheltenham,
Gloucestershire, G25 5DT
Tel: 01242 222878
Fax: 01242 243378

Unipower Owners Club
South Plain Cottage, Plummers Plain,
Horsham, West Sussex, RH13 6NX

Vanden Plas Owners Club
The Briars, Lawson Leas, Barrowby,
Grantham, Lincolnshire, NG32 1EH
Tel: 01476 573660

**Vanguard Phase I & II
Owners Club**
7 Priory Close, Wilton, Salisbury,
Wiltshire, SP2 0LD

The Vauxhall Droop Snoot Group
28 Second Avenue, Ravenswing Park,
Aldermaston, Reading, Berkshire,
RG7 4PX
Tel: 01734 815238

**Vauxhall PA/PB/PC/E
Owners Club**
333 Eastcote Lane, Harrow,
Middlesex, HA2 8RY
Tel: 0181 423 2440

Volkswagen Owners Club (GB)
PO Box 7, Burntwood, Walsall,
Staffordshire, WS7 8SB

Volvo Enthusiasts Club
4 Goonbell, St. Agnes, Cornwall,
TR5 0PH
Tel: 01872 553740

Volvo Owners Club Ltd
18 Macaulay Avenue, Portsmouth,
Hampshire, PO6 4NZ
Tel: 01705 381494
Fax: 0181 866 7172

VW Cabriolet Owners Club GB
29 The Crossways, Stonecross, East
Sussex, BN24 5EH
Tel: 01323 769286

PICTURE ACKNOWLEDGEMENTS

The author and publishers offer their sincere thanks to those who supplied illustrations for this book. Every effort has been made to trace those photographers who took the historical pictures reproduced. We apologise for any omissions of credit.

ADT Auctions: 231

Beaulieu Motor Museum: 54, 55(t), 73, 75(b), 79(t), 80, 92,94, 96, 110(t), 111(t),115, 117, 123, 132, 133, 144, 145(t,b), 146(t), 147(b), 156

Chris Bennett: 174

Brooks: 233(t)

Peter Burn: 162, 163, 221(m,b), 222, 259(b), 260

Andrew Dee: 57(b), 59(t), 77(m,l), 89, 106, 128, 134, 207(t), 208

Demon Tweeks: 43(t,m,b)

Focalpoint: 58(b)

Guy Griffiths: 50, 51, 52

Christopher Love: 8, 38-42, 153

Andrew Morland: 58(t), 59(b), 95, 101, 104(t), 109, 114, 118, 119, 120(b), 121, 129, 138, 140, 154, 155, 164(t), 166, 170(t)

Manufacturers: 18-22, 56(b), 82, 112(m), 116, 130, 131, 164(b), 165, 180, 202, 204(t,m,b), 206, 207(b), 218, 219(b), 220, 221(t), 223(t,b,bl)

Monitor: 246(tr)

David McLavin: main Healey picture on front of jacket

Richard Newton: 147(t), 173(t)

Andrew Orr: 1, 184-189 Endpapers

Quadrant Picture Library, from *Autocar and Motor*: 23-33 except 23(b), 211

Reed Illustrated Books: 60, 76(t), 81 (Ian Dawson), 83, 88 (Nicky Wright), 91 (Wright), 97, 98 (Dawson), 99(t), 103(t), 107 (Dawson), 110b (Wright),

122, 124(t), 125(br), 126 (Dawson), 139 (John Lamm), 146b (Dawson), 150 (Jasper Spencer-Smith), 157 (Wright), 160t (Dawson), 167, 168t (Dawson), 171t (Dawson),172, 173(b), 175(t), 176, 177, 182 (Wright), 183 (Wright), 55(t,b), 56(t), 203, 205(t), 246(tl), 247, 259t (Dickie Bird), 261, 262

Tony Saunders: 66(t)

Sotheby's: 232(b)

David Sparrow: 120(t), 170(b)

John Stanley: 9(t,b), 10(t,b), 11, 12, 13, 14, 15, 16, 17, 23(b), 34-37, 44-49, 53, 64(t), 77(mr), 90(t), 93, 99(b), 100, 102(t), 108, 112, 113(b), 136, 137(b), 141, 142, 143, 148, 149, 150(b), 151, 152, 158, 159(b), 160(b), 161,168(b), 169, 175(b), 178, 179, 181, 205(b), 212-217, 224-230(t), 232(t), 233(b)

Jim Tyler: 190-201, 209

INDEX

A

A-series see Austin A
A series engines 205, 208, 209-16
Triumph Herald, Rauno 112, 226, 229
AB Svensk Bilprovning 18
Abarth see Fiat Abarth 850 TC
Abarth, Carlo 141
AC Ace 162-3
AC Aceca 163
AC Buckland 162
AC Cobra 33, 42, 163
AC Greyhound 33
ADT Auctions 231-2
advertising 123
aerodynamic styling 26
air cooled engines 30, 124
Alfa Romeo 53, 219
Alfa Romeo 2.0 GTV 56
Alfa Romeo Duetto Spider 126
Alfa Romeo engines 126, 158, 159
Alfa Romeo Giulia 126
Alfa Romeo Owners' Club 55, 56
Alfa Romeo Proteo Project 158
Alfa Romeo Spider 158-9
Alfasud Sprint 55
Alfier, Giulio 170
Alford, Chris 42
Chris Alford Racing 43
alloy engines 30
Alpina see BMW Alpina B7
Alpine see Renault Alpine A110
        Rootes Sunbeam Alpine
Altenbach, Peter 153
aluminium construction 108, 130
Alvis 64
Alvis T21 range 137
Amery, Heathcote 23
Ami see Citroen Ami
Anglia see Ford Anglia
Arese Style Centre 158
Armstrong Siddeley engines 85
Armstrong Siddeley Star
        Sapphire 29
Arrow see Rootes Arrow range
Ashman, Jonathan 14, 15

Association of Racing Drivers
Schools (ARDS) 39, 43
Association of Specialist Car
Manufacturers (ASCM) 46, 48
Aston Martin 173, 180
Aston Martin DB series 33, 112, 173, 180
Aston Martin DBR1-300 30
Aston Martin DSB 146-7
Aston Martin engines 173
Aston Martin International 46
Aston Martin Lagonda 59, 146
Aston Martin Vantage 147
Atlantic see Austin A90 Atlantic
auctions see car auctions
Audi 80 101
Audi 200 101
Audi engines 119
Audi Quattro 101
Austin, Herbert 75, 203
Austin 16 205
Austin A30 205, 206, 207, 208-9
Austin A35 8, 12, 13, 29, 70, 207, 208-10
Austin A40 Devon 105
Austin A40 Farina 12, 13, 28-9, 70, 207, 209
Austin A40 Somerset 105
Austin A40 Sports 105
Austin A55 Cambridge 71, 79
Austin A70 Hampshire 105
Austin A90 Atlantic 105, 160, 161, 205
Austin A99 Westminster 29, 92, 160
Austin Atlantic see Austin A90
Atlantic
Austin Birmingham Bedford 203, 205
Austin Cambridge see Austin A55
Cambridge
Austin Countryman 29, 70, 205
Austin Devon see Austin A40
Devon
Austin engines 203-10
Austin Hampshire see Austin A70
Hampshire
Austin Mini 8, 13, 19, 20, 26,

207, 208, 210
        see also Universal Power
Drives Unipower GT
Austin Mini Cooper 108
Austin Mini Cooper S 112-13, 207, 208
Austin Mini Cooper S MkII 22
Austin Motor Company 203-11
Austin Princess 204
Austin Seven Mini 27-8
Austin Somerset see Austin A40
Somerset
Austin Westminster see Austin A99
Westminster
Austin-Healey 8, 160
Austin-Healey 100 series 26, 105, 160-1, 205
Austin-Healey 3000 26, 98, 224-9
Austin-Healey gearboxes 137
Austin-Healey Silverstone 51
Austin-Healey Sprite 8-9, 22, 23, 26, 207-8
automatic gearboxes 117, 157
Avenger see Rootes Avenger range

B

B-series engines 207
Baillie, Alan 178
Baker, David 55
Banham, Peter 161
Barber, Malcolm 233
Barchetta see Ferrari 166 Barchetta
        Fiat Barchetta
Baxter, Raymond 13, 14, 19
Beart, Francis 153
Beauford Cars 48
Beetle see VW Beetle
Bentley see Rolls-Royce Bentley
Bentley, W O 53
Berlina 53, 110
Berlinetta see Ferrari 275 GTB/4
Berlinette see Renault Alpine A110
Bertone designs 56, 120, 155, 156, 167
Bilbie, Barnie 160
Birmingham Bedford see Austin
Birmingham Bedford

Blatchley, John 177
BMC 204, 206
see also Austin
MG
Morris
Riley
Standard
Triumph
Vanden Plas
Wolseley
BMC 1800 64
BMC B-series 64
BMC C-series 29
BMC engines 100, 109, 112-13,
205-6, 208
BMW 29, 223
BMW 2.8/3.0 CS 107
BMW 3.0 CSL 107
BMW 6 series 122
BMW 320 56
BMW 328
BMW 507 222-3
BMW 1500/1800 97
BMW Alpina B7 122
BMW CC 56
BMW engines 97, 107, 122, 162,
163
BMW 'Executive Express' 107
BMW Isetta 12, 13, 97
BMW M1 122, 175
BMW M6 122
BMW Z3 222
BN series see Austin-Healey 100
series
body filler 196
body shells 194-5, 196, 199
body styling 26-7, 28, 29-30, 33,
47, 53, 63, 98, 118, 122, 126, 128,
138, 140, 145, 150, 172, 173, 180,
181,
see also Bertone designs
Farina designs
Giugiaro, Giorgetto
Pininfarina designs
Borg-Warner gearboxes 117
Bosch fuel injection 101, 157
Boxer see Ferrari 512BB Boxer
Brabham, Jack 30, 93, 179
braking systems 127, 129, 132,
135, 140, 156
Bristol 400 series 22, 30, 33, 166
Bristol Aeroplane Company 166
Bristol engines 33, 162, 163
British Grand Prix 39
British Leyland 112, 137, 205,
210, 223
British Leyland Triumph TR5 P1
128
Brooks 233
Brown, Sir David 147, 173, 180,
231
Browning, Peter 64, 224-9
Buckland see AC Buckland
Bugler, Colin 59
Buick 103
Bulmer, Charles 22

C

Californian see Rootes Hillman
Californian
Callum, Ian 180
Camargue see Rolls-Royce
Camargue
Cambridge see Austin A55
Cambridge
Capri see Ford Capri
car auctions 9, 230-3
car dealers 9, 43
car events see classic car events
car inspection 199
car magazines 9-10, 50
car renovation 190-3
car rebuilds 190-3
car restoration 17, 53, 190-201
car restoration costs 190-2
car runs 10-11, 38, 54
introductory pack 39, 43
carburation see individually named
systems
Carrera see Porsche Carrera
Carson, Tim 51
Carter carburation 156
Castle Combe circuit 52
Castle-Miller, Tony 141
Caterham Seven 44, 46, 152
see also Lotus Seven
Celica see Toyota Celica
Chamois see Rootes Chamois
Chapman, Colin 130, 131, 152
Chesil Speedsters 48
Chevrolet see General Motors
children
motor sports for 39
Chisholm, Martin 232-3
Chrysler Corporation 118
Chrysler engines 166
Citroën 60, 170, 219
Citroën, Andre 120
Citroën 2CV series 12, 13, 62
Citroën D series 19, 20, 22
Citroën Ami 6, 62
Citroën BX GTi 106
Citroën CX 121
Citroën DS range 120-1
Citroën DS23 Pallas 120, 121
Citroën Dyane 62
Citroën engines 106
Citroën GS 20, 121
Citroën SM 21
Citroën Traction Avant 120
Citroën/Maserati SM series 121
Clark, Jim 130, 178, 179
Classic Car Of The Year 8, 16
classic cars
definition 8-11, 54
future classics 18-22
preservation of 50-1
classic car events 50-3, 258-61
cleaning cars 200
Climax see Coventry Climax
Clutton, Sam 50
Cobra see AC Cobra
Colchester Racing Developments

Merlyn 42, 43
Colombo engines 182
column gear change 105
competition cars 30, 38-43, 123
competition licences 39, 40, 43
competitions see car runs
'Competitors Yearbook' 39
Consul see Ford Consul
Continental R see Rolls-Royce
Bentley Continental R
Convair see General Motors
Chevrolet Convair
Cooper, John 14, 112, 113, 141,
153
Cooper 500 53, 153
Cooper Car Company 112
Cooper Climax 30
Corner, Neil 52
Corniche see Rolls-Royce Corniche
Cortina see Ford Cortina
Corvette see General Motors
Chevrolet Corvette
costs of restoration 190-2
Coucher, Robert 13, 15
Countach see Lamborghini
Countach
Countryman see Austin
Countryman
Coventry Climax 178, 179
Cresta see Vauxhall Cresta

D

D-series engines 205
Daimler Dart see Daimler SP250
Daimler Double Six 20
Daimler Majestic Major 29
Daimler SP250 138
Daimler see also Jaguar
Dakar Cars 48
Dare-Bryan, Val 108
Dart see Daimler SP250
Dauphine see Renault Dauphine
Daytona see Ferrari Daytona
DB series see Aston Martin DB
De Dion suspension systems 146
De Tomaso see Ferrari De Tomaso
Dechaux, Charles 20
Dellortus carburation 131
Delta see GSM Delta
Demon Tweeks 42, 43
Devon see Austin A40 Devon
Diana project 86
Dickson, Alex 12, 13
Dinky cars 36
Dino see Ferrari Dino
disc brakes 127, 132, 140, 156
Dolomite see Triumph Dolomite
donor cars 46, 47, 48
see also kit cars
Downs, G 59
driving techniques 40, 41
drum brakes 129
Dubonnet suspension systems 97
Duncan, Ian 206
Duncan Dragonfly 206

E

Earl, Harvey 139
Eaton superchargers 180
Ecclestone, Bernie 53, 153
Ekland, Britt 213-14
Elan see Lotus Elan
Elise see Lotus Elise
Elite see Lotus Elite
emission regulations 155, 174
Engel, Elwood 67
engines 21, 22, 26, 27, 28, 29, 70, 76-7, 124, 202-11
    air-cooled 30
    alloy 30, 124
    rear-mounted 65
    side-valve 205
    twin cam 129, 131
    transverse 154
    see also individually named engines
England, 'Lofty' 53
equipment see tools and equipment
Escort see Ford Escort
Espada see Lamborghini Espada
Esprit see Lotus Esprit
eventing see classic car events
Evernden, H I F 177
'Executive Express' see BMW Executive Express
exports 23

F

Fairlane see Ford Fairlane
Fairlane Committee 86
Falcon see Ford Falcon
Farina designs 12, 13, 26, 29, 79, 80, 177, 207
Feeley, Frank 173
Fellows, Peter 46
Ferguson Formula cars 101
Ferrari 178, 221-2
Ferrari 166 Barchetta 162, 163
Ferrari 250 182
Ferrari 275 GTB/4 182-3
Ferrari 288 GTO 167
Ferrari 308 GT4 155
Ferrari 308 GTB/GTS 167
Ferrari 328 167
Ferrari 400 GT 157
Ferrari 512BB Boxer 60
Ferrari Daytona 182
Ferrari De Tomaso 60, 170
Ferrari Dino series 21, 108, 155, 167
Ferrari F1 10
Ferrari F40 182
Ferrari Owners' Club 60
Ferrari P series 182
Ferrari Type 166 52-3
FIA 38
Fiat 110, 115, 157
Fiat 16V Coupé 219
Fiat 128 Coupe 83
Fiat 500 22, 72

Fiat 600 72
Fiat 850 Coupe 72
Fiat Abarth 850 TC 141
Fiat Barchetta 219
Fiat X1/9 83
fibreglass bodywork 104, 108, 114, 132, 139, 156
Firenza see Vauxhall Firenza
Flavia see Lancia Flavia
Flying Nine see Standard Flying Nine
Ford Anglia 26, 66
Ford Anglia 105E 26-7, 66, 67, 90
Ford Capri 86, 109
Ford Consul 66
Ford Consul MkII 111
Ford Consul Capri 90
Ford Consul Classic 90, 111
Ford Cortina range 8, 20
Ford engines 104, 109, 131, 148, 152, 163
Ford Escort 42, 66
Ford Escort MkII RS 2000 57
Ford Fairlane 123
Ford Falcon 123
Ford Formula cars 42, 43
Ford Lotus Cortina Mk1 130
Ford Motor Company 42, 108, 180
Ford Mustang 86, 123
Ford Popular 100E 66
Ford Popular 103E 78
Ford Prefect 66
Ford RS Owners' Club 57
Ford Scorpio 164-5
Ford Side-valve Owners' Club 66, 78
Ford Sierra 46
Ford Squire 66
Ford Thunderbird 139
Ford Zephyr 66
Ford Zephyr MkII 111
Ford Zodiac MkII 12, 110
formula cars 42, 43, 51, 101, 108, 153, 178
Formula Junior (FJ) cars 42, 112, 153, 179
FPF engines 178, 179
Frazer Nash Collectors Club 52
front wheel drive 27, 120
Frost, David 214-15
Fry, Tim 65
fuel injection 107, 128, 157, 181
fuel tanks 179
Fulvia see Lancia Fulvia
FWM engines 65

G

Gamma see Lancia Gamma
Gardner Douglas 48
Grinnall Cars 48
Garnier, Peter 21
Garrett, Ken 206

Gauntlett, Victor 147
gearboxes 117, 137, 157, 178, 183
General Motors Chevrolet Convair 30
General Motors Chevrolet Corvette 139
General Motors engines 156
Gibson, Tom 231-2
Ginetta G15 114
Girling 97, 156
Giugiaro, Giorgetto 56, 58, 156, 170, 175
Giulia see Alfa Romeo Giulia
Gordon, John 156
Gordon-Keeble 156
Gordini see Renault R5 Gordini
Graber, Carrosserie 137
Grantura see TVR Grantura
Green, Nick 46-7
Grey Lady see Alvis T21 range
Greyhound see AC Greyhound
Griffiths, Guy 51-3
Griffiths, Penny 51, 53
Griffiths Formula 51, 52, 53
GSM Delta 219
GTM 46-7
Gullwing see Mercedes-Benz

H

Haig, Betty 52, 53
Hall, Nobby 225, 226
Hampshire see Austin A70 Hampshire
hand built cars 49
    see also kit cars
Hayter, Don 98
Healey see Austin-Healey
Healey, Donald 99, 105, 129, 160, 207-8
Healey, Geoffrey 160, 207-8
Herald see Triumph Herald
Hill, Graham 21
Hillman see Rootes Hillman
historic cars see classic cars
Historic Sports Car Club 42, 43, 50, 53
Hofmeister, Wilhelm 107
Honda CRX Series II 116
Honda engines 93
Honda S series 93
Hooper 138
Hopkirk, Paddy 22
Hoyle, John 46-7, 48
Hudson-Evans, Richard 230
Humber see Rootes
Humphries, Cliff 225
Hunt, James 42
Hunter see Rootes Hunter
Hurlock, William 162
hydroelastic suspension 27, 64, 113
hydropneumatic suspension 121

I

Iacocca, Lee   123
Imp see Rootes Hillman Imp
independent suspension   28, 108, 132, 156
individuality
    in car design   218-23
insurance   39
Interceptor see Jensen Interceptor
Isetta see BMV Isetta
Islero see Lamborghini Islero
Iso   97
Issigonis, Alex   13, 16, 19, 20, 26, 27, 53, 64, 70,
    76, 207, 208
Ital Design   170
Ital/Marina   46, 48
Itala   50

J

Jaguar   23, 29, 51, 53, 134, 138
Jaguar 3.8 MkII   33
Jaguar C-Type   53
Jaguar Daimler 2.5 Litre V8   117
Jaguar Daimler SP250   26, 117
Jaguar E-Type series   53, 138, 154, 168-9
Jaguar engines   171
Jaguar XJ   180
Jaguar XK8   218
Jaguar XK150 series   23, 169, 171
JAP engines   153
Jensen Brothers   105
Jensen Interceptor   101, 105, 205
Jern, Erik   91
Jones, David   89
Jowett Javelin   100
JPE engines   152

K

K-series engines   205
K26 turbo engines   101
Karmann styling   122
Keeble, Jim   156
Kent engines   27, 66, 67, 130
Kettlewell, Mike   13
Kinch, John   56
kit cars   44-9, 109, 114, 152
Klanh, Quasar   108
Kume, Tadashi   93
Kyalami see Maserati Kyalami

L

Lagonda see Aston Martin Lagonda
Lagonda Cars   173
Lamborghini Countach   154, 174
Lamborghini engines   174
Lamborghini Espada   154, 174
Lamborghini Islero   154
Lamborghini Marzel   154
Lamborghini Miura   154, 174
Lancia 1600HF Lusso   110
Lancia Beta Monte Carlo   115

Lancia Flavia   110
Lancia Fulvia Coupe   110
Lancia Fulvia Sports   110
Lancia Gamma Coupe   55
Lancia MC   55
Lancia Zagato Sports   110
Larkin, Nick   13, 14
Larson, Gustaf   91
Le Mans   53, 129
Leake, Tom   12, 13
Lefebvre, Andre   121
Leonard, Paul   13
licences see competition licences
Liddon, Henry   112, 229
lifespan
    of cars   18
Lilley, Arthur   109
Lilley, Martin   109
Lima see Panther Lima
London Motor Show   12, 22-33, 64, 127, 160, 162, 171,
    173
Lord, Leonard   105, 160, 203-4, 206, 207, 231
Lotus   42, 44, 134, 220
    see also Ford Lotus Cortina MkI
Lotus Six   152
Lotus Seven   131, 152
    see also Caterham Seven
Lotus 20   178, 179
Lotus 21   178, 179
Lotus Elan series   21, 130, 131
Lotus Elan Sprint   131
Lotus Elise   220, 221
Lotus Elite   131
Lotus engines   179
Lotus Esprit S1   58
Lotus Owners' Club   58
Lucas   97, 128
Lusso see Lancia 1600HF Lusso
Lyons, William   171

M

McLaren   39
McLaren F1   175
MacPherson suspension systems
67, 73, 90, 122, 124, 25, 134, 164
Magnette see MG Magnette
Magnum see Vauxhall Magnum
Majestic Major see Daimler Majestic Major
Makinen, Timo   226
Manumatic systems   100
Marlin Engineering   46
Marples, Ernest   23
Martin, T   57
Marzel see Lamborghini Marzel
Maserati Bora   108, 170
Maserati engines   21
Maserati Kyalami   60
Maserati Merak   170
Matra Rancho   57
Matra Enthusiasts' Club   57
Maughan, Susan   216-17

Mayflower see Triumph Mayflower
Mazda   219, 220-1
Mazda MX-5   142-3, 219, 220
Meccano   36, 37
Merak see Maserati Merak
Mercedes-Benz 220SE   140
Mercedes-Benz 230-250-280 SL   140
Mercedes-Benz 300SL   181
Mercedes-Benz engines   181
Mercury Marine engines   103
Merlyn see Colchester Racing Developments Merlyn
Metropolitan see Nash Metropolitan
MF   8, 219
MG engines   129
MG Magnette MkIII/IV   80, 100
MG Magnette ZA/ZB   100, 129
MG Midget   98
MGA   26, 33, 98, 129
MGB   46, 47, 98-9
MGB GT   98-9, 103
MGC   98, 99
MGF   219
Micheloti, Giovanni   28, 54, 96, 128, 132
Middlebridge see Reliant Middlebridge
Mini see Austin Mini
Minx see Rootes Hillman Minx
Miura see Lamborghini Miura
model cars   36-7, 184-9
Montagu of Beaulieu, Lord   20
Monte Carlo see Lancia Beta Monte Carlo
Moore, Roger   212-13
Morgan, H F S   148
Morgan Car Company   127, 148
Morgan Plus 8   103, 148-9
Morris, William Lord Nuffield   75, 203, 204-5
Morris 1100   70, 210
Morris Minor   8, 13, 14-17, 70, 76-7, 205, 206, 207, 208
Morris Minor 1000   12, 17
Morris Minor Centre, Bath   17
Morris Minor Traveller   77
Morris Motors   203
Morris Oxford   71
Moss, Pat   226
Moss, Stirling   153, 178, 179
Moss gearboxes   148, 168
MOT tests   201
Motor Show see
    London Motor Show
    (Earls Court)
    Paris Motor Show
motor sport see car runs
Motor Sports Association (MSA)
38-9, 40, 43, 52, 54
Mulliner, H J   145, 172, 176, 177
Mulliner Park Ward designs   172
Mustang see Ford Mustang

N

Napier Sabre engines   53
Nash Metropolitan   207
National Motor Museum,
       Beaulieu   20
Nearn, Graham   152
Neyret, Robert   121
NG Cars   46-8
Niland, Stuart   57
Norton engines   153
Norwich Union RAC Run
NSU Ro80   22
Nuffield, Lord see Morris, William

O

Olga see Rolls-Royce Bentley
Continental R
Olympic see Rochdale Olympic
on the road restoration   193-4
       see also car restoration
Oulton Park circuit   53
owners' clubs   54-60, 262-3
Oxford see Morris Oxford

P

P4 engines   30
Pagoda see Mercedes-Benz 230-
250-280 SL
painting cars   200
Pallas see Citroën DS23 Pallas
Palmer, Gerald   100
Panther CC   58
Panther Lima   58
Paris Motor Show   20, 88, 120,
121, 132, 157
Park Ward   137
Parkes, Mike   65
Parnell, Reg   112
Pastiche   46, 48
Peagam   13
Peerless GT series   156
Peugeot 205 GTi   106
Phantom see Rolls-Royce Phantom
Phillips, George   129
photography   51-3
Pininfarina, Battista   126
Pininfarina designs   64, 70, 71, 75,
81, 115, 155, 157,   158, 159, 167,
172, 183
Pollard, Chris   14, 15
Popular see Ford Popular
Porsche, Ferdinand   124, 135, 150
Porsche, Ferry   150
Porsche 3.3 Turbo   60
Porsche 356 series   150-1
Porsche 911 series   134-5, 148
Porsche 924   59
Porsche 944   119
Porsche 924/944 Club   59
Porsche 928   60
Porsche Carrera   150, 151
Porsche engines   119
power steering   140
Prefect see Ford Prefect

Prescott Hill Climb   50
Pressed Steel   144, 145
prices   9, 12, 17, 27, 33, 46, 54-60,
230-3, 234-57
       of competition cars   42, 43
       of racing kit   42, 43
       see also costs
Princess see Austin Princess
       Vanden Plas Princess
professional restoration   197
       see also car restoration

Q

Quantum Sports Cars   48
Quasar-Unipowers   108
Quattro see Audi Quattro

R

RAC   38-9, 40, 43, 50, 52, 54
race schools see training schools
racing cars see competition cars
racing kit   41-2
racing kit suppliers   42, 43
Rancho see Matra Rancho
Range Rovers   103
Rapier see Rootes Sunbeam Rapier
Rea, Chris   10
rear-mounted engines   65
rebuilding see car rebuilds
Redele, Jean   132
Reliant GTE   104
Reliant Middlebridge   104
Reliant SE series   104
Renault   219-20
Renault, Louis   88
Renault 4CV   88, 132
Renault Alpine A110   132-3
Renault Alpine Owners' Club   133
Renault Dauphine   88
Renault Fiftie   219
Renault R5 Gordini   82
renovation see car renovation
replica cars   10
restored cars see car restoration
Rhodes, John   113, 141
Riley   203, 223
Riley 1.5   207
Riley 4/68   81
Riley 4/72   81
Riley engines
Rochdale Olympic   219
Rolls-Royce   180
Rolls-Royce Bentley MkVI   144-5,
176
Rolls-Royce Bentley Continental R
144, 176-7
Rolls-Royce Bentley SII   29
Rolls-Royce Camargue   172
Rolls-Royce Corniche   172
Rolls-Royce engines   144, 176
Rolls-Royce Phantom V   29
Rolls-Royce Silver Cloud   29, 172
Rolls-Royce Silver Dawn   144
Rolls-Royce Silver Shadow   172
Rolls-Royce Silver Wraith   144

Rootes Arrow range   118
Rootes Avenger range   118
Rootes Chamois Coupe   65
Rootes Hillman Californian   65
Rootes Hillman Imp   114
Rootes Hillman Imp Coupe   65
Rootes Hillman Minx   12, 84
Rootes Humber Super Snipe series
29, 85
Rootes Hunter   118
Rootes Sunbeam Alpine series   26,
63, 84, 118
Rootes Sunbeam Rapiet   63
Rootes Sunbeam Rapier III   84
Rootes Sunbeam Stiletto   65
Rootes Sunbeam Tiger   63
Rostyle wheels   98
Rotoflex suspension systems   95
Rover   8, 29-30, 137, 223
Rover 3.0   102
Rover 75   8, 12, 13
Rover 80   29
Rover 100   29
Rover 2000 series   19
Rover engines   73, 98, 99, 148,
149, 221
Rover P series   29-30, 102
Rover P5   29-30, 102-3
Rover P5B   103
Rover SD1   60, 73, 103
Ruby see Saab 900 Turbo
Rudd, Ken   163

S

Saab 900 Turbo   136
Sabre see Napier Sabre engines
Salvadori, Roy   112
Saville, Jimmy   216
Sayer, Malcolm   168
Scalextric   36
schools see training schools
Science Museum   52
Scribante, Aldo   179
Sears, Jack   130
Sebring bodywork   98
Sellers, Peter   213
Senna, Ayrton   43
servo braking systems   131
Setright, L J K   135
Shelby, Carol   162, 163
Shelby Mustang   123
       see also Ford Mustang
side-valve engines   205
Siddeley, John Davenport   75
Sierra see Ford Sierra
sill assemblies   192
Silver series see Rolls-Royce Silver
Silverstone see Austin-Healey
Silverstone
Silverstone circuit   39
Simca 1100   18
Smith, Sir Rowland   231
Somerset see Austin A40 Somerset
Sotheby's   232-3
spare parts   190, 191, 196

Spider see Alfa Romeo Duetto Spider

Alfa Romeo Spider

Spitfire see Triumph Spitfire

sports cars 26, 47-8, 175, 182

Sprint see Alfasud Sprint

Lotus Elan Sprint

Spyder see Ferrari 275 GTB/4

Squire see Ford Squire

Standard 8/10 12, 68

Standard engines 68, 69, 127, 128

Standard Flying Nine 127

Standard Vanguard Phase I 87

Standard Vanguard 6 96

Standard see also Triumph

Stanley Classic Model of the Year 187-9

Stanley One Hundred 62-181

Star Sapphire see Armstrong-Siddeley Star Sapphire

Stiletto see Rootes Sunbeam Stiletto

Stokes, Lord Donald 113, 218

stripdowns 193, 198

see also car restoration

Stromburg carburation 131, 205

SU carburation 80, 144, 205

Sunbeam series see Rootes Sunbeam series

Super Snipe see Humber Super Snipe

Surtees, John 155, 178

suspension systems 27, 28, 64, 108, 113, 124, 128, 130, 132, 134, 149, 156

see also individually named systems

T

T series see NG Cars

Taimar see TVR Taimar

Talek Marek engines 146

Targa roof options 128, 135, 167

taxis 205

Taylor, Simon 13, 15

Thornley, John 99

three-wheeled cars 97

Thunderbird see Ford Thunderbird

Tiger see Rootes Sunbeam Tiger

Toivonen, Pauli 121

Tojeiro, John 162

tools and equipment 191, 198, 199-200

Towns, William 59, 146

toy cars 35-7

Toyota Celica 60

Traction Avant see Citroën Traction Avant

training schools 38-43

transverse engines 154

Triumph Dolomite 54, 68, 95

Triumph Dolomite Owners' Club 54

Triumph GT6 95, 96, 131

Triumph Herald 28, 69, 96

Triumph Mayflower 127

Triumph Spitfire 95, 114, 219

Triumph TR series 26, 103, 127

Triumph TR3 127

see also British Leyland

Triumph TR5 P1

Triumph TR engines 109

Triumph Vitesse 73, 96

Triumph see also Standard

trucks and vans 203, 205

Turner, Edward 117, 138

TVR 220

TVR Grantura 109

TVR M Series 109

TVR Taimar 60, 109

twin cam engines 129, 131

TWR Design 180

Typhoon aircraft 53

U

Ultima Sports Ltd 48

Unger, Erness 108

upgrades 17

upholstery 197

Universal Power Drives Unipower GT 108

V

V4 engines 64, 110

V6 engines 60, 64, 104, 106, 119, 178

V8 engines 26, 29, 30, 48, 60, 73, 98, 102, 103, 117, 123, 138, 146, 147, 148, 149, 155, 156, 163, 166, 167, 170, 178, 179

V12 engines 20, 52, 154, 168-9, 174, 175, 182

V16 engines 158

value see prices

Vanden Plas 4 Litre R 92

Vanden Plas Princess 29

Vanguard see Standard Vanguard

vans see trucks and vans

Vantage see Aston Martin Vantage

Vauxhall Cresta 12

Vauxhall Cresta PA 94, 117

Vauxhall Firenza Coupe 89

Vauxhall Magnum 58, 89

Vauxhall Velox 94

Vauxhall Ventura 89

Vauxhall Viva 89

Velox see Vauxhall Velox

Ventura see Vauxhall Ventura

Vickers 203

Vincent engines 153

Vintage Sports Car Club 51-3

Viotti, Carrozzeria 53

Vitesse see Triumph Vitesse

Viva see Vauxhall Viva

Volvo PV444 91

Volvo PV544 91

VW Veetle 12, 13, 16, 124-5, 150

VW Beetle Cabriolet 124, 125

VW Bieber Cabriolet 125

VW Karmann Ghia 124

van der Vyver, Sid 179

W

Walker, Rob 179

Walklett brothers 114

Wankel engines 22

Ware, Charles 17

Ware, Michael 12, 13

Warwick see Peerless

John Watson Performance Driving Centre 39-42, 43

Weber carburation 72, 83, 131, 167

Weld-Forrester, Piers 108

Westminster see Austin A99 Westminster

Whitmore, Sir John 130

Wiggin, Maurice 144

Wilkins, Gordon 20

Wilkinson, Trevor 109

Williams, Dennis 98

Williams Renault 132

Wilson, Quentin 54

Wolseley 203

Wolseley 4/44 100

Wolseley 6/99 29, 92

Wolseley 15/60 12, 13, 74-5

Wolseley 16/60 74-5

Wolseley 1500 207

Wood & Pickett custom-built Minis 112

works cars 10, 112, 224-9

workshop manuals 198

World Sports Car Championship 30

Worth, Bernard 52-3

X

XK series engines see Jaguar engines

Y

Yamamoto, Keniche 219

Yorke, Susannah 215

Z

Zagato Sports see Lancia Zagato Sports

Zenith carburation 205, 206

Zephyr see Ford Zephyr

ZF gearboxes 178

Zobo project 69

Zodiac see Ford Zodiac

Zytec electronic management 180

Dreams can come true

Great Cars magazine, where you'll find the car of your dreams at surprisingly affordable prices.

Great Cars, the magazine for people who want more than "just another car".

Indulge in your passion for the very best, pore over the 1,000 plus cars for sale each month in Great Cars.

Great Cars magazine is available from W H Smith, John Menzies and other leading newsagents. Published on the first Friday of each month at £1.50. For further details call 01202 445500.

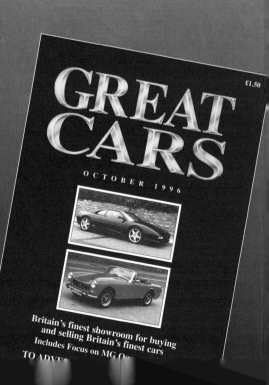

£1.50

GREAT CARS

OCTOBER 1996

Britain's finest showroom for buying and selling Britain's finest cars
Includes Focus on MG O...

TO ADVE...